MOSES'
WOMEN

ജ്ഞൽ

Also by Tuchman and Rapoport

The Passions of the Matriarchs
KTAV, 2004

ജ്ഞൽ

MOSES' WOMEN

෨෨෬෬

Shera Aranoff Tuchman

and

Sandra E. Rapoport

KTAV Publishing House, Inc.

Library of Congress Cataloging-in-Publication Data

Tuchman, Shera Aranoff.
Rapoport, Sandra E..
  Moses' Women / Shera Aranoff Tuchman & Sandra E.
Rapoport.
    p. cm.
  Includes indexes.   ISBN 978-1-60280-017-5

  1. Moses (Bible). 2. Women in the Bible. 3. O.T. Exodus—
Commentaries.
I. Rapoport, Sandra E. II. Title.

Published by
KTAV Publishing House, Inc.
930 Newark Avenue
Jersey City, NJ 07306
Email: orders@ktav.com
http://www.ktav.com
(201) 963-0102

With respect, gratitude and love, to my mother,
Freda Appleman Aranoff

ഌ S.A.T. ശ

ഌശഌശ

To Sam, my loving husband and best friend,
with my gratitude

ഌ S.E.R. ശ

TABLE of CONTENTS

৪০৫৪০৫

ACKNOWLEDGMENTS   xi

INTRODUCTION   xiii

BEFORE YOU BEGIN   xix

GENEALOGY OF MOSES   xx

PART I: MOSES' MOTHERS: A SLAVE AND A PRINCESS

    1 Yocheved, the Seventieth Soul   3

    2 Prosperity, then Slavery, for Jacob's Family   9

    3 Seductions by Righteous Women   11

    4 The Midwives Foil the Pharaoh's Schemes   15

    5 The Midwives are Called to Task   25

    6 The Midwives are Favored by God   28

    7 Shifra and Puah Defy the King   30

    8 The Midwives' Reward   35

    9 "Death by Drowning to All Newborn Sons!"   39

10 A Wedding, a Divorce and a Remarriage   42

11 Yocheved Gives Birth to a Son   45

12 Yocheved Builds an Ark   51

13 Miriam Guards Her Brother   56

14 Pharaoh's Daughter Discovers the Floating Basket   59

15 Princess Batya Rescues the Baby   66

16 Miriam Confronts the Princess   71

17 Princess Batya Commissions Yocheved to Nurse the Baby 76

18 Yocheved Brings Her Son to Princess Batya and
   He is Named Moses   80

PART II: MOSES MARRIES

19 Moses Becomes a Fugitive   89

20 Moses and the Kushite Woman   90

21 Moses and the Seven Shepherdesses   95

22 Zipporah Marries Moses   102

23 Zipporah Bears a Son for Moses   110

24 Moses Encounters God and Returns to Egypt   113

25 Serach, Asher's Daughter, Heralds the Redemption   116

PART III: MOSES AND ZIPPORAH IN THE DESERT

26 Moses, Zipporah and their Sons Take Leave of Yitro   123

27 The Incident at the Inn   127

28 Zipporah is Sent Away   140

PART IV: **MOSES RETURNS TO EGYPT AND
           EFFECTS THE EXODUS**

29 Moses in Egypt   145

30 Moses' Provenance   150

31 Moses Leads the Exodus   153

PART V: **THE AFTERMATH OF THE EXODUS**

32 Miriam the Prophetess Leads the Women in Dance
    and Song   157

33 The Well of Miriam   163

34 Batya, the Egyptian Princess, is also Saved   168

35 Hur, Miriam's Son   171

36 Zipporah Returns to Moses with Their Two Sons   176

37 Marital Abstinence in Preparation to Receiving God's
    Law   198

PART VI: **THE KUSHITE WOMAN REDUX**

38 Miriam and Aaron Speak about Moses' Kushite Woman   205

39 Miriam and Aaron are Chastised   219

40 God Identifies Moses as *His* Prophet   222

TABLE OF CONTENTS

PART VII: MIRIAM'S CODA: TRIAL AND REDEMPTION

41 The Punishment of Leprosy   231

42 Aaron Pleads for Miriam   234

43 Moses Prays for Miriam   243

44 God Sentences Miriam to a Brief Exile   247

45 The Israelites Wait for Miriam   249

46 The Death of Miriam   251

47 The Survival of the Women of the Exodus   259

HEBREW ENDNOTES   267

GLOSSARY OF TERMS AND SOURCES   305

INDEX OF SOURCES   319

GENERAL INDEX   323

ACKNOWLEDGMENTS

೫೦೮೩೫೦೮೩

In writing this, our second book, we were again blessed with loving and supportive family, friends and colleagues. The following individuals stand out because they have been unfailingly dependable and wise.

Wendy Amsellem and Maya Bernstein each critically reviewed our manuscript and offered insightful suggestions which enhanced our book. Beth Samuels rigorously analyzed our early chapters until her illness precluded further work. Sandra's sister, Dr. Diane M. Sharon, offered us important exegetical insights by encouraging us to concentrate on the biblical words themselves.

Sandra's son, Ben Rapoport, was invaluable to us in multiple ways: he was our in-house Information Technology department, our graphic designer—Ben composed our genealogy table—and he offered us a welcome male perspective in his review of our manuscript. Shera's husband, Alan, provided us with necessary historical perspective, and her son, Andy, offered an accurate numerical analysis of the post-exodus generation. Sandra's daughter, Sarah, offered a listening ear to textual quandaries, and 24/7 computer assistance. We extend an additional, special thank-you to our husbands, Alan Tuchman and Sam Rapoport, for their forebearance, support and able management of the home front during the past two years.

Bernie Scharfstein, our beloved publisher at KTAV, again gave us the necessary encouragement to take on the substantial challenge of writing this book. Adam Bengal, Bernie's worthy assistant, facilitated our project at every turn. Steve Siebert, patient and precise typesetter and friend, has once again formatted our book and

xii ∞∞∞∞ ACKNOWLEDGMENTS

produced it in its final, polished form. Chava Aranoff proofread our early chapters. Hertzliah Goldstein introduced us to current articles by Israeli Torah commentators, and proofread our Hebrew footnotes.

Sandra wishes to thank Rabbi David Silber and Devora Steinmetz, her teachers at the Drisha Institute, who have taught her to seek out and appreciate layered meanings in the Torah text.

Rabbi Haskel Lookstein, our rabbi and teacher, pointed us toward Rabbi Joseph B. Soloveitchik's expansive lecture on the exodus. It was Rabbi Lookstein's personal tape of the Rav's lecture that allowed us to hear the Rav's insights in his own voice. Also, we are grateful for Rabbi Lookstein's continued graciousness in providing a home at Congregation Kehilath Jeshurun for our Thursday morning study group. Finally, the women of Shera's Thursday morning study group continue to inspire us to grapple with the timeless Torah text.

INTRODUCTION

ഋരഋര

After completing my study group on the Matriarchs in Genesis, and the subsequent book it engendered, I felt a sense of relief and satisfaction. I really felt I *knew* those women. I knew how they thought and felt about their God, their husbands, their children, themselves. They became my mother, my sister, my daughter, my best friends. They accompanied me in my thoughts, and were there to help me deal with the joys and sorrows of my life. But soon after, encouraged by the women in my study group at Congregation Kehilath Jeshurun, an Orthodox synagogue in Manhattan, to continue the class, I began afresh, this time to study the women of Exodus, the second book of the Bible.

The story of Exodus is mainly the story of Moses, the unequalled prophet, leader and lawgiver. His lifelong mission is to lead the people of Israel, who have been enslaved in Egypt, to their destined land, Canaan. The Torah narrative relates the difficulties Moses encounters as he attempts to transform a primal horde into a civilized society as they travel toward their ultimate destination: the land that is rightfully theirs by virtue of the divine covenant with Abraham.

At first reading I found the women to be minimally active characters in the nation's story of slavery and redemption. Unlike the women in Genesis, women rarely speak in Exodus. And unlike the Matriarchs, who were so instrumental in managing their families—often even more so than the men—the women of Exodus are not granted a powerful biblical voice. In fact, the feminine dimension of life is pushed into the background and these women are not initially seen as protagonists.

In the story of Moses one can point to five female characters of some importance, but none of them constitute a major figure in the story.   They are Moses' birth mother, Yocheved; his sister, Miriam; the Pharaoh's daughter, who becomes Moses' adoptive mother; his wife, Zipporah; and the mysterious Kushite Woman. We are given no details about his relationship with his birth mother, sister or his adoptive mother.   Though no person is more central to Jewish history than Moses, of his life with his wife Zipporah and their children almost nothing is revealed.

Over the past fifteen years I have tried to understand the women of the Bible by analyzing and deconstructing biblical words, phrases, and sentences, aided by traditional Orthodox commentators and their *midrashic* explanations.   It is these interpretations, some thousands of years old, some very recent, that allow me to slip into the world of these women and join the women of the Exodus.

I entered the lives of these heroic Hebrew women who were enslaved by the pharaohs, isolated from their husbands, and even ordered to kill not only others, but their own children!   I followed them as they cooked and bathed in the fields; into their bedrooms and into their birthing rooms. I entered into their intimate thoughts, heard their private words, and observed their personal actions.   And I was impressed by their intrinsic faith in God in the face of unfathomable physical and emotional trials, and how they lived by that faith.   It is these women who are the true heroes of the spitritual and national rebirth.   The Talmud (Sotah 11b) actually credits these women's righteosuness as the determining factor whose merit brought forth the redemption from Egypt!

Through *midrash* I could focus closely on one family in particular.   I could hear a young Miriam astutely convincing her separated parents to reconcile, and could see the festivities of the re-wedding ceremony.   I could visualize the mother Yocheved's determination and feel her angst as she tries to save the life of her newborn son, doomed by the Pharaoh's murderous decree.   I could share the anxiety of the Princess of Egypt as she must decide if she will negate her father's command to let the Hebrew boy babies drown in the Nile or stretch out her arm to save one.   I read about the fugitive Moses' sojourn in Kush, and his relationship with the queen of that land, a story only alluded to in the biblical text.   Later,

I saw a stateless Moses at the desert watering well, observing carefully the young maidens as they drew water, and deciding on his future bride, Zipporah. I learned more of their marital relationship, which is barely mentioned in the text. I opened closed doors, and entered their private chambers, at night, in the inn. I was privy to unwritten conversations between Zipporah, after her separation from Moses, and her sister-in-law, Miriam. And finally, I was able to observe the development of a strong and beloved Miriam, who becomes one of the triumverate, along with Moses and his brother Aaron, as leaders of the Exodus.

Midrash is considered the "white spaces" between the black letters of the text, the unwritten, implicit part of the text that was passed down orally from generation to generation, alongside the explicit written words. Rabbi Moses Alschich, a sixteenth-century Torah scholar, in his commentary on the Torah portion of Chukat, states clearly that the Well of Miriam, which is not mentioned directly in the Bible, but is part of *midrashic* commentary, is a wellspring of the oral Torah and spirituality. He continues definitively that one should absolutely not think that the oral Torah falls beyond the confines of the written Torah. *Know*, he instruct us, *that in the written Torah is found all the oral Torah as well.* Rabbi Judah Aryeh Leib Alter, also know as the S'fat Emet, a late nineteenth-century scholar, refers to this as well. In his commentary on the same portion, he mentions that in fact Miriam's well, which is attributed to sustaining the thirsty Israelites during their trek in the desert, is in fact an allusion to the oral Torah, or *midrash*. Thus, according to the S'fat Emet, *the oral Torah accompanied the Israelites alongside the written Torah.*

Daniel Boyarin, a modern professor of Talmudic Culture at the University of California, Berkeley, in discussing *midrash*, states that the sovereign notion informing the present reading of *midrash* is intertextuality. In his book, *Intertextuality and the Reading of Midrash*, he recounts that *midrash* is, in fact, a radical intertextual reading of the Torah itself, and a *true reading* of the underlying meaning of the gapped biblical narratives. He understands that we cannot assume that there is a single, simple, correct interpretation of the text, and that the commentaries, through *midrash*, flesh out details of these dialectical and alternate readings.

Without reference to *midrashic* sources the women of the Exodus are but shadow figures. With *midrash* the women are fleshed out as real human beings. Through *midrash* the women in my study group were able to become intimately close to the women of Exodus, to observe them and to identify with them. And, as the class ended, the material for my next book was amassed.

As I entertained thoughts about the texts I had studied, I had an amazing realization. While the *midrash* does flesh out the stick-like figures in the text, the *p'shat*, or simple reading of the text, was itself astonishing. I realized that not only was the Talmudic statement regarding the righteous women of the Exodus as responsible for the deliverance of the Israelites from slavery an amazing statement, but in fact, *Moses' very life itself* was dependent upon these women. Following the biblical text, I realized that the life of Moses, the greatest prophet on earth, was continually saved by a woman. In the text of Exodus itself, his mother, Yocheved, saves him by hiding him from Pharaoh's murdering soldiers; his sister Miriam watches over him as his cradle is tossed about in the waters of the Nile; the Egyptian princess saves him as she draws him from the Nile and raises him as an Egyptian prince, in the very house of the Pharaoh who sought to drown him; and finally, his wife, in the mysterious story of their night at the inn, takes a flint and saves his life yet again.

So yes, the *midrash* as explicated by the commentaries develops these characters so that we know them intimately. But we needn't go beyond the written Torah text, which attests not only to the strength of character of these women, but clearly presents them as unequivocal heroes of the Exodus.

Along with the written and oral Torah, I feel that the indomitable spirit and soul of the Israelite woman is passed down from generation to generation in those who learn and assimilate these ancient texts. Studying these formidable women and imbibing their qualities, one cannot but have them inform one's own soul as well. In this vein, I need to acknowledge the five generations of women in my personal life who were and are my soul mates: My grandmother, Bina Appleman, *A"H*; my mother, Freda Appleman Aranoff; my sister, Gaya Aranoff Bernstein; my daughter, Micole Tuchman Koslowe; and now my granddaughters, Danelle Sophia and Natalia Meshi Tuchman. Each in her own way exhibits parts of those very same qualities that identified and embodied the women of the Exodus. To complete the inner circle, I must mention Alan Tuchman, my husband, who has been at my side and on my side for over thirty-five years. His steadfast love and constant encouragement is my anchor. My older son Ari is a confidante, and father *par excellence*. Andy, my younger son, continues to give us joy as he lives the varied aspects of his life with a serious integrity. The newest male addition, my grandson Charlie Hillel, son of Micole and Oren Koslowe, adds boundless joy to my life.

The writing of this book was interrupted by the untimely death of my daughter-in-law, Beth Samuels, of cancer. Her life embodied a love and appreciation of both the text and the spirit of Torah. It is this duality, permeated with enthusiasm and love, that she left behind for my son Ari, her husband; Dania and Natalia, her daughters; and for all of us whose lives she so enchantingly affected. Her intrinsic faith in God in the face of unfathomable physical and emotional trials, and how she lived by that faith, truly mark her as a righteous woman of *our* generation.

Once again, I owe thanks to my teachers, Rabbi Israel Rosenberg, *A"H*, and Rabbi Jack Bieler, rabbi of Kemp Mill Synagogue in Silver Spring, MD, who taught me not only how to learn, but how to extract the hidden essence from what I was learning; the body and soul of Torah. And again, the more I study, the more I realize that there is an infinite body of Torah knowledge I would like to learn and only an infinitessimal part that I have uncovered. I have accepted that Torah learning is a forever process, not an achieveable goal.

Finally, my genuine gratitude to my co-author, *chavruta* and friend, Sandra Rapoport, who labored with me—as we did in our first book—sentence by sentence, line by line and word by word, to create this exciting and vital book.

Shera Aranoff Tuchman

BEFORE YOU BEGIN

ॐ〰ॐ〰

Before you begin reading this book, there are three points to bear in mind.

First, *Moses' Women* has been written to correlate by chapter and verse with the Hebrew Bible, also known as the Torah. Although the book is intended to be read and understood on its own, the reader's appreciation is enhanced if one follows along with the biblical text. One can then glance backward, or look forward, to a sentence that has just been explained, or to one that will soon be explicated. This is important, for many pages in this book often are devoted to a few significant biblical words.

Second, long passages in italics are the authors' own paraphrased translations of the biblical narrative, and are not intended as literal substitutions for the biblical text.

Third, while our book is written in English, numerous passages are footnoted in the original Hebrew or Aramaic and appear in an "endnotes" section at the back of the book. Please bear in mind that this book was written to be read and understood *without* the necessity of comprehending these foreign language quotes. We have included them because the richness and poetic beauty of the Hebrew or Aramaic words often are diminished in translation, and those who understand the original Hebrew will appreciate the beauty of the ancient texts and will reap additional satisfaction in this extra dimension. To those who do not read Hebrew, the footnotes can safely be ignored without compromising the flow of our book.

GENEALOGY

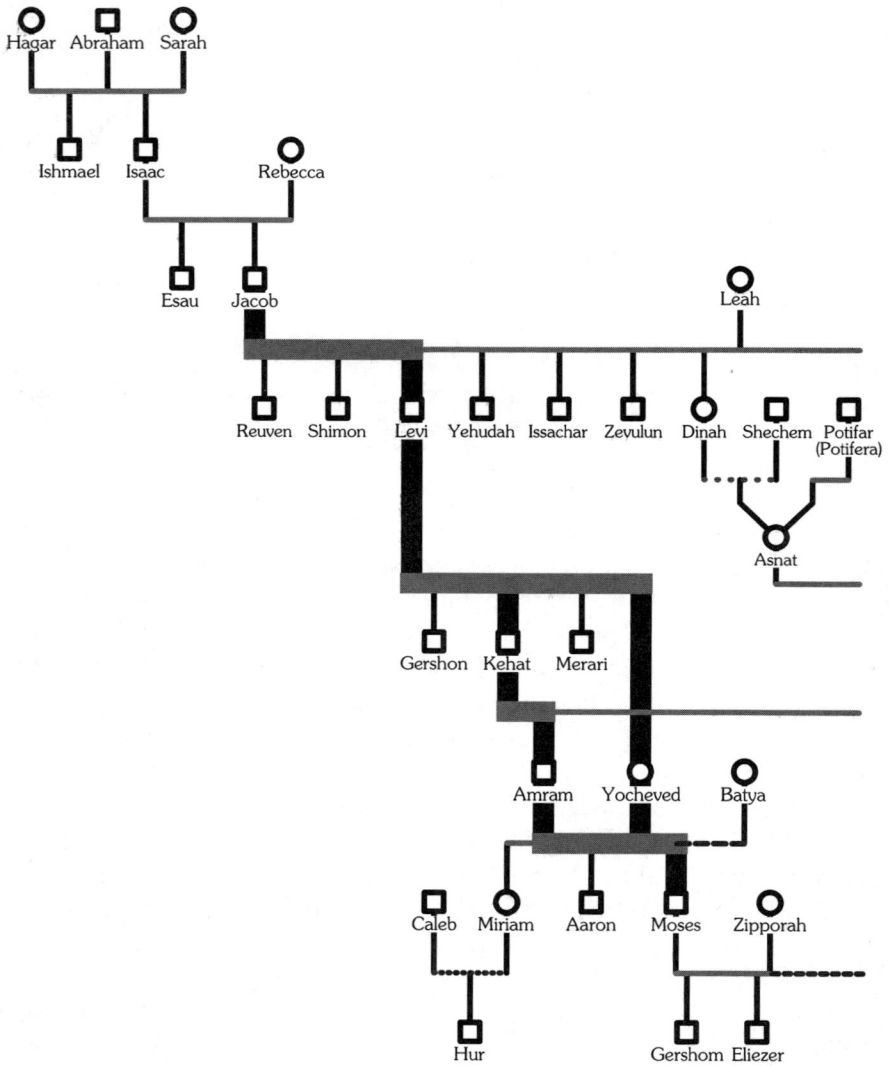

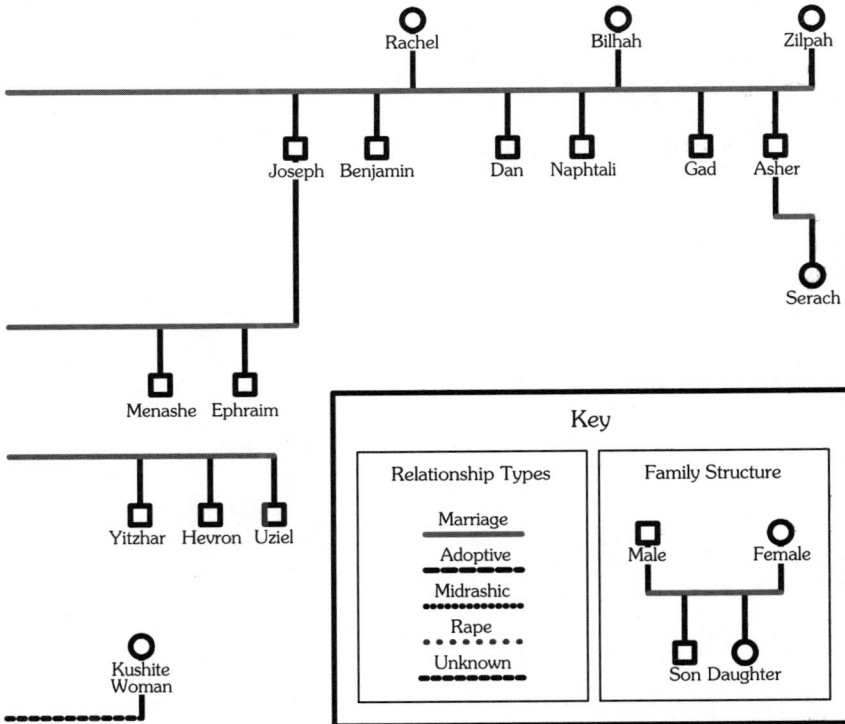

Rachel · Bilhah · Zilpah

Joseph · Benjamin · Dan · Naphtali · Gad · Asher

Serach

Menashe · Ephraim

Yitzhar · Hevron · Uziel

Kushite Woman

Key

Relationship Types

Marriage

Adoptive

Midrashic

Rape

Unknown

Family Structure

Male · Female

Son · Daughter

B. I. Rapoport

PART I

MOSES' MOTHERS:
A SLAVE
AND A PRINCESS

ഇരുഇരു

ONE

ဆလ္ဗဆလ္

Yocheved, the Seventieth Soul

GENESIS 45:28

And Israel said, "How abundant [are my blessings] that Joseph my son is still alive; I will go and I will see him before I die."[1]

GENESIS 46:26-27

All the souls that accompanied Jacob down to Egypt, the fruit of his loins . . . all the souls numbered sixty-six. And there were two sons of Joseph who were born to him in Egypt; thus all the souls of the house of Jacob who went down to Egypt numbered seventy.[2]

T he story of Moses, which generally is understood to begin in Exodus, the second book of the Bible, actually begins earlier. Already in Genesis chapter 45 (verse 28) the Bible is readying Jacob and all his household for the momentous journey from Canaan down to Egypt. In a dramatic turnaround, Jacob's long-lost son Joseph, who has risen to the exalted position of viceroy over all Egypt, has sent wagons back to Canaan to transport his aged father in relative comfort. Jacob had very nearly lost hope of ever seeing his son Joseph alive, and so is understandably prepared to uproot himself and his entire household, at Joseph's surprise summons, to follow his beloved son into Egypt.

As students of the text we must begin our inquiry into the life of Moses at the point where the Bible elaborates exactly *who* accompanied the patriarch Jacob on his journey into Egypt. Egypt is the place where the sons of Jacob—*b'nei Yisrael*—over the course of hundreds of years of debilitating servitude, emerge as the nation of Israel—*Am Yisrael*. Moses, the great redeemer, although born in Egypt and raised as an Egyptian prince, is in point of fact Jacob's great-grandson (through his mother's line). Thus, the verses in Genesis that enumerate one-by-one the Hebrew souls who crossed from Canaan into Egypt with Jacob (46:1-27) are laying the indispensable groundwork for appreciating Moses' provenance.

But Jacob is ambivalent about making the journey to Egypt. Once on his way, he seeks God's assurance before he leaves Canaan behind (46:1-3):

> And Israel took his journey with all that he had, and came to Beersheba, and offered sacrifices unto the God of his father Isaac. And God spoke unto Israel in the visions of the night, and said: "Jacob, Jacob." And he said, "Here am I." And He said, "I am God, the God of thy father. Fear not to go down into Egypt, for I will make of thee there a great nation."[3]

Once Jacob receives the divine reassurance that he is not taking a misstep by uprooting his household and relocating to Egypt, the Bible continues (46:26), listing the names of "all the souls belonging to Jacob that came into Egypt, that came out of his loins . . . and all the souls numbered sixty-*six*."

An exact count of Jacob's progeny, however, as set out in Genesis chapter 46 verses 8 through 25, yields the sum of sixty-*nine* people! The commentary the Maharaz solves this apparent arithmetic shortfall by a close reading of the Bible's next verse. This verse specifies that the head count includes only Jacob's progeny *that accompanied him on his journey into Egypt*. Therefore, reasons the commentary, subtracting both Joseph—Jacob's son *in Egypt*—as well as Joseph's two Egyptian-born sons, from the sixty-nine, yields the Bible's sixty-*six* persons who physically came down *with* Jacob into Egypt.[4]

Strangely, however, the very next verse in Genesis (46:27) states "all the souls of the house of Jacob that came into Egypt were *seventy!*" What are we to make of this descrepancy? One could think that the Torah is merely rounding up the count. But whenever the Bible belabors a seemingly-mundane matter such as the one here—where the Bible enumerates for twenty-seven verses the members of Jacob's family who accompany him down to Egypt—it is a signal to pay close attention. Especially here, where the text supplies different head counts, students of the text should pause and ask why verse 26 specifies sixty-*six* persons accompany Jacob, verse 27 states that the number is *seventy*, but the actual verses list the head-count at sixty-*nine*.

In fact, the number seventy is generally accepted as the historical head-count. So how can this difference be reconciled? Rashbam states simply that Jacob himself should be counted as the seventieth soul.[5] Ibn Ezra agrees that the fitting resolution is to include the patriarch Jacob in the count, thus bringing the total to seventy, because, in his opinion, Jacob is the moving force behind the descent to Egypt.[6] Both commentators ignore the biblical phrase (Gen. 46:26) that specifies that the head count is comprised of "the souls that *accompanied* Jacob down to Egypt, *the fruit of his loins.*" Logically, then, Jacob cannot be the seventieth soul because he cannot be considered the fruit of his own loins.

A fascinating body of *midrash* presents a fringe notion identifying Joseph's *wife* as the seventieth soul! The reader's first question must be, "How could Joseph's wife—presumably an *Egyptian* woman—be counted as one who was also *the fruit of Jacob's loins?*" Torat HaChidah suggests that Joseph's two Egyptian-born sons, who are included in the count along with their father Joseph, thus bringing the count from sixty-*six* to sixty-*nine*, were in fact born of a *Hebrew* mother, bringing the count to seventy.[7] But how could this be so, if Joseph was the first Hebrew emigre from the family of Jacob to settle in Egypt? To answer this question the commentary takes the reader back to the book of Genesis (ch. 34) and the rape of Dinah, Jacob's only daughter.

According to Pirkei d'Rabi Eliezer,[8] after Dinah was abducted and raped by Shechem, she became pregnant, and secretly gave birth to an illegitimate daughter who was named Asnat. The *midrash* relates that according to family mores, only the baby's death would have ameliorated the extreme disgrace to the house of Jacob. But instead, Jacob, the family patriarch, decreed that the illegitimate baby be banished from the family compound. She remained hidden beneath a thornbush where the angel Michael watched over her and saw to it that she was taken—perhaps by a passing caravan, perhaps he transported her himself—into Egypt. There, the baby was secreted into the house of Potiphar, a member of the Pharaoh's court, and was raised by Potiphar's wife, who was barren. She adopted the baby Asnat as her own.

The commentaries describe that before Jacob banished the baby Asnat, he ordered that a tiny amulet be made onto which was engraved the name of the house of Jacob (Rabbeinu Bachya),[9] or, suggests another *midrash*, the name of God (Pirkei d'Rabi Eliezer). Jacob attached the amulet to a golden chain and hung it about the baby's neck in order to both identify and protect her.

Decades later, when Joseph is elevated to the position of viceroy to the Pharaoh, the king bestows upon him an Egyptian name and an Egyptian wife. This young woman is none other than Potiphar's adopted daughter, Asnat (Exodus 41:45)![10] Chizkuni[11] suggests that Joseph instantly recognized Asnat's golden amulet as Hebrew in origin, and happily wed her, knowing she was his niece.

Still, a persistent question for modern Bible readers is, Why are there only *two women* enumerated in the biblical head-count in Genesis chapter 46? Surely there were others; Jacob's granddaughters, for instance. The answer lies in an understanding of who the two *enumerated* women are, as well as an examination of the lacuna, or space, that the text has deliberately left by specifying *seventy* souls, while a head-count only provides us with *sixty-nine*.

The two women enumerated in the original head-count as having come into Egypt with Jacob are Dinah, Jacob's only daughter, and Serach, Jacob's granddaughter, the daughter of his son, Asher. All the remaining "souls who descended into Egypt, fruits of Jacob's loins," are males. Consistent with biblical practice, the enumerations of names, generations, or genealogies generally specify only the males, as they constituted the phylogenic scheme for labeling purposes ("the house of Abraham," "the tribe of Judah," and so on). If a woman is enumerated there is an important exegetical reason for doing so.

Therefore, a better question might be: Why *are* Dinah and Serach mentioned in the original head-count? Why are these women mentioned at all?" *This* inquiry will lead us to our answer. Dinah is counted because she is the daughter of the patriarch Jacob. Important stories in Genesis have revolved around her, and for purposes of story closure she *must* be specified in the head-count into Egypt along with her twelve brothers or the reader will wonder if she had been left behind. As regards Serach, the daughter of Asher, she was understood by the *midrashists* to be an important, respected and even magical figure in the Israelite family. As we will discuss further on in this book, according to *midrash* Serach was entrusted with the secret code for the deliverance of the Hebrews from Egyptian bondage, and as such it was critical for her to have immigrated into Egypt with Jacob.

The Talmud's choice for "the seventieth soul" is a woman whom none of the *midrashists* have yet introduced. To understand its choice, we must peek ahead to the second chapter of the book of Exodus, where we encounter an unnamed Israelite woman, *a daughter of Levi.* She is busy planning to save her doomed Hebrew baby son. By keeping her unnamed, the Bible is building some suspense. But we will already have deduced her name, as she is our important missing link.

Bereishit Rabbah (94:9) interposes a short parable and solves the mystery. It asks rhetorically: "Have you ever in your life heard of a man who gives his friend sixty-six goblets, but then, adding three more, totals the count as seventy?!" The commentary has counted heads in the text, and even including Joseph and his two sons (the Egyptian branch of Jacob's family), its count still falls one short of seventy. The commentary then reveals the name of the seventieth soul who completes Jacob's family quorum in Egypt: **The seventieth soul is Yocheved, daughter of Levi, third son of Jacob and Leah.** The *midrash* tells us that Yocheved was conceived while the family was still camped in Canaan, and she was delivered as her mother's wagon lumbered into Egypt.[12] It is this infant girl Yocheved who is destined in years to come to give birth to Moses.

Now the text becomes clear. Of course Yocheved is not enumerated as one of the Bible's souls who accompanied Jacob down to Egypt; when Jacob began his journey Yocheved's mother was still swollen with child and very near her term. According to the Talmud (Bava Batra 123 a,b), it is only as Jacob's caravan rolled through the portals of Egypt that the head count was brought to the full complement of seventy with the propitious birth of Yocheved, Jacob's granddaughter.[13]

TWO

ଈଓଔଓଈଓଔଓ

Prosperity, Then Slavery, for Jacob's Family

EXODUS 1:1–13

A caravan consisting of Jacob's entire household, his eleven sons, their wives and all their worldly possessions, came down into Egypt at Joseph's behest and settled there. Many years pass in abundant prosperity, and eventually the generation of Jacob and his sons— including Joseph, the viceroy of Egypt—dies out. Still, Jacob's progeny increase abundantly and wax mightily, so that they overfill the province of Goshen, the land that Jacob first settled.

And there arose a new Pharaoh over Egypt whose dynasty neither knew nor recognized Joseph's seminal contribution to Egypt's very existence. This king incited the Egyptians to fear the children of Israel, who had grown profusely and multiplied super-abundantly into a nation who, by their sheer numbers alone, could constitute a threat to Egypt's might if ever they were to join with its enemies. So the Pharaoh called upon the Egyptians to cleverly plan and execute an inexorable scheme of oppressive edicts that would, over time, effect a genocide on the Israelites.

The Egyptians set abusive taskmasters over the Israelites, forc-ing them into hard labor building the stone cities of Pithom and

Ramses for the Pharaoh. Notwithstanding the staggering weight of this abusive bondage, the Israelites continued to produce multitudes of children and to fill the land, and the Egyptians were repulsed by their fecundity. So the Egyptians completely enslaved the Israelites, imposing ruthless tasks upon them.

THREE

෫෨෬෫෨෬

Seductions by Righteous Women

EXODUS 1:14

The Egyptians embittered the Israelites' lives with crushing labors, forcing them to make mortar into bricks and then to build cities, **and also causing them oppressive labor in the fields**.

We already have read (Ex. 1:11) that the Pharaoh enslaved the Israelites and forced them to build great storage *cities*. This verse (Ex. 1:14) is the first indication that the Hebrews also were enslaved in Egypt's vast and distant *fields*. Yalkut Shimoni focuses on this new information in the text and states that the Israelites were indeed enslaved in the fields *as well as* in Egypt's cities. The commentator explains that this enslavement in the outlying fields was even more insidious than the city labor. In this newest tightening of the oppressive noose, the Egyptians, as the sun was setting on the day's hard labor, restrained the Israelite *women* in the cities, while compelling the Israelite *men* to a forced march into the countryside, where they collapsed from exhaustion.[1]

Once in the fields, even if there were only an hour of light left, Rashbam adds that the Egyptians whipped the depleted Israelite men to plow the earth and harvest the grain.[2] Ramban elaborates, explaining that the Egyptians prodded the Israelite men with

11

beatings and curses, forcing them—after their backbreaking stonework and their trek into the countryside—to dig ditches and shovel offal. All manner of filthy field labor was heaped upon the fatigued and dispirited men, with the object of rendering rest an impossibility.[3]

The Egyptians' goal was none other than to physically debilitate the Israelites to the point where they would utterly lose their will to procreate. In one generation, they reasoned—two at the most—the Hebrew population would be so depleted as to be rendered ineffectual and near extinction. The taskmasters, seeking to insure the success of their nefarious plan, kept the sexes segregated: the women were to sleep in the cities, and the men in the the fields. Yalkut Shimoni explains that amazingly, the Israelite women foiled the plan. Surreptitiously and under cover of night they stealthily made their way to their husbands' outlying camps. There, foregoing sleep, the women prepared hot food and restorative drinks for their men. After the meal, the women continued to provide for their husbands' needs, comforting their bodies and their minds. "The Egyptians will never enslave us completely!" was their rallying cry. And their revived husbands rested in their arms.[4]

The Talmud (Sotah 11b) is more explicit, declaring outright that the women of that enslaved generation are forever to be known as *righteous women*, whose merit enabled the redemption of the Children of Israel from their bondage in Egypt. The Talmud explains the women's extraordinary behavior in the face of nearly certain detection and punishment. In the evening, after the day's work, at the hour the women wearily made their way to the river to draw water for bathing and cooking, the Almighty caused tiny fishes to swim into their water urns, halving their labors. The women, laden now with their ration of water and sustenance, heaved their two urns—one for bathing, the other for cooking—and carried them off to the fields. There, they built fires and cooked the evening meal, and prepared make-shift baths while awaiting their husbands' return. Then, using the heated water from the cleansing urn, these women carefully bathed their husbands' bodies of the stone dust, animal dung and caked grime that was the badge of their existence. They anointed their husbands' limbs with soothing plant oils, and literally fed them the day's meal, bringing the food to their lips when the men had no desire or ability to feed themselves.

Thus refreshed, the night air a cooling respite from the burning Egyptian sun, the women led their husbands, one-by-one, to seek their conjugal privacy between the hillocks in the fields. The women kept to this routine month after month, until they found themselves with child and were unable to endure the nightly trek from the city. Only when the early pangs of labor began did the Israelite women endure the trek back to the fields to deliver their babies in secret.[5]

Rashi is sensitive to the delicate heroism of the Israelite women here. The women's nightly seduction of their husbands—in order to insure that their generation not die out—was not only fraught with authentic physical danger, but also was an emotional minefield requiring the women to navigate with skill. In the privacy of their desert trysts, the Israelite women took out their hand mirrors and used them in an elaborate seduction mime. Each woman first made a show of gazing at herself in her mirror, pointing out her physical attributes, seeking thereby to arouse her husband. Next, she nestled up to her exhausted mate, playfully showing him their joint reflections and whispering teasingly to him, "Tell me, am I not more beautiful than you?" With their cajoling words and mirror play the determined Hebrew women thus aroused their enervated mates, engaged in intimate acts, and conceived and ultimately bore their children in the desert brambles.

The Israelite women's desert seductions of their husbands was considered by God to be an act of enormous faith, and worthy of immortalization. Much later on in the Book of Exodus (38:8), when the Israelites are building the desert sanctuary (the *mishkan*), Rashi explains that Bezalel, the *mishkan's* artisan, fashioned the holy wash-basins from the donated hand-mirrors of the daughters of Israel. The commentator explains that Moses, who oversaw all the Israelites' donations to the Tabernacle, initially despised these mirrors, which he thought of as instruments of vanity and entice-ment and therefore unworthy of inclusion. God Himself intervened, instructing Moses to accept the women's donation unconditionally, "For their mirrors are more dear to me than all the other offerings. It is through use of these mirrors that the Israelite women foiled the Egyptians and were able to beget hosts of children."[6]

Avivah Gottlieb Zornberg, in her book, *The Particulars of Rapture, Reflections on Exodus*, speaks to the essence of the

Israelite women's courageous act by juxtaposing them against none other than the mighty Pharaoh: "Since his edict is one of separation, of effective sterilization, the women's efforts naturally tend towards reunion." (p. 58) Zornberg suggests that the women's "dynamic, loving game" with the hand-mirrors (p. 61) in effect transformed the Pharaoh's attempt at sterilization of the Hebrews into an act of their redemption, by stimulating their husbands' desire and thence leading to their pregnancies and the birth of multitudes.

With the passage of time it became evident to the Egyptian taskmasters that their scheme to deplete the Hebrew population's numbers had failed—in reality it had boomeranged—as Hebrew women were giving birth in even greater numbers than before. Thus the Egyptians' evil design took an overtly deadly turn. Bechor Schor explains that the Egyptians resolved to put all the Hebrew male babies to death. The commentator implies that the Pharaoh could not have begun his genocide so blatantly several years back with this step—the outright massacre of the Israelites' sons— because the Hebrews were, then, still at the height of their strength and confidence. Only after the passage of years of backbreaking labor, the consequent erosion of their will, and the inevitable unraveling of their community's social fabric, could the Pharaoh even broach this murderous tactic.[7]

FOUR

୫୦୯୫୫୦୯୫

The Midwives Foil
the Pharaoh's Schemes

EXODUS 1:15–17

*So the King of all Egypt spoke to the Hebrews' midwives;
the name of the one was Shifra and the name of the second,
Puah. And the King said to them: "When you attend at the
birthing of the Hebrew women, and you see that they are in
the last throes of labor and are upon the birthing stone, if
they deliver a boy child you are to put him to death; if it is a
girl child, allow her to live." And the midwives feared God,
and they did not do as the king of Egypt told them; they
enabled all the children to live.*[1]

Verse 15 introduces a subtle but telling change in the subject of
the sentence from plural noun (*the Egyptians embittered. . .*
Exodus 1:14) to the singular (it was the King of Egypt himself who
spoke . . .). Since the inception and implementation of the Pharaoh's plot to decimate the Israelite people in the Torah text (Ex.
1:10), all the action by Egypt has been described as behavior by the
many. Ohr HaChayim notes this switch to the singular in verse 15.
The king of Egypt, it would appear, is about to act alone. Was he
fed up with his henchmen, disgusted that they were foiled by the

Israelite women and proved ineffectual at blocking the women's continued fertility? It would seem, according to the commentator, that while the king enacted the first stage of his genocidal scheme with the complicity, the consent, and the cooperation of the Egyptian people, the process proved to be too slow-going to suit the king. Here in this verse we are witness to his change of tactics. The singular language (*So the **king of Egypt** spoke to the Hebrews' midwives*) indicates not only his impatience but also his desire to keep his new murderous stratagem secret for as long as possible. Thus he spoke directly to the two midwives without an intervenor. The king is intent on lulling the Hebrew women into a false sense of safety, encouraging them to call upon the midwives for assistance, as was their wont, in their late stages of labor. The king sought to avoid, for as long as possible, publicizing his new killing scheme, in order to prevent pregnant Hebrew women from reacting defensively and secreting their pregnancies and deliveries even from the midwives.[2]

Students of the text should query how, if the Israelite women were giving birth to an overabundant number of babies (Ex. 1:12), these two midwives, named in verse 15, were sufficient to assist them. The king of Egypt, in his diabolical cleverness, summoned only these two midwives for a private audience in order to reveal his killing scheme for their ears alone. Ibn Ezra explains that these two named midwives were, without doubt, the chiefs of a corps of more than 500 midwives in Egypt. In fact, the midwifery corps was a steady source of revenue for the royal treasury. For every birthing she assisted, the midwife received a fee, and in turn she paid over a set portion to the king's tax collector.[3]

The commentator is leading the reader to a deeper understanding of the Pharaoh's nefarious motivations. We can deduce from Ibn Ezra's exegesis that the Egyptian king's brutal blood lust against the Israelites exceeded even his insatiable gold lust. We are witness that the king of Egypt sought the Hebrews' utter subjugation and ultimate annihilation, notwithstanding that he would, in the process, thereby destroy both his source of slave labor and a reliable stream of revenue.

Verse 15 also presents a verbal ambiguity that invites the possibility that the summoned midwives were *Egyptian* women. Kli Yakar introduces this minority opinion and explains that the Torah text could be read as follows: "The king of Egypt said to the midwives **for** the Hebrews . . . ," instead of "The king of Egypt said to the Hebrew midwives. . . ." Otherwise, says the commentator, why would the Torah text, just two verses ahead (Ex. 1:17), state that "the midwives feared God?" He reasons that if they had been *Hebrew* women that phrase (*the midwives feared God*) would have been superfluous.[4] He offers the solution that perhaps some of the midwives were Egyptian, and ordinarily not God-fearing women. Still, the Torah tells us that these midwives momentarily felt the fear of the Hebrews' God when faced with Pharaoh's command to murder the Hebrew male babies. Certainly murdering the very beings they were commissioned to bring safely into the world would have gone against the midwives' maternal natures, regardless of their nationality.

Verses 15 and 16, ostensibly a straightforward and cold-blooded edict to murder, also are imbued with seeming grammatical inconsistencies, inviting close reading and interpretation. Students of the text will note that verse 15 begins with the words "The king of Egypt spoke to the Hebrews' midwives . . . ," but the verse stops mid-phrase, never actually telling us what the king said. All we apparently learn from the *p'shat*, or simple reading of verse 15, are the names of the two midwives. The reader is left a bit anxious, filled with foreboding and expecting yet another grim royal edict. We are left dangling, worrying about what exactly the king said to them. The tension is partially resolved in the next verse, 16, which *once again* opens with the words "And the king said to them . . . ," here we read of his obscene edict to the midwives to kill the Hebrew male newborns. The question reverberates: *What* did the king say to the summoned midwives *in verse 15*?

Alschich notes that indeed the king spoke to the midwives twice: first in verse 15, and again in verse 16, and that each conversation touched on discrete matters. We discern this from verse 16's repetition of the phrase "And the king said. . . ." The king's *un*recorded words to the midwives in the first conversation were, according to the commentator, nothing short of an outright proposition! Only out of consideration for the midwives' honor did the text withold the king's request to bed them, relegating it to the *midrash* as one of the Torah's many "secrets."[5]

This astonishing disclosure is supported by both the *midrash* and the Talmud. Midrash Lekach Tov[6] explains that the king's illicit proposition to the Hebrew midwives is hinted at in the midwives' response in verse 17. There the Torah text states that the midwives, fearing God, "did not do as the king of Egypt **told** them." The Hebrew words for "he said" and "he told" have been used in the text as both *VaYoMeR* or *DiBeR*. The king's proposition to the midwives is inferred from the words **DiBeR aLeHeN**, translated as "he told them." The *midrash* is struck by the change in the text from "he said" (*VaYoMeR*) to "he told" (*DiBeR*). In verses 15 and 16 the word *VaYoMeR* is used twice; it is only in verse 17, where the Torah is narrating the midwives' refusal to hew to the king's command, that the text changes the Hebrew verb to *DiBeR*. "The midwives did **not** do what the king of Egypt **told** them . . . ."

The question on the reader's mind should be why the word *DiBeR* connotes sexual proposition. In Torah analysis such an inquiry is often resolved by a proof-text. Here, the *midrash* brings as proof—of the notion that *DiBeR* in this context implies seduction—the Torah's words in Gen 39:10, narrating the story of Joseph in the house of Potiphar. In that verse, describing Potiphar's wife's relentless and daily attempts to seduce Joseph, the Torah uses virtually the same Hebrew word, *DaBRaH*, saying "And it came to pass as **she told** Joseph repeatedly, day after day, and he did **not** hearken to her . . . ."

In both verses, in Genesis and here in Exodus, the scene is one where a person in power is speaking to persons who are in servile positions, where a refusal can mean punishment, imprisonment, or death. Yet both verses also record heroic disobedience. In Genesis Joseph narrowly escapes Potiphar's wife's sexual depradations, and here, in Exodus, the midwives actively ignore both the king's murderous edict as well as his sexual demands. And finally, in both verses where the Torah text uses the word *DiBeR*, the seducer is an Egyptian noble and the objects of the seduction are Hebrews. These verbal and narrative similarities indicate that the *midrash* has selected a convincing proof-text, reinforcing for the reader the heroism of the midwives.

This insight into the midwives' strength of character is further enhanced if we view their disobedience in light of the Talmud's injunction against illicit sexual relations. In Sanhedrin 74a, the Talmud[7] states the three commandments that a person may not transgress even at the point of threat of death. They are: first, worshipping false gods, second, engaging in illicit sexual relations, and third, committing murder. The Hebrew midwives were more courageous and righteous even than is commonly appreciated. In fact, Rabbi Adin Steinsaltz,[8] in his commentary on this section of the Talmud, explains that the rule that a person must forfeit his life rather that engage in illicit sexual relations applies only *to men*. For this reason, the fact that the midwives held themselves to the strict moral code even though they were not required to do so, is to their credit. Here in verse 17 the reader will view the evidence of the midwives' exceptional valor in upholding **all three** Talmudic strictures in face of enormous pressure. The Torah tells us that the midwives first "feared God" with an abiding awe; they feared *not* the "divine" Egyptian king.[9] Second, they refused the Egyptian king's demands for sexual favors; and third, they ignored the king's murderous edict, allowing the Hebrew babies to live.

Verse 17, rich with layers of meaning in the context of the midwives' heroism, continues to provide still another clue to their defiant behavior. The Talmud[10] (Sotah 11b) focuses on the Hebrew word following *DiBeR* in the phrase *DiBeR* **aLeHeN** (meaning "told **them**"). The verse says: "they did not do as the king of Egypt told **them**." The Talmud explains that the Hebrew phrase *DiBeR* **aLeHeN** is a strange iteration in Hebrew. The text should better have used the Hebrew word *LaHeN*, which translates exactly as "to them." The verse's word *aLeHeN* really translates as "*toward* them." It is from this awkward word that the Talmud's sages deduce that the Egyptian king approached the Hebrew midwives in an improper manner. The text's use of *aLeHeN* teaches us that the king sought sinful sexual favors from the midwives, and that to their credit the women were not seduced by the awesome power of his station.

To resolve the use of the word *aLeHeN*, translated awkwardly as "toward them," Rabbi Adin Steinsaltz, in his commentary on this section of the Talmud, suggests that the best way to read the word is not with an *aleph*, but with an *ayin*. In this way the word *aLeHeN* becomes its own homophone, sounding the same but spelled differently, and having still a different meaning. Spelled with the Hebrew letter *ayin*, *aLeHeN* means "**on** them." And, as Rabbi Steinsaltz says, quoting the Ri"f, a seventeenth-century Talmudist, "this assuredly refers to a demand for sexual intercourse. The essence of this interpretation is that the king sought to subjugate the Hebrew women utterly; by use of intolerable edicts as well as by physical domination."[11]

Rashi confirms this with a biblical proof-text. He states unequivocally that the word *aLeHeN* refers to the king's demand for sexual favors. Rashi's proof is Genesis chapter 29 verses 21 and 23 where Jacob, having worked seven years for his uncle Lavan, demands his agreed-upon marriage to his cousin Rachel so that he can "come **to her.**" The Hebrew word there is a familiar one: *aLeHa*. The clear meaning in the context is to join in sexual intimacy. And once more, two verses later, the Torah text states that Jacob "came **to her**," and the Hebrew word used is the familiar *aLeHa*. There, too, as Rashi noted, the word *aLeHa* is used to connote sexual activity.[†] [12]

The commentaries, having resolved for the reader what the king of Egypt *implicitly* said to the Hebrew midwives in verse 15, now tackle the *explicit VaYoMeR* (*he said* . . .) of verse 16. In verse 16 the Torah tells us outright that the king told the midwives: *When you attend at the birthing of the Hebrew women, and you see that they are in the last throes of labor and are upon the birthing stone, if they deliver a boy child you are to put him to death; if it is a girl child, allow her to live.*

Two questions immediately come to mind. First, how could the Pharaoh have even thought that his murderous plan would remain undetected? Would not the Hebrew mothers discern that their babies were being "born dead," and soon cease to call upon the midwives to assist in their births if they became associated with "stillbirths?" And second, as Siftei Chachamim asks,[13] why did the Pharaoh decree that all the *boy* babies should be put to death? Surely, to better fulfill his annihilation scheme, it would have been more logical for him to destroy the *girl* babies, for while the male of

---

[†]Of course, unbeknownst to Jacob, the woman he joins in his marriage bed is not his beloved Rachel, but her sister Leah. The reader is invited to refer to the authors' first book, *The Passions of the Matriarchs*, pages 208-210, where we discuss this in depth.

the species can in theory impregnate hundreds of women, it is the indispensable female who must give birth to each newborn one at a time. Even if, according to Sh'mot Rabbah[14] (1:8), the Hebrew women miraculously gave birth to six babies at once!

As to the first question, Ohr HaChayim explains that by allowing about half of the Hebrew newborns to be born alive—*i.e.*, the girl babies—the Hebrew mothers were not likely to detect that anything was amiss. Perhaps infant mortality in that time and place was very high under ordinary circumstances. For undernourished and overworked slaves, it might well have been 50%. Thus the Hebrew mothers would not soon connect stillbirths to the midwives attending them. Perhaps the realization would be made over time that the stillbirths were males and the live births females, but in the meantime the king would have effected part of his genocidal plan.[15]

The Talmud explains that the Pharaoh suggested to the midwives that they employ a secret detection technique while assisting at the Hebrew mothers' births. He reminds the midwives that when the baby is about to be born, if its face is oriented downward, it will be a boy; if it faces upward, it will be a girl [sic]. In this way, he suggests, the midwives could detect the baby's gender surreptitiously, and do their killing unbeknownst to the mother, even before the infant exited the birth canal.[16]

The commentary on Torah Temima is stunned that the Pharaoh would think it necessary to coach the experienced midwives in birthing procedures! The commentary explains that the Talmud has inserted that vignette to enlighten us about the Pharaoh's attempt to circumvent, in advance, the midwives' expected abhorrence to killing the newborns. The Pharaoh underestimates both the midwives' repugnance and their courage. He suspects that they would balk at outright killing of the newborns, and so presents them with a way to kill the male babies undetected, while the mother is still in extreme labor, and before the baby has taken its first breath. The king expects that the midwives will not consider such behavior to be outright murder.[17] He whispers to the two midwives that just a finger's press to the newborn boys' nostrils will be sufficient to kill him, and no one will be the wiser.[18] As for the girl babies, the Netziv explains that the Pharaoh was suggesting a passive neglect. If the girl babies happened to be born alive, the midwives were to let them be.[19]

Bechor Schor reminds the reader, who by now appreciates the Pharaoh's perfidy and his obsessive hatred for the Hebrews, that although the Pharaoh is determined to annihilate the Hebrews from his midst, he still desires to keep his killing scheme secret. It is for this reason that the king asks the midwives to simulate miscarriages and stillbirths with the techniques described, rather than to commit blatant murder in the light of day.[20]

Rashi explains that the Pharaoh's particular obsession with annihilating the Hebrews' *male* babies has its genesis in his astrologers' prediction that a male not yet born was destined to be the Hebrews' future deliverer.[21] The king is smug in his plans, thinking that by secretly co-opting the midwives he will secure his instrument to murder, and moreover, if his astrologers are correct, he will cut off any hope of the birth of a deliverer as well. In effect, the Pharaoh thinks he will kill off the despised Hebrews and their deliverer with this one clandestine stroke. His last step into perdition, which will entail escalating his scheme to outright extermination on a public and grand scale with the cooperation of all Egyptians, is still to come.

Verse 17, the reader will recall, states that *the midwives feared God, and they did not do as the king of Egypt told them; they enabled all the children to live.* Most commentaries understand this verse to mean that the midwives engaged in two independent actions. First, they disobeyed the Pharaoh's demand for sexual favors (as we described earlier in this chapter), and second, as the Netziv teaches us, they took affirmative steps to keep **all** the Hebrew newborns alive, regardless of their gender.[22] The Talmud (Sotah 11b)[23] expands the midwives' heroic actions, describing in detail that the midwives defied the Pharaoh's murderous scheme by going so far as to nourish the newborns with necessary food and drink. Ibn Ezra adds that the midwives spared no effort and used all means at their disposal to deliver live Hebrew babies.[24]

The midwives' courage in foiling the Pharaoh's edict elicits one tribute after the other from the Torah commentaries. The commentaries are sensitive to the excruciatingly difficult and dangerous, high-stakes tableau that is being enacted in the Egyptian palace, and they illuminate it for us here. The king himself—not an underling, not even a viceroy—is giving them a secret order to kill. We must understand that these midwives not only were members of the enslaved population, but also that they were *women*, and, as such, in that time and that place, they qualified as chattel in his eyes, and existed only to do the divine king's bidding. Perhaps that is another reason that the commentaries understand and explicate for us the sexual demands inherent in the king's words to the midwives; the Pharaoh understood that sexual subjugation is but another way to bend another to your will and also to quash her inclination to refuse or protest.

In this light, the reader can begin to appreciate the true heroism that the midwives exhibited by refusing the Pharaoh's sexual demands and by transgressing his explicit order to murder the boy babies. That they went to extraordinary measures to deliver a 100% record of live Hebrew babies—in a time of excruciating slavery, undernourishment and under royal warrant to do the precise opposite—shows the reader in a dramatic manner the mettle of these Hebrew women. The commentaries describe in detail the midwives' actions in defiance of the Pharaoh.

Sh'mot Rabbah (1:15) explains that after the Pharaoh's secret edict to the midwives, not only did they *not* engage in the murder of the Hebrew boy babies, but while attending at the birth of destitute mothers, they also went beyond the purview of their midwifery role; after they assisted in the baby's delivery, they went knocking on the door of a wealthier woman nearby, seeking food and drink for the new mother and her needy family.[25] Ohr HaChayim reveals that before the Pharaoh selected them as his instruments to murder the Hebrew babies, the midwives considered their job well done if they assisted at each birth and moved on to the next, leaving the newborn in the care of its mother. Providing food and drink to the newborns was not within their expected province. After the king's murderous edict, however, the midwives redoubled their efforts so that none of the newborns in their care would die. Their intention was not only to assist in as many live Hebrew births as they could, but also to increase the Hebrew birth rate on their watch. They were particularly concerned not to lose even one baby, if it were within their powers to keep it alive. The midwives sought to remove themselves as completely as possible from the shadow of the king's murderous scheme. [26]

Sh'mot Rabbah explains,[27] in the apotheosis to the discussion of the midwives' actions in defying Pharaoh, that not only did they do whatever was physically possible to ensure live births, but also that they implored God to assist them. The *midrash* describes the intense drama of the birthing moment. When the midwives are about to deliver a Hebrew baby who is in danger of being strangled by the umbilical cord, or who could be blinded by birth trauma, or who might be born with a deformity, or whose limbs were in danger of being severed during an impossible birth, the midwives resort to the highest power they know; they stand before the Almighty and pray. The *midrash* then supplies their unrecorded prayer: "Master of the Universe, You know that we have transgressed the edict of the Pharaoh. It is *Your* will that we seek to uphold. Oh, Creator of the Universe, please allow this newborn to emerge whole and perfect." According to the *midrash*, God's response to this powerful combination of heroic action and intimate prayer is immediate and complete: He heeds their prayers, and the babies are born whole and healthy.

FIVE

༺ღ༒ღ༻

The Midwives are Called to Task

EXODUS 1:18-19

And the King of Egypt summoned the midwives, and he asked them, "Why have you done this thing?! And [why have you] kept the babies alive?" And the midwives responded to the Pharaoh, "Because the Hebrew women are not like the Egyptian women; they are like CHaYoT; and before the midwife arrives to [assist] them, they already have given birth."[1]

The midwives are summoned to the palace, and must be terrified for their lives. They have transgressed the king's explicit orders, and fear that now they will be called to task, certainly censured, perhaps thrown into prison or even executed for their disobedience. Ohr HaChayim is surprised that the king's opening question to the midwives is phrased in the positive declarative (*Why have* **you** **done** *this thing?*) rather than in the negative (*Why did you* **not** **kill** *the babies as I ordered?*).[2] The commentaries suggest, in response, that there must be an additional subtext to the king's question. Sforno supplies an answer. The Pharaoh demanded that the midwives explain why they deceived him;[3] he had expected them to kill the Hebrew boy babies, and instead he sees that on the contrary, the babies' number is increasing. He must be astonished

25

that the lowly midwives dared to disobey his edict. It is interesting that he summons them to an audience in the first place, allowing them to defend themselves. Perhaps the king needs the midwives' services too much to do away with them outright.

The Netziv[4] provides an insight into the Pharaoh's knowledge of the Hebrew midwives' righteousness. The commentator explains that the king did not ask the midwives why they did not kill the Hebrew boy babies with their own hands. It is likely he even expected that they would refuse such an order categorically, on the strength of their moral beliefs. The Pharaoh knew that the law of Israel prohibited spilling of another's blood to the point of requiring oneself to be killed in his stead. The king appreciates that the midwives, who are necessary to him if he is to effect his killing scheme, are walking a dangerous tightrope. They must do his bidding or face punishment or death for disobeying a royal order; they also are compelled by their moral and religious compass to hew to their God's commands not to commit murder. The king's question, therefore, could have been, "why did you go out of your way to keep them alive?" in direct defiance of the spirit of his genocidal edict.

The midwives' conciliatory response to the king's summons ("*Because the Hebrew women are not like the Egyptian women; they are like CHaYoT; and before the midwife arrives to [assist] them, they already have given birth!*") hinges on the definition of the word *CHaYoT*. According to the *p'shat* or simple meaning of the text, it would seem the midwives are saying that while the Egyptian women require the services of a midwife, the Hebrew women do not, and they give birth before the midwives arrive on the scene. A common translation of the word *CHaYoT* is "wild creature," and Rashi interprets the midwives' excuse to Pharaoh ("they are like *CHaYoT*") to mean that the Hebrew women are likened to creatures of the field, who give birth without the services of a midwife.[5] The word *CHaYoT* contains the familiar root word *chai*, meaning "life." Bechor Schor explains that the Hebrew mothers are as proficient as the midwives in *bringing forth life*, even from their own wombs.[6] Ohr HaChayim adds that the Hebrew women thus were able to assist at one another's birthings, dispensing with the need for a professional midwife.[7] We can understand from these commentaries that the midwives are explaining to the Pharaoh that for all these reasons, they are not being called in to attend at the birthings of the Hebrews' babies.

Onkelos translates *CHaYoT* differently, to mean that the Hebrew mothers are "intelligent and knowledgeable."[8] Sforno says that the midwives explain to the king, "The Hebrew mothers are so canny in the ways of midwifery that if we were to attend at the births and attempt anything, however slight, that was not completely according to protocol, the Hebrew women would sense it instantly, and would never again summon us to assist at a Hebrew birthing."[9] Kli Yakar adds that the midwives are explaining to the king that they arrive at the birthing beds of the Hebrew women right *after* the babies have been born; in time to clean up the infant, and hear its first cries.[10] Sha'arei Aharon puts into words what the reader by now must begin to intuit. The commentator describes their explanation to the king: "The Hebrew women are giving birth without us. They deliberately delay calling us in until it is time to deliver the afterbirth. They do not allow us to attend to the newborns at all; they employ us only to assist them with their own needs after childbirth is done. We worry that the Hebrew mothers have begun to suspect us."[11] Ohr HaChayim adds, "The Hebrew women are so clever that they hide the early evidence of their pregnancy, so that they announce a false due date. They surely have a feeling that something is amiss."[12]

Ibn Ezra sums up the enormity of the Hebrew mothers' courage and strength as they defied Pharaoh and continued to have children against almost inhuman odds. The commentator states simply and eloquently that the Hebrew women were possessed of a life-force that beat powerfully in their hearts.[13]

Thus, it is the midwives' indomitable heroism in the face of the Pharaoh's pressure to commit infanticide, together with the Hebrew mothers' undaunted fortitude in continuing to have children throughout the darkest days of unending enslavement, that earns them the eternal sobriquet of "righteous women."

SIX

ഇരുഷ്ഠഗ

The Midwives are Favored by God

EXODUS 1:20

And the Lord favored the midwives; and the people multiplied and grew exceedingly mighty.[1]

The first part of this verse states that God favored *the midwives*, while the second portion of the verse seems not to follow, because it states how *the people* were favored. The commentaries address the relationship between the first and second parts of this verse. Ohr HaChayim[2] presents the simple reading of the text, stating that God favored the midwives by granting that the Hebrew women gave birth to many babies. In this way, the commentator continues, the midwives' reputation swelled along with the birth rate. It was considered a credit to the midwives that the Hebrew mothers whom they attended brought forth many healthy babies. Thus the midwives' fear that the Hebrew mothers would suspect them of foiling their healthy births was not realized.

Bechor Schor further helps us to appreciate the dynamic at work between the midwives and the Hebrew mothers. He explains that the mothers did not suspect that the midwives were harming their newborns; to the contrary, the heightened birth rate set that

28

potential fear to rest. But even if the Hebrew birth rate *had fallen* noticeably, the commentator assures us that the midwives would *still* not have been suspected of foul play. The trust between each mother and her midwife was so strong that each mother was confident that her midwife had only *her and her baby's* best interest at heart.[3]

Still the question persists for students of the text: Why does the Torah specifically state in the first half of our verse that *the Lord favored the midwives?* What was the specific "favor" or benefit that accrued to them? Sh'mot Rabbah explains that the benefit granted to the midwives was that God caused the king of Egypt to believe their explanations for the increased Hebrew birthrate. That the Pharaoh did not vent his ire on them was in the nature of a miracle, given the king's murderous scheme to do away with the Hebrews entirely. Had he perceived that the midwives were deliberately undermining his orders, there is no question that he would have harmed them grievously, if only to set an example for those who betrayed his trust.[4]

The Netziv builds on Sh'mot Rabbah, and explains that God's kindness to the midwives was to insure that the king's attention was diverted from them. When the Pharaoh saw that attacking the problem of the Hebrew birth rate from the vantage point of the birthing bed did not yield him what he desired—namely, a slackening of the Hebrews' fertility—the readers quite rightly might have feared for the midwives' welfare. How would the Pharaoh react to this failure? Would he throw the midwives into prison, or even have them put to death? The commentary tells us that *the Lord favored the midwives* by causing the king to bypass them entirely. He chose to relegate them to the sidelines, and to concentrate on his scheme of murder on a grand scale. The midwives quite literally faded into the background because they were no longer of any use to the Pharaoh, and he ignored them completely. This falling out of favor saved the midwives' lives.[5]

SEVEN

ഇൽഇൽ

Shifra and Puah Defy the King

EXODUS 1:15

. . . The name of the one was Shifra and the name of the second, Puah.[1]

The story of the midwives is far from ended. At this juncture, however, before we continue discussing the life-and-death drama that will play out in the Pharaoh's palace and in the homes of the Hebrews, we must hark back to verse 15 of Chapter 1 of Exodus. The reader will recall that that verse, which we discussed at length in Chapter 4, named the chief midwives whom the king of Egypt had called to a private audience. In the subsequent biblical verses, the midwives' actions and their interactions with the Pharaoh, are recorded at length, while their identities have been sidelined. Now their identities come to the fore.

In verse 15 the king of Egypt privately addresses the two Hebrew midwives, named in the text as Shifra and Puah. These pivotal women are specifically named in the Torah, and they become important as the story of Moses unfolds. Also, many commentaries associate the women's midwifely behavior with their given names, which are dissected at length. In fact, we learn much about how the midwives perform their important roles from the commentaries' discussion of their names. The Netziv opens the discussion by stating the *p'shat*, or simple explanation of the text, when he informs us that at the outset, the Torah is recording these women's names for posterity, because Shifra and Puah are the names of the two women who stand up to the king of Egypt and are uncowed.[2] Bechor Schor states outright that naming them in this verse of the Torah—the only mention of their names in all five books of Moses—was divinely intended. Recording the names of Shifra and Puah, and the reiteration of their names by countless future generations who recount their valor with every reading of the book of Exodus, is quite simply a way to memorialize them and bring honor to their memory. We must never forget that Shifra and Puah stood fast in the face of the mightiest monarch in the known world, and contravened his direct order to murder the Hebrew male newborns. Their lives were literally on the line, or, as the commentary eloquently reminds us, they held their own lives in the palms of their hands in order to save their fellow Hebrews.[3] The names Shifra and Puah stand for this selfless bravery.

The Talmud and the commentaries are fascinated with these two named women. Who are Shifra and Puah? If they are simply one-time heroines, with no further connection to our story, we would lose the depth of their characterization. For this reason, we welcome the discussions of their provenance. Rabbi Yehoshua David Hartman,[4] a modern commentator, states unequivocally that of course Shifra and Puah are not merely two ordinary women. The Talmud[5] (Sotah 11b) embellishes on this concept and recounts a discourse between Rav and Shmuel, the founders of the Babylonian Academies, on the identities of the two midwives. According to Rav, the two women are a mother and daughter team, with "the one" who is mentioned first in the text being the primary midwife and "the second" being her assistant. He identifies the first as Yocheved, and the second as Miriam. Shmuel also identifies the first midwife as Yocheved, but names the second as Elisheva, Yocheved's daughter-in-law. The reader now must identify two *new* women, Miriam and Elisheva! We recall the name of Yocheved from Chapter one of this book. Yocheved is "the seventieth soul," the daughter of Jacob's son Levi, born as Jacob and his entire family were entering the portals of Egypt. The woman Yocheved is destined to be none other than Moses' mother. Miriam and Elisheva, however, have not yet appeared on the Torah proscenium, but we know they, too, are destined for greatness. The Maharal[6] explains that the Torah text has not yet mentioned Yocheved and Miriam (and Aaron and Elisheva) out of honor and courtesy to Moses. Once Moses' birth is recorded (in upcoming verses), the Bible calls the other important biblical personae—his mother, Yocheved, his father, Amram, his sister, Miriam, his brother, Aaron, and his brother's wife, Elisheva (in Ex. 6:23)—by name.[7] In keeping with the Maharal's interpretation, and for the sake of the flow of our story, we will identify Shifra and Puah as Yocheved and Miriam, respectively.

The reader should bear in mind, however, that many commentaries consider the names Shifra and Puah to be descriptions of the *roles* of the two women rather than their proper names. Sh'mot Rabbah first explains that the name Shifra derives from the root of the Hebrew word *L'SHaPeR*, meaning "to cleanse and beautify." The midwife named Shifra loyally served the pregnant Hebrew women, wiping the amniotic blood from their babies' nostrils, and washing and swaddling the newborn before placing it in its mother's arms. The commentary's second explanation is based on a word play. Because Shifra's skilled midwifery also allowed the Hebrews' birth rate to climb, Sh'mot Rabbah points out that the Hebrew word used in the Torah for "increase and multiply," *PaRu*, is incorporated into Shifra's name, *SHePaRu*, because she caused the Israelites to increase and multiply in defiance of the Pharaoh's edict to kill all the Hebrew male babies. The third explanation of Shifra's name reflects the fact that her repeated acts of assisting in thousands of live, healthy births glorified her—*SHaPRaH*—in the eyes of the Almighty.[8] Ba'al HaTurim introduces a fourth etymological reading of the name Shifra. The commentary explains that her name also hints at her role as the midwife who often resuscitated the newborns by inserting a tube into the baby's nostrils and blowing air into the little one's lungs. The Hebrew word for this tool (similar in sound to *shofar*, the ritual horn that is blown to herald the new year) is *SHeFuFeReT*.[9]

As for Puah, Rashi explains that her name is an onomatapoeia for the vocalization or sound associated with her behavior. The girl named Puah calmed the newborn by muttering words and nonsense sounds like *poo-ah, pooh-ah* to comfort its cries. The commentator says that Puah's sing-song speech to the Hebrew newborns became her trademark.[10] The sounds she expressed became her name over time. "Go call the one who comforts the babies, who says *pooh-ah* to them!" can readily be seen as the rallying cry when the Hebrew mothers were in the final throes of their labor. Tosfot (Talmud Sotah 11b) goes further, ascribing to Puah the important task of making her comforting *pooh-ah* sounds into the ears of the laboring mothers, perhaps wiping the mothers' perspiring brows and whispering nonsense sounds to them during the arduous birthing process.[11]

Sh'mot Rabbah[12] (1:13) relates a *midrashic* anecdote concerning Shifra, Puah and the Pharaoh, which further illustrates how their names reflected their function as well as their character. The commentary explains that the name Puah can also mean "to appear, or to stand before," from the Hebrew root-word *HoPHiYa*. Apparently Puah, when challenged by the king about the Hebrew births, in an exhausted moment of anger challenged the monarch and exclaimed: "Woe unto this man when God comes to collect retribution from him!" The Pharaoh became filled with wrath and sought to kill the girl. Her mother, Shifra, true to her name, "beautified" her daughter's words, interceded on Puah's behalf, and placated the Pharaoh, saying: "Pay no heed to the girl, she is young and is having a childish tantrum." In this artful way Shifra calmed the king's anger, and thus averted a potential tragedy.

The Talmud (Sotah 11b) here presents Puah—whom it identifies as Miriam, Moses' older sister—as possessing amazing gifts. We have already seen that she is an able assistant to Shifra, calming and talking to the newborns and to the birthing mothers; that she is fearless even in the face of the Pharaoh; and that she toils alongside her mother, identified as Yocheved, helping to care for the Hebrew infants. Now, the Talmud assigns to the girl Miriam the gift of prophecy as well.[13] In an astounding pronouncement the Talmud states outright that the girl Puah, whom it acknowledges to be Miriam, speaks with divine inspiration, prophesying to all that her mother is destined to give birth to the great redeemer of Israel. The reader must appreciate what dark and hopeless times Shifra and Puah—Yocheved and Miriam—are inhabiting. They are serving their Hebrew brethren by bringing new souls into the world, but what a world! Unending decades of servitude precede them, and only whispers of secret astrological predictions of a redeemer are heard. That the young Miriam is heard prophesying that the redeemer of Israel is soon to be born is at once thrilling and terrifying. What if Miriam is correct in her prophecy, and what will the Pharaoh do when he hears these predictions?

Kli Yakar points out that Miriam's prophesying underlines her other name, Puah. The Bible's use of the name Puah, which originates in the root word *peh*, meaning "mouth," hints to us that Puah's—or Miriam's—spoken words are important to the biblical story. Paired with Shifra, whose name is translated to mean "to beautify," the girl's prophecy is understood to mean that her mother will enjoy a miraculous rejuvenation, a beautification similar to that enjoyed by the matriarch Sarah many years before. Yocheved will miraculously return to her youthful beauty, and will soon give birth to Israel's redeemer.[14]

EIGHT

❧❦❧❦

The Midwives' Reward

EXODUS 1:21

And it happened that because the midwives feared God, [He] made houses for them.[1]

We return now to the Bible's narrative describing the consequences of the midwives' courage. The reader will recall that in verse 20 the text states that *the Lord favored the midwives* by allowing the Hebrews to multiply greatly and increase in strength. This next verse continues this thought, adding a third consequence of their bravery, the "making of houses." What does this curiously worded phrase mean? The *p'shat* states that God is the subject of the sentence, and that *He* made houses for the midwives. But the Netziv recognizes an ambiguity in the text's wording (*who* actually made the "houses" and what exactly are they?) as he addresses the question of the subject of the sentence. The Netziv explains that the Bible text deliberately fails to explain the identity of "the maker" of the houses, thus leaving room for two interpretations. If "the maker" is the Lord, then the houses in question are an additional reward for the midwives' valor.

But if the Biblical text intends that "the maker" of the houses is the king of Egypt, then we must conclude, as does the Da'at Zekeinim,[2] that the houses are not a reward, but a form of house arrest for the midwives for having disobeyed the king's command to kill the Hebrew male newborns. Thus, the king moved the midwives into his personal servants' quarters in order to keep a close watch on their comings and goings among the Hebrews. Sha'arei Aharon adds that the phrase "built them houses" refers specifically to the king's housing the midwives where their movements were extremely restricted. They were no longer free to venture out among the Hebrew mothers, and could not even leave the house without first seeking the king's express permission.[3] The Netziv continues that this latter interpretation (that the Pharaoh eventually resorted to keeping the midwives quasi-prisoners), signals the commencement of the Pharaoh's unsheathed genocidal scheme, and we will see that this follows closely in the text.[4] Sha'arei Aharon concludes that when the king realized that the midwives were not prepared to commit the clandestine killing of the Hebrew babies as he had commanded them, he ceased to rely on them at all, kept them under house arrest, and thereafter resorted to outright murder and terror.[5]

In *Mei Ha-Shiluach*, the Ishbitzer Rebbe's commentary on the Torah, the chassidic master uses this Torah verse (*because the midwives feared God, [He] made houses for them*) as a springboard for a discussion on the differences between fear of God and fear of a person of flesh and blood. He teaches that when a person fears another mortal, this can cause within him disquietude and anxiety, emotions that in essence define the word "fear." In contrast, when one has fear of God, the emotions evoked are the precise opposite. The midwives in our verses, the Ishbitzer explains, experience a true fear of God that in effect constructs a psychological haven which yields a peace of mind so great that it overrides the natural fear of a flesh-and-blood king. This is the reason the Torah pairs "fear of God" with "building houses;" the houses referred to in the text need not even be made of bricks and mortar. According to the Ishbitzer they are the emotional bulwarks that the midwives' true fear of God provides for them.[6]

Rabbi Joseph B. Soloveitchik ("the Rav")[†] credits the Hebrew

---

[†]Soloveitchik, J. B., Public lecture on the weekly Torah portion of *Sh'mot* (Exodus), at Yeshiva University in New York City on December 30, 1980. From the private recordings of Rabbi Haskel Lookstein.

midwives with actively maintaining Jewish life in Egypt during the darkest days of the Pharaoh's edicts. The Rav explains, "I would say this phrase [*He made houses for them*] actually means that the *meyaldot* [the midwives] became the leaders." The term "house," continues the Rav, implies the idea of responsibility. "The midwives were entrusted by the Almighty with the leadership and the authority to lead and to teach" the Hebrew slaves in Egypt. Not only that, but by their heroic acts of refusing to comply with the Pharaoh's murderous scheme and standing up to the tyrant to his face, the midwives modeled courage of the highest order as well as a deep compassion for the unborn children. The people raised the midwives to heroic status and God immortalized their place in history by "making houses for them."

Rashi's interpretation of this verse is that the phrase "the houses" refers to the three great dynastic families of the Hebrews: the priestly dynasty, the Levite dynasty, and the monarchical dynasty.[7] At this point in the story of the Jewish people the Hebrews have multiplied greatly, so that the twelve sons of Jacob, who emigrated to Egypt as a sprawling family of seventy souls, have reproduced mightily, until Jacob's descendants are now considered tribes, or great families, each in its own right. Sha'arei Aharon explains that in such situations, each individual family represents a discrete dynasty.[8] From this verse the commentaries derive that Yocheved and Miriam, the heroic Hebrew midwives, are rewarded with the privilege of being the matriarchs of the dynastic houses of the Israelites. Yocheved, the mother of Aaron, Moses and Miriam, is destined to be a progenitor of *all three* dynasties: the priestly, the Levite, and the monarchical houses.

The Talmud[9] (Sotah 11b) engages in a spirited discussion about Yocheved's three children, the undisputed heroes of the Book of Exodus. The Talmud is eager to assign rewards to these heroes, and while we are only at the beginning of the Exodus story, and still have not officially "met" Moses or Aaron in the text, the Talmud deals with this issue now, because we have just witnessed Yocheved and Miriam's heroism in the face of Pharaoh's pressure. The Talmud here identifies Yocheved's reward for her heroic midwifery. It is that her three children, born in a time of darkness and bondage, will each grow in deeds and stature so as to ultimately merit being named as the heads of the Israelite dynasties. The Talmud also describes the reward of the second midwife, Miriam, Yocheved's eldest child, in the same terms. Rav and Shmuel set the parameters of the discussion. Rav states that the rewards referred to in our verse of the Torah text, that *[He] made houses for them*, is referring to the "house" or dynasty of the priests, which emerges from Aaron, and the dynasty of the Levites, which emerges from Moses. Shmuel adds that the dynasty of the Israelite monarchy, beginning with King David, emerges from Miriam.

While it is known that King David is from the tribe of Judah, and Miriam from the tribe of Levi, the Talmud and *midrash* connect Miriam to the Israelite monarchy through marriage. Unfortunately, the Bible text itself nowhere explicitly mentions either Miriam's marriage or her progeny. It is Rashi, summarizing the Talmud and *midrash*, who teaches us (Exodus 17:10) that Miriam is said to have wed Caleb, son of Yephuneh or Chetzron, and to have given birth to their son, Hur.[10] The Torah text (Numbers 13:3, 6) clearly states that Caleb is a leader of the tribe of Judah. Both men are Israelite heroes during the forty years of desert wanderings after the exodus from Egypt,[†] and King David is descended from them.

[†]Caleb is renowned as one of the two Israelite spies (the other is Joshua) to have had the courage to speak up to Moses—in the face of vociferous opposition by the other ten spies—saying that the Israelites indeed possessed the ability to capture the land of Canaan (Numbers 14:6-24). Hur, along with Aaron, Moses' brother, is credited with assisting Moses in the miraculous victory of the Israelites over the Amalekites in their first pitched battle after the exodus from Egypt. Hur and Aaron each held one of Moses' arms aloft for the duration of the battle, giving the fledgeling nation the courage to smite their enemy (Exodus 17:10-13).

NINE

๛เงิ๛เงิ

"Death by Drowning
to All Newborn Sons!"

EXODUS 1:22

And the Pharaoh commanded his entire nation as follows:
every newborn son you shall fling into the Nile; but all the
daughters you may allow to live.[1]

It was a time of misery and fear in the homes of the Hebrews in
the land of Egypt. Ironically, it was also a time in which a glimmer
of hope pierced the dark days of backbreaking slavery. The reader
will recall our mention in Chapter 7 that the young girl Miriam was
prophesying among her people that the redeemer was destined to
be born from her mother. In this verse of the Bible we witness the
king of Egypt's nationwide edict to the Egyptians to drown *all*
newborn male babies in the Nile. We are led to inquire: What is
the urgency that suddenly compels the king to escalate his killing
scheme to this obscene level? Rashi explains that on the day that
Yocheved gave birth to her son Moses, the Pharaoh's astrologers
announced, "Today was born the deliverer of the Hebrews! But we
do not know whether the deliverer is Egyptian or Hebrew. However, we can foresee that this redeemer's end will be caused by
water." This is the reason that in a seeming sudden move, the king

is here commanding even the Egyptians to drown "*every* son that is born," not restricting his edict only to Hebrew babies.[2] The royal astrologers have a murky vision of the birth of a redeemer, and are unable to discern whether he is born to a Hebrew mother or to an Egyptian. From that day, it would seem, *all* babies born in Egypt were to be killed by drowning.

It is fascinating that the Egyptian astrologers had a clear vision that the redeemer's birth was imminent, but that they were stumped as to his definitive nationality. Was he Egyptian, or was he Hebrew? Of course, from the position of hindsight the reader is aware that Moses, the predicted redeemer of the Hebrews, is *both* Hebrew—born of a Hebrew slave—*and* Egyptian—rescued and raised by none other than the daughter of the Egyptian king, as we will explain fully in coming chapters. The Maharal is quick to point this out in his discussion of the astrologers' prediction. They were not far off the mark.[3]

Sh'mot Rabbah (1:18) tells us that on that fateful day, after the Pharaoh was given the news of the birth—or the conception—of the redeemer by his royal astrologers, he gathered all the people of Egypt and explained the nation's predicament, asking that they yield up to him, as a patriotic sacrifice, all their newborns for a period of nine months. The king at once was issuing both an edict and an appeal, playing upon the Egyptians' long-lived dependency on the slave labor provided by the Hebrews, and, as Ohr HaChayim explains, upon their repugnance of the Hebrews' fertility.[4] He was in effect telling his people, "If you want to keep these Hebrews as your slaves, you must make the human sacrifice of your own newborns for a period of nine months, until we are assured that the redeemer's birth is no longer a threat." The wily and murderous king also feared for his own crown, knowing that with the ascension of the redeemer, he would lose everything. Sh'mot Rabbah continues that the Egyptian people resisted his edict to drown their own children, protesting incredulously that it was beyond comprehension that the Hebrews' redeemer should be of Egyptian birth; surely he would be born of a Hebrew mother.[5]

According to Akeidat Yitzchak, while the Pharoah announced to the gathered Egyptian multitude that his edict was across-the-board and applied to *all* his subjects—Egyptian and Hebrew alike—he secretly let it be known to the Egyptians that he would be enforcing the edict only against the Hebrews. Engaging in this public fiction ensured the king of two consequences: first, that his Egyptian subjects would aid him in his killing scheme, and second that the Hebrews, while doubtless distraught at the prospect of losing their newborns, would be mollified somewhat by their belief that this bloodthirsty monarch was not sparing even his own peoples' babies in his paranoid quest for the redeemer. The Pharaoh's goal was first to co-opt the Egyptian populace, and then to annihilate the purported enemy.[6] The king's strategy was not misplaced. Yefei To'ar confirms that in response to the groundswell of Egyptian resistance to sacrificing their own babies to the king's extreme fear of this reputed redeemer, the Pharaoh backed down from his command, but only with regard to his Egyptian subjects. Concerning the Hebrew boy babies, his edict stood until the day, months hence, that the infant Moses was set adrift in the Nile by Yocheved. Once Yocheved's son was set adrift in the water, the royal astrologers' predictions were set to rest. On that day the killing stopped.[7]

TEN

ಬುಲ್ಲಬುಲ್ಲ

A Wedding, A Divorce
and A Remarriage

EXODUS 2:1

And a man from the house of Levi went out and took [in marriage] the daughter of Levi.[1]

Rashbam identifies the text's mystery "man from the house of Levi" as Amram, and names "the daughter of Levi" as Yocheved.[2] The Bible text introduces this Israelite couple at this juncture because it is readying the reader for the events following the birth of their third child, who will be none other than Moses. The commentator Chizkuni explains that the Bible is narrating in this verse a marriage which actually had taken place some years ago, some time *before* the Pharaoh's murderous edict. In fact, Amram and Yocheved already have two children, Miriam and Aaron.[3] This verse places Amram and Yocheved squarely in the midst of the Hebrews' darkest days in Egypt, and they will not be untouched by the Pharaoh's genocidal plans. The reader is expected to take note that even Yocheved, the heroic midwife, is not exempt from the horrors of the king's murderous scheme. The verses that follow will detail how she and Miriam go to great and ingenious lengths once again to foil the Pharaoh. This time the newborn they rescue is

Yocheved's own son and Miriam's infant brother, and they earn textual immortality as a result.

This verse states that Amram "went out" and "took [in marriage] a daughter of Levi." Addressing the odd phrasing of the text, The Talmud (Sotah 12a),[4] in a fascinating and lengthy discourse, rhetorically asks, "Where did Amram go?" Many commentators consider just this question, and their answers allow us to appreciate the extreme hardships that the Hebrews faced in Egypt, even as concerns the basic human right to marry and procreate. The Talmud's rhetorical response to its own query is that Amram "went out" at the advice of his daughter Miriam. It elaborates that apparently Amram, who was a man of great stature and a leader of his people, was distraught as he witnessed his people's newborn sons meet death by drowning at the hands of Pharaoh's soldiers. He cast about for some solution to ease his own and his brethren's pain, and ultimately decided that the Hebrew slaves should refrain from having children at all, thus foiling the king's plan by depriving him of babies to fling into the Nile. So Amram publicly divorced Yocheved his wife, explaining his rationale to all. Thereupon, in agreement, all the Hebrew husbands followed suit. According to Kli Yakar, the Bible's statement that Amram "went out" is a euphemism for just this "divorcing" behavior.[5]

This untenable situation prevailed, according to the Talmud, until Miriam took her father aside and exhorted him, saying: "Father, *your* pronouncement to all our brethren is even more harsh than the Pharaoh's! For while the Pharaoh's edict condemns to death only the *male* babies, your prohibition affects *both* male and female unborn Hebrew children. Pharaoh's edict destroys their *mortal* existence, but your decision affects the mortality *and* immortality of the Hebrew people, as it prevents the birth of *all* future Hebrew generations. Furthermore, if we are forced against our will to comply with the king's edict, *perhaps* it will succeed in wiping out all the Israelites, but there is always the finite possiblity that his evil scheme will *not* be entirely successful, and that a remnant of the Hebrews will survive. On the other hand, words issuing from your mouth—the words of a respected and righteous man—pronouncing a ban on procreation, will surely come true."

The Talmud continues, stating that Amram saw the truth in his daughter's argument, and heeded her words. He arranged for

Yocheved to be returned to him, and, in public panoply, recon-secrated his marriage vows. Following his public example, all the Hebrew men retook their wives. The public act of *re-taking* their wives is the reason this verse ends with the phrase "and *he took* a daughter of Levi." Amram's "taking" was their public re-marriage, and was intended to set an example to all the Israelites. Amram's revocation of his ban on procreation was greeted as it was intended: a reaffirmation of hope in the future, of belief in an ultimate redemption. The Talmud emphasizes that Amram's re-marriage to Yocheved was enacted with great public spectacle. In full view of the community the couple's children, Miriam and Aaron, danced in front of the bride's palanquin as she approached her husband-to-be, and that even the heavenly angels rejoiced at their reunion.

Concerning the term "daughter of Levi," the Talmud asks whether the text could really be referring to Yocheved—the daughter of Jacob's son Levi, who was born one hundred and thirty years before. According to Rashi,[6] the unborn Yocheved was still cocooned within her mother's belly when Levi's wagons jolted into Egypt. Yocheved was born as her father's wagon passed between the walls of the city, so, as we have already described, she is counted as the "seventieth soul" who came down into Egypt with the patriarch Jacob. Should the now-venerable Yocheved accurately be termed a "daughter," or young woman on the brink of marriage? The Talmud's sages respond affirmatively that this grown woman most certainly is Yocheved, the daughter of Jacob's third son Levi. Yocheved's advanced chronological age at this point in the Torah text is dismissed by the Talmud's sages. They state that Yocheved is able to become pregnant with Moses in the same miraculous way that the matriarch Sarah gave birth to Isaac in her advanced age: she enjoyed a rejuvenation. The Talmud (Bava Batra 119b)[7] explains that the Torah text calls Yocheved a "daughter" in this verse to teach us that her entire body returned to its youthful suppleness, any wrinkles she had disappeared, and her youthful beauty returned to her intact, as she appeared in the days of her youth. It was in this state of youthful rejuvenation that Amram re-took Yocheved as his wife in the public ceremony described in the Talmud.

E L E V E N

ഇരുഇരു

Yocheved Gives Birth to a Son

EXODUS 2:2

And the woman became pregnant and gave birth to a son;
when she saw that all was well with him she kept his
existence secret for three months.[1]

The Bible attempts to hold the reader in slight suspense by
continuing to withold the names of the main characters of this
drama. In the previous verse, it was the Talmud and the commentaries who named "the man from the house of Levi" and "the
daughter of Levi" as Amram and Yocheved. Here the text narrates
the birth of their baby boy, an unnamed son. Perhaps the lack of a
name reflects the precariousness of the infant's very existence. A
glance at the Torah text will bear this out. After the first part of
verse 2, the cantillation, or trope, indicates that the reader should
pause audibly after the words "and gave birth to a son." This
common pause is nevertheless eloquent for the reader, because we
know, after all, that we have just read in the book of Exodus, that
the birth of a boy child in a Hebrew household under the shadow of
the Pharaoh's murderous edict is not a time to rejoice. So we
pause in our reading, and reflect on the mix of emotions swirling in
the hearts of Amram and Yocheved. They delight in a healthy birth
under the extreme conditions of bondage; they tremble at the

unimaginable horror of having their newborn son torn from their arms and flung to a watery grave in the Nile. Also, given the Talmud's elaborate description of the Hebrew people's rekindled hope for an imminent redemption, the murder of their leader's newborn son would cast the Hebrews into a pit of despair. All this is hinted at by the text's wording.

Even so, the commentaries express delight that the story of the redemption of the Children of Israel is imminent at last, with this announcement of the birth of Yocheved's son. Yehuda Nachshoni[2] eloquently points out that the Torah is excessively sparing of details about Moses before his rise to greatness. He emphasizes that the one concrete fact we are given in these first two verses is that Moses is born of mortal parents. This essential fact distinguishes him from mythological heroes or icons of other religions who claim descent from gods. Nachshoni extrapolates a pillar of the Jewish faith from the narration of Moses' earthy, human origins. He explains that we derive from this verse that the proper progression of the development of man's spirituality is the elevation from the earthbound to the Godly. According to the *p'shat*, Amram and Yocheved's newborn son has relatively inauspicious beginnings. This is borne out by the second half of our verse, which states that Yocheved is moved to hide him from the eyes and ears of Pharaoh's police. It is into this desperate human condition that Moses is born.

The commentaries delve into the meaning of the phrase "and she saw that all was well with him" or "she saw that he was good." Rashbam interprets the phrase at its most elemental level, meaning that Yocheved gave birth to a son, and gratefully saw that he was breathing on his own and that he had all ten fingers and toes, thus appearing on all accounts to be a healthy newborn.[3] Ibn Ezra states simply that Yocheved saw that her newborn son's face was beautiful.[4] Sforno adds that in Yocheved's eyes her baby was even more beautiful than ordinary newborns.[5] And according to the Netziv, the Bible's statement that Yocheved "saw that he was good" informs us that she was relieved that her newborn son exhibited none of the weaknesses or abnormalities that babies of older mothers sometimes exhibited. Notwithstanding her rejuvenation, Yocheved understandably heaved a sigh of relief when she was able to give birth to a normal, fully formed baby.[6] That he was also objectively beautiful was a bonus for which she had not even thought to pray. Sha'arei Aharon[7], also explaining the text according to its simple meaning, says that Yocheved saw that her newborn was a quiet baby, and that he did not cry excessively. It was the infant's contented nature that allowed her to hope that she might be able to keep his birth a secret, hiding him for the first three months of his life.

The Talmud[8] (Sotah 12a) departs from these *p'shat* interpretations. Some of its sages suggest that Yocheved's baby was born circumcised, others that after his birth her house was filled with light. Torat HaChidah bases the circumcision suggestion on a word play. The verse's Hebrew word *oTo,* meaning "him," also means "his sign." The commentary explains that when Yocheved beheld her newborn son and pronounced him "good," she was referring to the fact that he was born already circumcized, without a foreskin, which was, even at that time, universally known as "the sign" of the Covenant for a Hebrew male.[9] The Talmud associates the phrase "and she saw that he was good" with the familiar phrase at the beginning of the Bible, "and God saw the light, that it was good." The similarity of phrasing leads some of the Talmud's rabbis to associate "good" with "light-filled." Certainly in this context it is plausible that the birth of Yocheved's healthy son—conceived and born amidst darkest torment and slavery, to a couple who had feared procreating and witnessing the progressive infanticide of their people—would bring joy and light into their world. It is highly unlikely that Yocheved in her birthing bed, holding her newborn son in her arms, felt anything other than intense gratitude to God that her son was healthy and well. Ohr HaChayim gently points out that it is the Talmud and commentaries who parse the verse's spare words to bestow these added interpretations, thus increasing our understanding of the text.[10]

The Bible reader must be genuinely concerned for Yocheved at this juncture, and terrified for her baby's life. We have learned that the Pharaoh is so obsessed with his astrologers' prediction of a newborn redeemer meeting his end with water that he has enlisted his soldiers to patrol the Hebrew camps, root out expectant mothers, and wrest their newborn sons from their arms to drown them in the Nile. In this atmosphere of paranoia and headcounts, we are incredulous that the Torah texts tells us that Yocheved is able to keep her newborn baby's existence a secret for three months!

Traditional biblical exegesis explains this three-month period in different terms. The Talmud[11] (Sotah 12a) explains that Yocheved is able to avoid the Egyptian spies for her baby's first three months of life because the Egyptian soldier assigned to watch her house began keeping his accounting starting with her public remarriage to Amram. What the Egyptian failed to take into account was that Yocheved had become pregnant three months *before* her separation from Amram. At her public remarriage ceremony she was already three months along, but she did not show, and it is even possible that neither she nor Amram, who had been living apart from her, was aware of her pregnancy. She gave birth to her beautiful baby boy at the end of her full nine months of pregnancy, but the king's spy did not come seeking her child until nine months of her renewed married life had passed, by which time her baby was three months old. The Malbim[12] explains that the Hebrew women were able to keep their expected due dates secret from the Pharaoh's spies because their nocturnal treks into the fields to comfort their husbands were unbeknownst to the Egyptians. The Pharaoh's police believed that they were effectively living celibate lives.

Rashi[13] agrees that Yocheved was able to avoid the Egyptian spies because of the three-month lag, but he differs as to its rationale. Rashi (in his comment on Exodus 2:3) explains that Yocheved gave birth to her baby boy prematurely, at a term of six months and one day. He posits that she became pregnant upon her remarriage to Amram, and was able to hide her newborn son because the Egyptians, who began counting on the date of the remarriage, did not come seeking a baby until nine months had passed. By then she had already been hiding the baby for three months, since his early birth.

Chizkuni presents still a third scenario. He agrees with the Talmud that Yocheved had become pregnant before she and her husband Amram separated, and that in fact she is three months along in her pregnancy on the day of their remarriage. But he differs from the Talmud in that he believes, with Rashi, that Yocheved gives birth prematurely, at six months. If this is so, Yocheved's pregnancy timeline fortuitously foils the Egyptian spies:

she becomes pregnant three months prior to her remarriage, and the Egyptians begin counting at day one of the remarriage, unaware that the fetus is already three months at day one of the remarriage. Then, at three months into her remarriage Yocheved, at six months into her pregnancy, goes into premature labor and gives birth to a son. The Egyptians are not fools, reminds Chizkuni. They begin checking the Hebrew homes when a woman could be six months along in her pregnancy. They are fully aware that a baby born at six months can be viable. But Yocheved is saved by this premature birth of her son *three months before the Egyptians began checking*, because unbeknownst to anyone, she had been three months pregnant with Amram's child on the day of their remarriage. The Netziv specifically tells us that it is when the Egyptians knock on her door[14] that Yocheved realizes she may not be able to hide her son for much longer. She greets the Egyptian police at the door and of course she is *not* swollen with child because she had given birth prematurely three months previously! And, as the Torah tells us, she had been hiding her newborn son for nigh onto three months.[15] Chizkuni tells us that Yocheved meets Pharaoh's police at the door, and equivocates, explaining, "I *was* pregnant, but the premature baby was born dead, so I buried it in the river.[16] The police search her house, and finding no baby, nor any outward physical signs that Yocheved is nursing a newborn, they leave her alone.

Because of her newborn son's quiet nature, combined with the fortunate fact that the Egyptians did not come seeking her baby until three months had passed after its birth, Yocheved is able to devise a plan for saving its life. Virtually every person reared in the Western tradition is familiar with the image of Yocheved weaving a reed basket for the baby Moses. But Pirkei d'Rabi Eliezer presents a different and ingenious scenario. The commentary tells us that in the months prior to launching her baby son in her reed basket, Yocheved had dug a secret underground bunker beneath the floor of her house, and lined it with blankets. It is into this underground receptacle that she places her newborn son, and foils the Egyptian police when they come to check for Hebrew male babies.[17]

As we have seen from this extended discussion of verse 2:2, the commentaries want the Bible reader to appreciate the confluence of ordinary and miraculous circumstances that allowed Yocheved to deliver her son in secret, and moreover to keep his presence concealed from the Egyptian police for a period of three months. Unfortunately, as the next verse indicates, this reprieve ended all too soon.

TWELVE

ഹൗഌഹൗഌ

Yocheved Builds an Ark

EXODUS 2:3

And she was no longer able to hide him, so she fashioned for him an ark of bullrushes, and she sealed it with mud and pitch; and she placed the boy within it, and she set it [adrift] among the reeds [growing] at the river's edge.[1]

T he Netziv presents an image of the Egyptian police surrounding Yocheved's house and knocking on the front and back doors simultaneously. We can assume that this was their *modus operandi* throughout the Hebrew camp for the duration of the Pharaoh's killing edict. They thereby cleverly sought to thwart any last-minute escape attempts by Hebrew mothers desperate to save their newborns. Their ominous pounding signaled to the resourceful Yocheved that it was time to set the second part of her plan into motion. The reader will recall that the *midrash* allowed us to glimpse her ingenuity when it told of the tiny underground bunker that Yocheved dug under her earthen floor in order to keep her newborn son out-of-sight but close-at-hand for his first three months of life. Now, however, she can no longer keep her son hidden and silent. The Egyptian police have escalated their zealous killings. They are growing desperate to find and dispose of the predicted Hebrew redeemer. The king's astrologers had predicted his birth nine months previously, perhaps in response to an unrecorded dream by the Pharaoh,[2] and their celestial indicators were still heralding his existence. For this reason, according to Sh'mot Rabbah, the Egyptian police surrounded each Hebrew home and, blocking the exits, pushed their way into the homes of women of child-bearing age. The soldiers dragged with them from house to house an Egyptian baby whom they beat or prodded, forcing it to cry. Their intention was thus to root out any hidden Hebrew baby, who, upon hearing the wail of the Egyptian child, would instinctively respond with an answering sympathetic cry, revealing his hiding place.[3]

Yocheved is growing desperate. She has enjoyed a three-month period during which she nursed her son and kept him close, but she saw that the Egyptian police were becoming increasingly vigilant. Her son was beginning to turn over, and furthermore, according to Ibn Ezra,[4] she could not keep his burblings muffled from the ears of her Egyptian neighbors. She is poised between two heartbreaking alternatives. Her "Scylla," or first alternative, is to take no action and keep her baby son at home. If she chooses this course each passing day will bring her closer to the day when she will witness his certain death at the hands of Pharaoh's militia. On the other hand, her "Charybdis" is to set the baby adrift in the nearby river. If she chooses this course, the chances are great that he will either be discovered and killed, or that he will die of exposure to the elements. Either choice will likely result in her baby's death. Yocheved chooses the latter course because it offers a shred of hope, while, according to Ibn Ezra,[5] the other alternative would result in her witnessing his death *for certain.*

So Yocheved weaves an ark out of reeds and bullrushes, making it as sturdy and as stable as possible, and of a size to fit her three-month-old son. The Bible text is explicit in its narration, telling us that she daubed it inside and out with hardened mud and pitch, fashioning a water-tight craft. According to Rashi, Yocheved skillfully lined the baby's ark with insulation that would act both as a waterproofing and as a shock absorber. She was preparing against the obvious eventuality that water could seep inside; she also cleverly daubed it on the outside so that if it bumped up against the rocks its precious cargo would not suffer.[6] Sha'arei Aharon suggests that Yocheved built the ark from a lightweight wood that would stay afloat even if the river's waters became choppy. Her ark was built to float atop the waves and not to become submerged.[7]

Rabbeinu Bachya explains that Yocheved's labor was also an inspired tactical solution to the prediction of the royal astrologers. The reader will recall that according to Rashi the root of the king's nine-month killing spree is his astrologers' prediction that the birth of the Hebrews' redeemer was imminent, and that he would meet his end in water. Rabbeinu Bachya is filled with admiration for Yocheved. He explains that knowing this prediction, she cleverly devised the stratagem to cast her baby afloat in a seaworthy life-craft, leaving him in the river just long enough so that if perchance her son were the predicted redeemer, the astrologers' prediction would be satisfied, and the king would withdraw his edict. The commentary explains further that because the astrologers' magic was not definitive, Yocheved was hoping that they would register only that their prediction had come to pass (*i.e.,* that the baby was in the river), and not that the baby boy remained alive.[8] Chizkuni says that she sought a withdrawal of Egyptian vigilance so that she could go back and retrieve her son in stealth.[9]

Alschich, in a paean to Yocheved, rhapsodizes that she *alone* is to be credited with saving her son's life. The commentary says that it was her own handiwork—and not her husband's—that fashioned her son's waterproof ark. We have only to look closely at the Bible text to read that *she* fashioned an ark of reeds, and *by herself* sealed it with mud and pitch. *She alone,* says the commentator, launched her baby's ark in the marshy waters at the river's edge. Alschich emphasizes that this is not insignificant. The traditional men's work of building an ark and painting it with mud and tar was done even more artfully by Yocheved. Says the commentator, her skilled woman's hands which had brought uncounted Hebrew babies into the world and administered lifesaving measures should justly be those selfsame hands that create the vehicle for her own son's salvation.[10] As it happened, it was another woman's hands that were to draw Yocheved's son from the waters.

Rav Soloveitchik[†] notes that "it is interesting how the verbs which are used here (Ex. 2:3) are in the *feminine* gender:" *And*

[†]Please see chapter 8 where we cite the public lecture by J. B. Soloveitchik on Exodus.

she was no longer able to hide him, so she fashioned for him an ark of bullrushes, and she sealed it with mud and pitch; and she placed the boy within it, and she set it [adrift] among the reeds [growing] at the river's edge. The Rav reasons that the Torah is indicating to us that "Yocheved did it!" And where is Amram, her husband? Why is he not mentioned at all in this episode? "Apparently," says the Rav, "he had no voice, because the leadership was taken away from him. It was given to Yocheved and to Miriam." Implicit in this verse, then, according to the Rav, is the revelation that here has been a tacit shift in authority and leadership among the Hebrews from Amram, the Levite elder, to Yocheved and Miriam, his wife and daughter, the two heroic midwives.

Ibn Ezra explains that the river bank where Yocheved placed her ark was known as the river's edge, or in Hebrew, *SuF*. The commentator teaches that *SuF* denotes not only the shoreline, but also the tall reeds that grow there.[11] We learn from Bechor Schor that Yocheved placed her ark amidst the tall reeds on the river bank. She gathered, under cover of night, a trove of river-reeds which she used as the raw material for the ark. The commentator tells us that Yocheved's ingenious plan was to weave the ark of the reeds at the *SuF* so that the ark would be camouflaged once she launched it amongst them.[12] Her son's floating cradle would be virtually invisible to those walking on the shore or bathing near the river bank! According to Rashbam the ark remained invisible only from the vantage point of a person standing on the shore and looking seaward. Yocheved was unable to shield the ark from the vantage point of a person bathing farther out in the water and who might be looking towards the shore.[13]

There is a difference of opinion in the Talmud (Sotah 12a) concerning the body of water into which Yocheved places her son. Rabbi Eliezer says that the Bible's use of the word *SuF* is an indication that she placed him into the *YaM SuF*, or Sea of Reeds.[14] Rabbi Shmuel bar Nachmani says that she placed him in "the River," known in all of Egypt as the Nile.[15] The commentary on Torah Temima resolves this dispute, stating that the *YaM SuF* or Sea of Reeds reaches as far as the Nile River within Egypt proper, thus making either body of water accessible to Yocheved.[16] Regardless of which body of water actually sheltered her baby son, once the ark was placed afloat amid the marshy reeds, the Pharaoh's astrologers informed the king that the threat posed by the Hebrew boy babies was averted, and that whoever their redeemer was, he had met his fate in the waters.[17]

Thus, Yocheved's plan to save her baby son, conceived in desperation months before when the boy was born in secret, and executed painstakingly and in constant dread, has met with success. Not only has she kept her own son alive under the noses of the Pharaoh's murdering militia, but she also heroically manages to save all Hebrew babies born henceforth. According to Sha'arei Aharon,[18] the king withdraws his killing decree and relaxes the vigilance of his militia once Yocheved places her baby in the waters. Yocheved has cast her own baby adrift, entrusting him to her God. She charges her daughter Miriam to keep watch over him.

T H I R T E E N

ഒറങ്ങൊങ്ങ

Miriam Guards Her Brother

EXODUS 2:4

*And his sister stood [in the reeds watching] from afar, in
order to ascertain what would befall him.*[1]

Yocheved steps back into the marshy reeds at the shore, and, as
Sha'arei Aharon[2] says, she entrusts her daughter Miriam to watch
over the basket so that the rushing water does not overturn it and
drown the child. Bechor Schor[3] states that Yocheved was adamant
that her daughter Miriam, who had been her loyal helper
throughout this Egyptian nightmare, should stand by the shore and
keep watch over the baby. Miriam chose her spot with care. The
Netziv[4] states outright that God's divine providence is at work here.
Unbeknownst to Yocheved, her placement of Miriam as guardian
over the baby was a human manifestation of a divine plan. Sforno[5]
suggests that Yocheved likely hoped that the basket would be found
by a kindhearted Egyptian woman, taken into her home, and the
boy raised as a foundling. The alternative, that her hard-won baby
son would perish, was insupportable to this woman who had spent
years breathing life into other women's babies. So great is her
sadness, ambivalence and frustration as she places her baby's basket
in the water that as she watches it float away she taps her
daughter's head and cries out, "Ah, Miriam, where is your prophecy

now?!" (Sh'mot Rabbah 1:22[6]) Yocheved is only human, after all, and wishes fervently that Miriam's juvenile boast—that the redeemer of the Hebrews would be born of her own mother—would come to pass, thus saving her son. The Talmud's version of this episode[7] (Sotah 13a) has Amram—and not Yocheved—admonishing his daughter. Amram had been quick to praise the young Miriam months before, according to the Talmud, when Yocheved gave birth to their son. At that time he hugged Miriam in a spontaneous gesture of joy and hope. Here, in this moment of anguish, both parents are *midrashically* losing some of their optimism as they watch their helpless baby son borne on the water's current, drifting further and further away from them. Rabbeinu Bachya[8] infuses some hope into the scenario, relating that the Bible text states that Yocheved charged Miriam as the sentinel precisely because she secretly wished that in this way her daughter's prophecy would come to pass, and her son would be saved. The Netziv[9] agrees, saying that Yocheved possesses such courage and faith that she places her daughter Miriam on watch precisely in order to witness and report the manner of his salvation, so hopeful is she that he was born for a higher purpose.

Yocheved's baby son, floating alone and unprotected, literally adrift between life and death, safety and discovery, is completely vulnerable, and, from the point of view of a first-time reader, is surely doomed. But the Talmud[10] (Sotah 11a) and Rabbeinu Bachya[11] suggest that the floating baby boy was watched over and protected by the *shechina*, or divine presence. Rabbeinu Bachya contends that when a righteous soul is in danger, this causes the protective *shechina* to come to his aid.

One could say that Yocheved's planned act of casting her helpless baby adrift in the waters was inspired rather than merely desperate. For we will see that Yocheved's son, as she correctly intuited, is not an ordinary Hebrew baby, but, as the Egyptian soothsayers foretold, is destined not merely to survive, but to be raised above his slave roots to greatness. Ibn Ezra[12] posits that the boy's slave environs would have posed a hindrance to his effectiveness as a future leader of the Hebrew masses. He needed to rise to his stature at a real and figurative distance from his Hebrew brethren, so that they would accord him due respect and fear. This helpless floating baby boy, whose fate is the immediate focus of the Torah narrative and of the women who bore and nurtured him, is ironically destined to be saved from the waters that should by all the laws of nature entomb him. Moreover, according to Malbim,[13] against all odds and with an even greater degree of dramatic irony, Moses is destined to be raised as a prince among princes within the loving embrace of the selfsame Pharaoh who had condemned all Hebrew boy babies to death! Rashi[14] quotes the *midrash* as saying that not only was Moses raised among the princes, but that as a young man he was elevated by the Pharaoh to oversee the members of his royal court. The reader thus is aware that life's drama overtakes these biblical actors, and as Miriam dutifully stands in the river reeds and watches, her brother's basket is even now floating into the view of the next woman who will save his life.

FOURTEEN

ഔൽഔൽ

Pharaoh's Daughter Discovers the Floating Basket

EXODUS 2:5, 6

And Pharaoh's daughter went down to the river to bathe, while her handmaidens walked on the riverbank; and she saw the ark amidst the reeds, and she sent her maid, and she retrieved it. And she opened it, and she saw [him]—the boy—and lo, the lad was crying; and she had compassion for him, and she said, "This [baby] is one of the Hebrew children."[1]

The floating basket with its precious human cargo is dislodged from its marshy *cul-de-sac* and begins drifting slowly across the river. Coincidentally, at this precise moment, a royal bathing procession makes its appearance at the shore. Sha'arei Aharon[2] describes that it is a blisteringly hot morning and the Pharaoh's daughter is preparing for her cooling ablutions. Her handmaidens are walking nearby, but at a bit of a distance, according to Ohr HaChayim,[3] in order to afford the princess her requisite measure of privacy. Only the princess' personal maid is at her side when she

59

looks out over the cooling water, perhaps anticipating her imminent reprieve from Egypt's sweltering heat, and sees a basket bobbing gently in the reeds.

What appears, according to the *p'shat*, to be an amazing—very likely a miraculous—confluence of circumstances (that is, Yocheved's drifting baby is rescued by none other than the king's daughter), is invested by the commentaries with enormous spiritual significance. Pirkei d'Rabi Eliezer explains that the Pharaoh's daughter was down at the river's bank that morning because she was afflicted with a persistent skin rash that was irritated by the palace's hot water baths. Sh'mot Rabbah even specifies that her skin ailment was a type of leprosy.[4] The ailing princess was therefore wont to visit the river every morning, where she could bathe in its cool and palliative waters.[5]

The Malbim[6] annotates his reasons for terming this entire episode miraculous. First, notwithstanding any skin ailment she might have had, the commentator says that it is highly unusual that a royal princess would venture out of her palace to bathe in a quasi-public place. The rules of royal decorum certainly dictate that her bathing be in private. So her coming down to the river bank to bathe on the precise morning and in the exact spot that Yocheved set her baby adrift is propitious in the extreme. Second, how fortunate that the princess' ladies in waiting opted to take their morning stroll along the riverbank in the opposite direction from the princess (and incidentally the floating basket) out of deference to her. Says the commentator, the royal attendants were daughters of the king's officers, and very likely would have tattled on the princess had they been with her when she retrieved the floating basket. In fact, Torah Shlema explains that the princess' courtiers were not strolling idly along the river bank just to give the princess her privacy. Rather, says the commentator, they were searching the shore for live Hebrew babies that might have washed up on the tide. They made a sport of throwing those still-breathing infants back into the river in order to adhere literally to the Pharaoh's edict.[7] She might even have so feared the consequences of transgressing her father's edict that she might not have saved it at all! It was therefore another small miracle that the attendant who remained by her side even as she ventured into the waters was her personal maid, a lifelong servant and loyal retainer who had been the princess' servant since her birth. This maid's longtime service coupled by her lowly station dictated that she was in no position to question the princess' behavior, and that out of love for her princess she kept their doings a secret. It was yet another wonder that the princess could even see the basket, as it was well camouflaged in the reeds and nearly invisible from the shore. The commentary asks, what if it were a chance bather that morning—and not only the baby's sister Miriam—who had been nearby and watched the princess retrieve the basket? We must conclude that this, too, is miraculous. And finally, that the princess was able to retrieve the ark from the water without anyone (save her loyal maid) being the wiser, caps the array of miracles that protect Yocheved's son.

Torah Temima[8] poses an interesting dilemma. It is known that the Pharaoh worshipped the Nile as a powerful god, and for that reason he would never have used its waters in which to bathe or cleanse himself. We must ask, therefore, whatever was the princess thinking, emerging from the palace to use the holy river for her bath? Was she not restricted by her father's strong pagan beliefs? The commentator responds that on the contrary, her outright flouting of her father's idolatry by bathing in the Nile is an express indication that she repudiated her father's beliefs.

Chatam Sofer[9] delves into the philosophical reasons that the daughter of the king would risk her father's ire by bathing in the "holy" waters of the Nile. The commentator explains that the princess had parted ways with her father on the theological issue of who is the god of the Nile. Her father, the Pharaoh, had progressed from merely worshipping the river to declaring himself master of the river and its very creator! The princess has been privately troubled that her father, upon ascending the throne, ignored the well-known story of the Nile's recent and abundant blessings for Egypt. The accepted lore was that Jacob, the patriarch of the Hebrews, upon departing from an audience with the prior Pharaoh, blessed him with the blessing of plenty, saying, "God grant that the Nile will rise up to your legs!" True to Jacob's words, in the years following his public iteration of the blessing of the Nile the country enjoyed freedom from drought. Over time, *the new king, who did not know Joseph*—the Hebrew viceroy whose bold brilliance saved the country from starvation years before—began to promulgate the myth that he alone was the source of the Nile's beneficence. It is at this juncture that the princess departs from her father's credo. She firmly believes, as do many of the country's common folk, that Egypt's plenty must be traced to the Hebrew patriarch Jacob. It is for this reason that she bathes in the river's waters. She is expressly flaunting her disbelief that her father is the god of the Nile.

Still, the Rav[†] encourages us to appreciate the princess' grave inner conflict and her transformation from obedient royal daughter to rebel. Perhaps up until that fateful early morning bath she had never experienced her father's murderous edict up-close, and her personal belief system had never been tested. Now, however, is the moment of truth. She is facing a floating basket which surely contains a hidden baby, and in the hair's-breadth between the Torah's words *she saw the basket floating within the shore [reeds]* and *she stretched out her hand and took it* (Ex. 2:5), the princess must make the momentous decision to save the baby or to turn away. The Rav imagines her internal dialogue: "Did my father condemn this child to death? Is my father the devil himself, the incarnation of evil? But this is impossible! Yet the truth is that my father instructed the Egyptians to kill, and this child was condemned by my father." This flash of epiphany leads the daughter of the Pharaoh to cast her lot on the side of good, and so without hesitating she reaches out her arm to grasp the basket.

The Talmud[10] (Sotah 12b) teaches us that so evolved was the princess' soul, that her immersion that morning served as her symbolic conversion, her transformation from pagan to believer. Rashi[11] expounds on the Talmud, stating clearly that this immersion was her deliberate conversion from her father's beliefs to her newfound religion. It wounds her sense of justice that the Hebrew babies, sons of the sons of the patriarch Jacob, source of the Nile's blessings, should be relegated to the river's depths. For all these reasons, the princess' intellectual and moral imperative does not allow her to turn away from what is surely a Hebrew baby floating on the Nile. Her soul is cleaving to the baby's plight.

The stage is set, then, and we can envision the biblical tableau. The daughter of the autocratic Egyptian Pharaoh is, according to Alschich, stepping *into* the Nile's waters[12] with her loyal maid close

---

[†]Please see chapter 8 where we cite the public lecture by J. B. Soloveitchik on Exodus.

by. Floating in the river reeds—all but indistinguishable from the marsh that surrounds it—is the basket carrying Yocheved's baby son. Miriam, the baby's sister, is standing out of sight, keeping watch over her brother's basket as Yocheved instructed her. The princess squints into the sunlight, seeing what she thinks is a floating cradle. Bathing in the waters of the "holy" river is one small transgression of her father's theology; but if she reaches out to save a floating Hebrew baby she will be taking an irrevocable—probably an unforgivable—action. Whatever the princess does next will inform her life forever. The Bible tells us (in verse 6) that the princess hears the baby's cry. The princess' heart—already rebellious, already softened toward the unfortunate children of Jacob, already transformed—melts. According to Alschich,[13] it is at this precise moment that the Pharaoh's daughter is transformed from a pagan princess into a rightous woman.

Pirkei d'Rabi Eliezer[14] tells us that Pharaoh's daughter reaches out her hand, grasping the edges of the basket to draw it near. Miraculously, the commentary relates, an unexpected and unforeseen miracle occurs. The princess' livid skin sores are healed before her eyes! The princess, astonished and breathless, is aware of the nexus between the floating basket and her cure. She resolves aloud, almost as an oath to the God who has healed her, that she will preserve the life of the Hebrew boy inside the basket.

We have seen that this momentous event—the resolution to save the Hebrew baby from the Nile—is, paradoxically, both the catalyst and the apotheosis of the princess' spiritual conversion. Accordingly, the commentaries begin the call her by her new name: Henceforth, Pharaoh's daughter is known also as "Batya." Pirkei d'Rabi Eliezer[15] explains that she is worthy of this name—translated from the Hebrew as "daughter of the Almighty"—because by rescuing one soul from death, she has performed the moral equivalence of rescuing an entire world. Conversely, says the commentary, one who consigns to death even one Hebrew soul has in effect committed a murder of an entire world. In light of the commentary's juxtaposition of the act of Batya and the acts of her father, the reader appreciates that Pharaoh's daughter has allowed her compassion and spirituality, and not her father's immoral pagan beliefs, to rule her. In this manner she elevates herself above her father's execrable behavior. Pharaoh's edict to drown all Hebrew

male babies was a horrific attempt to destroy the entire universe of
the Children of Israel; his daughter's act of saving this one Hebrew
baby from certain death in the Nile was the antithesis of his evil,
and was recognized as such in the *midrash* and in the Book of
Chronicles.

The First Book of Chronicles, in chapter 4, verse 18, is the
one place in the Scriptures that links the daughter of the Pharaoh to
the name "Batya." There, the text refers to "the Jewess . . . Batya,
the daughter of the Pharaoh."[16] The Talmud[17] (Megilla 13a) first
asks rhetorically, "Why was the daughter of Pharaoh called 'a
Jewess?'" Its answer, based on our verse in Exodus 2:5, is that she
renounced her father's idolatry and became converted in the waters
of the Nile. The Talmud continues that Chronicles names Batya in
that verse, specifically to identify her as the mother of "Yered," an
alternative name for Moses. The Talmud's second rhetorical question is "How could the text refer to Batya as Moses' *mother* when
she surely was not the woman who bore him?" The Talmud
answers that she who raises an orphan in her home and takes him
to her bosom as her own is regarded in the eyes of the Almighty as
if she bore him herself. The Talmud[18] (Sanhedrin 19b) concurs,
summarizing the principle of adoption in a poetic manner:
Yocheved *bore* the baby, and Batya *raised* him; therefore he is also
called Batya's son.

Torat HaChidah[19] literally equates the princess' act of pulling
the baby from the Nile to the act of giving birth. She delivered him
from the waters which at once were lifegiving—allowing him to bob
safely in his basket—and deadly—rough and fast-flowing, and could
overwhelm the basket in an instant. If she had not acted at the
moment she did, it is likely that the basket would have been inun-
dated and the baby lost. The princess' act of stretching out her arm
and retrieving Yocheved's basket is as vital, says the commentary,
as Yocheved's act of giving the baby life. Both acts gave life to
Moses.

Ma'ayna Shel Torah[20] explains that this reference in Chronicles is expressly to remind us that the name of "Batya," or
"daughter of the Almighty," was given to the princess as a sign of
gratitude to the woman who saved the baby Moses from the Nile.
The commentary tells us that God, in renaming the princess, told
her "You have named one of my children 'Moses,' likewise will I

name you 'my daughter.'" Says the commentary, the princess' act of compassion in the midst of pervasive perfidy transformed her from "daughter of the Pharaoh" into "daughter of the living God." Rav Sa'adia Gaon[21] says it plainly: The princess' actions are differentiated explicitly from her father's. He is evil incarnate, while she is the essence of righteousness.

In the manner of a reward to Batya for her bravery in rescuing and mothering the baby Moses, the Scriptures in the First Book of Chronicles (4:15,18) states that she is wed to Caleb, the son of Yephuneh. As we explained earlier in Chapter 8, Caleb is one of the true heroic figures of the post-Exodus generation. By linking Batya to Caleb in this most honorable fashion, the Scripture is bringing the lapsed Egyptian princess into the fold of the nascent Israelite nation in a definitive way.

The difficulty for students of the text is that the commentators (notably Rashi) have stated that Miriam, Moses' sister, was wife of Caleb![†] It is unlikely that Caleb was married to both Miriam and Batya. The solution is that the rabbis and the oral tradition so revere both these women that they link them both with their generation's equivalent of a valiant knight. Caleb was a leader and prince in Israel, and was a fearless and honorable man who stood against his fellow tribal leaders and reported truthfully about the Israelites' ability to conquer the land of Canaan. The Talmud[22] expressly matches this "rebel" with Batya, because she, too, was a fearless figure who stood her ground against her father's paganism and murderous edicts. According to the sages, both Caleb and Batya were righteous rebels, and thus were well matched. Similarly Miriam, whom readers have already noted was a feisty, brave and prophetic young woman of Israel, was considered a fit mate for Caleb. Whether Caleb was actually married to the two women, perhaps at different times, is not clear either from the Talmud or Chronicles. What is important for the reader is that both women possessed the qualities that made them the prime women of their generation, both of them fit to wed Caleb, the generation's premier man.

[†]See our dagger footnote at the end of Chapter 8 for an explanation of Miriam's marriage.

FIFTEEN

ಬಂಛಬಂಛ

Princess Batya Rescues the Baby

EXODUS 2:5, 6

And Pharaoh's daughter went down to the river to bathe, while her handmaidens walked on the riverbank; and **she saw the ark amidst the reeds, and she sent her maid, and she retrieved it.** *And* **she opened it, and she saw [him] -- the boy -- and lo, the lad was crying; and she had compassion for him, and she said, "This [baby] is one of the Hebrew children.**[1]

T he Bible text plainly states that she *saw the ark*. According to the Netziv,[2] the princess was the *only one* to see it, which is an indication that divine protection was already at work on her behalf. The stage is set, says the commentary, for the princess to safely retrieve the Hebrew baby from the Nile. Her retinue of courtiers had continued their early morning constitutional following the path of the river, but climbed out of range of the princess. Their view of the princess' bathing place was obstructed, and even if they had stopped to glimpse her, the reader will recall that Yocheved's cannily woven ark was completely camouflaged within its marshy cul-de-sac.

Thus, virtually alone at her bath, with only her loyal maid by her side, the princess is safe from the fear that her aggressive courtiers may report to the Pharaoh that his daughter has transgressed his decrees. Torah Shlema[3] embellishes the text's simple phrase (*and she saw the ark*), injecting a touch of the miraculous to the incident. He explains that the princess' retinue consisted of thirty ladies-in-waiting who were loyal not to the princess but to the king and his officers. The Bible's statement that *she* saw the ark is a hint to the reader that notwithstanding the crowd of ladies along the river bank, only the princess—and no one else—spied the floating ark in its thicket of reeds.

The Talmud[4] (Sotah 12b) paints a picture of the princess' courtiers that is darker than that of the commentaries. The text states that only *she* (the princess) saw the ark because at that moment in time only the princess and her loyal maid were left on the river bank. Instead of being just out-of-sight, however, the courtiers were close enough to the princess to witness her outstretched hand as she prepared to rescue the Hebrew baby. The Talmud relates that the royal courtiers admonished the princess, saying, "Mistress, all the world knows that when a king issues a decree, even if the whole kingdom disobeys it, at least the king's own children and members of his household must uphold it! How can you, the daughter of the mighty Pharaoh, transgress your father's decree to drown all the Hebrew babies?" The angel Gabriel, who was sent by the Almighty to watch over the spiritually transformed princess, caused the sand to shift beneath the courtiers' feet, and they were buried alive under a landslide of sand and rocks. In this manner the princess' imminent desire to retrieve the basket and save the Hebrew baby was not revealed.

The Bible text states in verse 5 *and she sent her maid and she retrieved it*. The plain meaning of the text, according to Rashi[5] and numerous commentaries, is that she dispatched her private maid to wade into the Nile to retrieve the basket that was out of her reach. But there is a discussion in the Talmud[6] on this point. Because the Bible's word *aMaTaH* translates as "her maid" as well as "the length of her arm," some sages say the Torah verse means she sent her personal maid, and some say she reached out her arm to retrieve the basket. The Netziv[7] beautifully reconciles the two interpretations, saying that both versions of the word could be at work simultaneously in the text. According to the Netziv, the princess *sent her personal maid away* with the excuse to fetch something back at the shore, while she herself *reached out her arm* to retrieve the basket. The spiritually transformed princess wanted this act of redemption to be accomplished without witnesses.

Legends abound about the length of the princess' arm. If the ark was hidden amid the reeds in a marshy cul-de-sac far from the shore, how could the princess retrieve it by simply reaching out her arm? The Chafetz Chayim reminds us that commentators who translate the verse to mean *and she reached out her arm* implicitly accept that the distance was too great to reach, but that the princess' arm miraculously grew by many lengths, thus enabling her to save the child herself. Rabbeinu Bachya,[8] for instance, says that her arm stretched to sixty lengths! The Chafetz Chayim[9] extracts an object lesson from this interpretation. He explains that even though the princess was entirely aware of the length of her own arm, and that her short reach would never allow her to retrieve the basket, *still* she reached out her arm. He learns a vital lesson from this righteous Egyptian princess: Even if it may seem to our human sensibilities that it is impossible to save a human life, or even to achieve a goal we have set our sights upon, *still*, like the Pharaoh's daughter, we must stretch out our arms and make that valiant attempt. God's miracles might work in a seemingly natural way, thus allowing us to achieve our seemingly impossible goal. Here, for instance, who is to say that God did not send a small wave to the ark's reedy hiding place, pushing it out to the princess' outstretched hand just at the moment that she so urgently reached out for it? In this way is the princess able to reach the basket and draw it close to her.

The Bible next tells us that the princess opened the basket *and she saw him—the boy.* Certainly this statement is obvious. Rashbam[10] explains that when the princess opened the basket the first thing she saw was that it was a *male* baby, and further, that he was circumcized. At that moment there was no doubt that he was a hidden Hebrew baby who had been sent out onto the river. An attentive reader might ask, why does the text add the extra phrase, "the boy?" It should rather have said *either* "she saw him," or "she saw the boy." It seems redundant that both phrases are included. In fact, the Talmud[11] (Sotah 12b) asks this same question. It responds that the princess saw two things: Of course she saw the boy, but according to the sages she also "saw" the *shechina*, or spirit of God, hovering over him. Aggadot Yam HaTalmud[12] teaches that only a spiritually transformed princess would have merited the ability to "see" the *shechina* in this way. The Talmud continues, saying that the boy was swaddled in a tiny version of a grown man's marriage cloak. Yocheved had draped the cloth over her son before setting him adrift, with the hope that if he were found and saved by an Egyptian woman, perhaps she would raise the boy to adulthood and the marriage canopy. Alternatively, notwithstanding Yocheved's fervent prayers that her son would be saved, she understood the grim reality that at best her floating basket only postponed his death. For this reason the Maharaz[13] suggests that the baby in the basket was swaddled in a tiny cloak resembing a shroud. Yocheved wanted her son to meet his fated destiny, whatever God had in store for him, appropriately clothed.

This verse, so ripe with meaning and nuance, presents still another fascinating word play. The Bible tells us that *she saw him—the boy—and lo, the* **lad** *was crying*. The reader might pause and ask whether the verse itself is contradictory: If the basket contained a baby, why does the Torah say it was a "lad?" The Netziv[14] explains that the verse is written to reflect the princess' surprise. She opens the basket expecting a two-day-old infant, and beholds a chortling three-month-old! This was another confirmation in the princess' mind that he was a Hebrew baby. She was aware that in those desperate times the Hebrews grew adept at devising clever means of hiding their babies from the Pharaoh's murdering soldiers. It crosses her mind as she beholds the plump baby that this boy's mother was clever indeed to have hidden it for such a long time. Her transformed heart goes out both to the baby and to its no-doubt broken-hearted mother.

The princess' decision to reach out her hand and save the baby is momentous, and the reader should appreciate that it is hard-won. Alschich[15] describes the internal debate that the princess conducts in her mind before arriving at her decision. "If I am compassionate to this child, and rescue him from the river, surely my father will hear of my deed and he will have me killed. For how could he tolerate my saving the life of a Hebrew baby boy? And even if I could do this, it would be impossibly difficult to raise this beautiful baby in my father's house, within the very walls of his palace!" The commentator explains that the daughter of the Pharaoh is on the horns of a life-and-death dilemma: She yearns with all her soul to act in a humanitarian manner and save the baby, but those selfsame righteous instincts fly in the face of the Pharaoh's killing edict. The princess understands that her father despises, in an irrational way, the flesh and blood of the Hebrews. How can she act morally and at the same time not transgress her father's edict?

Aggadot Yam HaTalmud[16] injects a rationale that will solve both problems: save the baby, yet not threaten the princess' life. The commentary argues that by retrieving the Hebrew baby from the river, the princess does not actually transgress the letter of the king's edict. His command was to *throw the Hebrew male babies into the river!* This decree already was complied with, when Yocheved relinquished her son to the river's waters in his floating cradle.

The Torah text continues that at that moment the baby began to cry, further arousing the princess' compassion and tenderness, and she says aloud, "This is certainly one of the Hebrew babies." Miriam, overhearing the princess' remarks, steps out from behind the tall reeds and addresses the princess.

SIXTEEN

༺෴༻

Miriam Confronts the Princess

EXODUS 2:7, 8

And his sister said to the daughter of the Pharaoh, "Shall I go and summon a wet nurse for you from among the Hebrew women, to nurse the child for you?" And the Pharaoh's daughter said to her, "Go." So the girl went and summoned the child's mother.[1]

The Bible's exquisite drama is heightened here when Miriam steps out of her marshy hiding-place and confronts the princess. The reader must appreciate that this is by no means a meeting of equals. First and foremost, as these verses stress, Miriam is in the presence of *the daughter of the Pharaoh*, whose raiments, bearing, and the majesty of her position, are in stark distinction from Miriam's sodden and dripping humble slave dress. Abarbanel[2] says that Miriam is perhaps fifteen years old at the time, so she is surely aware of the sheer audacity of a slave girl approaching the daughter of the king, especially during the princess' private *toilet*. The girl's heart must have been pounding with trepidation as she broke from the reeds on an impulse. According to the Malbim,[3] Miriam's innate courage is augmented by a divine spark. Her young body, shot with adrenaline, supplies the bravado she needs to speak to the princess.

71

Abarbanel[4] explains that the impetus to speak was born of the girl's having closely followed the early morning events from her hiding place in the river reeds. When she saw the princess reach out her arm and grasp her baby brother's basket, Miriam waded ever closer, still undetected, to see what the princess would do once she opened the ark. The commentator says that Miriam was able to detect the princess' tenderhearted nature by watching her reaction to the baby. Upon hearing the princess' words, uttered spontaneously and with a heart of compassion, Miriam was emboldened to reveal herself.

Miriam's audacious words to the princess are *Shall I go and summon a wet nurse for you from among the **Hebrew** women, to nurse the child for you?* The question arises, Why would the princess agree so readily to a Hebrew wet nurse; surely she would have been more comfortable with an Egyptian woman nursing this foundling? The Malbim[5] explains that the girl's innocent question led the princess to examine, in an instant, the issue of *who* would best nurse this hungry, crying child. Even if her instinct would have been to give the baby to an Egyptian wet nurse from the complement of royal servants, the commentary tells us that Miriam's suggestion of a Hebrew nurse made instant sense to the Pharaoh's daughter. Even though she was raised among the upper crust of Egyptian society, she was under no illusion about either her courtiers or any servant summoned to nurse this child. She had an instantaneous insight that if she were to give the baby over to an Egyptian woman, it was virtually certain that the woman would comply with the Pharaoh's overriding edict and kill the infant. The princess was taking no chances. She readily agreed to Miriam's offer to fetch a nurse from among the *Hebrew* women.

Alternatively, some commentaries create a time gap in this verse of the Torah text. The scene at the river bank, one would think, took minutes, or perhaps at most an hour to unfold. The princess, ready for her morning bath, is anxious for the water's soothing refreshment. She is blessedly alone in the water with only her longtime personal maid by her side. Miriam is watching from the cover of the bullrushes as the princess reaches out and retrieves the floating cradle from its marshy hiding place. Instead of speaking up, some commentators suggest that Miriam hung back and continued to watch as the princess commanded her loyal maid to run and fetch a wet-nurse to feed the crying baby. They theorize that the princess first dispatches her *amah* to bring her an *Egyptian* nursemaid for the infant. We can envision the early morning mist being burnt away as the Egyptian sun rises ever higher in the sky, illuminating the river scene. The princess has no doubt reached into the floating cradle and taken out the squalling baby. She coos to him and pats him, and she even delights in her ability to momentarily soothe him. She scans the beach, anxiously watching for the return of her *amah* and the contingent of Egyptian wet nurses. When at last they arrive, to the princess' consternation, as each woman confidently bares her breast to suckle the hungry baby, the Talmud[6] (Sotah 12b) explains that the child spits out each unfamiliar breast and renews his cries of hunger and frustration. Ohr HaChayim[7] suggests that desperate to comfort the baby, the princess even attempts—futilely, of course—to nurse him herself.

It is at *this* propitious moment, hours after Miriam has set up her vigil among the bullrushes, that she breaks from her hiding place and approaches the princess with her suggestion of a *Hebrew* nurse. Miriam has seen that the princess is nearly frantic, needing desperately to satisfy this child. Miriam's instinct—to wait until the baby is hysterical with hunger, and the princess is at the end of her tether—has paid off. When she offers to fetch a Hebrew nurse for the princess, the royal response is a laconic *Go!* Miriam's plan, which the Bible tells us is to fetch the baby's own mother, will surely succeed now. Her three-month-old baby brother has been accustomed to nursing only from Yocheved's breast, and only just that morning has had his last feeding. The Talmud[8] (Ketubot 60a) discusses that a baby of that age assuredly recognizes and even craves the woman who nurses him. Thus, when Miriam fetches Yocheved as the baby's "nurse," the thirsty babe, recognizing his mother's sight, touch, smell, sound and taste, surely suckles hungrily. The absence of his wails is music to the princess' ears, and the reader can readily appreciate that she would certainly agree out-of-hand to hire the "nurse" permanently.

The Netziv[9] is intrigued by the repetition in verse 7 of the Hebrew word *LaCH*, meaning "for you." In verse 7 Miriam asks the princess: *Shall I go and summon a wet nurse **for you** from among the Hebrew women, to nurse the child **for you**?* The commentary infers from the double use of the phrase "for you" that

Miriam understood that for a Hebrew girl and a Hebrew nurse to have a hand in rescuing a Hebrew male baby was courting death. But if she were to seek the wet nurse *in the name of the princess* ("for you"), and if the wet nurse herself were to nurse the babe at the princess' behest ("for you"), both she and the nurse would be protected. The Malbim[10] continues this reasoning, explaining that even if the Hebrew child is nursed by a Hebrew woman, no Egyptian would raise a hand to interfere if it is done *in the name of the princess* (that is, "for you").

Following this amazing conversation between the slave girl and the princess in verse 7, verse 8 of the Bible text then narrates, *So* **the girl** *went and summoned the child's mother.* The Hebrew word for "the girl" is *aLMaH*, an unusual word whose plain meaning is "maiden," but which also derives from the root word "to conceal, to hide, or to disappear." The Talmud[11] (Sotah 12b) explains that the word *alma* teaches us that Miriam cleverly and instinctively **concealed** the fact that she was the baby's sister. Rashi[12] adds that her omission **hid** from the princess that both she and the wet nurse she would eventually present to the princess had a powerful ulterior motive to save the foundling: that they were the baby's sister and mother! The third meaning of the word *alma* ("to disappear") is elucidated in this verse by the Netziv.[13] He points out that after the princess sends Miriam on her errand to fetch a Hebrew wet nurse, Miriam **disappears** from this portion of the narrative. The next conversation is between the princess and the wet nurse; Miriam never returns to the princess, sending Yocheved alone. The commentary explains that Miriam's disappearance is significant, because it was understood that the princess would have given the girl a substantial reward for her timely efforts. Miriam's failure to reappear sent a message to the princess that the girl neither sought nor desired any remuneration for her service. She acted purely on the baby's behalf.

The Malbim[14] adds an observation that the confluence of events that the Bible has just described—that Miriam intervenes with the princess, and is permitted to fetch Moses' biological mother to be his wet nurse—are surely miraculous. We can clearly see a divine providence in the fact that in the midst of the black and desperate days of a genocide, circumstances conspire to allow the baby Moses to be nursed within the bosom of his family. According to the commentary, the fact that the chosen wet nurse is Yocheved, the baby's Hebrew birth mother, allows Moses to develop an awareness of his nation and his birthright. The baby who is fated to be raised in the palace of the Pharaoh will also come to appreciate that he is descended from the tribes of the Hebrews. The Bible is assuring us that not only is Moses no longer a foundling, but also that he is raised by his two "mothers," with a double dose of majesty and responsibility.

SEVENTEEN

Princess Batya Commissions Yocheved to Nurse the Baby

EXODUS 2:9

The daughter of Pharaoh said to her, "Take this boy and nurse him for me, and I will pay you for this." So the woman took the boy and nursed him.[1]

This is the first of only two times that the Torah text brings together Moses' birth mother and his adoptive mother. The dramatic irony is high, as the reader knows that Yocheved, the baby's birth mother, has hidden her pregnancy as well as this baby's very birth from the king's soldiers; both Yocheved and Miriam know that they are the "foundling's" birth family; and the reader knows that there is nothing Yocheved desires more than to see her son spared from the Pharaoh's death decree. We can imagine her relief and ecstacy when Miriam bursts into their hovel, embraces her mother, and pulls her by the arm. The text does not record this joyous moment between mother and daughter, but it allows us to envision it. Perhaps she said, "Mama, he is saved! The Pharaoh's daughter has had pity on him and she seeks a wet nurse to stop his cries. I have volunteered *you* to be his nurse! Say nothing, just go to the princess." Perhaps the Torah does not reveal this snatch of dialogue for the very reason of its brevity and immediacy. Yocheved cannot respond to her daughter; she turns and runs to the river bank. Yocheved, standing now before the princess, knows that the woman she faces holds the key to her son's life in her hands.

Princess Batya is oblivious to this intense personal drama that is being played out at her behest. Understanding this dramatic subtext, this verse's spare words resonate for the reader.

According to the Abarbanel and the Talmud (Sotah 12b), the connection between Princess Batya and Yocheved is stronger even than their mutual love for the same baby. The commentary and the sages of the Talmud derive this from the Bible's use of the unusual Hebrew word that Princess Batya uses when Yocheved presents herself at the river bank as a potential wet nurse. The princess, instructing Yocheved to **take** *this boy and nurse him for me*, uses the peculiar Hebrew word *HeiLiCHi*. The Abarbanel points out that the more appropriate word would have been the Hebrew word *KeCHi*, translated more generally as "take," or even *HoLiCHi*, according to Sha'arei Aharon,[2] which means "take him away." Abarbanel[3] responds that the strange Hebrew iteration of **take** *this boy* is a conjunction of the two Hebrew words *Hey! LaCH-He*, meaning "Here! This boy is yours." The Talmud[4] goes so far as to say that the princess' use of this unusual Hebrew word is— unbeknownst to Princess Batya—nothing less than an unwitting prophecy about Yocheved. Read properly, says the Talmud, the Hebrew word really means "take him, he's yours!"

The reader appreciates that the sages understand the Talmud's amazing interpretation to mean that the Torah is inserting a biblical hint that the princess, who is instrumental in saving the baby Moses, "understands" on some subliminal or spiritual level that she shares this baby with Yocheved.

This notion is strengthened by the next part of the princess' command: *Take this boy* **and nurse him for me**. The text reveals that the princess is already possessive about this foundling. Rabbeinu Bachya[5] explains that the princess stresses "for me" in her instructions to Yocheved because she expects Yocheved to nurse *only the princess' baby* and no other.

Torat HaChidah[6] interposes a bit of *midrashic* conversation, allowing the reader to appreciate the princess' genuine and intelligent concern for the foundling, and for the health of its nurse. The commentary continues in the same vein as this Bible verse, adding to the princess' instructions to Yocheved: "Always bear in mind that you are nursing this baby *for me*; as such, you must conduct yourself in the manner of one who is nursemaid to a prince, accepting all the honor and servility that others will show you. In addition, I will see that you are supplied with the most costly of delicacies. You must nourish yourself with the best foods so that your milk will be clear and fortifying. You must not stint in obtaining for yourself even the most treasured of edibles if you should find that you desire them, for you are now the nursemaid to the son of the daughter of the king! As such, you must cease your other work, and devote all your energies exclusively to nurturing this child. But do not be concerned, because I am the princess, and I will see that you are well compensated."

The text reveals only silence on the part of Yocheved throughout this brief but emotionally-charged episode. The commentaries find this textual silence unsatisfying. They are aware, as is the reader, that Yocheved's biblical silence reflects a heart so full with her cognizance of the miraculous that mere words fail her. What can she actually say, after all? Can she thank the princess for giving her her heart's desire and placing her own son in her arms after she consigned him to the river? Of course she cannot utter this truth. So in the Torah text we encounter only silence from Yocheved. The commentary Torah Shlema[7] inserts another astonishing *midrashic* conversation between Yocheved and Princess Batya, this time giving voice to the textually silent Yocheved. After the princess instructs her to *Take this boy and nurse him for me*, the commentary adds Yocheved's words: "But princess, I fear your father's decree! How can I do your bidding and keep this Hebrew baby alive in the face of your father's edict?" And the princess' response to Yocheved appears in this verse of the Torah text: "You will nurse the baby **for me**." The implication, according to the commentary, is that the textual phrase "for me" is not merely a statement of possession by the princess about this foundling. It is also Yocheved's shield, her defense to Pharaoh's soldiers, who have been ordered to interrogate any Hebrew mother who is found nursing a male baby. Princess Batya's statement that Yocheved will nurse the baby "for me" is Yocheved's royal warrant, the essential sovereign imprimatur allowing her to give sustenance to her son without fear of reprisal.

The Torah text's next phrase—*So the woman took the boy and nursed him*—is the fulfillment of Yocheved's unarticulated hopes. Sh'mot Rabbah[8] (1:25) provides a touching insight into the balancing of the divine scales in Yocheved's favor. The commentary explains that at the precise moment that Princess Batya gives the foundling over to Yocheved to nurse, the Almighty presents Yocheved with a small portion of her Heavenly reward. The Almighty reasoned that Yocheved had spent years toiling under wretched conditions to breathe life into newborn Hebrew babies; it was a fitting boon that her own newborn son should be returned to her now from the brink of death. Yocheved's ecstacy at being granted this precious time to hold her baby to her breast and watch him grow is only minimally mitigated by the knowledge that after he is weaned he will leave her humble protection for the majesty of the palace. He is, after all, destined to be raised as a prince.

EIGHTEEN

໖ඏ໖ඏ

Yocheved Brings Her Son to Princess Batya and He is Named Moses

EXODUS 2:10

And the boy grew, and she brought him to the Pharaoh's daughter, and he was her son; and she named him Moses, because she said, "For I drew him from the waters."[1]

Yocheved weans her son, and according to Sh'mot Rabbah[2] (1:26) when the boy is twenty-four months old she brings him to the Pharaoh's daughter. This meeting is fraught with emotion and significance. At its most basic level, it must be wrenching for Yocheved to part with her son this second time, separating him from the only home and family he has ever known. The reader can envision Yocheved taking the toddler by his hand and walking this last bittersweet walk together. She must have explained to him that they were setting out on an adventure, and that he would soon have a beautiful place to live, new playmates and importantly, another mother. The Torah text is eloquently spare in its details: *and she brought him to the Pharaoh's daughter, and he became her son.* Yocheved had received the baby directly from Princess Batya at the

80

river bank two years previously, and here we are told that she delivers the thriving toddler back into the princess' waiting arms. Yocheved's roiling emotions are her own. She must be reminding herself that her gratitude is boundless, that her son is alive and well, that he will not be raised in abject servitude, but as a prince of Egypt. Any sadness she feels as she turns him over to the princess must be relieved by the adoration on the other woman's face as she greets and embraces the boy. The Malbim[3] points out that it is part of divine providence that the princess' heart *still* yearned for the boy even after twenty-four months have passed. The time apart from the baby did not cool her desire for him, nor did she have second thoughts about having rescued him. Yocheved saw all this when she beheld the princess. She understood that the princess' passion had not waned, and so she was less reluctant to give her son into the princess' waiting arms.

From the princess' standpoint, the emotions that fill her are anticipation and elation. She is of course unaware of the emotional drama being enacted in front of her. To her, it is an incidental meeting of wet nurse and employer. The main object of the rendezvous is to transfer the cherished lad from temporary nurse to adoptive mother.

The Rav[†] emphasizes that the daughter of Pharaoh well understood that notwithstanding her taking custody of the baby, she appreciated that she was not the mother of Moses. The Rav understands the gravity of the dual sacrifice that Batya is making: First, that she resolved two years before to rebel against her father, the most powerful potentate in the known world, in order to take a moral stance and save a Hebrew baby from drowning. This in and of itself is sufficient to label her a hero. And second, at this very moment of taking the hand of the toddler from Yocheved, Batya also is making a second sacrifice. Gazing at the boy she truly understands that he is hers only on loan. According to the Rav, while Batya had been prepared to adopt the boy as her son unequivocally from the moment she drew him from the Nile, here, in a flash of insight, and at the moment her heart's desire would appear to be granted, she understands that he can never be truly hers. She is

---

[†]Please see chapter 8 where we cite the public lecture by J. B. Soloveitchik on Exodus.

granted a glimpse into Moses' future, and sees that her personal happiness in raising this child pales in significance to his more important role as leader and redeemer of a people. This boy's place, says the Rav, is not destined to remain in the palladia of the Egyptian empire, and Batya must absorb her disappointment and appreciate the fleeting nature of her custodianship of the boy. This almost superhuman emotional sacrifice coupled with her first important break from her father's moral clutches elevates Batya to the pantheon of righteous women of the exodus.

Once Yocheved has presented the toddler at the palace and he is standing at attention before the princess, the Torah text tells us *she named him Moses, because she said "For I drew him from the waters."* Ibn Ezra[4] explains that the name "Moses" is an Egyptian name translated into the Hebrew. Untranslated, his Egyptian name was "Munius." There is much discussion among the commentators about *who* named the boy. Was it Yocheved or was it the princess? The Torah text states, *and she named him Moses, because she said, "For I drew him from the waters."* On a *p'shat* level, or after a simple reading of the verse, it would appear that it was Princess Batya who named him, because it was she who drew him from the waters. Further, following Ibn Ezra's commentary, the name Moses was a translation from the Egyptian, the *lingua franca* of the princess. Torat HaChidah[5] also understands that it was the princess who named the boy, but for a different reason. The commentator states boldly that because Princess Batya rescued the boy from death on the river, she gave the boy a new life, and thus her action served *in lieu* of natural childbirth. For this reason it was she—the princess—who named the boy *Moshe*, meaning "I drew him from the waters," so his name would stand as an eternal reminder that she was his second mother.

It is considered a tremendous honor for Princess Batya that the text has her naming the boy "Moses." Ibn Ezra,[6] who has stated that her act of drawing the baby from the waters was equivalent to giving birth to him, goes even further, saying that the Egyptian princess named the boy *in the Hebrew language.* Thus the Bible text honors her by recording the name she designated, in the exact manner she chose. Perhaps the princess learned Hebrew either from the chatter of her Hebrew palace slaves, or she learned it in the twenty-four months between her finding the basket and the moment of exchange, in anticipation of her adopting the boy. Or perhaps she inquired about a Hebrew name for him as a measure of respect for his Hebrew origins. Chizkuni[7] adds that the princess learned the Hebrew language as part of her affinity for the Hebrew people and her spiritual conversion. Her act of naming him in Hebrew was a commemoration of the miracle that the Hebrews' God kept the baby alive in order that she might be the one to "pull him from the waters."

On the other hand, Abarbanel[8] interprets this verse to mean that it is Yocheved—and not the princess—who names the boy "Moses." The reader is mindful of Yocheved's extraordinarily difficult task of ceding her son to the daughter of the Pharaoh. Abarbanel must also appreciate this, and he expressly differs with Ibn Ezra. According to Abarbanel, the verse's pronouns refer exclusively to Yocheved. The verse states, and **she** brought him to the Pharaoh's daughter, and he was **her** son; and **she** named him Moses, because she said, "For I drew him from the waters." Abarbanel states that these female third-person pronouns refer exclusively to Yocheved. He reasons that the verbs here: "she brought" the boy to the daughter of the king, and "she named him," echo the prior verse's verbs "and she took" the boy, and "she nursed him." The boy's birth mother named him "Moses," a Hebrew name, because that was her spoken tongue. Yocheved thus brought eternal honor to the boy's adoptive mother, by according him a Hebrew name that meant "the princess drew him from the waters." This detail is so important to Abarbanel that he describes another rare extra-textual conversation between the two women. Yocheved, upon delivering the boy to the hands of the princess, says to her, "Mistress, I have named the boy 'Moses' in order to commemorate the moment when you found him and drew him from the waters." And the princess acknowledged the wisdom of the name, and the honor accorded to her, and the boy's name remained "Moses."

Thus, according to Abarbanel, both Moses' "mothers" shared the act of naming him.

According to Rabbeinu Bachya,[9] it is significant that the name "Moses" remains unchanged throughout the five books of the Torah, and that God uses only the name "Moses" in his numerous conversations with him. The redeemer of the Israelites, the paradigmatic prophet, the great teacher and law-giver retains until his death the name assigned to him by Yocheved and Princess Batya. This is so, agrees Abarbanel,[10] notwithstanding ample precedent in the Bible for changing the given names of the iconic figures (to Abraham from Abram; Sarah from Sarai; Israel from Jacob). Such a name change does *not* occur to Moses. The name his mothers gave him remains his name for posterity.

The Malbim[11] adds that psychologically, Moses' name (*I drew him from the waters*) had a humbling effect on him, serving as it did as an ever-present reminder *to him* of his origins. He was always aware that he "was pulled from the waters" by his adoptive mother. Moses thus embodied the essential blend of humility, as he was the son of a slave woman, and confidence, as he was also the son of a princess.

The commentaries raise a rhetorical question that perhaps has been on some readers' minds: How can Pharaoh's daughter name the Hebrew baby "Moses," which means "I drew him from the waters?" Surely by the baby's very name the Pharaoh's daughter is damning herself, admitting to her father and to all Egypt that she transgressed the Pharaoh's edict and saved a Hebrew boy baby from death! Aggadot Yam HaTalmud[12] addresses this precise question, explaining that the princess' act of retrieving the basket was perhaps not a technical violation of her father's edict. The commentary explains that the Pharaoh's edict (*throw all the newborn male babies into the river!*) was not as straightforward as it seemed at first. We have already learned, for instance, that while the edict stated "*all* the male babies," it was understood by the Egyptians to exempt *their* newborn sons. Likewise here, the commentary explains, the Pharaoh's daughter was relying on the generally accepted practice that once the newborn Hebrew babies were "thrown into the river"—thus adhering to the letter of her father's edict—if by some miracle any such babies escaped drowning and lived, it was permissible for them to be raised as Egyptians in Egyptian households.

Thus, as regards the princess, while her act in saving the Hebrew baby was by any estimation courageous (she was, after all, the Pharaoh's daughter, and there was no telling how the king would react to his daughter's saving a Hebrew baby), she was prepared to defend her "traitorous" act by pointing out that she did not transgress the letter of his law. The proof of her belief that her act would escape punishment is that she named the boy *I drew him from the waters.* If her act were an unambiguous violation of the king's law, it is unlikely that she would have named him in a way that blatantly admitted to the transgression. It is because her act fell into the gray area of what was an acceptable practice that the princess was able not only to save the baby Moses, but also to name him for her courageous act and bring him into the palace and raise him as the Pharaoh's adopted grandson.

There is a well-known *midrash* that illustrates just how integrated Princess Batya and her adopted son were in the court of the Pharaoh. Sh'mot Rabbah[13] (1:26) recounts that Princess Batya was accustomed to bringing the toddler Moses to sit with the Pharaoh in his throne room while he was holding court. The boy was beautiful to behold, and became a favored pet of the king and the courtiers. One day, in a playful mood, the toddler Moses reached out and took the Pharaoh's crown from atop his head and placed it upon his own. The entire court gasped, and the king's soothsayers took it as an omen that the princess' adopted son was covetous of the kingdom. They even demanded that the king put the boy to death at once to prevent him growing up to usurp the crown. The Pharaoh, who the *midrash* says was wont to kiss and coddle the boy like a doting grandfather, was reluctant to agree. Yitro, an advisor to the Pharaoh (or the angel Gabriel appearing in the guise of a courtier according to Yalkut Shimoni 2:166),[14] suggested a test. "Bring before the lad a vessel containing a chunk of gold and a glowing coal. If his hand goes forth to retrieve the gold, it will be a sign that he covets the kingdom. If his hand grasps the coal, it will be a sign that he took the king's crown in child's play, and we must let the boy live." The test appealed to the king and his suspicious courtiers, and the vessel was placed before the boy as he sat on the princess' lap. The boy naturally stretched out his hand toward the gleaming gold, but the angel Gabriel caused his hand to veer toward the glowing coal instead. The boy burned his fingers and thrust them into his mouth for relief, thereby singeing his lips and tongue. The test satisfied the king and his courtiers that the boy posed no threat to the crown. Thereafter, Moses was left with a pronounced lisp.

This *midrash* has at its core the fact that the princess presented Moses at the palace as her own, and that the king accepted
him as her son, held him close and treated him with paternal affection, though perhaps thereby arousing envy and suspicion in some
of the Pharaoh's close advisors.

Sforno[15] assesses Moses' name not as recording a historic
truth about his beginnings, but as a prediction of Moses' future
greatness. The commentary explains that just as Moses was "pulled
from the waters" and rescued from a certain death, so, too, was
Moses always destined to "deliver other souls from their suffering."
Ibn Ezra[16] adds that perhaps it was part of the divine plan that the
future redeemer was raised in the palace. His princely upbringing is
not merely incidental to his personality; it is essential to his role as a
leader of multitudes. The commentary suggests that Moses was
raised in the palace in order to elevate his intellect and character to
a level far above that of the Hebrew slaves. They had a great need
for a leader who was not from among them; for one whose stature
towered far above the abyss of their unending servitude. Further,
from a psychological vantage point, they were more likely to accord
Moses the awe and respect due him precisely because he was *not*
raised as a slave. Moses' palace upbringing lent him a royal bearing, a commanding authority, and level of erudition that the future
redemption demanded.

PART II

MOSES MARRIES

NINETEEN

བོལྕཏྰོལྕ

Moses Becomes a Fugitive

EXODUS 2:11-15

And it happened that the years passed and Moses grew to manhood. He left the palace one day to walk among among his brethren, and he saw how they suffered and endured their burdens. On that day he witnessed an Egyptian man beating a Hebrew man, one of his brethren. And Moses looked this way and that, and seeing that there was no one else about, he stepped into the fray. He struck the Egyptian a death blow, and then hid him in the sand. On the next day Moses went out again, and he beheld two Hebrew men fighting one another. And Moses said to the one who was the aggressor, "Why do you strike your friend?" And the man retorted, "Who appointed *you* to be ruler and judge over *us*? Are you thinking of killing me, too, as you slew the Egyptian yesterday?" Thus Moses understood that truly the events of the previous day were widely known. The news reached even to the ears of the Pharaoh that Moses had slain an Egyptian taskmaster, and the king sought to have Moses killed. So Moses fled Egypt and the Pharaoh's death warrant.

TWENTY

৪০৫৪০৫

Moses and the Kushite Woman

EXODUS 2:15

And Pharaoh heard of the thing [that happened] and sought to kill Moses; so Moses fled from before the Pharaoh . . .[1]

The Torah narrates in a few short phrases that Moses' heroic act of defending a Hebrew slave against an Egyptian taskmaster sealed his fate. With this act, Moses' life was altered from one of unquestioned privilege as adopted grandson of the king, to that of a capital criminal and traitor to the crown. A royal death warrant was posted for him, and Moses' only recourse was to flee for his life.

The Bible's account skips from its mention of Moses' flight from Egypt to his appearance some time later at the well in Midian. The medieval *midrashic* work entitled *Divrei HaYamim Shel Moshe*[2] expounds upon this ostensible time gap in the narrative, and relates at length and in exquisite detail Moses' years *between* his flight from Egypt and his arrival in Midian. According to this fascinating *midrash*, Moses escaped Pharaoh's soldiers, found himself in the land of Kush, lent his warrior's hand to the Kushite king in battle, and became a beloved hero and husband to the Kushite queen. The details set forth in the story offer insight into the man Moses is becoming, and into the man who appears at the

90

well in Midian years later to champion the seven daughters of Yitro, the priest of Midian.

When Moses realized that his impulsive defense of the Hebrew slave—and his killing of the abusive Egyptian taskmaster—was considered a grave act of treason against the Pharaoh causing a death decree to be placed on his head, he fled Egypt without a backward glance. Moses understood that his life as prince of Egypt was over. His hybrid self—part Hebrew, part Egyptian—posed a serious threat to the Pharaoh because of the astrologers' longtime predictions of a redeemer who *now* fit their profile. Furthermore, the Hebrew slaves did not appear to want him as their champion, either. So he set out into the desert and prepared to forge his own destiny.

According to the *midrash*, Moses' escape was a difficult one. Moses had been easily surrounded and apprehended by Pharaoh's ubiquitous militia, and he was taken to the palace dungeon to be slaughtered. Divine intervention placed the archangel Michael at Moses' side, the angel altering his own form and features so that he became the double of the royal executioner. Simultaneously, the angel caused the royal executioner's face and form to transform into that of the prisoner Moses! Without hesitation, the archangel lifted the executioner's own sword and slew him, appearing to all observers to have slain the prisoner Moses. In the ensuing confusion the archangel led the real Moses out of the palace dungeon, through the gates of Egypt, and deposited him in the desert beyond the Egyptian border, at a distance of a three-days' journey on foot.

In a fury at having harbored a traitor in his midst and then having allowed him to escape punishment and death, the Pharaoh redoubled the burdens heaped on his Hebrew slaves, embittering their lives and increasing their suffering a hundredfold.

During that same time frame, the desert kingdom of Kush was at war with the Kingdom of Kedem. Bilaam, the biblical sorcerer, had encouraged the destruction of the Children of Israel in Egypt and now insinuated himself into the kingdom of Kush as advisor to King Nikonos. When King Nikonos left Kush with his armies to fight a protracted war against Kedem, Bilaam aroused the Kush populace to rebel against their absent king and to install him as monarch, with his two evil sons as officers over the people. As king, Bilaam caused a great wall to be erected around two sides of the city of Kush, and a great moat to be dug on the third side.

Guarding the fourth side was a ditch filled with poisonous snakes and scorpions, effectively closing off the city of Kush from invaders. In addition, no person was permitted either to enter or leave the city.

Upon the successful conclusion of the war of Kush against Kedem, King Nikonos and his victorious armies returned home. At the Kush city limits they were greeted by the new fortifications, and they mistakenly thought their Kushite countrymen had built the defenses against potential invasion from other hostile kingdoms. It was only when the Kushites prevented entry even to King Nikonos and his soldiers on the orders of "King Bilaam" that King Nikonos understood that his kingdom had been stolen from him, and that he would have to fight a bitter and protracted battle to regain it. He and his solders fought fiercely, but Bilaam's Kushites had the fortification and the advantage, and Nikonos' troops were war-weary, and were unable to take back the city. Still, Nikonos lay siege to Kush for nine years.

It was during this nine-year siege that a thirty-year-old Moses effected his escape from Egypt. On his flight through the desert he encountered King Nikonos' army as they lay in siege against Kush. They generously offered to share their rations and water, so Moses tarried among them and quickly gained their favor. Moses eventually spent a period of years in the camp of King Nikonos, who grew to love Moses. The two spent many hours in discussion, each treating the other as a comrade and fellow member of exiled royalty. Moses gained the trust and admiration of king and soldiers alike, so that the king eventually appointed Moses as commanding officer of his militia. This state of affairs continued until King Nikonos took ill and died.

The Kushite milita consulted among the officers and men and decided to elevate Moses to be their king, reasoning that there was no one like him among the Kushite people. They conferred upon Moses the honor of wedding the Kushite queen, widow of King Nikonos. The *midrash* states that though Moses was wed to the Kushite queen he did not cohabit with her, distancing himself from foreign flesh in keeping with his Hebrew God. Moses' great sword was his bed partner, and the Kushite queen could not draw near to him.

On the third day of Moses' reign he was approached by the Kushite soldiers, who explained to him that after nine years of siege they desperately missed their families and their homes, and they sought his advice. So Moses, whose heart went out to his men, devised a military strategy for an audacious, lightning attack to regain Kush. He cautioned the soldiers to follow his directives precisely, hoping that with luck they would soon be sleeping in their own beds once more. Moses instructed his men to climb the nearby mountains and gather the hatchlings of the white stork, who nested in the heights above Kush. Clad in full armor and mounted on war horses, Moses led his army into the vile snake pit that guarded the fourth entrance to Kush. He had his men toss the stork hatchlings into the snake pit as they rode through it, diverting the snakes and allowing their army safe passage. As Moses had predicted, he and his army were thus able to breach Kush's defenses and retake the city in fierce hand-to-hand combat. Bilaam the sorcerer, the usurper king, magically disappeared from Kush and resurfaced back in the court of the Pharaoh along with his two sons.

The liberated and elated Kushites showered their devotion onto Moses, and he lived among them as their beloved monarch and leader, adhering to God's law for many years.

The years passed and Moses' Kushite queen confided to her closest advisors that Moses has kept himself apart from her for all this time. She yearned for a true husband and suggested that they appoint a king and leader from among the descendants of King Nikonos, replacing Moses, who after all was a stranger among them. She rallied the wives of the rulers of the Kushite states behind her, and appealed to the officers of the militia to replace Moses. And Moses' generals approached him, saying, "Sire, you are our beloved king and commander, and no one can replace you in our hearts and on the battlefield. But the Kushite queen is reasonable. We need to continue the Kushite monarchy through the line of Nikonos. So please, help yourself to the riches and booty of our kingdom, and return to your home in peace."

So Moses, in essence a stranger and interloper even to the Kushite people whom he had befriended, championed and ruled wisely for nearly half a century, accepted his destiny and left their midst, an exile once more.

The Abarbanel suggests that the extensive *midrashic* narrative of Moses in the Kushite kingdom places Moses' at age twenty when he escaped Egypt and fled for his life. Allowing for his years on-the-run and four decades as a ruler of Kush, Moses was middle-aged, as the Torah later confirms, when he arrived in Midian. Abarbanel[3] opines that if in fact this *midrash* is true, the Bible omits any reference to Moses' pre-Midian years because they were, in Torah terms, merely a dalliance. Moses was being primed to step up to his role as God's messenger.

This, then, is the man Moses whom the Torah text tells us traveled to the desert kingdom of Midian and positioned himself at the well.

TWENTY-ONE

ഏരുജ്ഞൽ

Moses and the Seven
Shepherdesses

EXODUS 2:15-20

> . . . *So Moses fled from before the Pharaoh. And he settled in the land of Midian and he settled at the well. Now the priest of Midian had seven daughters; they arrived [at the well] and drew water, and they filled the water troughs so as to water their father's flock. And the shepherds came and drove them away; and Moses rose up and rescued them; and then he watered their flock. They returned to Reu'el their father, and he said to them, "Why did you hurry back [from the well] today?" And they told him, "An Egyptian man saved us from harm at the hands of the shepherds, and he also drew the water and watered the flock." He said to his daughters, "So where is he? How could you just leave him there? Go, summon him to break bread with us."*[1]

The commentaries wonder why the Bible text twice uses the Hebrew word *VaYeSHeV* in verse 15, meaning that Moses *settled* in Midian and also that he *settled* (or sat) at the well. Abarbanel explains that the two statements of "he settled" indicate that Moses may not have appeared in the land of Midian directly after he fled from Pharaoh. The commentary posits that the two-time use of the phrase "he settled" indicates that perhaps Moses first "settled" in the land of Kush, and years later he arrived in Midian, where he "settled" by the well. It was at the well in Midian, Moses' second stopping place, that he met his destiny.[2]

Whether Moses settled in Midian directly after he escaped the Pharaoh, or whether he settled there after having been in Kush for many years, the fact remains that he had committed a capital crime in Egypt and was a wanted man. The Pharaoh had put a purse on Moses' head, and he was, by any interpretation, a fugitive. Moses understood that his chances of detection were lessened if he kept out of the public eye, so he secreted himself in an unknown, far-flung province. He therefore spent years in Kush, according to the *midrash*, and afterwards settled in Midian.

Ibn Ezra suggests that the essence of verse 15 is that the Pharaoh's spies were everywhere, and that they were abroad even in the land of Midian. Therefore, Moses' first "settlement" in Midian would have been in its outskirts, where he occupied himself unobtrusively as a shepherd, where the chance of his being recognized was minimal.[3] It was only after the passage of years, when Moses perhaps felt safer, that he "settled" a second time, now by the town's well, a more populous area. It is at this point in the story that Moses encounters the seven shepherdesses.

Moses' motivation for settling at the well in Midian may have been more basic. After the passage of many years Moses was existentially alone. He felt secure enough from his pursuers after all this time to venture confidently into the public domain, which in biblical times meant stationing oneself at the town well. According to Rashi, Moses must have been taught the mythic story of his great-grandfather Jacob, who had stationed himself at the well in Padan-Aram and there fell instantly in love with his future wife, Rachel.[4] Levush HaOrah, a supercommentary on Rashi, adds that Moses was so desirous of finding his perfect mate that he risked settling himself at the public well. It is likely that Moses also knew that the Hebrew patriarch Abraham, when seeking a proper wife for his son Isaac, dispatched his most trusted servant to the land of his fathers, who found the girl Rebecca watering her father's flocks at the well. Perhaps Moses was subconsciously hoping that his appearance at the well would likewise put an end to his loneliness.[5]

Verse 16 opens with with words, *Now the priest of Midian had seven daughters; they arrived [at the well] and drew water, and they filled the water troughs so as to water their father's flock.* The Bible is speaking in the narrative voice, and because it has just situated Moses at the well, we are invited to observe the goings-on through Moses' eyes. He watches these seven young women arrive at the well, driving their substantial flock before them. He might be thinking, Who are these women? The Bible answers this unwritten question, informing us that they are the daughters of the Priest of Midian. Abarbanel adds that the seven young women are virgin sisters, the eldest and the most notable of whom was named Zipporah.[6] Ibn Ezra adds that the Bible's "Priest of Midian" is Yitro.[7] But if this is so, why would the daughters of Midian's high priest, according to Chizkuni,[8] be tending his flocks and watering them at the public well? Is this not a task for servants? Sh'mot Rabbah explains the behind-the-scenes drama.[9]

It seems the Priest of Midian, after years of serving false gods, had been doubting his service and seeking a spiritual truth. For some time before Moses appeared at the well in Midian, Yitro already had begun to distance himself from the priestly service, explaining to the Midianites that it was time to pass the mantle to a younger man who could serve them better. He expunged all the priestly vestments and accoutrements from his home, returning them to the Midianites, thus engendering their scorn and derision.

As a result, Yitro, the former high priest of Midian, has now become a pariah in the city where he once was revered. No man would agree to be in his employ, and neither would the village shepherds agree to tend his flocks. For these reasons his seven maiden daughters, who until recently had never ventured out to the well unattended, were driving Yitro's flock before them in their haste to complete the task before the other shepherds arrived to taunt them in their newly-lowered status. Sh'mot Rabbah (1:32) adds that they had pressed themselves to arrive at the well earlier than usual because they actually feared the brutish shepherds, who had become emboldened by Yitro's lowered circumstances. Stripped of the implicit protection of their father's status as high priest, Yitro's seven daughters were now prey to the shepherds' leering stares, lewd remarks, and groping hands. They had been fortunate so far in eluding their tormenters, but they knew they were vulnerable at the well, and could be trapped and helpless there, with no one to come to their aid. Hence they arrived early, seeking—in vain, as it happens—to water the sheep and be gone before the shepherds arrived.

According to the Netziv[10] the seven women did in fact arrive before the shepherds, and were well into the laborious task of drawing the water and filling and refilling the troughs when the shepherds arrived. Moses watched them at their tasks.

Moses observed as the seven young women made their way to the mouth of the well, and began with businesslike efficiency to group the sheep alongside the empty troughs, unload the water jugs, lower the well buckets, and ferry the water to fill and refill the troughs as the thirsty flock drank its fill. Alschich explains[11] that Moses thought that these young women were unlike any others he had ever before observed; most other women, upon arriving at the town well, would have immediately engaged whoever was present in casual conversation at the very least. And if the man at the well happened to be a stranger to the town, how much more so would the women have engaged in curious questioning of him. He expected them to ask him his name, and from where he had traveled. But on the contrary, these maidens—while they had certainly noticed his presence at the well because when they arrived there was no one else about—consciously paid him no mind. It was obvious that they were shy of this handsome stranger. Moses also noted that the girls did not chatter or gossip among themselves as they completed their duties. The commentary derives this from the Torah text's description of the maidens' chores that morning. Verse 16 states that *they arrived [at the well], they drew water, and they filled the water troughs in order to water their father's flock*. This unembellished, almost hasty phrase teaches us that the seven maiden daughters of the priest of Midian did not comport themselves as ordinary shepherdesses. This was not lost on Moses, who sat by the well and observed.

Alschich continues that Moses watched as the burly shepherds arrived at the well and eyed the seven maidens. The women did not make eye contact with the men or greet them in any way, so that Moses saw that there was no familiarity among them.[12] He understood that these maidens held themselves apart from the other

shepherds. Perhaps he wondered whether they were really shepherdesses at all.

On the fateful morning that Moses coincidentally chose to
settle at the well, he watched as a violent scene unfolded. Da'at
Zekeinim narrates the action.[13] The men chafed as they waited
their turn at the well, and they balked at the slow, inexpert hands of
the unaccustomed shepherdesses. The impatient shepherds rose
up, hoisted the young women, manhandled them, barred them from
the mouth of the well, and tossed them into the watering troughs.
Their objective was to humiliate the seven maidens, and to prevent
them from completing their watering task. The shepherds had been
biding their time, and attacked them when they were only seven
women ranged against a throng of determined men. The Netziv
states clearly that the shepherds' intent was vicious; they intended
no less than to rape them.[14]

The women, though they had been sheltered by privilege until
now, fought mightily, according to Alschich, and set up a din of
protest.[15] Simultaneously, Moses rose up from his place by the
well. The time for watching had ended, and this man, who had
been raised in a palace and was a fugitive before the Pharaoh
because he had come to the aid of a defenseless slave, was once
again poised to put his own life in danger to rescue these seven
maidens. Torah Shlema reminds the reader that in his essence
Moses remained a prince, a proud and valiant champion of the
defenseless victim.[16] Alschich is in awe of Moses' brave audacity,
his almost automatic response to the women's cries for help.
Moses had seen enough to know that the maidens' cries would have
been fruitless had he not been sitting by the well at that exact
moment. Their situation was hopeless but for his serendipitous
presence, so he stepped into the fray. His anger propelled him.
He was but one enraged man pitted against the many. Granted, he
was a fit, fighting man, and these men were but shepherds, but they
had him outnumbered. The matter was not simply one of priority
of watering rights. Moses assessed the situation in an instant, and
saw that the shepherds had blood in their eyes. With a war cry of
his own, Moses overcame the shepherds by dint of surprise, speed,
and expert wielding of his heavy staff. The Bible states, in verse
17, *Moses rose up and rescued them; and then he watered their*

flock. Moses' heroism allowed the seven daughters of the erstwhile priest of Midian to return to their ancestral tent unharmed.

Their father is surprised at their early return from the well, and the maidens respond in verse 19 that *An Egyptian man saved us from harm at the hands of the shepherds, and he also drew the water and watered the flock.* Alschich says that after their explanation of the morning's events their father understood that his daughters had been rescued from their tormenters by a man with superhuman strength who appeared as if out of nowhere, and disappeared immediately afterwards.[17] But the commentaries are curious why they tell their father that the man was an Egyptian. How did they discern that he was from Egypt? Is it likely that Moses, a fugitive from Egypt with a price on his head, would have dressed himself in Egyptian clothing? Abarbanel says that it must have been Moses' accent that disclosed his Egyptian origins.[18]

Yitro is filled with gratitude and is anxious to meet the man who championed his daughters. He is also a true man of the desert and, according to Sforno, practiced gracious hospitality to wayfarers.[19] How much more so is Yitro now keen to open his home to this stranger—perhaps an Egyptian—who interceded on behalf of his daughters, saving them from extreme harm. So Yitro inquires of his daughters in verse 20, *Where is this man? How could you just leave him there? Go, summon him to break bread with us.* Sh'mot Rabbah (1:32) explains that beyond the *p'shat* or straightforward explanation that "breaking bread" means Yitro sought to invite Moses to share a repast, the term also means "to take a wife."[20] The *midrash* understands that once Yitro heard his daughters narrate the brave rescue at the well that morning, his fatherly heart was already calculating that the heroic stranger might find more than just desert hospitality in his tent. Perhaps Yitro thought the man might find one of his seven daughters to his liking. After all, the local men had spurned his daughters after Yitro publicly resigned his role of high priest of Midian. Eligible men were scarce, and Yitro was hopeful.

The instant he commanded his daughters to *Go, summon him to break bread with us!* the *midrash* tells us that it was Zipporah who flew from the tent and raced back to the well to summon the stranger.[21] Just a short while before, the young women had fled back home after Moses rescued them, without offering him hospitality, so leery were they of strange men. Alone among Yitro's daughters it was Zipporah, the *midrash* explains, who—once her father gave his implicit permission to welcome the stranger—gave vent to her fascination and inchoate desire and sought him out.

TWENTY-TWO

ೞೞೞೞ

Zipporah Marries Moses

EXODUS 2:21

Moses consented to dwell with the man, and he gave his daughter, Zipporah, to Moses.[1]

The Bible text moves swiftly from Yitro's invitation to Moses to share a meal in his tent, to Moses agreeing to an extended stay. The curious reader might wonder if he or she has missed some of the action that surely took place between the end of the last chapter of this book and the current chapter. The commentary HaMa'or Shebatorah agrees that more occurred in Yitro's Midianite tent than is described in the Torah text, or why would the text read *Moses consented*? The commentary hints at an unrecorded conversation between Yitro and the heroic stranger. The *midrash* suggests that once Yitro had engaged Moses in a night of wide-ranging discussion, he invited Moses to tarry with him for an extended visit, and he also offered Moses one of his daughters in marriage.[2] The *p'shat*, according to Rashi,[3] is that *Moses consented* to come to dinner, to stay in Midian, and to marry Yitro's daughter. Sforno explains that *Moses consented* to be a shepherd for Yitro's flocks.[4]

The commentaries are fascinated by the Torah's first word in verse 21, *VaYo'el*, which can mean not only "he consented" but also "he swore." In fact according to the the Talmud (Nedarim 65a) the definition of *VaYo'eL* is "and he swore."[5] Thus far, we have explained the verse using the translation of the word to mean *Moses consented.* But since the word can also mean *Moses swore,* we are led to examine the Midianite drama more closely. After Yitro and Moses sat talking long into the night, what could have been the subject of Moses' oath to Yitro? Once Yitro learned of Moses' provenance, Rashi tells us that he demanded that as a condition of giving him Zipporah as a bride he made Moses swear never to depart Midian without first obtaining his father-in-law's blessing.[6] According to Sh'mot Rabbah (1:32) Yitro has heard, through desert lore, how Moses' great-grandfather Jacob, after toiling for more than twenty years as a shepherd for his father-in-law Lavan, fled Lavan's home with his wives and grandchildren.[7] Yitro sought to prevent a similar occurence.[†] Moses *consented, swore* as much to Yitro, and was given Zipporah as his wife. And, true to his oath, years later Moses does seek and obtain Yitro's blessing before he departs Midian to return to Egypt to face the dangers and wonders that await him there.

A more unsettling *midrash,* quoted in Yalkut Shimoni, relates another reason for the oath that Yitro extracts from Moses. This *midrash* suggests that Yitro desired to raise his daughter's first-born son as his own, and made Moses swear to agree to cede the boy to him to raise in his own tradition.[8] Alschich explains that Yitro, remaining troubled by the desert stories about the children of Abraham—Moses' ancestors—is fearful that if he gives his beloved first-born daughter to Moses to wed, Moses will follow in his ancestors' familial footsteps and will send away his first-born son just as Abraham exiled Yishmael. Moreover, Yitro worries that Moses will shunt aside his Midianite wife after she has served her purpose, and will marry an Israelite woman so that she will bear him children of the Covenant. The commentary posits that Yitro explains his fears to Moses, and extracts a promise that if he gives Zipporah to Moses for his wife, Moses will in turn give to Yitro the couple's first-born son to raise as his own.[9]

This *midrashic* notion that Moses somehow swore to Yitro that he could raise his future first-born son, is disturbing. Alschich

---

[†]We refer the reader to our first book, *The Passions of the Matriarchs*, p. 285, where we discuss this incident.

even exclaims that this story is enough to melt the reader's heart![10]
How could we believe that Moses would consent to such a thing?
Sha'arei Aharon understands that Moses had taken the measure of
his host, and appreciated that Yitro had already denounced the
Midianite priesthood and was questing for spiritual meaning. Moses
knew that in future years his oath to Yitro would become merely a
discarded formality since they would be living under virtually the
same roof, and Yitro would ultimately adopt Moses' faith.[11] All this
of course comes to pass.

Alternatively, Rabbeinu Bachya explains Moses' *midrashic*
behavior, and the speed with which he melted into Yitro's bucolic
household, as the rational behavior of a man fleeing for his life. By
happening upon Yitro's daughters at the well in Midian, and thereafter marrying Zipporah and becoming part of Yitro's household,
Moses coincidentally insured his safety from Pharaoh's questing
spies. The *midrash* tells us that the Midianite priests—even a
former priest such as Yitro was—enjoyed a measure of immunity
from Egypt's sovereign tentacles. For this reason Yitro's tent and
his holdings were a sanctuary and haven for Moses. Moses was a
wanted man, and being taken back alive to Egypt would have meant
certain death. Hence the text's statement *and Moses swore.* He
would have agreed to almost anything in order to insure that he
remained safely ensconced with Yitro in Midian.[12]

The Torah text continues, saying, *and he gave his daughter,
Zipporah, to Moses.* Torah Shlema once again quotes at length
from the *midrash Divrei HaYamim Shel Moshe,* to enlighten the
reader as to why it is Zipporah who is selected for this brave
stranger. The *midrash* tells a fascinating tale of Zipporah's intervention and salvation of the stranger Moses from a Midianite prison,
his acquisition of his mighty staff in an Arthurian contest, and his
ultimate marriage to Zipporah.[13] This commentary enriches the
reader's appreciation for the bond between Zipporah and Moses.
According to the *midrash,* when Moses came upon the well at
Midian he was on the run from the Pharaoh's soldiers. When Yitro
summons him to his tent after Moses saves Yitro's daughters from
the shepherds, Yitro inquires, "From where do you hail?" Moses
answers him honestly saying, "I am Moses," and relates to Yitro all
the events in Egypt leading up to that day. Yitro, desiring the king's
ransom that was promised to the one who captured and returned

Moses to Egypt, imprisons Moses on the spot, ordering rations of stale bread and rancid water for him, and planned to present Moses to the Pharaoh's soldiers when next they passed through Midian.

But Yitro's maiden daughter, Zipporah, had lost her heart to the stranger Moses when he rose up and single-handedly saved her and her sisters from the molesting shepherds at the well that fateful morning. So she secretly defied her father Yitro and for a period of seven years daily brought wholesome food and drink to Moses in the Midianite jail. As it neared the time for the Pharaoh's soldiers to return to Midian, Zipporah cleverly said to her father, "Did you know that the prisoner you locked away years ago is still alive? Moreover, I have heard him every day entreating his God to punish you for imprisoning him unjustly." Yitro replied, "I have never in my life heard of a man surviving in prison for seven years without proper food and drink! Let me go and see this man for myself." So Zipporah accompanied her father to the Midianite jail where Moses was found hale and hearty, words of praise for his God on his lips. Yitro freed him immediately, out of awe for the man Moses and his God.

Abarbanel continues the tale, describing that in the meantime, a thick staff—later identified by all as the miraculous staff of God—had been planted in Yitro's field, and over the years no one had been able to pull it free. After Yitro frees Moses from the Midianite jail, as a further test of Moses' apparent powers, he dares Moses to try his hand at uprooting the fabled staff, promising his daughter Zipporah's hand in marriage if Moses is successful. The commentary explains that Moses gripped the staff and pulled it out in one try, thus winning his bride.[14]

Pirkei d'Rabi Eliezer, an ancient *midrash*, embellishes this tale, describing the staff's provenance.[15] The commentary identifies Moses' miraculous staff of wonders as having been created by God at twilight on the first day of Creation, then passed on to Adam in the Garden of Eden, and thence from father to son through the years to Noah, Abraham, Isaac and finally to Jacob, who brought it down to Egypt and passed it on to his son Joseph. At Joseph's death his worldly goods were confiscated by the Pharaoh, and the fabled staff was given over to one of the king's magicians. Now Yitro had, in his youth, been a member of the Pharaoh's court, and he had watched Joseph wield the staff and had coveted it for its miraculous qualities. When his beliefs began to change and he fled Pharaoh's palace, Yitro took the magic staff with him and planted it in his garden in Midian. There it remained for years, repelling anyone who attempted to come close enough to touch it. Moses, upon arriving in Yitro's tent after rescuing his seven daughters at the well that morning, entered the garden, and recognizing the staff by its distinctive markings, gripped it and pulled it from the earth with ease. When Yitro saw this, he peered at Moses more closely and divined that he was destined to be the one to redeem the Children of Israel from Egypt. Because Moses was worthy, Yitro bestowed upon him as a prize the hand of his daughter Zipporah in marriage, and Moses remained in Yitro's household as master shepherd over all his flocks, for forty years.

The Torah text offers the reader little insight into the relationship between Moses and Zipporah. Verses 21 and 22 are laconic in the extreme, stating only that *Moses consented to dwell with the man, and he gave his daughter, Zipporah, to Moses, and she bore him a son.* Elsewhere in the Bible the narrator offers the reader clues as to the affection—or lack thereof—between a man and his wife. This occurs, for instance, in Genesis 29:18 and 31 when the Bible explicitly states that *Jacob loved Rachel,* and further, that *Leah was hated.* In contrast, here the reader is left to infer the relationship between Moses and Zipporah. And because of the spare Torah text the commentaries are conflicted as to the nature of their relationship. Did Moses love Zipporah?

Alschich answers this question in the negative. The commentary says that the Torah states plainly that *Moses consented to remain with the man* for the simple reason that it was Yitro's comradeship that Moses desired. He was not seeking a wife, and it was not his desire for Zipporah that kept him in Midian.[16] Hegyona Shel Torah agrees, using the Bible's phrase **and he gave** *his daughter, Zipporah, to Moses* as his proof-text. The commentary points out that had Moses been in love with Zipporah the text would have stated instead, *and* **Moses took** *Zipporah, Yitro's daughter.* This would have been a clear textual indication that Moses volitionally took Zipporah as a mate. As it reads, however, the implication is clear according to the commentary. Not only was Moses not cleaving unto Zipporah, but it was Yitro who was cleaving unto Moses![17] Moses was indifferent to Zipporah.

Zipporah fulfilled the age-old function of a prized daughter serving to unite one clan with another. She was the apple of her father's eye, and he sought to bestow her upon the stranger who had come to mean so much to him. What better way to keep Moses by his side than to cement the connection by a marriage to his daughter Zipporah? And while the Netziv agrees that the marriage of Zipporah and Moses lacked reciprocity, he explains it differently. The reason lay in Moses' character. The commentary tells us that a signal characteristic of Moses is that he was first and foremost a loner. He neither required nor desired a helpmate.[18]

The name of Zipporah is not mentioned in the Bible's story of Moses in Midian until verse 21. Until now, the episode in Midian has unfolded with only an undifferentiated mention of "the seven daughters" of the Priest of Midian or "his daughters." It is this compact verse that links the episode's three main characters: Yitro ("the man"), Moses, and Zipporah, and even alludes to their marriage. What is absent from the text, however, is any mention at all of characteristics that would define this woman who becomes Moses' wife. Bible readers are accustomed to slightly more detailed textual references about the women who attracted and wed the biblical heroes. For instance, we recall from the story of Jacob's first meeting of Rachel at the well in Padan-Aram (Genesis 29:17) that the Torah text informed us that Rachel was beautiful of face and form. Likewise, earlier in Genesis (24:16) we read of Isaac's future wife, Rebecca, at the well. There the Bible text told us that she was compassionate and quick to assist Eliezer, the thirsty wayfarer. We also learned that she was exceedingly beautiful. Here, in the absence of any textual mention of Zipporah's characteristics, it is the commentaries who eagerly and generously flesh out the physical as well as personal dimensions of the woman who weds the fugitive Egyptian shepherd, the man destined to be known throughout the millennia as "Moses the redeemer."

In a fascinating and uniqe *midrash*, Torah Shlema harks back to the dramatic well scene and poetically narrates the action through Moses' eyes. "As I sat by the well in Midian a group of shepherdesses approached the watering place with their bleating flock. One of the maidens stood out from the others, and my eye was drawn to her modest stance, her calm demeanor and her stately carriage. After I chased away the aggressive shepherds I learned that her name was Zipporah, and I told her that one day soon I would make her my wife."[19] The commentary continues, drawing from the sound-alike root-word *ZaPHRaH*, meaning "morning."[20] The *midrash* says that Zipporah was the most beautiful of all of Yitro's daughters, and that her lovely face glowed with exertion and happiness so that her countenance lit up the early morning scene.

The commentaries elicit Zipporah's personal qualities from the definition of her name, which translates as "bird." The reader will recall in chapter 21 above when an exasperated Yitro commands his daughters to *Go, summon the stranger to break bread with us!* that it is Zipporah who runs back to the well to fetch Moses. There, we quoted the *midrash* (Sh'mot Rabbah 1:32) analogizing Zipporah's flight to summon the heroic stranger to the quick flight of her winged namesake. Here, Rabbeinu Bachya continues to derive the maiden's qualities from her name. He points out that just as the bird is categorized in the Bible as a ritually pure creature, so, too, is the maiden Zipporah like her namesake. She is destined to become purified of her father's pagan beliefs, to be converted to monotheism, and to be a fitting partner for Moses.[21]

Ohr HaChayim bases his understanding of Zipporah from a close reading of verse 21. In that verse the Bible mentions Moses' name twice; once to say that Moses consented to settle with Yitro, and once again to say that Yitro gave his daughter Zipporah to Moses. The commentator says the dual mention of Moses' name in this verse is unnecessary, except as a hint to the careful reader. Ordinarily, as it was the second reference to Moses in the same verse, it would have sufficed for the text to say *and he gave Zipporah his daughter to him*. But from the reiteration of Moses' name the commentary learns that the Bible is verbally linking Moses with Zipporah. The Torah intends for the reader to derive that Zipporah is Moses' counterpart.[22]

Torah Shlema caps the commentaries' understanding of Zipporah. He reminds the reader that it was Zipporah who, according to the *midrash Divrei HaYamim Shel Moshe*, sustained Moses during his seven years in the Midianite prison, daily risking her father's wrath and grave punishment to do so. Her quiet strength and understated bravery and devotion to Moses elevate her to the same level of righteousness and integrity as the Bible's matriarchs. She trod the same path to Godliness as did Sarah,

Rebecca, Rachel and Leah, and adhered to the commandments taught to her by her husband, Moses.[23] She was one of the heroic and fabled "righteous women" of her generation.

TWENTY-THREE

৪০৪৪৪

Zipporah Bears a Son for Moses

EXODUS 2:22

And she bore him a son, and he named him Gershom, because he said, "I was a stranger in a foreign land."[1]

The text does not state that Zipporah became pregnant with Moses' child, only that *she bore him a son.* Typically the Bible's format for announcing a birth is to narrate the fact of the pregnancy and then the birth, in a formulaic manner. The commentary Chizkuni notices this omission, and suggests that as this was Zipporah's first pregnancy her body remained taut and did not show the pregnancy until she was very near term.[2] Hence this verse *and she bore him a son*, comes on the heels of the prior verse narrating her marriage to Moses.

The commentaries offer a flurry of observations about the Bible's statement *and he named him Gershom, because he said, "I was a stranger in a foreign land."* Ibn Ezra belabors the obvious, pointing out to the reader that it is Moses—not Zipporah, and not Yitro—who names his son.[3] To the contrary, Torat HaChidah diverges from the *p'shat*, suggesting that notwithstanding the grammatical awkwardness, it was Zipporah who named the boy. She was determined that her firstborn son would *not* be given over to her father to raise, despite Moses' prior agreement. In fact, the

110

commentary suggests that Moses relied on Zipporah's honor to prevent their firstborn son from being raised with Yitro's beliefs. Zipporah justly named their son "Gershom" because she knew Moses had been a newcomer and *a stranger in a foreign land*, and he had made the promise to Yitro against his will.[4]

The name "Gershom" is a simple combination of two Hebrew words, *GeR* and *SHoM*, meaning literally "stranger there." According to Rashbam, the simple meaning of the boy's name is its correct one. Moses was merely commemorating that his son was born in a far-flung land.[5] The ambiguity in this verse concerns Moses' explanatory phrase "I was a stranger in a foreign land." Why does Moses speak in the past tense (*I **was** a stranger . . .*), and to which foreign land is Moses referring?

The Chatam Sofer deals with the issue of Moses' use of the past tense, which he claims refers to the land of Egypt. Even though Midian clearly qualifies as a "foreign land" to Moses, his use of the past tense indicates that Midian has become his home, and is no longer "foreign" to him; Midian has offered him succor and pleasure, peace, and a wife and child, and—not insignificantly—a safe haven. While Egypt is Moses' birth place, it was in Egypt that he was hunted down and declared a capital criminal, forcing him to become a fugitive. Egypt thus forfeited the emotional link associated with one's birth home and became "foreign" to Moses. By naming his son "Gershom" Moses is expressing gratitude to God for delivering him to safety from the hands of his Egyptian pursuers.[6]

Abarbanel suggests that by so naming his son Moses implies that it was in the land of Kush that he **was** *a stranger in a foreign land*. The commentary says that according to the *midrash* Moses was a stranger in Kush first, before he arrived in Midian. Egypt is not considered in Abarbanel's equation because Egypt was Moses' birthplace, and was not a "foreign land."[7] And because Midian adopted him and sheltered him, it was his current home, and Moses felt no foreignness in Midian.

On the contrary, Chizkuni suggests that Midian is the "foreign land" to which Moses refers in his rationale for naming his son. The commentary reasons that even though by the time of Gershom's birth Moses had become Yitro's son-in-law and a fixture in Yitro's tent, as well as an accustomed shepherd in the fields and at the well in Midian, he was never accepted as a Midianite. He was still considered by the Midianite denizens to be a parvenu and a newcomer.[8] It is interesting that all the enumerated commentaries, with the exception of Chizkuni, interpret this verse based on Moses' own internal designation of himself as a "stranger." Only Chizkuni takes the verse's rationale outside of Moses himself, and references it in the manner he is perceived by those around him. The reader can empathize with Moses in both of these posited situations; he is an outsider wherever he goes, and he also carries his "otherness" with him. Is it any wonder that after being a fugitive for forty years he named his son "Gershom," meaning "a stranger there?"

Malbim agrees that Moses is referring to Midian—and not Egypt— as the "strange land." But the commentary's reasoning relies not on the lands themselves, but in Moses' deepest yearnings. According to the Malbim, though Moses was physically present in Midian, even the joyous birth of his son served only to remind him that his place was elsewhere. Moses' heart was in Egypt because his brethren were there. Moses was biding his time until he could return to Egypt and redeem his brethren from bondage. In the meantime, by so naming his son, he was reminding Yitro and Zipporah that he was only sojourning in their land. He remained a stranger there; his heart was elsewhere.[9]

TWENTY-FOUR

ഇൽ൫ഇൽ൫

Moses Encounters God

EXODUS 2:23-4:17

The years pass, and the Bible tells us that the king of Egypt dies and the Children of Israel sigh in anguish, and buckle under the oppression of their slavery. But the time is ripe and unbeknownst to them their redemption is nigh, as God hears their cries and recalls the divine covenant with the Hebrew forefathers, Abraham, Isaac and Jacob. God is presently readying the redeemer of the Children of Israel.

Moses has been living all these years in Midian, as shepherd to Yitro's extensive flocks. In search of ever-more-fertile grazing land Moses leads the sheep far into the Midianite desert, until they are grazing at the very foot of God's Mountain at Horeb. It is as he tends the sheep at Horeb that Moses sees a thorn-bush that is alight with flame, yet the bush is not consumed! Moses' curiosity is kindled, and he strays from the grazing path to investigate this unusual phenomenon. God sees that Moses is drawing near to the burning bush and calls out to him from its midst: "Moses, Moses!" And Moses answers, "I am here."

Chapters 3 and 4 of Exodus contain the narration of Moses' incredible conversation with God through the medium of the burning bush. First, God instructs Moses to draw no closer to the burning bush, and to remove his shoes out of respect for the holy place.   God reveals that He is God of Moses' forefathers, and Moses hides his face from this divine revelation.   This becomes the template for this biblical conversation between God and Moses, as God explains that He has chosen Moses to act as His emissary and lead the Children of Israel out of bondage into the promised land flowing with milk and honey, and Moses repeatedly demurs.   "Who am I that you would choose me to go to Pharaoh?"

Moses is understandably terrified to return to the land that caused him to be a fugitive some forty years ago, and God repeatedly reassures him, saying, "I will be with you."   God instructs Moses to speak to the Hebrew elders and to say in God's name, "Verily I have remembered you (*PaKoD PaKaD'Ti*)[1], and I have seen what was done to you in Egypt."   God tells Moses to request of the Pharaoh that he allow the Hebrews to take a three-day journey into the desert to sacrifice to their God.   God warns Moses that the Pharaoh will refuse his request to leave, and will respond only to force.   God will then call upon His awesome strength and will utterly destroy Egypt through miracles, so that the Egyptians will ultimately eject the Hebrews from their midst, with great wealth given from the Egyptian women to their departing Hebrew counterparts.[2]

Moses replies, "But they will not believe me."   And God gives Moses two signs that His omnipotence will accompany Moses into Egypt.   God first turns Moses' staff into a writhing snake before his wondering eyes, and only Moses' grasping of its tail turns the snake back into the inanimate walking staff.   Next, God turns Moses' hand white as snow with the dreaded leprosy, and then reverses the terrifying marvel by returning Moses' flesh back to normal in an instant.   God further presages the plague of transforming the waters of the Nile into blood, and instructs Moses that he will perform this demonstration of God's might to the disbelieving Hebrews as well as to the intransigent Egyptian king.

Moses interjects yet another objection saying, "But my Lord, I am not a man of words, nor have I ever been thus, and I am slow of speech."   God's impatience is evident as He responds once again to the reluctant Moses, "Who but I gave mankind a mouth?   And who is it who determines if a person will be dumb or deaf, sighted or blind?   Is it not within my power to do this?   For I am the Lord! Now, go!   For I will guide your mouth and I will teach you what to say."

Still Moses persists, and begs to be excused from God's mission. "I beg you, my Lord! Send whomever else you wish." Moses' last objection ignites God's wrath, but He offers Moses an accomodation. He says that Aaron the Levite, Moses' brother, is an able speaker, and furthermore that Aaron is even now setting out on the desert path to meet Moses. "When he sees you his heart will be filled with gladness. You will be able to speak through Aaron, who will utter your words for you. And I will be with you both, and I will teach you what you must do. Aaron will be your spokesman to the people, and you will be his guide."

This last exhortation silences Moses' objections once and for all, and God instructs Moses to take the staff in hand, as it will be with this staff that Moses will perform God's miracles.

TWENTY-FIVE

༄ఌ༾ఌ

Serach, Asher's Daughter, Heralds the Redemption

EXODUS 3:16, 3:22, 4:31

*Go and gather the Elders of Israel and say to them, 'The Lord, God of your fathers, Abraham, Isaac and Jacob, revealed Himself to me, saying, "**Verily have I remembered you**, and I have seen what is being done to you in Egypt."'*[1]

*And **every woman** shall ask of her neighbor objects of silver and gold, as well as clothing, and shall give them to her sons and daughters, for you shall be victorious over the Egyptians.*[2]

*And the people believed [Moses] when they heard that **God remembered** the Children of Israel. . . .*[3]

God's conversation with Moses at the burning bush was significant on several levels. First, of course, is Moses' reluctant but eventual acceptance of his role as God's messenger to the people and to the Egyptian Pharaoh. But equally momentous is God's emphatic statement in chapter 3 verse 16 that the redemption is imminent. God's words, *verily have I remembered—PaKoD*

116

PaKaD'Ti in Hebrew—have been awaited for hundreds of years. The people have labored and suffered, witnessed their newborn sons drowned before their eyes, and have despaired of redemption. Their lives, the lives of their parents, and the future lives of their children have become mired in slavery. They know no other way of life. Pharaoh is their master.

The Bible's double-use of the Hebrew word for "remember" as spoken by God to Moses is therefore highly significant. God knows that Moses will have a nearly impossible job convincing the Children of Israel that "God has truly remembered" them. Their entire existential being is that of slaves, and they will not leap to embrace this fugitive stranger's announcement of impending redemption. They will doubt him, will surely direct their anger against him, and will not rush to upset the status quo and anger the Egyptian king. The *midrashists* have therefore woven a rich tapestry explaining the Torah's use of this emphatic phrase, *verily have I remembered.*

The commentaries say that the Bible's doubling of the word "remember" was an encrypted code that God transmitted to Moses at the burning bush in order to assist him on his mission to return to Egypt. Pirkei d'Rabi Eliezer[4] explains that such double words appear rarely in the Torah, and these in particular—because of their future momentous power—had been passed down in trusted whispers from father to son beginning with Abraham, then to Isaac, thence to Jacob, from Jacob to his favored son, Joseph, and from Joseph to his brothers. Throughout the years of the Children of Israel's unending bondage in Egypt, Jacob's sons died off one by one, and the future redemption's secret code—*PaKoD PaKaD'Ti*— was transmitted ultimately, according to the Talmud[5] (Sotah 13a), to his eldest surviving issue, Asher's youngest daughter and Jacob's granddaughter, Serach. In this way, if someone calling himself "the redeemer" were to present himself to the Children of Israel, the elders would be able to judge whether or not he had in truth been appointed by God, by discerning if he possessed this secret code. It therefore fell to Serach, the daughter of Asher, (known in the *midrash* as Serach bat Asher) to confirm the veracity of any such putative redeemer. She alone possessed the knowledge of the code words. It is for this reason, according to the *midrash*, that the Torah says in verse 16 that God commands Moses to first *go to the elders.* The most revered of all the elders was Jacob's granddaughter, Serach. She would confirm Moses' authenticity, paving the way for his acceptance first by the other elders and then by the Children of Israel.

God's emphatic statement of remembering—*PaKoD PaKaD'Ti*—is that special quality of divine memory that will free one who has no hope.[†] For this reason the elders will be aghast as well as hopeful when, later on in the Exodus story, Moses returns to Egypt with his brother Aaron at his side and announces that he has been sent by God to redeem them from slavery. Moses reveals to them, in that future meeting, God's three signs: the miracle of his staff that becomes a snake; the sign of his leprous hand; and the ability to transform the waters of the Nile into blood. Moses also speaks the encrypted phrase—*PaKoD PaKaD'Ti*—to disclose to the elders of Israel that redemption is imminent. The elders consult Serach bat Asher. They reveal all that Moses has shown to them, and she remains skeptical until they also reveal to her the code words that he had brought to them from God's mouth: *PaKoD PaKaD'Ti*. Immediately, recognizing the fabled code, Serach's ancient eyes become alight with excitement, her wrinkled visage transformed in ecstacy as she points to Moses: "*He* is the man who will redeem Israel from Egypt!"

Ibn Ezra explains[6] that this is the reason the Bible states, in chapter 4, verse 31, that *the people believed Moses when they heard that* **God remembered**. The momentous power of *PaKoD PaKaD'Ti*—*verily have I remembered*—first revealed by God to Abraham generations earlier, was destined to be confirmed by the daughter of Asher. It was Serach, granddaughter of Jacob and cousin of Moses, who confirmed Moses' bona fides to the elders of Israel and heralded the redemption. She was also a legendary wise woman who appears and reappears in *midrashic* lore over the course of eight centuries of Jewish history. The *midrash* credits Serach bat Asher with the knowledge that Joseph had not died a terrible death, but that his brothers had sold him to the caravan of

---

[†]Readers will note that the Bible used the same root word, *PaKoD*, when it told us that "God remembered the matriarch Sarah" (Gen. 21:1) and opened her womb after she had endured decades of childlessness. The authors dealt with this issue in depth in Chapter 7 of their first book, *The Passions of the Matriarchs.*

Ishmaelites. She is also one of the seventy original souls who migrated into Egypt with Jacob, and the Talmud (Sotah 13a) has her pointing out to Moses the secret burial place of Joseph's bones on the eve of their exodus from Egypt. She is mythically present from the time of Abraham through the advent of Israel's servitude in Egypt, until the kingdom of David arises centuries hence, and according to Otzar Ishei HaTanach[7] is one of the fabled nine persons in Jewish history whose death is never recorded and who is said to have entered the Garden of Eden alive as a reward for her righteousness.

Beth Samuels[†] likened Serach Bat Asher to "an Eliyahu figure who appears and reappears throughout the generations, a wise woman who, according to the *midrashim*, is immortal. In every generation where she appears, Serach is the authority, the leader. Serach is a catalyst who transforms us—through her sensitivity, wisdom and teaching—from a state of darkness to a state of redemption."

Harking back to Moses' revelation at the burning bush, the reader will recall that in addition to the words *PaKoD PaKaD'Ti*, God also foretold a nearly unbelievable reversal of events. God predicted that as part of the redemption the Israelites would ultimately vanquish the Egyptians, and that **every woman** *shall ask of her neighbor objects of silver and gold, as well as clothing, and shall give them to her sons and daughters.* The commentaries ask pointedly why this prediction is restricted to the women? Why will the Egyptian women cede their wealth exclusively to their Israelite counterparts?

According to Nehama Leibowitz,[8] the Egyptian women are returning to the erstwhile Hebrew slaves the valuable objects and jewelry that they had acquired from the Hebrew women over the years. In the wake of the Pharaoh's genocidal edict to murder the Hebrew male newborns, the desperate and ingenious slave women had bartered their valuables and clothing, begging the Egyptian women to overlook their hidden babies. Over the years, the Hebrews' homes became bereft of all valuables, while the Egyptians'

[†]Beth Samuels delivered a lecture entitled "Who is Serach Bat Asher?" at the 25th Anniversary Dinner of the Drisha Institute in New York City in May of 2004. This quote is drawn from her talk.

homes swelled with the wealth they acquired from the Hebrew women as bribes—mostly unavailing—to save their babies' lives. The commentary explains that God's prediction is a poetic reversal: when God redeems the Children of Israel, the slave women will have the upper hand, and the Egyptian women will give up their valuables and fine clothing to them. In reality, says the commentary, they are returning the valuables to their true owners.

It is not coincidental, says Leibowitz, that it is the *women* who are requesting the Egyptian wealth. It was the women who righteously enticed their husbands to continue to procreate, who bore their children against impossible odds, who stood up to the Pharaoh, and who, in the face of death, bartered for the life of each child one-at-a-time. For these reasons the women are spared attending their redemption in slave rags. God's prediction is that the Israelite women shall clothe their children in the fine raiment they requested of the Egyptian women once the redemption was upon them. Such was the hopeful message that Moses was to bear to his enslaved Israelite brethren.

PART III

MOSES AND ZIPPORAH
IN THE DESERT

ഇൻൽഇൻൽ

TWENTY-SIX

ಹಃಡಹಃಡ

Moses, Zipporah and their Sons Take Leave of Yitro

EXODUS 4:18-20

And Moses returned to Yeter his father-in-law, and he said to him, "Please give me leave to return to my brethren who are in Egypt, in order that I may see for myself whether they are still alive." And Yitro told Moses, "Go peacefully." For God had told Moses [while he was] in Midian, "Go, return to Egypt, for all the men who sought to kill you are already dead." So Moses took his wife and their sons and he set them upon a donkey, and he set out on the return path to the land of Egypt. And Moses had in his hand God's chosen staff.[1]

The Bible meticulously narrates that after his revelation at the burning thorn-bush, Moses returned from his desert isolation to the tent of his father-in-law Yitro. According to Chizkuni[2] Moses returned leading Yitro's flocks homeward for the last time. He was embarking on God's mission and truly did not know if he would ever return to Midian. Rashi explains Moses' return to his father-in-law in ethical terms.[3] Moses was honor-bound to consult with Yitro before embarking on his return trip to Egypt because Moses had sworn to his father-in-law, in Exodus 2:21, that he would never depart from Midian without first seeking his blessing.[†] The Talmud (Nedarim 65a) concurs, and narrates a *midrashic* conversation between Moses and God.[4] Recalling Moses' oath to Yitro, God instructs him while he is still in the Sinai desert: "You swore an oath while in Midian; now return to Midian and seek absolution from your oath."

Upon his return to Yitro's tent Moses is greeted by his father-in-law, by his older son Gershom, and by his wife Zipporah, about to give birth to their second child. According to the Ramban,[5] Zipporah had been pregnant when Moses left Yitro's tent months ago to lead the flocks to distant fertile pastures. Moses has returned in time to witness his second son's birth, beg leave of Yitro, bundle his wife and sons onto a donkey and return to Egypt as God commanded him in 4:20. It would seem that Moses has no time to spare.

It is fascinating that God's instructions to Moses—both textual and *midrashic*—display God's understanding of Moses' most personal concerns. First, preempting Moses' fears, God reassures Moses that he is free to return to Egypt notwithstanding that he fled there years before and remained wanted for a capital crime. "You can return to Egypt. Those in Egypt who sought your death are themselves dead, and no longer pose a threat to your life." And second, God understands that Moses might think that God expects him to pick himself up immediately and head down to Egypt, without stopping first in Yitro's tent. But in the *midrash* God is instructing Moses that a man's oath freely given should be honored. After Moses is released from his oath to Yitro, God's expectation is that Moses "leave Midian behind and return to Egypt." After his revelation at the burning bush, Moses has been transformed from Yitro's shepherd into God's servant. It was past time to set out on the path to bring about the promised redemption.

Sha'arei Aharon[6] presents a possibility that months before, Zipporah and Gershom had in fact accompanied Moses into the desert of Horeb when he shepherded Yitro's flocks, pitching their tent in the grazing lands in the foothills of Mount Horeb. Thus, Moses' return **to Yitro's tent** in 4:18 was in time to allow

---

[†]See Chapter 22 above, where we discussed Moses' oath in detail.

Zipporah to give birth to their second child in the comfort of her childhood home and with her sisters about her, to beg leave of Yitro, and to bid the old man goodbye.

Still, the predominant *p'shat* reading of verse 4:20 is that *Moses took his wife and their sons and he set them upon a donkey, and he set out on the return path* **to the land of Egypt**. Ramban[7] recounts a fascinating *midrashic* conversation between Yitro and Moses when Moses and Zipporah were preparing to set out on the desert journey to Egypt. "So tell me, Moses. Where are you bound for now?" "For Egypt," he replied. "Egypt! In the name of Heaven why would you want to take my daughter and grandsons *into* Egypt? Egypt is the one place everyone is seeking to *escape!*" And Moses responds, "In the coming months there *will* be a great exodus from Egypt, and our people will journey from there to stand at the foot of Mt. Sinai, where they will hear the pronouncements of the One God. I will lead this exodus, and I will stand on God's mountain. Should not your daughter and grandsons witness this greatness?" And Yitro gave Moses his blessing. *Go peacefully.*

In fact, according to the 20th-century commentary of Meshech Chachma,[8] it is Moses' faith in God's promise of redemption that allows him to take Zipporah, Gershom and their newborn son out of Yitro's comfortable oasis home and subject them to the rigors of desert travel and the certainty of hostilities once they arrive at their destination. And according to the *midrash*, if Moses were to arrive in Egypt leading a donkey carrying his wife and children, his credibility with the skeptical Children of Israel would be enhanced. They would appreciate how certain Moses must be of the veracity of God's promise of imminent redemption. For otherwise, they would reason, it is inconceiveable that Moses would bring his wife and sons—one a newborn—to a place of bondage and constant danger. This putative redeemer, this man Moses, must place great store in God's promise. Perhaps, the lifelong slaves will think, just perhaps, the redemption really is at hand!

The power of God's word can be tangible and awesome, but it also can be mystical and incalculable, according to the biblical commentaries. The Midrash Tanchuma, Sh'mot Rabbah and Ba'al HaTurim refer to God's word to Moses in Midian (4:19): *Go, return to Egypt*. The implicit question is why the Bible states again in

4:19 that God told Moses to *Go, return to Egypt,* when God had already given Moses this command at the burning bush in chapter 3. Midrash Tanchuma[9] explains that God's voice is the medium of miracles and wonders. Moses was introduced to God's voice at the burning bush, and there God outlined for Moses his mission to redeem the Israelites, and offered him reassurances and magical signs. But according to the *midrash* God's reiteration to Moses in Midian to *Go, return to Egypt* is meant to be understood as only *half* of God's message. Miraculously, God's voice simultanously spoke both to Moses in Midian *(Go, return to Egypt),* and to his brother Aaron in Egypt! God's concomitant word to Aaron in Egypt (4:27) was: *Go forth and greet Moses who is on his way in the desert.* The *midrash* implies that while the great miracles are still to come—the plagues, the splitting of the Red Sea, the giving of the Torah—God's will is generous enough to encompass the relatively minor miracle of uniting brothers who have endured half a century of separation under fraught and daunting circumstances, and ensuring that mutuality and gladness fill their hearts as well as commonality of purpose.

This is the reason, says the *midrash,* that the Bible tells us in 4:19 what God instructs Moses, and in 4:27 in parallel language, what God instructs Aaron. God had assured Moses at the burning bush that he and Aaron would be partners in the forthcoming redemption. Thus, God's bifurcated voice in chapter 4— simultaneously spoken but heard differently by Moses and Aaron worlds apart but to a single purpose—is the fulfillment of His promise to Moses. God knows that when Moses encounters Aaron in the desert on the way back to Egypt Moses will recall God's promise to him and he will be reassured. Moses' God is the God who keeps His promises, be they seemingly trivial or of enormous consequence.

These simultaneous iterations by God to Moses and Aaron appear in the Bible separated by three verses. The *midrash* explains that by this placement we learn that God's voice is bracketing a miraculous and momentous occurrence. It behooves us to pay close attention to what befalls Moses and Zipporah in the intervening verses that are strategically placed between the bookends of God's words.

TWENTY-SEVEN

ഇരുഇരു

The Incident at the Inn

EXODUS 4:24-26

And it happened on the way, at an inn, that God encoun-
tered him and sought to kill him. And Zipporah took a flint
and cut the foreskin of her son, and she touched his legs;
and she said, "For you are like a bridegroom of blood to
me." Thence, it instantly withdrew from him; thus she said,
"A bridegroom of blood for circumcisions!"[1]

Moses and Zipporah have left Midian behind. Zipporah has taken leave of her father and her home and is venturing, for the first time in her sheltered life, into the vast desert terrain that separates Midian from Egypt. Her husband Moses, a courageous but solitary man, a shepherd and a thinker, has disclosed to her and her father that his God has spoken to him and instructed him to return to Egypt in order to redeem the Hebrews from their slavery. Moses is on foot, leading the donkey that is carrying his wife Zipporah and their sons Gershom and newborn Eliezer. They plod westward, the only humans as far as the eye can see as they cross the endless sunbleached dunes.

Elie Wiesel, in his essay "Moses: Portrait of a Leader,"[†] suggests that in order to understand the incident at the inn we must first appreciate that Moses has still not fully shed his reluctance to return to Egypt. We recall that Moses had patently expressed this reluctance to the Almighty when God gave him his mission at the burning bush. In Wiesel's words, "Moses gathered his family, bid his in-laws farewell and set out on his return journey, albeit with noticeable lack of enthusiasm. That very night he stopped at an inn. Why not rest the night? And thus postpone the moment when he would meet once more those brothers he had expected never to see again." It is Wiesel's thesis that Moses felt he had been betrayed by his brethren, who had informed the Pharaoh's men that he had slayed the Egyptian taskmaster. So even though Moses allowed God to convince him to return to Egypt as redeemer of the Israelites, at this moment Moses is still dragging his feet, so-to-speak. It is at this point in the text that we encounter Moses, Zipporah and their tiny caravan.

Finally, the desert night is upon them, and the travelers stop at a tented settlement, at an inn that accepts desert wayfarers. It is while Moses, Zipporah and their sons are secluded at this inn that they experience one of the strangest incidents in the entire book of Exodus, a Biblical book that is rife with miracles as well as supernatural occurrences.

This incident is narrated in three verses between God's command to Moses to *Go to Egypt* and God's command to Aaron to *Go forth and greet Moses*. It has been called one of the most obscure or incomprehensible vignettes in the Bible. The 20th-century Torah commentator Yehuda Nachshoni[2] articulates the intellectual puzzlement that is expressed by Torah scholars when they are faced with these verses. Nachshoni poses the questions that surely crowd the reader's mind: If God has appointed Moses as His messenger to Pharaoh and as the redeemer of the Hebrews, why then does God accost Moses on his way to Egypt and attempt to kill him? Was it, as some commentators say, that Moses faced the death sentence because he failed to circumcise his newborn son Eliezer? And if Moses and his wife have encountered some grave

---

[†]Weisel, E. (1976), *Messengers of God: Biblical Portraits and Legends*, (New York, Simon & Schuster), p. 190.

danger at the inn because he did not circumcise his newborn son, why then is it Zipporah—and not Moses—who circumcises the infant? And whatever can Zipporah mean by her first cryptic pronouncement *A bridegroom of blood are you to me!* when the death force is upon Moses, and her parallel remark after he has been spared: *A bridegroom of blood for circumcisions!* Furthermore, continues Nachshoni, it is unclear whom precisely the angel of God sought to kill; was it Moses or was it his newborn son? The commentary specifically acknowledges his thanks for the collected wisdom of the commentaries and the *midrash*, with whose help we can begin to make some sense of this incident at the inn.

According to Rashi[3] the straightforward reading of the verses is that God sought to kill Moses because he failed to circumcise his newborn son while they were still all together in Midian. Because Moses delayed consecrating his newborn son to God, he faced dire punishment on the road to Egypt. The Talmud (Nedarim 31b) elaborates, saying that in those days circumcision was not a simple matter. What might appear to readers to be a simple course of action—Moses should have circumcised Eliezer in Midian and then left for Egypt—is in fact more complex. The Talmud presents[4] Moses' dilemma: *If I circumcise Eliezer while I am still here in Midian, the boy is in danger if we travel immediately. I would have to wait here for at least three days afterwards to ensure his safe recovery. Yet God has commanded me to "Go, return to Egypt!" I am forbidden to delay setting out on God's mission.* Circumcise and wait, or leave for Egypt directly? Such was Moses' quandary according to the Talmud. In light of this, why then did Moses face punishment by death? The Talmud suggests that the inn itself holds the answer.

Akeidat Yitzchak explains that a very human Moses chose to delay the circumcision and to spend the night at the inn before pressing on toward Egypt.[5] The reason for his choice was that Moses was not yet a man of God. He still desired his wife by his side, and he sought time for marital intimacy at the inn. The commentary says that had Moses been thinking logically he could have circumcised his son even when they had stopped at the inn. That he did not do so, but further delayed performing the circumcision, is the reason for God's wrath. Moses could have—and according to Akeidat Yitzchak Moses *should* have—circumcised Eliezer either before leaving Midian, or even upon arriving at the inn.   In either case Moses then should have left the baby in the care of Zipporah, striking out alone for Egypt.   That he did neither is the reason God confronts Moses *on the way at the inn.*

The Netziv explains this present confrontation between Moses and God as having its origins in Moses' spiritual transformation.[6] According to the commentator, when Moses first confronted God at the burning bush in chapter 3 and removed his shoes out of respect for the holiness of the place, Moses began—perhaps unbeknownst even to himself—his ascent into holiness.   God's intent was that from the encounter on Mount Horeb Moses would become the quasi-holy vehicle for the redemption of the Children of Israel.   God would engineer the momentous event, and Moses and his brother Aaron would carry out God's wishes.   The problem, according to the Netziv, is that Moses' spiritual transformation proceeded more slowly.   In his human and thoughtful fashion, Moses was absorbing his new role, and after his discourse with God, he reluctantly assumed the mantle of redeemer.   We must appreciate that back on the ground, so-to-speak, amidst his family in Midian, Moses was hard-put to remain entirely God's messenger.   He was dutiful son-in-law, enamored husband, father of a newborn.   His new mission was pulling him away from all that was familiar to him, and he was temporarily without moorings.   Heeding God's command to hasten to Egypt, he postponed the circumcision of his newborn son, brought his small family along with him into the desert, and took comfort from the nearness of his wife in a desert inn.   All of these behaviors were understandably human, and precisely what God did *not* require from the newly anointed redeemer.

God's confrontation of Moses at the inn that night was unexpected and very nearly fatal.   Moses was completely un-prepared for it.   He was engaged in the prosaic acts of settling his family for the night.   This is contrasted with the incident on Mount Horeb, where Moses, although surprised and awestruck at the vision of the burning bush, had been a solitary shepherd who spent his days in contemplation and meditation.   He accepted God's presence there, and was as prepared on Mount Horeb as he would ever be to confront the Lord for the first time.   Contrariwise, when God con-fronted Moses at the inn Moses' reaction was one of paralyzing fear.   He quite simply did not expect God's abrupt appearance to him there. Moses was not in a state of readiness to meet God on His terms, having not yet made that critical transition from husband and father to Man of God.

Rabbi Adin Steinsaltz, in his commentary to the Talmud on this incident (Nedarim 31a), confirms the Netziv's understanding of Moses' near-fatal misstep.[7] Says Steinsaltz, Moses was punished by God at the inn for the reason that instead of rising above his worldly and corporeal needs, Moses succumbed and allowed his own needs to control him. As God's anointed, He was expected to give priority to his spiritual self. Instead, his son remained uncircumcised, and he was dallying en route to Egypt.

HaMa'or Shebatorah explains[8] that one might think that as God's anointed, Moses could have delayed the commandment of circumcision with impunity, as he was already on his way to fulfill God's previously articulated command to return to Egypt. Had he stopped to circumcise his son he would have delayed returning to Egypt. Moses was in a seemingly impossible situation. But according to the commentary, because there *was* time to fulfill *both* of God's commandments, Moses was held to God's exacting standard.

Still, the textual difficulty is glaring: *God encountered him and sought to kill him.* Despite the wording, the commentaries reject the notion that God sought to eradicate the man He had selected and appointed redeemer of the Children of Israel. Rashbam laconically states that it was an angel, not God Himself, who encountered Moses at the inn.[9] Sforno adds that the angel who encountered Moses was the designated angel of the *brit*, the angel of the covenant. This specific angel threatened Moses with death because he had bypassed the commandment to circumcise his newborn son and bring him into the covenant with God.[10] It is Rashi who names Eliezer, Zipporah and Moses' newborn, as the uncircumcised son whom God jealously—and angrily here—desires to enter into the covenant.[11] The Talmud, too, (Nedarim 32a)[12] understands verse 24 to mean that God's threat was directed not against Moses, but against the uncircumcised newborn itself.

Contrariwise, Sha'arei Aharon posits that God is angry that Moses' and Zipporah's *firstborn* son, Gershom, was still as-yet uncircumcised. Readers will recall our discussion in chapter 22 that Yitro had required as a condition of Moses' marriage to Zipporah that their future firstborn son would be raised in Midianite tradition.

Here, the commentary suggests that God is angered that Moses has not taken the first possible opportunity to circumcise Gershom now that he is out of Yitro's purview.[13] The commentary suggests that Moses reasoned, "Since the *brit* has been delayed until now, I will wait until we arrive in Egypt and *then* I will circumcise him." We will see that it is this critical delay that nearly costs Moses his life.

Sha'arei Aharon explains that a close reading of verse 24 yields a hint to the reader that this was a terrifying *warning* to Moses rather than the angel of death come to exact *punishment*. The Biblical term for "God" in this verse, *YKVK*, is understood to represent the "*merciful* God." Had the verse used instead the word "*Elokim*"—the Biblical reference for "God of *judgement*"—our understanding of the verse would have been completely different. Thus, according to the *midrash*, the angel that encountered Moses was one of mercy, because it waited until Moses and his tiny caravan had reached the inn before accosting him. In contrast, the angel of judgement would have accosted Moses on the way, while he was trudging through the blistering sand dunes, and the danger to Moses in those circumstances would have been dire indeed.[14]

HaMa'or Shebatorah agrees, saying that the spirit that Moses encountered was surely the spirit of divine mercy. This merciful angel sought only to hurry Moses along, urging him to reach the sanctuary of the inn before complying with God's command to circumcise his newborn son. God's merciful angel did not seek to exact Moses' death.[15] Nachshoni explains that the supernatural encounter was not intended as a sinister one; rather it was initially a divine phenomenon whose purpose was to signal that the time had come for the circumcision.[16] Only when Moses apparently ignored the angel's presence did its mission revert to one of punishment.

This "angel of God," or manifestation of God's presence, caught Moses completely unaware. The *midrash* explains that Moses and his wife already had retired for the night. God's abundance concentrated itself in Moses' room at the inn, and quite literally filled it to bursting. Moses' only previous encounter with the spirit of God had been in the wild and barren spaces of the desert mountains, where Moses had been readying himself to accept God's presence in solitude and contemplation. Also, on the slope of Mount Horeb there was plenty of space for God's spirit to inhabit. Here at the inn, says Abarbanel,[17] Moses is confronted by the enormity of God's presence after he has been busily occupied with the most mundane and corporeal of human needs. Not only is Moses unprepared for God to "find" him here, but God's abundant presence nearly suffocates him. An unready Moses is greeted by a virtual tidal wave of divine spirit, and he is paralyzed with fear. Says the commentator, at that moment Moses perceived his own imminent death. The lesson that Moses must absorb, teaches Abarbanel, is that as God's chosen prophetic messenger Moses was expected to exist in a solitude of contemplation so as to be prepared to accept God's revelations at any time, day or night, even at the inn.

What manner of physical or mental paralysis overtook Moses at the moment that *God encountered him and sought to kill him*? The commentaries present a picture of a stunned and shocked Moses, surprised into muteness and rendered nonfunctional in the overwhelming presence of God in the room at the desert inn. The thoughtful Bible reader might counter with the query that Moses already has stood in the presence of the Lord and conversed with Him on Mount Horeb; how, then, can we accept his utter paralysis here? The reader only has to envision Moses, Zipporah and the isolated desert inn, and if possible, imagine the sudden, unexpected manifestation of God's glory appearing in their room in the gloom of the desert night. Abarbanel laconically states that Moses panicked and went into shock.[18] Bechor Schor[19] explains that the circumstances instantaneously plunged Moses into a state of existential angst, so that he was as immobile as a corpse. The Netziv embellishes upon this and explains that the enormity of the glory of God appearing to Moses in the desert inn rendered him immobile.[20] The commentator reminds us that Moses felt himself essentially unworthy of God's mantle, as was evidenced by his equivocation with God at the burning bush. God's sudden appearance to him at the inn was a burden he simply could not shoulder. It incited in Moses a radical alteration to his fundmental being, causing a paralysis born of terror, indecision and need. The Malbim summarizes Moses' physical and emotional state by saying that God's surprise presence to an unprepared and unholy Moses caused the man to shudder to his very foundations.[21] In that split second Moses was rendered utterly unable to think or act.

The issue for the reader is how did Moses survive this brush with death?

The next verse presents the biblical reader with the undisputed champion of this episode, Moses' wife, Zipporah. *And Zipporah took a flint and cut the foreskin of her [newborn] son. . . .* Moses is lying inert in their room at the inn, and Zipporah is in a turmoil of her own. She knows she must act to save her husband, but what should she do? The reader cannot but be struck by the contrast between Moses' disabled passivity born of his existential terror, and Zipporah's nearly instantaneous thought coupled with action. The Torah does not allow any hesitation between the words *He sought his death* at the end of verse 24, and the opening words of verse 25, *And Zipporah took a flint . . . .* According to Abarbanel,[22] in the instant between seeing her husband in the throes of a near-death experience and picking up the flint, Zipporah's ability to wisely, correctly and instantaneously infer both the causation and its antidote mark her as heroic.

What impelled Zipporah take the action she did (*and she cut the foreskin of her [newborn] son*)? It is undisputed that Zipporah was not privy to Moses' vision of God's exalted presence in their room at the inn. God revealed Himself only to Moses on that night. Bechor Schor[23] explains that Zipporah's keen insight took over, so that she immediately began scrutinizing her husband's actions, searching for any act of his that might have led to his present predicament.

Sh'mot Rabbah (5:8)[24] answers the question on every reader's lips: How did Zipporah know that Moses' life hung in the balance *because of a circumcision*? The *midrash* narrates the bizarre scenario. At that precise instant Zipporah watched in horror as God's messenger angel enveloped the supine Moses and swallowed him whole from the top of his head until his genitals. The Talmud[25] (Nedarim 32a) narrates this same incident, adding that it was *two* angels of the Lord who assaulted the inert Moses: The angels of divine Wrath and divine Anger swallowed Moses' entire body, from his head down, and from his feet upwards, stopping suggestively at his genitals. Because Moses' genital area was the only part of his body exposed to her view, the rabbis explain that Zipporah was able instantly to infer that therein lay the essence of the problem, as well as the solution.

According to Alschich,[26] Zipporah instantly deduced that Moses' dire predicament was due to one of two possibilities.

Perhaps God was angered that Moses had wed her—a Midianite—thereby desecrating himself after having spoken face-to-face with the Lord at the burning bush.   Alternatively, perhaps God's anger was incited by Moses' delay in conducting the ritual circumcision of their newborn son.   She reasoned immediately that her best course of action was to perform the circumcision herself, and she fervently hoped that her courageous act would solve both exigencies.   By performing the required *brit* she assumed that she would thereby nullify in God's eyes any unseemly aspect of her marriage to Moses; also, her consecration of their son via the *brit* would placate the Lord if the absence of the *brit* were the reason for Moses' punishment.   Either way, Zipporah took the flint in hand and, in the process of consecrating her son, released Moses from his crisis.

Chizkuni[27] adds that Moses' paralysis overtook him in front of Zipporah's eyes, and in a flash of prophecy it was revealed to her that *she* must be the one to act.   The Talmud[28] (Avodah Zara 27a) engages in a discussion about whether a *brit* performed by a woman is permissible.   Rabbi Adin Steinsaltz's discussion of the Talmud's passage on this issue cites the Rambam's comment that a woman is fit to perform the circumcision in a situation where no male is present and able to act.[29]   The Talmud suggests that Zipporah might only have begun the circumcision and that Moses completed it after he recovered from his crisis.   There are numerous opinions on the legal technicalities of such a circumcision.   But a plain reading of the Torah text points to the essence of verse 25: *And Zipporah took a flint and cut the foreskin of her [newborn] son*.   Moses' wife, Zipporah, daughter of the high priest of Midian, mother of Moses' two sons, performed the circumcision on their baby son while Moses lay incapacitated in the desert inn.   It is undisputed that her bold action saved Moses' life.

*And Zipporah took a flint and cut the foreskin of her [newborn] son, and she touched **his** legs . . . .*   The Torah text seems clear at first reading: After Zipporah circumcised their son, she took the excised foreskin in her hand and placed it *at Moses'* feet.   Says Rashi, Zipporah *threw* the skin at Moses' feet.[30]   We can appreciate that Zipporah, terrified that her action might not be in time to save her husband, threw down the foreskin almost like a gauntlet, implicitly saying, "It is done!   The boy is now consecrated unto the Hebrew God!   Now release Moses from your grip!"   Ibn

Ezra would agree, saying that Zipporah cast her baby's foreskin at Moses' feet so as to appease whatever evil spirit held him in thrall.[31] Chizkuni adds that she might have intended that the blood of circumcision would atone for and expunge Moses' paralysis.[32]

Because the Torah phrase is ambiguous—*whose* legs did Zipporah touch?—some commentaries suggest that the Bible's words might mean that Zipporah touched the legs *of her newborn son* during or after her act of circumcizing him. Chizkuni states that this interpretation naturally fills in the text's ambiguity, for of course she held the baby's legs while performing the *brit*.[33] But Perush Yonatan also presents a third possibility; that Zipporah threw the baby's foreskin at the feet *of God's messenger angel* who appeared in their room at the inn that night.[34] Zipporah's purpose was to present her baby's foreskin to the angel as an unambiguous offering: Her baby's covenantal foreskin in lieu of her husband's life. In a time-worn method of primitive exchange or appeasement of an angry deity, Zipporah boldly acted in the only way she knew.

These three interpretations are set out clearly in the Talmud (Yerushalmi, Nedarim chapter 3:9).[35] There the rabbis summarize the issue as follows: If the Torah text meant that Zipporah placed the foreskin at *Moses'* feet, she sought thereby to demonstrate to the angel of God that Moses' sin in failing to timely perform his son's *brit* in Midian has been expiated. If the Torah text meant that Zipporah tossed her baby's foreskin at the feet of *the angel,* her intention would have been clear to God's messenger: "Your mission is accomplished. Moses' son is now circumcized. You can leave Moses in peace and return to your Master!" And finally, if the meaning of the Torah text is that she touched the feet of *her baby son,* the crisis of ritual would have been averted by her bold act of performing the required circumcision itself, and her husband would have been released from his paralysis.

After Zipporah circumcised her son while Moses lay paralyzed, the Bible relates that she said, *"For you are like a bridegroom of blood to me."* This biblical phrase is strange and puzzling, and would seem to be nearly unintelligible. But we can appreciate the nuanced interpretations of the commentaries who assist the reader by parsing and examining this biblical phrase.

Of course, the first question on the reader's mind is *Who and what is the 'bridegroom of blood?'* Whom is Zipporah addressing? Rashi says that she is addressing her baby son Eliezer.[36]

Though this may seem strange at first, we can easily envision Zipporah comforting her baby son, cleaning up his blood after the circumcision, and saying, "My husband might have been killed tonight but for your blood that I have let!" In fact, Sh'mot Rabbah[37] presents an embellishment to the Torah's mysterious phrase. The *midrash* allows the reader to see and hear as Zipporah addresses her baby while she swaddles him after the circumcision. According to the *midrash*, Zipporah is musing aloud to her baby saying, "With your blood, the blood of the *brit*, my bridegroom has been spared!"

Ibn Ezra confirms that the "bridegroom of blood" in our biblical verse is the newborn baby.[38] The commentator, along with Sha'arei Aharon,[39] explains that according to the rabbis, a baby boy on the day of his *brit* is referred to by his mother and the other women present as a bridegroom, or *chatan*, in honor of the consecrated new life that is symbolically beginning with the ritual circumcision.

Chizkuni,[40] on the other hand, contends that it is Moses who is the "bridegroom of blood." When Zipporah says *"For you are like a bridegroom of blood to me,"* she is addressing her husband, and continuing in her heroic mode she takes the blame for this entire terrifying episode onto her own shoulders. Chizkuni places the emphasis on the Bible's phrase as follows: *For you are like a bridegroom of blood to me*. Zipporah is saying to her paralyzed husband that when he married her—a Midianite and not a Hebrew—he *became* her "bridegroom of blood." For by his continued act of having intimate physical relations with her, his Midianite bride, he has violated the code of the Hebrew God and may be is liable for death as a consequence. She is worried that the Hebrew God had placed a blood penalty upon Moses' head at the time he wed her, and that this near-death episode is therefore indirectly her fault.

Rashbam[41] and Alschich[†] summarize this episode and allow us to hear Zipporah's unrecorded thoughts and words: "This blood of our son's *brit* will serve to salvage my bridegroom from a death sentence. My husband kindled his God's wrath either because he delayed circumcising our son, or because he wed me. But whichever 'sin' brought him to this terrible state, this blood ceremony I have just performed will atone for it and return my husband's life to me."

[†]Please see our discussion beginning at the bottom of page 134.

The reader understands now that Zipporah's "bridegroom of blood" speech is her pronouncement that her bold act has caused God to spare Moses' life. The Torah's next verse—the third and final verse in this episode—confirms this understanding. The Bible tells us, *"Thence it instantly withdrew from him."* According to Abarbanel,[42] the angel of death receded from Moses following Zipporah's wielding of the flint. The Netziv[43] adds that Moses' awful encounter with God's angry and wrathful messenger angels is abruptly brought to a close after Zipporah's heroic act. Truly, then, Zipporah has saved the day. Sh'mot Rabbah[44] states unequivocally that but for Zipporah's decisive act of wielding the flint, Moses would have been lost. Her bold action vanquished the spirit of a vengeful death by circumcising her son and thereby rescuing her husband.

Zipporah is justifiably jubilant after the departure of the angel of death, and the closing phrase in this episode at the end of verse 26 is, fittingly, in her voice: *And she said, "A bridegroom of blood for circumcisions!"* The simple reading of the text might interpret this as Zipporah's reiteration of her "bridegroom of blood" comment in verse 25, except for the fact that here in verse 26 the word "circumcisions" appears in the plural. Sforno[45] and other commentaries interpret the phrase as referring simply to the two technical parts of the circumcision surgery itself.

Midrashically, we learn that an elated Zipporah first explains to her revived husband that she has performed the *brit* and chased away the angel of death. Thereafter, Zipporah marvels to her husband that the act of circumcision—a ceremony of blood—must have been the awaited antidote to his paralysis, because he returned to life immediately after she had performed it. According to Abarbanel[46] the word "circumcisions" appears here in the *plural* because there were *two* opportunities for Moses to perform the circumcision on his son, and he missed both of them. Moses could have performed the *brit* either before he left Midian, or when they arrived at the inn. So important was this blood ritual of circumcision to the Hebrew God that even Moses—God's chosen messenger—was on the brink of death because he failed to perform it. According to the Torah text, that he did not succumb to the death-like paralysis that overtook him was due to Zipporah's quick thinking and bold action. She unquestionably saved his life. The

Maharal[47] states that the immediate departure of the angel of death following the *brit* confirmed for Zipporah that it was the importance of the circumcision—or its fateful absence—that lay at the essence of the night's bizarre happenings.   And Zipporah, in her love for Moses, is relieved that it was the *brit*—and not his marriage to her—that was the cause of his crisis.[48]

Thence, it instantly withdrew from him; **thus she said**, *"A bridegroom of blood for circumcisions!"* Before this terrifying episode draws to a close, the Torah allows us to infer that the angel of death had withdrawn *because of her*. It does this by the use of an often-overlooked, two-letter Hebrew word. The pivotal Hebrew word is *aZ*, meaning **thus** or therefore.   The word connects in causality what comes before it in the text and what follows.   Here, we are meant to understand that the angel of death's withdrawal and Zipporah's second "bridegroom of blood" pronouncement are connected causally.   Torah Shlema[49] presents a beautiful *midrash* about Moses' recognition of this causality, and the fulcrum is the word *aZ*. According to the *midrash*, we must jump ahead in the story of the redemption of the Children of Israel to the miracle of the splitting of the Red Sea.   We see that the Hebrews are able to cross the sea on dry land while Egyptian soldiers are drowned in the flood of the returning waters.   Viewing the scene from the opposite shore, Moses and the Children of Israel break out in an exultant song of praise to God, affirming their spared lives and God's miracle of salvation.   This Song of the Sea, presented in the Bible at Exodus 15:1-19, is delineated in the Torah scrolls by poetic indentation and special formatting.   And the very first word of the Torah's narration of this song of exultation is the word *aZ*, the same word that the Bible uses here.

The *midrash* inquires, "Why did Moses begin the Song of the Sea with the word *aZ*?" The *midrash* responds that Moses is harkening back to his own salvation that night at the desert inn, when Zipporah saved his life by performing the *brit* on their son. "She gave me back my soul that night. For the Torah says, **Thus** *[aZ] she said, [you are] a bridegroom of blood for circumcisions!"* The careful Bible reader is led by the commentary to appreciate that in the near future Moses himself will acknowledge, via his echoing use of the word *aZ*, that Zipporah saved his life.

TWENTY-EIGHT

ଅଓଷଓଓଷ

Zipporah is Sent Away

EXODUS 4:27-29

And God said to Aaron, "Go forward into the desert and greet Moses." So he went and met him at God's Mountain, and he kissed him. And Moses told to Aaron all the words of God with which He had sent him; and all the signs with which He had commanded him. And Moses and Aaron went forth . . .[1]

It was after the incident at the inn that a revived Moses, once again leading the donkey that carries his wife and sons, continues his journey to Egypt. The Bible tells us that Moses' brother, Aaron, who had also been instructed by God—as was Moses—to venture into the desert in order to meet up with his brother, ultimately meets Moses in the vicinity of God's Mountain.

We can appreciate the poignant scene. Moses and Aaron see one another from afar, then approach each other under the blazing desert sun. Perhaps Moses is fearful of meeting up with the brother whom he has not seen or contacted for at least 40 years. After all, he has been charged with the awesome mission to redeem the Children of Israel, and Aaron has been designated his second-in-command, his sergeant-at-arms, his mouth-piece. Moses is the one who will speak with God, and Aaron will translate for the Pharaoh

140

and to the Hebrews. Will Aaron, the elder brother—and by rights the one to whom fealty is traditionally paid—accept this chain of command and yield to his younger and hitherto-absent brother? Moses, who has fought an Egyptian taskmaster, lived on his own in the desert for decades, vanquished all intruders, and matured into a man who speaks to God, is yet sufficiently human and humble that he is apprehensive about the unknown brother who is striding purposefully toward him through the baking sand dunes. For all these reasons the final spare words in verse 27 speak volumes: *and he kissed him.* Aaron, beholding his long-lost brother after half a lifetime, stretches out his arms and embraces and kisses him. The Torah does not need to embellish. The brothers greet one another with love and longing, and all their fears evaporate in the desert air.

That is no doubt the reason that the Bible narrates subtly, in verse 29, after Moses explains the mission and chain-of-command to Aaron in the intervening verse, that the two go forth *as one.* Curiously, the verb "to go" in verse 29 is in the *singular* form even though it refers to both Moses and Aaron. The inference is that though the brothers were two people, they were of one mind in fulfilling God's stated mission to redeem the Children of Israel.

No doubt there is a lingering question in the reader's mind: Where are Zipporah and their two sons? Why does the Bible state *And Moses and Aaron went forth,* with no mention of Zipporah? Yalkut Shimoni and Rashi respond to this query by elaborating on the *midrashic* conversation between Moses and Aaron. According to Yalkut Shimoni,[2] when Moses and Aaron greet one another Aaron grasps his brother, embraces him, clings to him with overwhelming affection, and kisses him. Aaron asks Moses, "My brother, where have you been hiding yourself all these years?" Moses answers, "I have been in Midian." Rashi[3] continues the *midrashic* conversation, telling us that Aaron looks up at Zipporah and the boys astride the donkey and says to Moses, "And who are these, pray tell me?" Moses responds, "This is my lawful wife whom I wed in Midian, and these are our two sons." To wit Aaron asks, "Where are you leading them?" And Moses answers, "To Egypt." Aaron is stunned, and chides Moses gently saying, "Here we are, agonizing over the families who have been born under the yoke of the Pharaoh, and you are preparing to add your young family to this suffering multitude!" Duly chastened, Moses turns to his wife who has witnessed this exchange, and gently tells her, "Return to your father's house in Midian." Zipporah then turns the donkey around and with their two sons she returns to Midian.

Siftei Chachamim[4] continues this compelling reasoning. The commentary explains that Moses was concerned lest the Egyptians enslave Zipporah the moment she sets foot in Egypt. Out of concern for her he sent her back to Midian. The Maharal[5] confirms this shift in dynamic from Moses-as-husband-and-father to Moses-the-redeemer, saying that when Moses turned away from the receding figure of his wife and sons and continued on foot to Egypt, only his brother Aaron was by his side. Moses was on an impossibly difficult mission, and he understood that having a wife and children by his side would make him vulnerable and would be an untoward distraction. The Bible bears this out when it tells us in verse 29 that only *Moses and Aaron went forth.*

PART IV

MOSES RETURNS
TO EGYPT

৪৩৪৩

TWENTY-NINE

๛๏ฆ๛๏ฆ

Moses in Egypt

EXODUS 4:29-6:15

Moses and Aaron travel on foot into Egypt. There is no mention in the Bible text about how Moses must have felt as he entered the portals of the kingdom that he fled half a lifetime ago. The text tells us only that once there, Moses and Aaron convened the elders of the Children of Israel, those members of the Hebrews with the age and spiritual maturity that would command the community's respect. We can imagine that they must have met in a deserted field after dark, when slave and taskmaster alike were asleep, or perhaps they crowded into a secure house with a sentry posted by the entrance. The excitement was palpable but subdued; what was being plotted that night was a rebellion against the mightiest kingdom in the world. Every man in the room faced certain death at the Pharaoh's whim if the meeting were known in the upper reaches of the king's court. That it was being done with the sanction of the Hebrew God would have made no difference at all to the king's executioner.

The Bible explains that Aaron spoke to the elders with Moses standing at his side, explaining about Moses' revelation at the burning bush, and about all that God had instructed him about the impending redemption of the Children of Israel from bondage. Anticipating their skepticism—they were understandably leery of

145

risking all on the promises of a putative redeemer—Moses uttered the secret code words: *PaKoD PaKaD'Ti, verily have I remembered*. This code had been jealously hoarded over the course of three generations, and once spoken by Moses it heralded for the gathered elders that their redemption had begun, and that Moses was their chosen liberator.[†] Moses also performed the signs that God had shown to him at the burning bush: He changed his staff into a serpent; he tucked his healthy hand beneath his cloak and when he removed it he held it out for all to see that it had become white with leprosy; he tucked it away again and upon removing it a second time it was healthy once more; and he demonstrated for them his ability to turn water from the Nile into blood. Moses performed these wonders before the eyes of the convened elders, and they acknowledged him as God's instrument. Believing that Moses was sent to redeem them from their misery, the elders prostrated themselves out of relief that redemption and retribution were nigh.

Thereafter Moses and Aaron sought an audience with the Pharaoh and they appeared before him saying, "Thus said God, the Lord of Israel: Let my people go, so that they might celebrate a feast to me in the wilderness." Pharaoh's response was, "Who is 'God' that I should hearken to his commands to release the Children of Israel? I do not know 'God,' and moreover I will not let Israel go." Moses and Aaron then presented the king with a compromise request for a three-day pilgrimage for the Children of Israel in order to sacrifice to the Hebrew God, telling the Pharaoh that such a sacrifice was needed "lest He smite us with a pestilence or by the sword." But the king of Egypt was not moved and haughtily said to Moses and Aaron, "Why do you come to interfere with these people and their work for me? Leave me and return, both of you, to your own vocations, and let my slaves be."

In a vicious act of spite to Moses, Aaron and the Hebrews, the Egyptian Pharaoh then issued a new edict, commanding that his own officers should henceforth no longer provide the Hebrew slaves with the straw necessary for them to make their quota of bricks. He commanded the slaves to gather their own straw, saying that their required daily quota was not to be dimished by even one brick per

------

[†]Please refer to chapter 25, where we discuss the issue of these secret code words.

slave. "For the slaves are lazy and slothful, and they seek a vacation to go and sacrifice to their God. Let them work even harder so that they will have no spare time in which to plot this foolishness!"

Even the Hebrew officers were beaten by the Pharaoh's soldiers, who taunted them saying that they were falling down on their task of ensuring that the slaves keep up with their quota of bricks. So the Hebrew officers cried out and inquired of the Pharaoh, "Why are you dealing with your slaves in this manner—not giving us straw with which to make our quota of bricks?" And the king responded in a maniacal tirade, "Lazy! You are all lazy! If you have the spare time within which to sacrifice to your God, then go, now, and use your spare time to work for me, the god of Egypt! Gather your straw in your own time, and you shall still deliver to me the undiminished tally of bricks!"

When the Hebrew officers left the presence of the Pharaoh downcast and exhausted, they met Moses and Aaron who were standing in the king's courtyard anxiously awaiting word of what the Pharaoh's anger had wrought. The officers rounded upon Moses and Aaron and cried out at them in anger and defeat, "Let God see you and judge you harshly. For you have caused us to be despised even more in the eyes of the Pharaoh and his officers! You have placed in their hands an additional sword with which they will slay us!"

The reader can appreciate Moses' present predicament: On the one hand, he has dutifully conveyed God's message to the Pharaoh, but on the other hand this message has caused his brethren greater suffering. Moses, recognizing the justice in their angry accusation and experiencing his own empathic misery at being the cause of his brethren's tribulation, turns to God for an explanation.

The man Moses who will question God in chapter 5 verse 22 asking, *My Lord, why have you increased the misfortune of your people?* is the apotheosis of his two signal and formative encounters with God. First, of course, Moses had spent much of his time in Midian as a lone shepherd, leading his flocks into the barren wilderness seeking grazing land. When God approached him on Mount Horeb Moses was taken by surprise, and over the course of an astounding and fateful face-to-face conversation with God Moses came to understand that he was God's chosen messenger. But at that time Moses did not yet understand that God expected him to be an *exclusive* "man of God." The incident at the desert inn, when Moses came face-to-face with God's angel of death, proved to Moses that he could not continue to straddle both the world of human passions and the realm of spiritual solitude.

Moses had sent Zipporah back to the safety of her father's house, and consequently he freed himself to do God's bidding at any time, day or night. It is this spiritually "ready" Moses who is confronted by the angry Hebrew officers in Egypt. They accuse him and Aaron of inciting the Pharaoh to increase their burdens. Moses has nursed an affinity for the suffering Hebrew slaves since his youth, and the reader recalls it was his defense of a Hebrew slave that led to Moses' exile half a century before. We will see that Moses' concern for the welfare of the Hebrew slaves henceforth becomes his chief *raison d'etre*.

The Torah text here (Exodus 5:22) states that Moses "returned to God" and asked him, "My Lord, why have you increased the misfortune of your people, and why have you sent me here if this is to be the result?" The careful reader will recognize that *this* Moses is a different man from the Moses in Horeb or the Moses at the inn; *this* Moses is ready and able to speak with God *at any time.* And he capitalizes on this privilege in his first self-initiated conversation with God. Moses confronts God on behalf of the suffering Hebrews, seeking God's reason for adding to his people's burdens. He tells God, "Since I came to Pharaoh and spoke to him in Your name he has added greatly to his evil burdens upon these Hebrews, and still You have not delivered Your people." God responds, "Presently you will see what I will yet do to the Pharaoh. With a strong hand will he send out the Hebrews, and with a strong hand will he chase them from his midst."

Moses' despair over the Hebrews' increased misery at his hands is assuaged by God's next revelatory pronouncement. God announces to Moses (Exodus 6:2) "I am the Lord." The implication is that God's might—while it has been inchoate since Creation and throughout the lives of the patriarchs and matriarchs—will henceforth be unleashed in all its terrible power upon the evil of the Egyptian king and his subjects. God reaffirms for Moses his covenant with his forefathers, which includes the promise of the gift of the land of Canaan, the land in which they had lived. God also reponds to Moses' most fervent expressed concern, saying "I have also heard the groans of the Children of Israel under the bondage of the Egyptians. I have remembered my covenant."

God gives Moses his next set of instructions, as follows: "Therefore, tell the Children of Israel 'I am God, and I will bring you out from under the yoke of the Egyptians. I will deliver you from enslavement to the Egyptians, and I will redeem you with an out-stretched arm and with great judgements. And I will take you to be My people, and I will be your God. I will then bring you to the land that I have designated to your forefathers, and I will give it to you for an inheritance. I am the Lord.'"

So Moses told the Children of Israel all that God had revealed to him, but they paid him no heed, so short were their tempers and so great were their burdens.

God's next instruction to Moses is to return to the Pharaoh, king of all Egypt, and to reiterate to him that he must send the Children of Israel out of his land. Moses, having suffered the humiliation of powerlessness and insufficiency as the aftereffect of the last time he spoke to the Pharaoh, confronts God as follows: "Understand that the Children of Israel have not heard my words that you instructed me to tell to them. How, then, will Pharaoh hear my words given that I lack the powerful gift of speech?" God's response is to address both Moses and Aaron concerning His plans for the Children of Israel and for the Pharaoh: That He will bring the Children of Israel out of bondage in Egypt.

THIRTY

๛౧ะ౧౩

Moses' Provenance

EXODUS 6:14-26

*These are the heads of their fathers' households; the
children of Reuven, the firstborn of Israel . . . and the
children of Shimon . . . . And these are the names of the
sons of Levi: Gershon and Kehat and Merari . . . . And the
sons of Kehat are Amram . . . . And Amram took his aunt,
Yocheved, as his wedded wife, and she bore him Aaron and
Moses . . . . This is Aaron and Moses whom God instructed,
'Take out the Children of Israel from the Land of Egypt in
their multitudes.'*[1]

The Torah takes a fascinating detour here, in the midst of the
drama of Moses' and Aaron's confrontation with Pharaoh and the
king's vicious redoubling of the Hebrew slaves' labors. Seemingly a
non sequitor, the text begins to chronicle the genealogy of Moses
and Aaron. The verses begin by naming the children of Jacob—
also known as Israel—the patriarch of the twelve sons who emigrated to Egypt during the course of a great famine, and who eventually grew over several generations to comprise the hundreds of
thousands of Hebrews subjugated and enslaved by Egypt's king.

The reader is treated to a summary of begats that is subtly
momentous. This interlude presents the reader with a number of

important "firsts." These verses are the first time that the Bible mentions the names of Yocheved and Amram, mother and father of Moses and Aaron; the first time that Moses' lineage is explicitly traced from the patriarch Jacob to Levi, his third son, through Levi's middle son, Kehat, Amram's own father, and inexorably to Aaron and Moses, Amram's sons. Although this book already has chronicled the story of Moses' birth and exile and told the story of the women who championed him, the reader should remember that nowhere in the first chapters of Exodus did the Bible ever mention Moses' parents by name. It was the commentaries—Rashi, Rashbam, Chizkuni, Kli Yakar—along with the Talmud, who had identified them.[†] The Torah text only told us cryptically, in Exodus 2:1, that *a man from the house of Levi went out and took [in marriage] the daughter of Levi.*

According to the Malbim,[2] the Bible's interruption of the story and interjection of this genealogy of Moses and Aaron is deliberate. It is designed to set the reader's mind at ease about the provenance of the man Moses to whom God has entrusted the awesome mission of forcing the Pharaoh's hand, liberating the Children of Israel from centuries of slavery, and leading them to the land that God promised them. The commentary says that the reader comes to appreciate through these verses that Moses and Aaron were truly selected from all of Israel and from the "first family" of the patriarch Jacob. Amram, Moses' father, is identified through his father's line as Jacob's great-grandson, and Yocheved, Moses' mother, is Jacob's granddaughter. Amram marries his Aunt Yocheved, and their children are Aaron, Miriam and Moses. Miriam's sibling relationship to Moses is not mentioned here in Exodus 6 because the text is immediately concerned with elucidating only the provenance of the two brothers who hold the Hebrews' lives in their hands each time they enter the Pharaoh's court. Miriam's genealogical tie to Moses and Aaron is discussed later on in Exodus, and is explicitly highlighted in the Book of Numbers, the fourth of the five books of the Bible.

In Numbers 26:59, Miriam's relationship to Moses and Aaron is spelled out clearly. There the text states, amidst the apportioning

---

[†]Please refer to chapter 10, where we elaborate upon the story of Moses' parentage.

of the land to the various named families and tribes: "And the name of the wife of Amram is Yocheved, the daughter of Levi, who was born to Levi in Egypt; and she bore for Amram Aaron and Moses, and Miriam, their sister."[3] There, in an unambiguous verse far removed from the intense drama of the Exodus, Yocheved is named as daughter of Levi, Jacob's third son; the wife of Amram; and the mother of the three heroes of the Exodus story, Moses, Aaron and Miriam.

Apart from the importance of setting out Moses' indisputable genealogy for purposes of assuring the reader of his Abrahamic bona fides,[†] the Ma'ayna Shel Torah[4] points to another reason for the interruption of the story in Exodus 6. The commentary explains that the Torah intends to explicitly remind the reader that Moses and Aaron, though they certainly loomed larger-than-life, were in fact born of a mother and father who were Hebrew slaves. More prosaic beginnings could hardly be imagined. Notwithstanding their humble origins and their documented frailties, this biblical saga demonstrates that these men rose to become prophets and leaders *par excellence*. Their enduring glory is due not to any high-born privileges they enjoyed as of right, but rather to their individual works and deeds, yielding destinies they forged for themselves. And the commentary ends with a simple but nonetheless enduring lesson: We can learn from the example set by Moses', Aaron's— and yes, Miriam's life, as well—that every person possesses an inherent ability to realize his or her full potential to lofty heights. It only remains for each person to apply himself with rigor. Nothing is impossible, teaches the commentary; each of us can strive to achieve the greatness of a Moses, Aaron, or Miriam!

[†]The text is explicit that Moses was the great-grandson—through his mother—of Jacob, the third of the Hebrew patriarchs. The reader will recall that the patriarchs are Abraham, Isaac and Jacob, and that God had long ago promised to Abraham that though his seed was destined to be enslaved in Egypt, they would be redeemed from that place and would inherit the land of Canaan. This divine promise—or covenant—of progeny, redemption and inheritance of a designated promised land is a banner to the Hebrews as they emerge from Egypt as an undisciplined multitude, on the verge of becoming a nation of laws.

THIRTY-ONE

໖ଉ໖ଉ

Moses Leads the Exodus

EXODUS 7:1-15:19

The Haggadic[†] centerpiece of the book of Exodus occurs in these chapters. We read of the sensational drama of Moses confronting the mightiest monarch in the known world with the words of the Hebrew God as his sole weapon and armor. This is followed by the Pharaoh's eventual capitulation after suffering plagues of ascending severity, brought upon Egypt at Moses' behest as a result of the king's refusal to let Moses' people go. And of course the jubilant release of the Children of Israel from centuries of unremitting bondage is also described in detail.

The climax of the Exodus story is the parting of the Red Sea and the annihilation of the charioted Egyptian army in the flood of the waters after the Israelites have passed through its walls of water unscathed. In a spontaneous expression of relief and ecstasy, Moses and the Children of Israel sing out a song of praise to God who has twice saved them: First from the whip of the Egyptian taskmasters, and now from the pursuing army.

[†]The *Haggadah* is the text that accompanies the Passover *seder* service held annually in the form of a Jewish dinner banquet. The *Haggadah* tells the story of the Exodus from Egypt, detailing the deliverance of the Children of Israel from slavery to freedom.

PART V

THE AFTERMATH
OF THE EXODUS

৪০৪৪৪

THIRTY-TWO

Miriam the Prophetess Leads the Women in Dance and Song

EXODUS 15:20-21

And Miriam the prophetess, sister of Aaron, took the timbrel in her hand; leading all the women with timbrels and dances. And Miriam answered them, 'Sing unto the Lord, for He has become exalted! Horse and his rider has He thrown into the sea!'[1]

The Bible turns next to Miriam, according her full play after it sets out in poetic verse Moses' song exulting in God's miraculous victory over the Egyptian army. For the first time in its reference to Miriam, the Bible here names her *Miriam the prophetess*. Torah Temima[2] goes so far as to quote this phrase of the Bible as the proof-text that Miriam was one of the seven named Biblical prophetesses.[†] This important title also raises some questions. The reader will certainly ask, Why is this glorious and rarified title followed by the qualifying phrase *sister of Aaron*? We know, of course, that she is also Moses' sister. Why does the Bible not append Moses' name as well? According to the Talmud (Sotah 12b)[3] and Rashi,[4]

[†]The seven biblical prophetesses are enumerated in the Talmud (Megilla 14a). They are Sarah, Miriam, Deborah, Chana, Avigayil, Chulda and Esther.

157

the answer is that Miriam first prophesied before Moses was born. The reader will recall[†] that while she was still a young girl and Aaron's baby sister, Miriam prophesied that her mother was destined to give birth to the great redeemer of Israel. Hence the Bible's phrase in this chapter, *Miriam the prophetess, sister of Aaron.*

Another reason Miriam is linked here with Aaron, according to the Kli Yakar,[5] is that she and Aaron possessed equal levels of prophesying ability. Moses' ability to speak with God face-to-face certainly exceeded his siblings'—as well as all other prophets'—powers of prophecy. As the Torah hints in the phrase, *sister of Aaron*, Miriam and Aaron are siblings in prophecy.

As we read that *Miriam the prophetess, sister of Aaron, took the timbrel in her hand; leading all the women with timbrels and dances*, an inquiring reader might wonder that they even possessed drums and timbrels with which to dance and sing on the shore of the Red Sea. At the unexpected midnight signal to leave Egypt did the Hebrew women actually pause to pack their tambourines along with the riches of Egypt (Exodus 3:22, 11:2 and 12:35) and their personal effects?[‡] Rashi responds that the righteous women of the Exodus did, indeed, consciously add their drums and tambourines to their bundles as they prepared to flee Egypt.[6] So certain were these women—who had kept faith with the Almighty throughout the terrors of the Egyptian genocide by continuing to have children—that they would be redeemed, that they kept their celebratory instruments handy always. The miraculous redemption would not pass unheralded! And their faith was rewarded when they walked with the rest of the Children of Israel to safety through the dry sea bed, and then witnessed the thundering return of the waters of the Red Sea to drown the Pharaoh's pursuing chariots. First Moses and then Miriam broke out in songs of thanksgiving and relief to the Almighty. When Miriam led the women of Israel in dance and song they were ready; with their timbrels held aloft and their jubilant voices raised in melodic praise to God.

[†]Please refer to chapter 7, where we discuss Miriam's first prophecy.
[‡]As we discussed in chapter 25, the Torah text enumerates the treasure that the Israelites took out of Egypt, and it consisted of *objects of silver and gold as well as raiment.*

In discoursing on this verse, some of the commentaries raise the issue of the medieval Hebrew custom of interdiction against hearing a woman's voice in song. Sha'arei Aharon notes that while Miriam the prophetess took the drums and timbrels in her hand during her song, the Bible states that the men sang to God *without* drums and timbrels.[7] He reasons that the women, aware that their sweet voices raised in song could be seductively enticing to the men, accompanied their song with loud percussion, thus avoiding the prohibition by drowning out the sound of their voices. Torat HaChidah disagrees, stating emphatically that there was no question here of violating the ancient prohibition.[8] The commentary explains that during such a moment of utter sanctity—such as the jubilation following the miracle of the parting of the Red Sea—the prohibition against hearing women's voice raised in song is overshadowed by the holiness of the experience, when the divine presence is so clearly felt.

In the same vein, the Talmud (Brachot 24a)[9] derives the prohibition from the ancient verse in Song of Songs (2:14), wherein the lover explains to his beloved that her voice is sweetly arousing, and her form beautiful. Thus, it is not that the woman's voice *per se* is prohibited, but that in an unholy context it could arouse the men to impure thoughts and deeds. Here, we learn that given the godliness of the post-Exodus redemption, the women's voices were not only acceptable, they were desired by God and welcomed as praise from the righteous is welcome in heaven. Likewise, Miriam's drums and timbrels were not deliberate buffers, but were enhancements of the righteous women's ecstatic song of thanksgiving.[†]

Verse 21 of chapter 15 of Exodus comprises the entire one-verse "song of Miriam." The most striking element of the verse is that it is virtually identical to Moses' song which appeared in verse 1 of this chapter: '*I will Sing unto the Lord, for He has become*

[†]Nowadays, many who adhere to this prohibition still welcome women's voices raised in song in praise to God, during synagogue services, at the Sabbath and festival table, and while chanting grace after meals, and the like. The rationale is that during moments of holiness the prohibition is outweighed by the sanctity of the moment and modern sensibilities. For a complete discussion of this issue see article by Rabbi Saul Berman entitled "Kol 'Isha" in the *Rabbi Joseph H. Lookstein Memorial Volume*, pp. 45 ff, New York City (Ktav, 1980).

exalted! Horse and his rider has He thrown into the sea!'
Miriam's verse, however, begins with the words *And Miriam answered them.* Also, her song begins with the poetic command, *Sing!* or *Sing out!,* while Moses' song begins with the same Hebrew root-word but in a different tense, meaning *I will sing.* The commentaries engage in a flurry of discussion about the nature of Miriam's song. Is Miriam's song in response to Moses'? Given the close wording of Moses' and Miriam's songs, is the single verse quoted here the women's refrain to Moses' song? And finally, could there be more to her song than appears in this verse?

The *p'shat* or simple reading of verse 21 is that it is, as the verse states, a response by Miriam to Moses' song. The precise wording of Miriam's and Moses' words supports this reading. The *p'shat* would indicate that verse 21, Miriam's song, is the oft-repeated refrain to Moses' lengthy song. Surprisingly, the commentaries seem bent on assigning a broader role to Miriam and the women than merely singing the choral refrain in response to Moses. Rashi explains that Moses' song is directed to the men of Israel, whereby Moses "sang" and they answered him in kind; and Miriam's song is directed to the women.[10] Rashi is vague, though, in that he does not specify whether the women answer Miriam in the same manner that the men answer Moses. It falls to the Mechilta to add that Miriam's song was the counterpoint to Moses', and that the women of Israel responded to her words just as the men responded to Moses'.[11] We are invited to envision the Children of Israel, some 600,000 strong, having just escaped through the dry sea bed and witnessed the mighty sea closing in upon their charioted enemy. Their recent salvation was more of a palpable miracle to them, perhaps, than even the plagues of Egypt. Ma'ayna Shel Torah[12] explains that Miriam the prophetess with her ability to inspire the multitude in jubilant dance and song aroused the populace to a fervor such that in their state of rapture and relief they answered Moses and Miriam in this spontaneous song of thanksgiving. Their voices raised in a unison of praise and gratitude to God must have sounded like powerful, inexorable waves of sound rolling heavenward.

Chizkuni says that the women were in fact chanting the entire song of Moses, but that the Torah had already reproduced the entire song in verses 1 through 19, so all that was needed was for the Torah to reproduce Miriam's first verse, which was identical to that of Moses.[13] The commentaries are lining up to afford the women of Israel equal status with the men in this chapter of song exulting and praising the Almighty. In an amazing commentary on this verse, the Netziv goes even further and suggests that the women did, indeed, sing a lengthy song all of their own on the shore of the Red Sea. According to the Netziv this song is unpublished in the Torah text and what remains is verse 21, which is the refrain that Miriam sang as she led the women in responsive song after every verse. The commentary even says that verse 21 is Miriam's own inspired response to Moses' prophetic and spontaneous paean to God.[14]

Sha'arei Aharon[15] engages in a bit of word play based on the Torah's statement in verse 21 that Miriam responded *to them*—written in the Hebrew *masculine* form. The *midrash* explains that the Bible text is hinting to the reader in this verse that we must appreciate the bravery of the women of Israel, who kept their faith in God's ultimate redemption even throughout the darkest days of Egyptian servitude. We understand from this verse that the women's bold behavior in Egypt—enticing their husbands so as to continue to give birth in the face of death and genocide, bringing new Hebrew life into the world in defiance of the Pharaoh—is compared to ideal assertive male behavior. It is actually a mark of praise, says the commentary, that the Torah hints via its usage of the male pronoun, that the Hebrew women's sustained courage in the face of pervasive danger while in Egypt is likened to the behavior of a male warrior.

The Malbim makes the extraordinary statement that the rabbis agree that "all this"—the redemption from Egypt, the splitting of the sea, and the drowning of Pharaoh's army—was done specifically on account of the merit of the righteous women of Israel.[16] And it is for this reason that the *midrash* tells us that the women sang in one exultant voice with Miriam. The commentary explains that they were raising their voices in appreciation of the miracles that God wrought and their pivotal role in bringing about the redemption.

Similarly, when the Talmud (Megilla 4a)[17] states that women are required to read *Megillat Esther*, the Scroll of Esther, because they, too, were redeemed by God's miracle, Rabbi Adin Steinsaltz' comments echo our verse.[18]   Rabbi Steinsaltz clarifies that the women *must* read the story of the salvation from Haman not because they, too, were saved in the end, but precisely because they were *essential* to the salvation itself! After all, the miracle of Purim was effected by Esther.   The Tosfot,[19] in their comments on this Talmudic verse, drive the point home emphatically. They state that women were at the essense of the miracles of the three holidays of Purim, Chanukah and Passover. Esther's heroism vanquished Haman and saved the Jews of Persia; Judith slayed Holofernes, contributing to the victory of the Jews over the Greeks; and the heroism of the righteous Hebrew women in Egypt actually brought about the redemption of the Children of Israel from bondage. For this reason, says the Chatam Sofer,[20] Jewish women are *required* to read the Purim Megilla, kindle the Chanukah lights, and drink the four cups of wine at the Passover *seder*. The women were included in the persecutions and the redemptions, and they were essential to the salvations. Thus they merit their share in the glory as well as the responsibility of sanctifying these events even in modern times.

THIRTY-THREE

ℰℭℨℰℭℨ

The Well of Miriam

The legend of the Well of Miriam has its origin in Exodus 4:21, which states, *And Miriam answered them, 'Sing unto the Lord, for He has become exalted! Horse and his rider has He thrown into the sea!'* Bamidbar Rabbah[1] states that the miraculous well of water that accompanied the Children of Israel throughout their forty years of desert wanderings is attributed to Miriam's merit. Her act of singing spontaneous praise and glorification of God on the shore of the Red Sea in the aftermath of the rout of the Egyptian army sealed her immortality in Jewish history, and her presence deeded a precious gift to the Israelites: "spontaneous water, gushing freely from the depths of the desert itself."[†] Miriam's Well is, in the words of Avivah Zornberg, "essential but almost totally effaced in the Torah text." The Well of Miriam is never explicitly mentioned in the Bible. It is a creation of Biblical lore and is discussed in the Talmud and described in detail in the *midrash*.

Miriam's nexus to Moses and to the Children of Israel is water-related. We recall that she watched over Moses from the river reeds as Yocheved cast him adrift in the Nile; she saw Princess Batya draw him from the river's waters and pronounce him her own; she walked on dry land through the walls of the split Red Sea and watched as her people's tormentors drowned when the sea waters

---

[†]Zornberg, A. G. (2001). *The Particulars of Rapture: Reflections on Exodus* (New York: Doubleday), p. 232.

163

engulfed them; and she pronounced the words of the Song of Miriam and led the women in dance and song in praise and gratitude to God. Even Miriam's very name incorporates the Hebrew word for sea: *YaM*.

The Torah here—at the Red Sea—explicitly recognizes Miriam as an equal partner with her brothers as a hero of the Exodus story. In Exodus 15:20, in the verse preceding the Song of Miriam, the Torah pronounces her a "prophetess,"[2] one of the few times in the Bible that an individual is termed a prophet in the text. We must assume that naming her a prophet and delineating her truncated song—all of which closely parallel Moses' action earlier in the chapter—are meant to raise Miriam onto the proscenium where Moses and Aaron act as leaders to the people. Miriam is their partner in the eyes of God.

Torah Shlema refers us to the writings of the prophet Micah[†] (6:4), where Micah accords equal mention to the three siblings. In pronouncing words of God to the Children of Israel, Micah states, "For I brought you up out of the land of Egypt, and I redeemed you from the house of bondage; **and I sent before you Moses, Aaron and Miriam.**"[3] The commentaries enlarge upon the triumverate's duties and mission. Each of the siblings was a herald, a leader and a prophet. Radak interprets[4] the prophet Micah's phrase *and I sent before you Moses, Aaron and Miriam* to mean that God appointed all three as harbingers of the promised future redemption while the Children of Israel were embroiled in their labors. Their presence was a source of hope to the people that their deliverance was imminent. According to Metzudat David,[5] the three are listed together as heroes of the Exodus not only because they heralded the redemption, but also because they were the most fit *leaders* for the task of guiding the erstwhile slaves out of bondage and into the wilderness on their way to the promised land. Targum Yonatan[6] synthesizes the *midrashim* and explains that Moses, Aaron and Miriam were indispensable and critical to God's plan. Each prophet, says the commentary, played a pivotal role in leading the Children of Israel in the period following the Exodus: Moses

---

[†]Micah is the sixth prophet in the book in the Hebrew Bible entitled *Tre-Asar*, or "The Book of the Twelve Prophets."

was the giver and teacher of the laws; Aaron atoned for the people's sins; and Miriam instructed the women.

Yalkut Shimoni[7] presents a *midrash* that illuminates the unique character of the leadership that Moses, Aaron and Miriam each provided to the fledgeling nation. The commentary dramatizes God extolling his choices of leaders for His people. "Come and witness the difference between me and a king of flesh and blood! A mortal king would send before him messengers of state, expecting that the people cease in their labors and occupations and cater to the king's messengers, feeding and providing for them. Not so with me! For I sent before you three redeemers who required neither food nor provisions from the people. On the contrary, my three messengers provided *the people* with food and sustenance! The mannah that appeared every day for 40 years fed the people on the merit of Moses; the clouds of glory that hovered over the camp protected the people on the merit of Aaron; and the well of water that sustained you in the wilderness was on the merit of Miriam."

So inextricably bound was the well of water to Miriam's presence as a leader of the people that, according to the *midrash*, upon her death the well disappeared completely. Immediately after the Torah records Miriam's death in Numbers 20:1 it records the *absence* of water and the people's bitter complaints to Moses of thirst in verses 2 and 3. . . . *And Miriam died there and was buried there. And there was no water for the people; so they gathered before Moses and before Aaron. And the nation complained to Moses . . . .*[8] The Talmud[9] (Taanit 9a) confirms that the well of water disappeared at Miriam's death, but adds that it returned sometime thereafter so as not to leave the people bereft of a source of fresh water. The well's eventual reappearance is expressly tied to the continued merit of Moses and Aaron. Yet Rabbi Adin Steinsaltz asks, *If the well was thus returned to the people some time after Miriam's death, why was it necessary for it to have disappeared at all?* He responds that some sages insist that the returning well never recaptured the full glory that it embodied when Miriam was alive. We can assume that after Miriam's death, instead of a freely gushing wellspring, perhaps the water emerged as a trickle; and that the people were forced to wait longer for their water buckets and skins to fill up, a state of events that never occurred when Miriam was alive. Perhaps that is a reason for their bitter complaint for water to Moses as recorded in the Bible. Steinsaltz concludes that all this underlines that we must appreciate that Miriam's presence was the important essence of the well's existence.[10] Without her, the well was just going through the motions, so-to-speak, but did not function with enthusiastic spirit. This was Miriam's signal characteristic and it died with her.

The Well of Miriam retains its mysterious and magical quality even while it is referenced lavishly in the *midrash.* Sh'mot Rabbah (1:2)[11] asks, *What did the Well look like?* and presents a fascinating description. We are told that it was a honeycomb-shaped boulder that rolled with the people from encampment to encampment as they traveled through the wilderness. When the nation was at rest and the penants were flying above each tribe's camp, this selfsame boulder rolled to a stop in the center of the yard of the Tent of Meeting. There, the princes of each tribe ranged around the boulder, chanting for the rock to release its wellspring of waters. And miraculously, it did so.

The reader must bear in mind that the Bible nowhere explicitly mentions this honeycomb-shaped rock that miraculously spouted water. While the Children of Israel's desert experience is, naturally, preoccupied with finding and dispensing water to nearly three-quarters-of-a-million people, the water-giving rock that is referenced in the Torah is textually associated only with Moses. In Exodus 17:6 we read that Moses is commanded by God at Horeb to strike a rock with his staff, and that sweet water miraculously spouts from the rock at Moses' touch. Ironically, in later years and in a moment of uncharacteristic anger at the complaining and recalcitrant people, Moses strikes the rock yet again, disregarding God's command to *speak* to it in order to draw forth water for the thirsty people (Numbers 20:8-11). Rashi unifies the water-giving rocks referenced in the Bible and points out that the rock which Moses struck in anger refused to yield up its waters. That is the reason, he says, that Moses struck it *twice* (Num. 20:11). According to Rashi, the rock was the selfsame Well of Miriam, which held back its life-giving waters after Miriam's death.[12] The Torah explains (Numbers 20:12)[13] that after the episode where Moses *struck* this desert rock rather than speaking to it, he was ultimately prevented by God from later leading the Children of Israel into the promised land. How tragic that Miriam's Well, *midrashically* credited with sustaining her people in her lifetime throughout their desert wanderings, after her death becomes a focus of bitter contention among Moses, the people, and God.

THIRTY-FOUR

৪০ত৪০ত

Batya, the Egyptian Princess,
is Also Saved

The reader might be wondering about the fate of Batya. Whatever became of this complex and essential character in the Exodus saga? Yalkut Shimoni tells us that Batya—daughter of the Pharaoh, princess of Egypt, Moses' adoptive mother, and believer in the Hebrew God—was also the Pharaoh's firstborn child.[1] As such, according to Torah Shlema,[2] Batya should have perished along with the other Egyptian firstborns on the night that Moses brought forth God's angel of death upon the nation of Egypt.[†] This tenth and ultimate plague—the most horrific of them all—was the catalyst that caused the evil and obstinate Pharaoh to let the

---

[†]Exodus 12:29 states: *And it came to pass at midnight that God smote* **all** *the firstborn in the land of Eqypt, from the firstborn of Pharaoh that sat on his throne unto the firstborn of the captive that was in the dungeon, and all the firstborn of the animals.* This verse is often understood to mean that only the firstborn Egyptian *males* were slain, because an ambiguity in the Hebrew grammar is commonly interpreted as referring only to *male* firstborns. But because the text does state *all* Egyptian firstborns, it is still unclear whether firstborn Egyptian *females* were *also* smitten by the hand of God on that night. Because of this uncertainty, Batya, the Pharaoh's firstborn daughter, was potentially at risk of death.

Children of Israel go. Was Batya, Pharaoh's firstborn, slain by the plague of the death-of-the-firstborn?

The commentaries are loath to relegate the heroic Batya to an ignominious end. The night of the miraculous plague that slayed the Egyptian firstborn is etched into the national consciousness of the Jewish people. "And it happened, in the middle of the night" are the words of the Passover Haggadah repeated annually at the Passover *seder*. The *midrashists* connect this night of death, retribution and redemption to Batya's salvation. Sh'mot Rabbah (18:3)[3] states unequivocally that while *all the female* Egyptian firstborn did, indeed, perish along with the firstborn males on that fateful night, Batya, the Pharaoh's daughter, was the only firstborn Egyptian woman who was spared. The commentary on Proverbs 31:15, as explained in Torah Shlema,[4] agrees that Batya did not die along with Egypt's firstborn on that fateful night of death. In fact, the commentaries go on to immortalize her. The phrase from Proverbs that is associated with Batya is the 15th verse in the paean to Jewish "women of valor." The words *And she arose when it was yet darkest night* . . . are the textual hint that Batya was saved while her countrymen perished.

The *midrash* recounts two reasons for Batya's redemption. The first, of course, is that her salvation redounds to her utter righteousness. She was, after all, the privileged daughter of despotic royalty who nevertheless put her own life in danger to save and raise as her own a Hebrew baby whom she rescued from the Nile.[†] Her greatness also includes her ability to have perceived and recognized the presence of a beneficent and omniscient deity, the God of the Hebrews. Batya was never presented in the Torah as a "true" Egyptian. Her signal qualities as outlined in chapter 2 of Exodus include her open heart, her merciful instincts, and her heroic desire to save a life at a real risk to her own well-being. She is presented as the antithesis of her Egyptian father. In fact, the sensitive reader will deduce that these identical qualities of Batya's character are reflected in Moses! All this comprises the foundation for an astounding statement by Torah Shlema. The commentary pronounces that there exist gentile women of such exceptional

---

[†]Please refer to chapter 14, where we discuss at length Batya's rescue of baby Moses.

righteousness and worth that they are marked by history and for all time. The commentary identifies five women of the Exodus era as among these women: Asnat (wife of Joseph and mother of Ephraim and Menashe), Zipporah (wife of Moses), Shifra and Puah (the midwives), and Batya (daughter of the Pharaoh).[5]

In addition to Batya's righteouness, Yalkut Shimoni[6] advances a second reason for her salvation. The commentary states that Moses himself prayed that Batya's life would be spared. The *midrash* is reminding the reader that Moses remembered and loved his adoptive mother. Even after the passage of nearly half a century during which Moses has evolved from a prince, to a shepherd, and now to a man of God, he has not forgotten Batya. He remembers that she saved him, she raised him as a prince, and she loved him as a mother. In this light, one can imagine the aged Batya's joy when she learned that her adopted son, Moses, had returned to Egypt. It is possible that after Moses killed the Egyptian taskmaster so many years ago and was forced to flee for his life, Batya had absented herself from the Pharaoh's palace and took up residence in Goshen with the Hebrews. Certainly she had an established relationship with Yocheved, Moses' birth mother. The women's mutual affinity and love for Moses would have made it a natural place of refuge for Batya to lodge with the Levites.

Because the Torah text does not mention Batya again after Yocheved brings the lad Moses to the palace to be raised as Batya's son, we must rely on the *midrash* to fill in the details about the end of her life. We have seen that the commentaries are in awe of her courage, and *midrashically*, at least, they accord her the ultimate reward: eternal life.   Torah Shlema[7] recounts that nine biblical figures were permitted to enter Paradise without first suffering a corporeal death; among them is Batya, the daughter of Pharaoh. And so we have closure on the life of this remarkable woman. We see that Batya did not perish at the plague of the killing of the Egyptian firstborn. Nor did she drown with the Egyptian army at the Red Sea. She lived to witness and experience the redemption of the Children of Israel and the triumph of Moses over the Pharaoh. Perhaps the aged Batya even joined with Miriam and the righteous women of Israel as they danced and sang in praise and exultation.

THIRTY-FIVE

৪০ড়৪০ড়

Hur, Miriam's Son

EXODUS 17:8-13

*And Amalek came and attacked the Children of Israel in
Refidim. And Moses said to Joshua, 'Select from among us
[strong] men, and go and do battle with Amalek. Tomorrow
I will stand upon the hill, with the staff of God in my hand.'
And Joshua obeyed . . . and Moses, Aaron and Hur climbed
to the hilltop. And it happened when Moses raised his arms
that Israel triumphed; and when he lowered his arms
Amalek triumphed. And the hands of Moses were heavy, so
they took a stone and placed it beneath him, and he sat
upon it; and Aaron and Hur supported his arms—one on
each side of him—and his arms instilled confidence until the
setting of the sun. And Joshua triumphed over Amalek and
his people at the point of a sword.*[1]

It is amazing that in a book like the Bible—preoccupied as it is with
fertility, genealogy and provenance—we are not told whom Miriam
married, or even if she married; nor do we learn if she bore any
children. It is the richness of the oral tradition, in the words of the
midrash and the Talmud, that generously supplies these details.
Rashi, Da'at Zekeinim[2] and the Talmud (Sotah 12a) set out the
various names by which the Bible identifies both Miriam and Caleb,
her husband. For instance, Miriam is referred to as Efrat and

171

Azuva, and Caleb is known alternately as son of Chetzron and also as son of Yephuneh (1 Chronicles 2:18). Regardless of the nomenclature, however, the sources agree that Miriam married Caleb and that they had a son named Hur.

At this present mention of Hur (Exodus 17:10), we read of a man who is chosen, alongside Aaron, Moses' brother and second-in-command, to support Moses' arms and assist in ensuring a victory over Amalek. This heroic opportunity to so assist Moses is a great honor and was likely dispensed to a proven man of courage from among the Children of Israel. But because this is the first-ever mention of Hur in the Torah text, we are led to ask, *Who is Hur?* Rashi supplies the answer,[3] stating definitively that Hur is the son of Miriam and her husband, Caleb.[†] Mizrachi elaborates,[4] explaining that the Torah text mentions Hur with the implicit familiarity of a person who has already proven his mettle in the Exodus story. Indeed, says the commentary, Hur has more than just his status as Miriam and Caleb's son, and thus Moses' nephew, to commend him. The commentator states that Hur was a renowned leader and hero in his own right, and his name was commonly recognized in his day.

The Maharal[5] sees a pattern in the Torah's mention of Moses, Aaron *and Hur* together in this verse. We have mentioned above several textual references to the triumverate of Moses, Aaron *and Miriam*. The commentary appreciates the nature of this prophetic and essential triad to the people of the exodus, and thus links Hur to Miriam. In this first post-Exodus pitched battle between the erstwhile slaves and an armed enemy, we might have expected the text to mention, totem-like, the names of Moses, Aaron and Miriam, the three trusted and beloved leaders who led the Children of Israel out of bondage. In the absence of Miriam's physical presence overlooking that battle-torn desert valley, the closest the text can come to crediting all three prophets with this important victory over Amalek is to introduce Miriam's son as one of Moses' men-at-arms. Having one of *Aaron's* sons support Moses' other arm in this episode—after all, they, too, are nephews to Moses—would have missed the message the Torah is imparting. The text is hinting to us

---

†See our dagger footnote at the end of Chapter 8 for our discussion of Caleb.

that Hur, son of Miriam, the third link in the dynastic chain that brought about the redemption, plays a seminal role alongside Moses and Aaron in this battle as a worthy bearer of Miriam's standard. The commentary on the Maharal confirms this,[6] stating that Miriam's part in the people's victory over Amalek—their first military victory as a free people—is not merely nominal. On the contrary, her presence, in the person of Hur, her son, is *necessary* to the people's ability to overcome Amalek. By reading of Hur's presence as Moses' aide (in Exodus 17:10) we are expected to appreciate that Miriam's actual and even mystical nexus to the army of Israel is critical—not simply incidental—in order for them to prevail.

Later on in the exodus story, after the people have been wandering in the desert but before they receive the law from God at Sinai, Moses disappears up the mountain to confer with God. Before he departs from the camp the Torah tells us (Exodus 24:14[7]) that he puts the elders in charge, expressly singling out Aaron and Hur, saying that the people can approach these men in the event that any problems arise. Moses is absent from the camp for forty days and nights, and the people, accustomed to his presence and to turning to him at every juncture, grow frightened. Pirkei d'Rabi Eliezer describes that black day in detail.[8] The commentary tells us simply that the people forgot God. They recalled aloud only that while they were in Egypt the gods were always present and visible, and that the Egyptians were able to see their gods as they worshipped and sang to them. The people vociferously demand of their leaders that they fashion for them such a visible and material god: a golden calf. One of the leaders they turn to in fear and anger is Hur. Rashi, careful to ascribe to Hur the heroic provenance that is his due, reiterates that he is the son of Miriam and Caleb.[9]

Pirkei d'Rabi Eliezer sets the scene: The people are encamped at the foot of a looming mountain which periodically spews fire and smoke from its midst. Their leader Moses has climbed that mountain forty days earlier, and has not returned to them. They have been whipped into a frenzy by the dregs of their society, who have fed them tales of being abandoned and leaderless in the wilderness. "Better to have died in Egypt with full bellies than to wander in this wilderness to die of hunger and thirst! And where is Moses' God now, when we need Him?! Can you see Him? Of course not!

Moses has gone and left us, and so has his God! Let us compel Aaron and Hur to make us a new one!"

The reader can readily imagine the terrible sound and sight of thousands of angry, frenzied people converging upon Hur. Perhaps he emerges from his tent that is pitched on the foothills slightly above the people, Aaron at his side, and he confronts the throng. "Fashion us a god!" they shout.   Several burly rabble-rousers surround him pushing Aaron out of the way, wrench Hur's arms behind his back, and march him toward the cliff's edge. Hur stands his ground, tall and stalwart, and speaks aloud to the horde, rebuking them. "Ingrates! You have witnessed the greatest spectacle of God's power, the parting of the Red Sea and the drowning of the mighty Pharaoh's army, and still you doubt Him? You stand at the foot of God's Mountain, where Moses has gone to receive the word of God for you to live by. Have you forgotten God so quickly? The God who brought the plagues upon the Egyptians, the God who redeemed you from slavery? Faithless ones! Moses *will* return, and you will see that God has not forgotten you. Unhand me and return to your tents! Ready yourselves to receive the word of God!" In the silence following Hur's reprimand the instigators holding him captive shout to the mob: "What shall we do with him? He will not make us a god!" The mob responds in one roaring voice, "Kill him, kill him!" The lynchers wrestle with Hur and stab him to death, then throw his body from the cliff. The people, who had heard the truth from Hur's lips but rejected it, murdered him in cold blood. Aaron, restrained by the lynchers but witness to the tragic and gory scene, is held menacingly close to the cliff's edge. "Build us an altar, old man!"

The Chatam Sofer[10] picks us the story at this point, and underlines Miriam's seminal importance to the people of the exodus, while eloquently describing Hur's heroism and ultimate martyrdom. The Chatam Sofer tells us that at the Song of the Sea the Torah text inserts the phrase that the men *believed in God and in Moses, His servant.* In contrast, when it describes the women's reaction to the miracle at the Red Sea, the Torah has no concomitant phrase, stating simply that *Miriam the prophetess, sister of Aaron, took the drum in her hand, and all the women followed after her.* The commentary points out that for the newly-liberated men of Israel their belief in God was tied to the physical presence of Moses, their deliverer. This simplistic vision of their true savior led inevitably to their future construction of the golden calf when Moses was physically absent from the camp for forty days and nights and they feared him dead. The women of Israel, on the other hand, took no part in the death of Hur, and the subsequent construction and worshipping of the golden calf. Says the commentator, the women possessed a deeper understanding of their salvation, and reasoned that God had provided them with Moses, but had also provided them with other prophets, namely Miriam and Aaron. They did not despair at Moses' protracted absence. The men, believing Moses dead, attempted to compel Hur, Miriam's son, to build them a graven image of a new god. They reasoned that by this strategic move they would enlist the women, who placed great store in the leadership of Miriam and her son. The *midrash* goes on to reiterate that Hur resisted the frenzied mob of fearful and zealous men, and he denounced their behavior as cowardly idol-worship. Because Hur upheld the honor of the one God and resisted the mob's insistence that he construct a surrogate, they murdered him at the foot of God's Mountain.

To Hur's everlasting credit, his grandson, Bezalel,[11]—great-grandson to Miriam the prophet—was charged by God and Moses with the awesome labor of fashioning the vessels and stucture of the holy tabernacle. The Torah states in Exodus 31:2 and 3 that in naming Bezalel to this momentous task, God spoke to Moses saying, *Behold! I am calling the name of Bezalel, son of Uri,* **son of Hur** *from the tribe of Judah. And I will fill him with divine inspiration, insight and wisdom* in all his creative endeavors. Hur's memory was destined to live on in God's tabernacle.

THIRTY-SIX

ᏧᎦᏋᎦᏋᎦ

Zipporah Returns to Moses with Their Two Sons

EXODUS 18:1-27

Now Yitro, the Priest of Midian, Moses' father-in-law, heard about all that the Lord did for Moses and Israel, his nation; that God brought Israel out of Egypt. And Yitro, Moses' father-in-law, took Zipporah, Moses' wife, after he had sent her away. And also her two sons, the one named Gershom, because he said 'I was a stranger in a foreign land.' And the name of the one was Eliezer, 'For the God of my father has aided me, and saved me from the Pharaoh's sword.' And Yitro, father-in-law to Moses, and his sons and his wife, traveled to Moses in the desert where he was encamped, there at God's mountain. And he said to Moses, 'I am your father-in-law, Yitro, come to you; and your wife and her two sons along with her.' And Moses went out to greet his father-in-law, and he bowed low, and he kissed him, and they inquired of one another's welfare; and they came into the tent. And Moses told his father-in-law of all that God did to Pharaoh and to Egypt on Israel's behalf; of all the travails that beset them on the way and how God saved them.[1]

The reader last encountered Zipporah in Exodus 4:20 after the incident at the inn, in the wilderness between Midian and Egypt.

176

We watched as she bid farewell to her husband, Moses, and, at Moses' behest, returned with her two sons to her father's house in Midian. Moses then accompanied his brother Aaron back into the dangerous maelstrom of Egypt. Now, fourteen chapters later, after the momentous miracles of the plagues, the exodus from Egypt, the parting of the Red Sea and the victories over Egypt and Amalek, the Torah brings Zipporah and her father Yitro back onto the biblical proscenium.

Rashi asks why the Torah text specifically reminds us, in Yitro's words, that Zipporah is *Moses' wife, after he had sent her away?*[2] The commentary wants the reader to understand that Zipporah did not leave Moses of her own accord; that according to the *midrash* she returned to Midian with her newborn infant and young son to the safety of her father's house at Aaron's instigation and at her husband's suggestion. Chizkuni even reminds us that back in chapter 4 the Torah text nowhere said that Moses sent Zipporah away![3] Harking back to the text, it only states that *Moses placed them on the donkey.* Did this act by Moses' signify a formal "sending away," to use Yitro's words?

According to chapter 4 of Exodus, Zipporah very nearly accompanied Moses back to Egypt. It is the *midrash's* extensive description of Moses' desert encounter with his long-lost brother and Aaron's incredulous statement to Moses that Egypt was no proper place for his wife and children that placed Zipporah on the return road to Midian. The commentary states that it is only here, at chapter 18, that we learn the origin of this story. In bold Torah text we read for the first time that on the morning after the incident at the inn Moses had indeed "sent Zipporah away."

The Netziv explores Zipporah's mind-set after having been dispatched by her husband. The commentary teaches us that notwithstanding having been sent back to her father's house, Zipporah remained at all times "Moses' wife."[4] In fact, says the commentary, Zipporah pined for her husband, and her every thought was of him. Perhaps she thought, Was he safe? Did the Pharaoh's soldiers cast him into prison? Would she never see him again? The Malbim, on the other hand, examines Moses' reasoning[5] and tells us that while he did in fact send Zipporah away before returning to Egypt with Aaron, he had no dark motive for doing so; on no account did Zipporah displease him, nor did he grow tired of her. On the contrary, this phrase in the Torah text confirms that Zipporah remained "Moses' wife" *in his mind* even after he was constrained to send her back to Midian. He departed from her only until such time in the future as God would remember His people and redeem them from bondage, freeing Moses so that he could resume his life as her husband.

While some commentaries agree that Moses sent Zipporah back to her father's house as a matter of temporary practicality and safety, others hold to the opinion that Moses in effect divorced her when they parted ways on the desert path after the incident at the inn. According to the Mechilta, Rabbi Eliezer espoused the former opinion, and Rabbi Yehoshua presented the latter.[6] The reason the issue of divorce even arises in this context is that here, in Exodus 18:2, the Torah uses the Hebrew word *SHiLuCHeHa*, meaning *he sent her away*, referring back to Moses and Zipporah's last encounter in chapter 4. The term of art that is used in the Bible when referring to a divorce between a man and wife—see Deuteronomy 24:2[7]—is from the same root-word, *SHaLaCH*. The Torah's wording is careful and precise, and it is certainly possible that the Bible's use of the word *SHiLuCHeHa* here is meant to hint to the reader that Moses parted with Zipporah with some degree of finality. According to the Mechilta, Moses hastily wrote a bill of divorcement, rolled it up and thrust it into Zipporah's hand. We can readily envision Moses closing Zipporah's fingers around the scroll, the two of them staring into one another's eyes appreciating the serious necessity of the event. After all, Moses had reason to believe that he would be killed on sight when he set foot in Egypt. So by handing Zipporah the *get*, or divorce decree, he was setting her free to continue her life unencumbered by a husband who was still a wanted man. Also, Moses had already turned his mind and body toward Egypt and fulfilling God's awesome mission of changing the Pharaoh's mind and releasing the Children of Israel from centuries of bondage. Ohr HaChayim[8] agrees, stating that Moses thought that even assuming he would not perish on his mission, he sought to set Zipporah free of the certitude of a long wait for his return. There also was no question of his taking his sons from their mother. The newborn was a suckling infant, and Gershom was a young boy just past the toddler years, still needing his mother's arms. In "sending her away" Moses was closing the door on this bucolic interlude in his life and executing a *volte-face*, returning to the dreaded land of Egypt from which he had fled a lifetime ago.

The incident at the inn must have reinforced for him that his days as an ordinary shepherd, husband and father were ended, and that his focus needed to be directed solely upon God and his mission. Understanding all this, the rabbinic notion took hold that Moses parted from Zipporah via a *get,* the legal use of the term *SHiLuCHeHa.* And here, in Exodus 18, his (perhaps) former father-in-law repeatedly reminds Moses no fewer than six times of their former close relationship, hoping to soften the surprise that he has turned up on Moses' proverbial doorstep unbidden, on the eve of the giving of God's Law, with Zipporah and her two sons in tow.

Torat HaChidah explores the reunion in chapter 18 from Yitro's point of view.[9] The commentator explains that once Yitro heard the news from the passing caravans that Moses, as God's servant, had successfully led the Children of Israel out of bondage in Egypt, he gathered up his daughter, Zipporah, and his grandsons, and brought her to her "husband" at the foot of God's Mountain, in the wilderness beyond Midian. He brought her to Moses notwithstanding the *get*—or bill of divorce—that Moses had written for her. Says the commentary, the divorce decree that Moses hastily wrote for Zipporah was a divorce *on a condition*; a document that by its terms would only take effect in the event that a set of conditions would occur.[†] In Moses' and Zipporah's case, the document would have come into full force and effect *only if* Moses were *un*successful in his mission, or perished in Egypt, or if the Children of Israel never made it out of Egypt. Once Yitro learned that his beloved son-in-law had achieved his goal, he perceived his role as the one to re-unite the couple as husband and wife, because the conditional divorce decree never came into play.

Torat HaChidah[10] relies on the *conditional* nature of any divorce between Moses and Zipporah for the reason that as a

———————

[†]The commentary HaMa'or Shebatorah points out that in biblical times it was not unusual for a soldier on the eve of battle to grant his wife a conditional divorce. The theory was that by so doing he was performing a necessary kindness; for if he should be lost in battle, imprisoned and fails to return to her, she would be free to remarry. And if by the grace of God he returned home to her, the divorce would never have taken effect.

member of the first-family of the priestly class Moses would have been forbidden to marry a divorced woman, even if she had been his wife previously. And according to HaMa'or Shebatorah,[11] the reason the Torah even refers to Zipporah as *Moses' wife* in Exodus 18:2 is that whether or not Moses handed her a *get* before he parted from her; and regardless of whether that *get* was conditional, the Torah is stating clearly that all the time that Moses was in Egypt and Zipporah was on her own in Midian, she conducted herself as befitting Moses' wife. Says the commentator, Zipporah held herself aloof from all others, never so much as glancing at another man. In her mind *and in the eyes of all others*, Zipporah remained "the wife of Moses." It is for this reason that Torah Shlema states unequivocally that Zipporah was a worthy wife for the leader of Israel.[12] Her behavior was in keeping with that of the righteous women of the generation of Hebrew women who helped bring about the exodus. Thus, even the Torah here refers to her as *Zipporah, the wife of Moses.*

This interpretation allows the Torah text in chapter 18 to be read more easily, as there are numerous references in verses 1 through 8 to *Moses' father-in-law* and *Moses' wife*, without the qualifying word "former." Clearly the Torah text accepts that by the time of the reunion in chapter 18, Moses and Zipporah are once again—or still—married.

The commentator Akeidat Yitzchak is troubled by this reunion at the foot of God's Mountain.[13] He opines that the scene depicts a disruption of the natural familial order. It is the way of society, he says, for the husband to support his wife and children, providing for all their needs. In a situation such as the one that engulfed Zipporah and her two young sons, in the words of the commentary, she had been abandoned by her husband, notwithstanding his essential reason for forsaking them. In Zipporah's case she was fortunate enough to return to her father's house, which—because of Yitro's elevated station as Priest of Midian—was able comfortably to accomodate her and her young sons. Still, says the commentator, analyzed objectively, Moses the husband failed in his duties to Zipporah: First of all, he sent her back to her father's house after the incident at the inn where she saved his life. Second, he failed to support his wife and sons. And third, the *coup de grace* and the essence of these verses in Exodus chapter 18, Moses failed to send for Zipporah and his sons after he had effected the exodus from Egypt and the splitting of the Red Sea. According to the commentator, it was Moses' duty to send for Zipporah, not hers to seek him out.

Abarbanel concurs,[14] explicitly stating that when the rumors reached Yitro's tents that the exodus from Egypt had been effected and that Moses had survived and triumphed, the old man decamped and packed Zipporah and his two grandsons into a small caravan and journeyed to meet the Israelites at the foot of God's mountain. The commentator explains that the Israelite camp was not far from Yitro's Midianite home. In fact, Moses had led the people unerringly and camped with them in the same wilderness where he had grazed Yitro's flocks. The sere landscape strewn with rocks and desert plantings was Moses' home turf. We recall that Moses had led Yitro's flocks "into the wilderness beyond Midian," and spent years tending them there. It was a terrain he knew and understood, and, according to Abarbanel, it was where he connected mentally and spiritually to his God. For all these reasons, Abarbanel is incredulous and somewhat censorious that Moses failed to send for his wife and sons. He was out of immediate danger, his leadership was solidified, and he was camped and readying his people to receive God's law. How could he *not* send for Zipporah and his sons? Says the commentary, it behooved Moses—when at a resting point in God's mission—to honor his father-in-law, mollify his wife, and acknowledge his sons. When he failed to send for them, the aged Yitro breached accepted protocol and traveled to Moses.

In fact, Alschich adds[15] that Yitro's escorting of Zipporah to Moses is the older man's clever method of modeling the proper behavior for his son-in-law, avoiding an outright chastisement of him. The commentator is emphatic that Moses should not have abandoned Zipporah in the wilderness after the incident at the inn. At the very least he should have sent her back to her father's house under escort. Her escorted appearance in these verses at Moses' tent door is Yitro's intervention in the lonely stalemate suffered by his daughter.

Akeidat Yitzchak's core point is that by his negligent behavior in failing to send for Zipporah after the most dangerous part of his mission was completed, Moses allowed and passively encouraged his father-in-law, Yitro, and his wife, Zipporah, to demean themselves by traveling to the Israelite camp and presenting themselves at his tent door unbidden. This was a debasement, according to the Akeidat Yitzchak. Furthermore, according to the Torah text Moses failed to pay the newly-arrived Zipporah any attention whatsoever.

Hegyona Shel Torah[16] is exquisitely mindful of the scene, noting that this surprise family reunion takes place in the center of the Israelite camp, on the public stage. How awful for Zipporah to journey to her husband fearing that he might possibly spurn her before hundreds of curious eyes! Says the commentator, even appreciating that Zipporah's great love for Moses might have propelled her to journey to him without his having initiated the meeting, this does not release Moses from the culpability of publicly disregarding her honor by breaching spousal etiquette. The commentator is aghast that Moses failed to summon his wife and sons to witness the revelation at Sinai!

In this vein, Akeidat Yitzchak suggests that perhaps it was God who instilled in Yitro and Zipporah the desire to join up with Moses at that precise time, at the foot of God's Mountain. This divine impetus would have allowed them to override their scruple of pride and fear of humiliation, and to arrive in the camp in time for the giving and receiving of God's laws.

Kli Yakar expresses an acute appreciation for Zipporah's tenuous position.[17] He is picking up on the Hebrew meaning of her name—a female bird—and reminds us that Zipporah returned alone after sharing Moses' bed at the desert inn, remained for months in her father's household with her two "chicks," and now leads them across an expanse of desert to attempt a *rapprochement* with her husband. Her recent life resembles the flight of a lost bird, ever wandering in search of her nest. Kli Yakar empathically explains that the grief and uncertainty that Zipporah suffered during her wanderings back to Moses and God's mountain is sufficient reason for us to accord her great honor.

The commentators cover Zipporah with glory. After all, she saved Moses' life at the inn; bore him two sons; and returned, uncomplaining, to Midian while her husband embarked on his imperative and life-threatening journey into Egypt. Hegyona Shel Torah adds a layer of spiritual devotion to Zipporah's character.[18] The commentator says that Zipporah was the impetus behind Yitro's and her arrival at the Israelite camp. He suggests that

Moses' reason for not sending for her was to allow her just this opportunity to seek him out at the foot of God's Mountain, thus demonstrating for the world her commitment to his God. Whether Zipporah converted to Judaism right then, upon her reunion with Moses in chapter 18; or whether her earlier conversion in chapter 2 is simply stengthened by her arrival at Moses' camp, the commentary states unequivocally that it is to her credit that she returned to him of her own volition and did not wait until Moses sent for her. The reader is not surprised by the commentary's reading of these verses. After all, this is the Zipporah we have grown to know through the Torah text and the *midrash*: a woman of bravery, determination, perspicacity and decisive action. This is the Midianite woman, eldest daughter to a high priest, whom Moses married and who bore his sons; she is the woman he left, and the wife who is returning to his side in time to be converted to the laws of Moses and his God in full view of the congregation. Says the commentator, her return at this moment demonstrates that she is a true daughter of Israel.

And, according to Hegyona Shel Torah, because Zipporah was a true convert, her sons were considered converted as well.[19]

It is fitting that here, in Exodus 18:3, during this reunion of Moses and his family, the Torah text mentions Zipporah and Moses' two sons by name. The reader had been introduced to Gershom in Exodus 2:22, but this is the first textual mention of their second son, Eliezer, by name. The commentaries take this opportunity to explore the boys' identities.

The text reads, *And also **her two sons**, the one named Gershom, because he said 'I was a stranger in a foreign land.' And the name of the [other] one was Eliezer, 'For the God of my father has aided me, and saved me from the Pharaoh's sword.'*

The Netziv asks why the Torah identifies the boys, at Exodus 18:3, as **her** *two sons?*[20] It would have better fit into the style and cadence of the prior two verses if the boys had been identified as **Moses'** *two sons*, since Yitro had been identified as Moses' father-in-law, and Zipporah as Moses' wife. The commentator explains with exquisite sensitivity to the real drama being played out in front of Moses' tent that while of course Moses sired the boys, for all intents and purposes it was Zipporah who nursed them, mothered them, raised them and loved them, even after Moses sent her—and them—away, back to Midian, after she saved his life at the desert inn. The boys embodied Zipporah's nexus to Moses, and as we will see, the Torah text reminds the reader that their names, too, are a memory jog to Moses, as he bestowed names upon each of the boys according to milestones in his life.

Kli Yakar analyzes in depth the Torah's reasons for enumerating the boys' names at this precise point in the text.[21] The commentary imagines the conversation between Yitro and Moses as Moses ushers his beloved father-in-law into his tent. Perhaps Yitro—anticipating Moses' implicit query about Yitro's surprise appearance with Zipporah and the boys—seeks to preempt Moses objections. "My dear Moses, please accept our presence in your midst for the sake of my daughter, your wife, Zipporah. For she has been forced to live like a wandering bird, forever seeking her own nest, while in truth her place is at your side. And if that is insufficient to convince you—for perhaps it is not in a man's nature to feel his wife's pain—then accept our presence in your tent on behalf of your son Gershom. For you named him, precisely to remind you that you were a stranger in a foreign land. So surely you can have compassion upon your sons, who are strangers such as you, and who have never yet eaten at their father's table. And I know that you empathize with the soul of the stranger, as you have been a stranger in every land in which you rested your head. And finally, Moses, if you cannot greet your wife and sons for these compelling reasons, surely you can accept them into your tent on the strength of your baby son, Eliezer. For you, yourself, named him as a tribute to your God, the God of your father, who aided you and strengthened you in your plight. If you welcome young Eliezer into your tent, surely it is akin to welcoming the presence of your God into your midst, from which you cannot turn away."

Ohel Yaakov confirms that Yitro's move in bringing Zipporah to Moses along with the two boys was calculated to rekindle in him his dormant love for his wife.[22] Yitro was relying on the character of the Moses he had come to know and love, who—once confronted with his young family, especially with the wife of his dear sons whom he had named with care—would embrace them all figuratively as well as literally, and take Zipporah into his tent once more.

The Torah chooses this moment to explicate the names of Moses' and Zipporah's sons, and to reiterate the meanings of their respective names. *The one named Gershom, because he said 'I was a stranger in a foreign land.' And the name of the one was Eliezer, 'For the God of my father has aided me, and saved me from the Pharaoh's sword.'* The commentaries (Ibn Ezra, Sforno, Chizkuni, Ohr HaChayim) accept that it is appropriate to reacquaint the reader as well as Moses with the two boys, but they are also curious why Moses named the first son Gershom ("I was a stranger") and the second son Eliezer ("God was my help and savior"). Given that Moses was *first* saved by God from Pharaoh's sword and only *thereafter* was a stranger in the land of Midian, should he not have reversed the order and named his *first* son Eliezer and his *second* son Gershom? The reason for the order of the boys' names, says Ibn Ezra,[23] is that Moses fled the sword of Pharaoh and settled in Midian, where he was "a stranger in a strange land." His first son was named after that pervading sense of "otherness." Furthermore, Moses never felt secure from the reach of Pharaoh's spies and avenging soldiers throughout his sojourn in Midian, as he expected that the king's tentacles could snake out and grip him at any time, even in the desert beyond Midian. As long as the Pharaoh and his henchmen remained alive, Moses did not feel "saved." Sforno continues[24] that by the time his second son was born, he had already heard that the old King of Egypt had died and was replaced (Ex. 2:23), and that all who had sought to kill him had themselves died off (Ex. 4:19). *Now* Moses was able to name his infant son "God saved me," feeling for the first time that he was no longer a hunted man.

The Malbim delves into the wealth of emotion inherent in the boys' names, and states that the names offer a window into Moses' love for them.[25] We can appreciate that Moses quite possibly never thought he would live out his lifetime; after all, he was the subject of a fevered manhunt mounted by the greatest king of that era. So for him to have found a measure of peace in the tent of a stranger, and to have been granted solace in the arms of his wife—his host's worthy daughter—would perhaps have been sufficient unto themselves to cause Moses to be thankful. But he was blessed additionally, first with one son and then with another. Says the Malbim, Moses named his sons for the two formative events in his adult life.   First and formost, he named Gershom after his most seminal experience: "I was a stranger in a strange land."   Moses had been a stranger even in Egypt, the land of his birth, because his birth mother was a stranger, a slave and a Hebrew.   Also, his adoptive mother raised him in the palace, where his lowly birth kept him a stranger and apart from the Egyptian royalty.   After fleeing Egypt Moses was an outsider in the land of Midian, and remained, for all the days of his life, a stranger even among his chosen people. He lived among them and led them, but he was at all times God's servant.   "I was a stranger" was Moses' signal, formative characteristic, and his first-born son bore this name as his mantle.   Ohr HaChayim[26] states that these life experiences defined Moses, so that his existential nature was always to be "other."

And regarding the naming of his second son, Moses called him Eliezer because "God is my helper and savior." This second, but all-important theme also marked Moses. He was saved as an infant from Pharaoh's murdering soldiers by Yocheved and then by Batya. He escaped Egypt after having killed an Egyptian slave master, and found succor in another land. Moses truly appreciated that his very life was owed to the God who spared him, and so his second-born son bore *this* as his mantle.

And also her two sons, **the one named Gershom***, because he said 'I was a stranger in a foreign land.'* **And the name of the one was Eliezer***, 'For the God of my father has aided me, and saved me from the Pharaoh's sword.'* The Netziv notes the awkward phrasing of the Torah text when it mentions Eliezer in Exodus 18:4.[27] Usually, when itemizing a series of two, we would expect the text to state, "the name of the one is Gershom, and the name of **the second** is Eliezer." Here, however, the Torah takes pains to mention Moses' second-born son with the same verbal panoply as the first-born, calling him "the one" as well. The commentary, mindful that such verbal aberration in the Torah is always significant, states that this awkward phrasing is an indication that Eliezer, Moses' second-born son is, in fact, considered the chosen or special one; that from *him* will emerge Moses' lineage.

The reader should not be surprised to learn that Moses' first-born son will be skipped over and that his second-born son will merit God's covenant. For in the book of Genesis, which immediately precedes the book of Exodus in the Torah, the story of the Patriarchs followed a similar path. Of Abraham's two sons, Yishmael and Isaac, "the chosen one" was *not* Yishmael, his first-born; of Isaac's two sons, Esav and Jacob, "the chosen one" was *not* Esav, his first-born; and again, of Jacob's twelve sons, "the chosen one" was *not* Reuven, his first-born.   The overarching message that is revealed by these examples is that the patriarchal blessing and God's covenant will not necessarily devolve to the child who has the accidental good fortune to be born first: the rule of primogeniture.   Rather, the person's individual merit, his deeds and *modus vivendi* will dictate his fate.

As regards Moses' two sons, the Netziv is telling us that Gershom, the first-born, will likewise *not* merit his father's blessing and God's covenant.   That privilege will descend through Eliezer, Moses' second-born son, who merited this ascendancy.

What occurred to sideline Gershom? The Mechilta on this episode in Exodus 18 recounts the story that we told at chapter 22 of this book. The Mechilta explains[28] that when Moses, a stranger to Midian, asked Yitro for Zipporah's hand in marriage, Yitro said to him, "Promise me one thing and then I will grant you Zipporah as your bride." And Moses asked, "What is this one thing?" Yitro told him, "Your firstborn son will not be yours to raise, but will come to me to raise in idolatry. All your other issue you can raise in belief to your God." And Moses acceded to Yitro's condition. Still Yitro persisted, "Swear this to me." And Moses swore to Yitro, as the text states (Ex. 2: 21): *Moses swore.*

The ancient *midrashic* notion that Moses made a pact with Yitro before his marriage to cede his firstborn son to him to raise in idolatry is difficult for us to fathom, accept and reconcile with our understanding of who Moses is. Earlier in this book, at chapter 22, we discuss the meaning of this verse (Ex. 2:21), which in its *p'shat* interpretation states that *Moses consented to dwell with the man.* In its *midrashic* interpretation the verse means that *Moses swore, and dwelled with the man.* According to the *midrash,* Moses did the unthinkable, and promised his firstborn son to his father-in-law to raise in his own tradition. The commentaries, understandably troubled by the Mechilta, offer mitigating circumstances in Moses' behalf. And this *midrashic* explanation *of a midrash* is itself an unusual exegetical occurrence.   Torah Shlema even states that notwithstanding that it is highly unususal to offer commentary *on a midrash,* he nevertheless proceeds to do so because of the strange and bizarre notion that Moses would have consented to Yitro's plan.[29] The commentaries are at pains to offer plausible justification for Moses' assent. They want the reader to recall Moses' state-of-mind, and they paint a picture of the vulnerable hero, a fugitive from Egypt who was, at the time—he had not yet been selected by God to lead His people from bondage—a stranger in Yitro's house, reliant on and subject to his desert hospitality and laws.

Meshech Chachma[30] explains that the stranger Moses, having found respite and succor in Yitro's Midianite tent, and intellectual exchange with the lapsed Midianite priest, was confident he would convert Yitro to belief in the Hebrew God. Moses consented to Yitro's condition, suggests the commentary, because he never thought that the condition would come to pass. Moses saw that Yitro was seriously doubting his pagan beliefs, and assumed Yitro would voluntrily abandon those beliefs before such time in the future that a son would be born to Moses and Zipporah. And in truth, reminds the commentary, Moses was not too far off the mark, as Yitro does ultimately reject paganism and embrace Moses' God here in Exodus 18, though of course not in time to prevent the condition from coming to pass.

Torat HaChidah explains Moses' consent from a different psychological vantage point.[31] The commentary agrees that at the time that Moses consented to allow Yitro to raise his and Zipporah's future firstborn in the pagan tradition, he never expected the condition would arise. But Torat HaChidah's analysis, in contrast to Meshech Chachma, describes Moses' reliance upon Zipporah's—not Yitro's—righteousness. The commentary states that Moses understood his betrothed, and appreciated her essential moral nature. When he agreed to Yitro's terms in order to secure his consent to their marriage, he was calculating that if the time came, Zipporah would be able to prevail upon her father and retain the ability to raise their son according to the Hebrew God. The commentary reminds us that Moses had been a fugitive, a penniless stranger who had had no bargaining power in that pre-marital negotiation. The *midrashic* scenario presented is that once Moses and Zipporah married and had a son, Yitro positioned himself at their tent demanding that Moses live up to their bargain and cede his firstborn to Yitro to raise. The *midrash* continues that Zipporah, reluctant to part with her child, spoke up boldly, and countered to her father that *she* was in charge of their son, and that she refused to cede the boy to him. To wit Moses in effect shrugged his shoulders at his father-in-law's outrage, saying, "It's out of my hands. I was a stranger in Midian when I agreed to your condition; I was not privy to the native customs. I agreed to give you my first-born son to raise in your tradition, but how was I to know that in your country it falls to the woman—and not to the man—to decide on her baby's future. And see! Zipporah refuses to part with the boy!" The *midrashim* conclude that notwithstanding Zipporah's efforts, however, the dominant force of Yitro's tribal and personal prominence ultimately prevailed, and Gershom came under his grandfather's idolatrous tutelage. And as the Talmud (Bava Batra 109b)[32] and Meshech Chachma teach us, in the course of time Gershom sired a son of his own who became a priest to false gods.

The strange tale of Gershom's son—Moses' grandson—is told in chapters 17 and 18 of the book of Judges. As the text there states, it was in the time after Joshua's death, a time of moral and judicial vacuum; there was no king or leader in Israel, the people were rudderless, and every man behaved as he saw fit.[33] At that time a young Levite was an itinerant throughout the land, wandering from his home city in Bethlehem to seek his fortune. Rashi expounds on verse 7 of chapter 17 of Judges and makes the extra-ordinary statement that the itinerant Levite was the son of Gershom, who was none other than the son of our revered teacher and leader, Moses![34] This young man, far from home and a stranger wherever he went, wended his way to the mountain of Ephraim, and thence to the home of Micah, an Israelite man. Micah had strayed from God's way and had set up an altar to idols in his home on the mountain of Ephraim and installed his own son as a priest there to the false gods. When Micah encountered the young Levite man he was overjoyed to have come upon an authentic priest on his very doorstep. Micah begged the stranger to tarry in his home in order to teach him about the priesthood and to perform priestly rites for his temple of idolatry. He offered him food, clothing, shelter and the substantial sum of ten pieces of silver on the condition that the Levite remain in his home and serve as priest in the temple that Micah had established there.

The text next relates that the Levite consented to remain as a priest in Micah's house. Astonishingly, the wording of the phrase in Judges 17:11 (*The Levite consented to dwell with the man*)[35] is eerily similar to the phrase in Exodus 2:21 where Moses, a fugitive and likewise a stranger, consented to dwell in the tent of Yitro, the Priest of Midian. The Bible's phrase there is *Moses consented to dwell with the man.*[36] In the way of the Bible, the uncanny similarity of the two texts signifies a deeper connection, and in fact we read in Judges that the Levite young man consented to dwell with Micah, and that Micah treated him like a son.[37] The reader will recognize this theme: in Moses' story, told at Exodus 2:21, Moses remained in Yitro's tent as the son Yitro never had, and Yitro gave him his daughter Zipporah as his wedded wife. In both stories a young Levite man, an itinerant stranger, is prevailed upon by an established priestly figure to tarry in his home and become a member of his household. In striking contrast, however, in the tale in the book of Judges the Levite young man serves Micah's temple as a priest to idolatry.

Later on in the story in Judges, at chapter 18, members of the tribe of Dan happen upon the house of Micah and they recognize the voice of the Levite priest. They prevail upon him to leave Micah's house and to join them in their quest for their rightful portion of land. After their capture of the land, the Danites, with the Levite young man still in their camp, instead of reverting to their worship of the Hebrew God, became idol-worshippers. And verse 30 of Judges 18 delivers the text's body-blow to Moses' progeny as it says, *And the Children of Dan constructed the idol for themselves;* **and Yehonatan, the son of Gershom, the son of M[ena]she,** *he and his sons were priests for the tribe of Danites until the day of exile from the land.*[38] The Hebrew verse as written in the book of Judges finally identifies this Levite young man who is the son of Gershom. His name is Yehonatan. Then the text presents a rare oddity of Hebrew lettering: the name of Yehonatan's grandfather, listed as "Menashe," is spelled "Moshe" with the Hebrew letter *nun* as a super-script. Read without the superscripted letter *nun* Yehonatan's provenance becomes clear: this Levite priest-turned-idol-worshipper is son of Gershom, who is the son of Moses!

Rashi is astonished at this textual revelation, and his amazement reflects the words of the Danites when they happened upon the young Levite in Micah's house.[39] The verse in Judges (18:3)[40] allows the reader to appreciate their shock at seeing the Levite performing idolatrous rites. Said the Danites to the Levite, "I recognize your priestly voice in song! What could you possibly be doing here, so far from the Temple?" And Rashi completes the conversation: The Danites say, "You couldn't possibly be from the tribe of the Levites who are descended from Moses our teacher, can you?!" It is clear to the commentator that the confluence of the textual similarities between the story of the Levite young man in Judges 18, and the story of Moses in the tent of Yitro at Exodus 2—combined with the glaring textual aberration in the scribing of the *nun*—identify the young apostate as Moses' grandson. It is Rashi's opinion that out of respect for Moses' honor the letter *nun* was inserted so as to alter the name of the apostate's grandfather from Moses (*MoSHe*) to Menashe (*MeNaSHe*).[41] The reader must bear in mind that the text in Judges 18 nowhere mentions Moses' name. It is Rashi and the Talmudists who draw this inference and establish Yehonatan's provenance as Moses' grandson.

The Talmud (Bava Batra 109b) echoes this identification, quoting the story in Judges 18:30 where the text names the young Levite as *Yehonatan, son of Gershom, son of Menashe; he and his sons were priests to the Danite tribe.* The Talmud repeats the shock of the Danites that the Levite was in reality Moses' grandson, and Rashi, explicating this segment of Talmud, reiterates his reasoning, saying that the letter *nun* in *MeNaSHe* is superfluous.[42] Rabbi Adin Steinsaltz concurs. His comment on this segment of Talmud is that the "hanging" or superscript letter is an indication in the text that the word can be read *without* the *nun*.[43] Thus, according to the Talmud and the oral tradition, the apostate Levite youth is not the grandson of a man by the name of Menashe; he is the son of Gershom, who is the son of Moses.

It is fascinating that the rabbis of the Talmud and the transmitters of the oral tradition do not shy from naming Moses' grandson as an apostate. It may shock them; it likely broke their hearts. But as readers of the Bible are aware, the Jewish tradition depicts its larger-than-life heroes complete with weaknesses, so that they can be venerated and emulated realistically by future generations.

Moses' towering stature remains intact notwithstanding this *midrashic* revelation about his grandson.

Still, Moses fathered *two* sons with Zipporah, and Eliezer, his second-born, was by all accounts a credit to him and to his people. In fact, according to the Netziv, the wording of verse 18:4 in Exodus (naming Eliezer "the one" instead of "the second one") confirms that Eliezer—and not the firstborn Gershom—is the singular son of Moses.[44] Meshech Chachma even asks rhetorically why Moses did not name his *first* son Eliezer rather than Gershom, and responds that Moses did not want the name of God (*Eli*) to be associated with a son who would father the apostate Yehonatan.[45] We are left expectant that Eliezer will live up to his name, and according to the *midrash* this is borne out.

And **the name of the one was Eliezer**, 'For the God of my father has aided me, and saved me from the Pharaoh's sword.' It comes as a relief to the reader that the commentaries view this verse as a hint that Eliezer, Moses' second son, is destined to father revered and distinguished rabbinic progeny. Bamidbar Rabbah (19.7) and Yalkut Shimoni recount a *midrash* of a heavenly enounter between Moses and God.[46] The *midrash* says that when Moses went up the mountain to receive God's laws, he came upon the Master of the Universe studying the chapter of the Torah dealing with the red heifer, an especially involved and abstruse series of laws. God was saying, "And my son Eliezer taught that the law was thus-and-so," giving credit to the future Rabbi Eliezer who explicated the minutiae of this important law. To wit Moses said to the Lord, "Master of the Universe, the worlds of heaven and earth are controlled by your word; yet you nevertheless quote the law according to a man of mere flesh-and-blood?" And God responded, "Not a mere man of flesh-and-blood, but the selfsame Rabbi Eliezer whose opinion on the red heifer will be quoted *first* in the book of laws." Said a wistful Moses, "Would that I would merit having this scholar issue from my own loins!" And God replied, "I swear to you, my servant, Moses, that Rabbi Eliezer is indeed destined to issue from your loins!" So Moses—the redeemer of Israel, beloved servant of the one God, husband to Zipporah—was comforted; his second-born son, Eliezer, was destined to father progeny who would, like their patriarch, be revered teachers in Israel.

And Yitro, father-in-law to Moses, and his sons and his wife, traveled to Moses in the desert where he was encamped, there at God's mountain. And he said to Moses, 'I am your father-in-law, Yitro, come to you; and your wife and her two sons along with her.' And Moses went out to greet his father-in-law, and he bowed low, and he kissed him, and they inquired of one another's welfare; and they came into the tent. (Exodus 18:5–7)

The reader will recall that earlier in Exodus 18, before the digression about the names of Moses' two sons, we encountered Yitro bringing his daughter, Zipporah, and her two sons, to Moses' tent at the foot of God's mountain. The Torah invites the reader to envision the dramatic scene. Exodus 18:5 has Yitro approaching Moses' tent. We can imagine that Yitro has had to pass through various rings of security or circles of tribal Israelite princes surrounding Moses' sanctum, for as Torah Shlema tells us, Moses was on the level of a king.[47] There must have been quite a stir among the people in the camp, with rumors flying as Yitro and his entourage wend their way to Moses: "See who comes! It is Yitro, Moses' father-in-law. And see who is with him! Those boys must be Moses' sons, and the woman must be his wife!"

Though Moses has not been apart from his family for a great length of time as measured by the calendar, the reader must appreciate that he has undergone a radical change since he sent Zipporah and the boys back to Midian after their night at the desert inn. Moses has jousted verbally and intellectually with the mighty Pharaoh and his advisors; he has juggled the admiration and scorn of the Hebrew slaves; he has reestablished his relationship with his brother Aaron, erstwhile titular head of the Hebrews; he has been God's instrument of wonders and terrors as the harbinger and engineer of the ten plagues; and he has—with his generals to aid him—trimphantly guided the Hebrews out of Egypt and through the Red Sea, and led the fledgeling nation to victory over the army of the Amalekites. Finally, now, he and the Israelites have come to rest at the foot of God's mountain in the wilderness, where Moses had first established an intimate relationship with his God.

This is where we now encounter Moses, Yitro, Zipporah and their two sons in Exodus chapter 18.

Verse 5 presents Yitro, Moses' father-in-law, at the head of the tiny procession, followed by his two sons and lastly by his wife. Verse 6 has Yitro announcing to Moses—who, presumably, has come to his tent door in response to the summons—"I am your father-in-law Yitro, come to you; I have brought your wife and her two sons with her."   And verse 7 allows us to witness Moses' awaited reaction to this surprise. His past is thrust upon him in the person of Yitro, Zipporah and his sons at this perhaps inopportune time. We think, How will Moses greet them? The Bible supplies the answer: *And Moses went out to greet his father-in-law, and he bowed low, and he kissed him, and they inquired of one another's welfare; and they came into the tent.* Literarily, the circle is closed, and Moses, who was brought into Yitro's tent in Midian fourteen chapters previously as an itinerant fugitive and hero, now opens his own tent door to Yitro, who in turn comes to Moses as a wanderer of sorts, also needy in his fashion.

We are aware that Yitro's goal is nothing short of having Moses accept and gather Zipporah and their two sons to his bosom after their separation. Yitro is playing his trump card of father and grandfather along with that of revered and beloved advisor to Moses.   Torah Shlema verbalizes Yitro's *midrashic* conversation upon greeting his son-in-law:[48] "Moses, my son, open your tent to your family. At the very least, accept your two sons to your heart. For you have been preoccupied all this time with teaching the commandments to all of Israel, in the process ignoring the moral education and upbringing of your own sons. You consigned them to my daughter—your wife—but you deprived them of your presence." The Netziv presents Yitro's speech to Moses with a different slant:[49] "Open your tent to us. If not because you have pined for your wife and sons, then do so because I am asking this of you; *I*, your father-in-law."

The Torah text is clear. In verse 7 Moses invites his father-in-law into his tent, and not his wife and sons. Nowhere is there even a hint that Moses is discourteous to them, or that he is distressed at their coming to him. But a close reading of the *p'shat* allows us to infer from Moses' actions that *at that precise moment in time*, at the foot of God's mountain and on the eve of receiving God's law, Yitro was more important to Moses and to the biblical story-line than were Zipporah and her two sons. The Netziv explains that in full view of the gathered Israelites[50] Moses held open his tent flap for his father-in-law, and *not* to his wife and sons.

The Bible has allowed us to witness Moses' compassion, heroism, courage, humility, passion, resignation, fearlessness and dogged determination. All these qualities converged to make Moses the perfect man to serve both God and the Israelites, foil the great Pharaoh and redeem a people. Perhaps the Torah is now tacitly expressing that the time of Moses' passion—for Zipporah and their sons, for his solitary life as a Midianite shepherd—has irretreivably passed, and that even when presented with her physical presence, Moses sees only Yitro, his father-in-law, the teacher and thinker, his mentor and advisor. According to Ibn Ezra,[51] Moses' courtly gesture of greeting and welcoming Yitro accorded Yitro the honor that his age and enduring importance to Moses demanded. The next verses of Torah text bear this out.

The commentaries engage in spirited discussion about Yitro's presentation of himself and his daughter and grandsons at Moses' tent door. They bear in mind, as we do, that the opening verse of this chapter in Exodus begins with the words **And Yitro**, *the priest of Midian, father-in-law of Moses,* **heard** *about all that God did for Moses and Israel his nation; that God took Israel out of Egypt.* The commentaries ask, Why did Yitro bring Zipporah and their two sons to Moses at this precise moment? And what, specifically, did Yitro "hear?" The Talmud (Zevachim 116a) touches on these questions and sets out the three possible subjects that Yitro "heard" that could have induced him to uproot his daughter and grandchildren and travel through the Midianite desert to Moses' camp. Did he hear about the fact that the perfidious Amalekites attacked the released slaves at Refidim? Or did he hear about the miraculous splitting of the Red Sea? Or did he hear about God's Torah being given immimently to the Israelite nation?[52] This question is widely debated, and is not susceptible of resolution according to Rabbi Adin Steinsaltz.[53]

The commentary Kli Yakar postulates that Yitro had "heard" about the imminent giving of the Torah and God's law, and that *this* is what caused him to present himself at Moses' tent at the foot of God's mountain at this precise moment in time.[54] The commentary explains Yitro's motivation saying that the father in Yitro yearned for his daughter to be reclaimed by her husband

Moses. For after all, says the commentary, a husband and wife belong together, and the glory of the marriage relationship is the ability to coexist side-by-side with one's chosen soul-mate. This is no less than what Yitro wanted for his daughter Zipporah.

Predictably, then, the second great intractable rabbinic debate after discussing what Yitro "heard," concerns whether Yitro presented himself to Moses *before* or *after* the giving of the Torah. The question is not merely academic, because in the upcoming chapter 19 of Exodus Moses instructs the Israelites to separate from their spouses for a grace period leading up to and including the giving of God's law. The rabbis therefore inquire whether Moses would allow Zipporah back into his life at Yitro's behest, or whether here, in chapter 18, Moses already has issued the order of temporary separation of spouses and will not allow Zipporah to draw close to him.

For our purposes, and as regards the immediate action occurring in Exodus 18, we are most concerned with understanding Yitro's motivation and Moses' frame of mind when he opens his tent door and sees Yitro, Zipporah and his sons ranged before him. The Torah plainly states that Moses welcomed his beloved father-in-law. The absence of any biblical mention of Moses' reaction to seeing his wife or children must be taken as a statement that they were secondary to his new life as God's servant and Israel's redeemer.

All-in-all, Yitro succeeded in his bold move. The surprised Moses did not reject him and his daughter and grandsons. He welcomed Yitro into his tent, eager to resume the intense and meaningful discussions that marked their relationship. Once they were alone, Moses recounted in detail for Yitro all that God had done to Pharaoh and Egypt on behalf of the Israelites, and how God also had delivered them from the hardships they encountered after they had left Egypt. Yitro's response was to bless Moses' beneficent God and to offer up a burnt sacrifice to Him.

Yitro's lasting contribution to his beloved son-in-law and incidentally to the Children of Israel was his brilliant advice to Moses outlining a new method of judging the people. His system, readily instituted by Moses, enabled Moses to delegate brave and honest men who would judge the people. Yitro's innovative system ensured swifter justice to the multitudes and freed Moses to focus on larger issues of leadership. Once Yitro's tiered system of judges for

the emerging nation was in place, many commentaries hold that
Moses allowed his father-in-law to return to his own land, and
Zipporah and their two sons remained in the Israelite camp.

THIRTY-SEVEN

୫᎐Ꮿ᎐Ꮿ᎐Ꮿ

Marital Abstinence in Preparation for Receiving God's Law

EXODUS 19:1-15

The Children of Israel arrived in the wilderness of Sinai in the third month after the exodus from Egypt . . . and they camped before the mountain. And Moses went up to God, who called out to him from the mountain saying , 'Tell this to the House of Jacob and to the Children of Israel: . . . . You will be a special treasure to me above all the other nations. And you will be a kingdom of priests and a holy nation.' . . . And the people answered as one: 'All that God has said we will do!' . . . And God said to Moses, 'Go to the people and sanctify them today and tomorrow, and have them cleanse their clothing. **For they should be in readiness by the third day***, because on the third day God will come down to Mount Sinai in full view of all the people . . .'*
. . . So Moses descended the mountain and rejoined the people, and he sanctified the people and they cleansed their clothing. **And Moses told the people, 'Be ready for three days! Do not draw near to your wives!'**

The Children of Israel are encamped at the foot of God's mountain in the wilderness of Sinai expectant and willing, but also

198

fearful of what God would require of them in exchange for His gifting them with His laws. In verse 11 God instructs Moses to tell the people to ready themselves for the imminent revelation: *For they should be in readiness by the third day.* They are to spend two days cleansing their clothing and their persons in preparation for receiving God's presence among them on the third day. A close reading of the Torah text reveals that Moses adds a critical condition to his instructions to the people. In verse 15 Moses says, *Be ready for three days!* **Do not draw near to your wives!** The question thus arises, How did Moses make the leap in these verses from being *in readiness* to include *do not draw near to your wives?* Rashi responds that the Hebrew words for being *in readiness* (*HeYu NeCHoNiM*)[1] in verse 11 encompasses remaining separated from one's wife in verse 15.[2] Siftei Chachamim explains Rashi,[3] pointing out that both verses 11 and 15 use the same Hebrew word for being *in readiness—NeCHoNiM.* It is therefore a logical inference, according to the Mechilta,[4] that verse 11 should also adopt verse 15's textual partner—*separating from one's wife*—when instructing the people to make themselves ready to receive God's laws.

Sforno goes a bit further, justifying such a reading by explaining that the body as well as the spirit must be made ready for the acceptance of God's revelation.[5] Separating from one's wife for the prescribed three days will allow the body physical respite and focused concentration. This is the reason, says the commentator, that the text includes in Moses' instructions to the Israelites his expression of the requirement of sexual abstinence. It was God's intention that the people ready themselves body and soul to accept the divine presence.

The Talmud (Shabbat 87a) discusses the concept of abstention of sexual relations as it relates particularly to Moses.[6] When Moses instructed the people in God's name to purify themselves in preparation for their receiving the divine presence, he logically included himself in this prohibition, and abstained from sexual relations with Zipporah for this same time period. But the Talmud explains that Moses apparently went even further. Moses separated from Zipporah utterly: Moses inferred that if God desired the Israelites to abstain from sexual relations in preparation for their *one-time* encounter with the Almighty, how much more so should he—Moses—abstain from sexual intimacy *at all times*! For he was expected to be ready to accept God's face-to-face prophecy *at any moment* after the revelation at Sinai. Moses surmised—incorrectly, according to Rabbi Adin Steinsaltz—that the Almighty expected him to leave no room for human intimacy. This misconception was excusable, according to Rabbi Steinsaltz's understanding of Rashi, only because the divine presence hovered over Moses day and night. As regards all other mortal men it would be a forbidden excess for them to so abstain.[7]

The Talmud[8] (Yevamot 62a) discusses three important things that Moses initiated and that the Almighty assented to thereafter. The first of these is that he separated from his wife completely, even after the revelation at Sinai, when all the other Israelites were permitted to resume normal sexual intimacy with their spouses.[†] While the Talmud explains that God ultimately agreed with Moses and affirmed this strict personal behavior, the commentary to Torah Temima says that it may not been God's original intention to hold Moses to this higher standard for the rest of his life.[9] The commentary continues that it is possible that God would not have required such an unnatural code of behavior of a mortal man, even if that man were Moses.[10]

The proof-text for God's ultimate consent and even agreement with Moses' voluntary, complete sexual abstention is found in Deuteronomy 5:27-28. There, Moses is recapping the events that befell the Children of Israel. He narrates that after the receipt of the Torah at Sinai God told him to address the Children of Israel. *Go tell them, 'Return to your tents!' And as for you, remain here with me.*[11] From these seemingly innocuous phrases Rashi and the commentaries infer a wealth of meaning. Says Rashi, God was instructing Moses that the male Israelites were now released from the pre-Sinai prohibition and permitted to return *to their tents*, meaning that they could now resume sexual intimacy with their wives.[12] According to Torah Temima, it was widely understood that the Torah's words *return to your tents* referred

---

[†]The second thing that Moses initiated without God's express permission is that he added a third day of sexual abstinence to the Israelites' preparation for receiving the Torah; the third is that he smashed the two tablets of the law upon witnessing the worshipping of the Golden Calf.

euphemistically to returning to their wives and to their marital beds.[13]   But as concerns Moses, the commentary explains that Moses interpreted the phrase *as for you, remain here with me*, as his cue to remain apart from his wife even after the general three-day prohibition had ended.[14]   And Rashi is absolutely clear that Moses' conjugal separation from Zipporah in anticipation of receiving God's law ultimately merged into a complete and permanent separation from her bed ever afterwards.[15]   Moses understood God's phrase *remain here with me* to mean that because he was poised to accept God's prophecy *at any time*, and face-to-face, according to Sforno,[16] he could not *ever* resume marital relations with his wife.

In contrast to the Talmud (Yevamot 62a), Sifrei states that Moses' sexual separation from Zipporah after the revelation at Sinai was his response to a direct command by God. The *midrashist* relies for a proof-text on God's paean to Moses in Numbers 12:8, where God says, *mouth-to-mouth do I speak with him . . . he beholds the semblance of God. . . .* The reader is invited to ask, *what* does God tell Moses "mouth-to-mouth?" And Rashi quoting Sifrei responds that God specifically instructed Moses to remain separate from his wife so that he would always be in spiritual and physical readiness to speak with the Almighty.[17]

According to the Netziv, Moses' present austerity was even augured for the reader in the prior chapter, at Exodus 18:7.[18] There, we recall, the Bible narrates the scene of Moses' reaction to his father-in-law's surprise appearance in the Israelite camp at the foot of God's mountain. Zipporah and his two sons are standing with—or more likely behind—Yitro as Yitro presents himself to his son-in-law. *And Moses went out to greet his father-in-law, and he kissed him, and they each inquired as to the well-being of the other; and they went into the tent.* Even before God's instruction to the Children of Israel to separate from their wives for the three days prior to the revelation at Sinai, Moses—in full view of the entire encampment—escorts only his father-in-law into his tent, and not his wife and sons. The implication of the Netziv's commentary is that Moses had already shifted his focus from (wo)man to God. We need not even venture to guess what Moses and Yitro are discussing inside the tent. The Bible tells us at 18:8 that Moses was singing God's praises to Yitro. No doubt this was an opportunity for closure for Moses. He had spent years, the *midrash* tells us, discussing with Yitro the nature of God and man. Here at last he can close the book, so-to-speak, on those discussions with his father-in-law, the lapsed priest of Midian. The Bible says that in his tent that day Moses recounted for Yitro how the One God triumphed over the mighty Pharaoh and vanquished Egypt, specifically in order to save the Israelites. In fact, the Torah text at 18:10-11 makes it clear that after meeting with Moses Yitro blessed Moses' God, acknowledged Him who saved the weak in the face of the strong, and explicitly affirmed God's supremacy over all other gods.[19] Thus, it is evident that as he camped at the foot of Sinai, Moses' wife and sons no longer occupied a place of importance in his consciousness; Moses was utterly preoccupied with his God.

PART VI

THE KUSHITE
WOMAN REDUX

৹৩৹৩

THIRTY-EIGHT

৪০৫৪০৫

Miriam and Aaron Speak about Moses' Kushite Woman

NUMBERS 12:1

And Miriam and Aaron spoke about Moses, concerning the
Kushite woman that he took; for he took a Kushite woman.[1]

After God gives His law to Moses and the Israelites at Sinai, we
read immediately of the people's betrayal of God and their
fashioning and worshipping of a golden calf. Moses is stunned and
irate at their abandonment of the God who delivered them from
Egypt amid signs and wonders, and he smashes the tablets of the
law. Eventually Moses receives a new set of tablets after he has
appeased an angry God, and the biblical narrative continues as
Moses leads the grumbling Israelites through the wilderness over a
course of decades. During this time Aaron and Miriam function
along with Moses as a ruling triumverate. Moses speaks with God
and teaches and leads the people, and Aaron and Miriam, prophets
in their own right, function as essential liaisons between Moses and
the fractious Israelites.

Chapter 12 of Numbers, the fourth of the Five Books of
Moses, opens (12:1) with a cryptic narrative describing a conversation between Miriam and Aaron as they speak about their
sibling, Moses. According to the text, they are troubled about
Moses' "Kushite woman." The verse is vague and repetitive, and it

takes the reader by surprise. The text elicits a number of questions, each of which is important in light of the drama that follows. The commentaries ask, Who is the enigmatic "Kushite woman," and what are they saying about her?

Even before we address those issues, however, the verse presents a grammatical challenge. It begins by saying *And Miriam and Aaron spoke . . .* , but the Hebrew word for "spoke" appears here in the *singular feminine* conjugation, while the text describes a conversation where *both* parties—male and female—are speaking! In contrast, when the next verse again refers to both of them speaking, it *does* employ the *plural* conjugation. Rashi resolves this by explaining that in 12:1 it was Miriam who initiated the conversation, which explains why the verb is in the singular feminine form.[2] Ibn Ezra adds that while Miriam initiated the conversation, Aaron was an active participant, either expressly acquiescing to, or tacitly agreeing with her words.[3] It is for this reason, says the commentator, that *both* Miriam and Aaron are judged culpable and will be punished for speaking about Moses.

The reader should be intensely curious about the subject of their conversation. Who is the "Kushite woman" referred to in verse 12:1? Rashbam—along with Ibn Ezra and Chizkuni—quoting *Divrei HaYamim Shel Moshe*, identifies the "Kushite woman" as the reigning queen of Kush and the widow of King Nikonos.[4] Moses had wed her, according to the *midrash,* after he had fled Egypt and saved the Kushite kingdom from usurpers.[†]

Surprisingly, the Talmud[5] (Moed Katan 16b) identifies the "Kushite woman" as Zipporah. Questions the Talmud, "But her name is Zipporah, not 'Kushite!' This must mean that she is referred to in the text as 'Kushite' strictly for the purpose of emphasizing the contrast between Zipporah and other women. For as glaring a difference as there is between the skin color of the people of Kush—they are Ethiopians with black skin—and people whose skin is light in color, so, too, is there an obvious difference between Zipporah's deeds and those of the average woman." The sages of the Talmud are guiding us as we navigate this mysterious passage of Torah text. They interpret the strange epithet "Kushite

———————

[†]We refer the reader to chapter 20 above, "Moses and the Kushite Woman," where this episode is discussed in detail.

woman" to mean that Moses' wife, Zipporah, is exceptional. Torah Temima expands upon the Talmud, saying that Zipporah's righteous deeds and her special nature combined to make her stand out even among the righteous women of her generation.[6] According to Rashi, Zipporah was widely regarded as a beauty, so striking that she stood out from the crowd.[7] The commentary on the Maharal lauds Zipporah to the highest degree, saying that she walked in the path of the righteous daughters of Israel.[8] In the manifestation of her physical beauty as well as in her mode of behavior she echoed the greatness of the Hebrew matriarchs Sarah, Rebecca, Rachel and Leah.

A minority opinion interprets the phrase "Kushite woman" to mean that Miriam and Aaron were referring to Zipporah's black skin color. Ibn Ezra says that Zipporah, a Midianite woman, was a descendant of the Ishmaelites, who, as desert tent dwellers, were black-complexioned. Says Ibn Ezra, "Zipporah was nearly as black as the Kushites."[9]

But it is difficult to reconcile this reading with the facts. The Bible tells us that Zipporah was not Kushite, but Midianite. Further, just as the Midianite peoples' skin became baked brown by the desert sun, so, too, did the Israelites' skin become tanned. So there would have been no objective reason for Zipporah to have been termed a "Kushite woman." Moreover, as Alschich eloquently states,[10] to have referred to Zipporah as a "Kushite woman" for any other reason than as a compliment would have been impossible. For once Zipporah, the Midianite, had become converted to Moses' God, she was considered in everyone's eyes to be a Jewess, as authentic a Jewess as any Israelite.

The prevailing understanding is that the Bible's expression "Kushite woman" was used as a short-hand method of distinguishing Zipporah from her peers: she stood out, not because of her skin color, which was not appreciably different from their own, but because of her beauty and her courageous and steadfast character. The reader will recall that Zipporah alone, of all her sisters, was lovely enough to catch the eye of Moses at the well in Midian. Also, her unprecedented quick thinking and bold action saved Moses' life at the desert inn, and her tenacity and love for Moses and their sons allowed her to raise the boys in his absence. This is the woman who sought Moses out at Sinai, but who encountered a

changed man in his stead. Zipporah's husband had become transformed, through his partnership with the Almighty, from the
itinerant shepherd she married, into a man of God who no longer
had need of the comforts offered by a flesh-and-blood wife, regardless of her worth.

Still, the reader is in the dark about what Miriam and Aaron
actually say about Zipporah. The Netziv focuses on the second
clause of verse 1, *for he took a Kushite woman*.[11] This points to
the unarticulated subject of their discussion, says the commentary.
He interprets that phrase to mean that Miriam and Aaron were
discussing Zipporah, and that she was a Kushite. The commentary
ignores for the moment that according to the Bible Zipporah was
not a Kushite, but a Midianite. He focuses on the fact of her alien
status. What could the two have been saying? The Netziv suggests
that they surmised that Moses had instigated the prolonged marital
separation from Zipporah because he was in some way ashamed of
her Midianite—i.e., her non-Israelite—status; that she was not the
appropriate life partner for a leader of Moses' stature. The
commentator posits that Miriam and Aaron disagreed with what
they thought their brother had done, and felt it wronged Zipporah.
The fact is that she had long before been converted to Moses' God,
and Miriam and Aaron—and likely the people as well—did not
consider her to be a stranger among them.

Bechor Schor presents the converse of the Netziv's scenario.
He suggests that Miriam and Aaron feared that Moses had taken
Zipporah, the Midianite, as his wife because he shunned the Israelite
women and sought out the stranger.[12]   Unfortunately, the
commentator gives no hint as to why Miriam and Aaron might even
think this, let alone discuss it. Further, this does not explain the use
of the term "Kushite woman." Nor does this *midrashic* scenario
jibe with Miriam's proven textual attachment to her brother Moses,
and it also is inconsonant with the facts presented in the text in the
book of Exodus. We must remember that the young man Moses
was an Egyptian prince, and living as he did within Pharaoh's
palace he had no opportunity to meet or court an Israelite. Readers
should recall as well that no sooner had Moses' awareness of his
Hebrew birth status blossomed within him, then he was forced to
flee for his life after he struck and killed the Egyptian taskmaster in
defense of the Hebrew slave. As Da'at Zekeinim suggests,[13] it was

only Moses-the-fugitive who had any opportunity at all, however slim and improbable, to meet and wed an eligible female, and the Torah text deposits him at the well in Midian for the dual purpose of rescuing Yitro's daughters, and introducing him to his future mate and also to his mentor/father-in-law.

A third, more subtle scenario is proposed by the Chatam Sofer.[14] He suggests that as a conscientious convert to Moses' God, Zipporah kept so scrupulously to the strictures of the Hebrew faith and practice that her exemplary behavior was irksome to the fractious Israelites. Perhaps Miriam and Aaron were discussing that Moses' separation from such a woman was an unnecessary degradation of Zipporah.

We present these three scenarios in order to illustrate that the puzzle inherent in verse 12:1—what did Miriam and Aaron say about Moses, and who is the Kushite woman?—troubles not only thoughtful readers of the text, but the commentators as well. So eager were the commentaries to resolve these questions that they explored various scenarios involving Moses and Zipporah: that he no longer desired her because she was not an Israelite (the Netziv); that on the contrary, he desired her precisely because she was different from the Israelite women (Bechor Schor); and that she was too perfect an example of an Israelite for the peoples' peace of mind (Chatam Sofer).

Let us continue the quest for an understanding of the subject of this *tête-à-tête* between Miriam and Aaron. Rashi presumes that the two are discussing the fact that Moses has separated completely from his wife,[15] and that while Zipporah remains a respected presence in the Israelite camp, she no longer shares a tent with her husband. Implicit in Rashi's explanation, and in the discussion of many of the commentaries, is that Miriam befriended her sister-in-law Zipporah, and that the two women developed a close personal relationship. We can appreciate this intimacy, because both Miriam and Zipporah share a vital life-mission and *raison d'être*: loving and caring for Moses. Where Miriam left off watching over her brother after he was taken into the palace as a prince of Egypt, Zipporah assumed this mission when she married the fugitive Moses and began to build him a home in the wilderness beyond Midian.

Now, for the first time in the Moses narrative, the commentaries connect these two heroic women and allow us to glimpse their private conversations. This is the reason, according to Alschich, that Miriam speaks first in verse 12:1.[16] The commentary, appreciating Miriam's close affinity for her sister-in-law, suggests that Miriam is so troubled by Zipporah's presumptive loss of face among the Israelites because of Moses' absence from her tent, that she broaches the subject with her other brother, hoping that the two can propose a solution.

Rashi continues that Miriam happened to be standing with Zipporah when, in the prior chapter (Numbers 11:27), a runner announced to Moses that two Israelite men, Eldad and Meidad, were prophesying in the camp. Zipporah leaned over to Miriam and whispered, "Woe unto their wives! For it is a lonely life they will lead as wives of prophets of God. Their husbands will surely remain separate from them just as my husband has done from me." It is from this whispered confidence that Miriam realized that Moses no longer went to Zipporah's tent, and this, says Rashi, is what she disclosed to her brother Aaron in 12:1.

The Maharal explains that Zipporah, a discreet woman, would never ordinarily have initiated a conversation about her and Moses' physical intimacy.[17] She had kept her thoughts and feelings about her marital estrangement private all this time since the revelation at Sinai. It is likely that she did not even appreciate how much she revealed in the wistful aside to her sister-in-law.

Yalkut Shimoni[18] describes the conversation between Zipporah and Miriam in a slightly different context, and in greater detail. He explains that the impetus for the women's exchange was when Moses elevated the seventy elders to positions of prominence as judges among the Israelites (this took place in the prior chapter, at Numbers 11:25). There was a jubilant celebration, complete with a candle-lighting ceremony, throughout the encampment. Miriam, watching the display, opined to Zipporah, "The wives of these men must be so proud of their husbands on a night such as this one, marking their elevation to positions as assistants to Moses!" To wit, Zipporah responded in Miriam's ear, "Woe unto those women! From this night forward they are as good as barren; for their husbands will shun their beds." "How do you know this?" Miriam asked her. "From your brother," replied Zipporah. "For from the very hour that he was privileged to speak with the Almighty he forsook our marriage bed." The commentaries, in recounting these "conversations," demonstrate their exquisite sensitivity both to Zipporah's conjugal loneliness and to Miriam's dual loyalties. Miriam, ever her brother's protector, has naturally also befriended and allied herself with his wife. She will attempt to serve them both well by confiding the situation to Aaron and seeking his counsel. The reader will see that her attempt will have devastating consequences.

Sifrei[19] presents a more subtle scenario, wherein Miriam intuits Zipporah's change in marital status before her sister-in-law utters a word. Rather, according to the commentary, it is Miriam's sisterly eye and intuitive heart trained upon her sister-in-law that evokes, in *midrashic* terms, Zipporah's intimate secret. Sifrei rhetorically asks, "How does Miriam know that Moses has separated from his wife?" It answers that Miriam noticed that Zipporah, when she had arrived at the foot of Sinai so many months ago, had been meticulously groomed down to the intricate braiding of her hair. This bespoke her feminine anticipation of a reunion with her husband, Moses. Miriam must have noted and approved of her sister-in-law's fastidiousness.

But now, says the commentator, many months after the giving of the law at Sinai, Miriam has become good friends with Zipporah, and has observed that Zipporah has altered her toilette. To Miriam's keen eye, this change signaled her sister-in-law's subtle metamorphosis from a woman who had been wont to tastefully adorn herself in bracelets and headscarves in the feminine way, into a still-comely but plain-dressing woman. The *midrash* describes that Miriam is moved to privately inquire of Zipporah, "What has come over you that you no longer don your finery?" And Zipporah carefully answers her implicit query, "Ah, my sister, your brother never even noticed." Miriam understands, according to Sifrei, that Zipporah's change in behavior signaled that Zipporah and Moses had ceased having sexual relations even for the purpose of having more children, and that Zipporah was pining for her husband. Thus, Miriam took it upon herself to discuss the matter with her older brother, Aaron, and that is the conversation alluded to in the text at Numbers 12:1.[†]

[†]The reader will recall (from chapter 10) that according to the *midrash*, even as a young girl living in Goshen, during the darkest days of oppression in Egypt, Miriam assumed the role of conciliator and facilitator,

This verse presents still another issue, highlighted by the unique Hebrew grammar, but perhaps also raised in the readers' minds. The question is whether Miriam and Aaron spoke *in Moses' presence* or behind his back. And it is discussed by the commentaries because the Bible's precise wording is[20] that *Miriam and Aaron spoke* **within** (or **in front of**) Moses. Rashi[21] and the Maharal[22] consider verses 1 and 2 together for the purpose of interpreting the word **B'MoSHe**,[23] because the precise word appears in both verses, along with the word **BaNu**.[24] The prevailing question is how to read the three words, each preceeded by the Hebrew letter *bet*, functioning as a preposition and meaning loosely "with." Employing this plain-sense reading, in both verses 12:1 and 2 the text's word **B'MoSHe** means unequivocally *with Moses*, and the third word, **BaNu**, means *with us*. Thus, verse 1 would be interpreted as *And Miriam and Aaron spoke,* **with Moses present**, *concerning the Kushite woman that he took . . . .*

This reading—that Moses was actually present at Miriam and Aaron's conversation—puts a whole new perspective on this incident. This is the reading of verse 1 presented by the Ohr HaChayim.[25] The commentary reasons that Miriam and Aaron were issuing a private rebuke to their brother, reprimanding him about his marital separation from Zipporah. There is no doubt, according to Ohr HaChayim, that Moses was a party to the conversation, hearing every word spoken, though not responding verbally. This reading is consonant with the upcoming text of verse 3, which states, in a seeming *non sequitor*, that *The man Moses was very humble; more so than any person on the face of the earth.*[26] Says the Ohr HaChayim, it is an obvious inference from the text of verse 1 that Moses was present but silent during his siblings' rebuke, in light of verse 3's extended statement that *the man Moses was very humble*. What constraint—what humility—it must have taken on Moses' part to remain absolutely mute when confronted by his siblings' criticism!

-----

causing her estranged parents to resume marital relations. We are told that the result of her parents' reunion was her baby brother Moses. It is obvious that Miriam has retained the quality of character that defined her those many years ago. Clearly the *midrash* also connects Miriam's behavior in Egypt and her well-meaning intervention in Numbers 12.

Moses was surely torn between his perceived exclusive duty to his God, versus the concurrently pressing duty he owed to his wife Zipporah. By devoting himself exclusively to God, Moses was seen as holding himself above Miriam, Aaron and the other prophets among the Israelites. There was no possible way for Moses to "win" in this knotty situation, so he chose the road most compelling to him: continued exclusive devotion to his God, to the exclusion of his wife, and silence in the face of the justified and loyal rebuke of his sister and brother. This is the drama that has unfolded in verse 12:1 and which continues in verses 2 and 3.

And they said, Is it only through Moses that God speaks? For He also speaks through us! And God heard. And the man Moses was very humble, above all the people on the face of the earth.[27] (Numbers 12:2-3)

The next verse, Numbers 12:2, follows the siblings' discussion of Zipporah, and injects a second aspect to Miriam and Aaron's reproof of Moses. Miriam and Aaron, continuing their championing of Zipporah and chastising their brother Moses for abandoning his husbandly duties toward her, add another element to the discussion. According to Rashi,[28] they say, in effect, "We are all three of us prophets of God. God does not speak only through Moses! He speaks through us, as well. Yet we two have not separated ourselves from the ordinary ways of human nature; *we* still share sleeping quarters with our spouses. Why does Moses keep himself apart from Zipporah?" Sifrei abandons all subtlety here, confirming that the subject of the discussion was Moses' utter cessation of sexual relations with his wife after the revelation at Sinai.[29]

Ibn Ezra adds that this conversation reveals Miriam and Aaron's misconception about their prophesying ability.[30] They here equate their spiritual power with that of Moses. They further assume that Moses' marital separation is merely his whim, and that it does not have God's approbation, reasoning that cohabitation is not forbidden to *them*.

According to the Netziv, Miriam and Aaron were not equating themselves with Moses so much as they were harking back to their forefathers, Abraham, Isaac and Jacob. The forefathers—though they were all of them prophets who also spoke with God—still maintained intimate physical relationships with their wives throughout their lives.[31]   That is the basis for their reproof of Moses over his marital separation from Zipporah.   They did not comprehend that Moses' relationship with God exceeded that of the patriarchs.   Nor did they yet perceive that Moses' relationship with God was unique and all-consuming, obviating the need for any intimate human contact whatever.

Alschich agrees that Miriam and Aaron are as yet unaware that Moses' level of prophecy is infinitely greater than theirs.   In an interesting slant the commentator characterizes their comments in this verse as affectionately uttered.[32]   They may be meddling in matters which Moses and God do not wish them to discuss, but they are doing so out of love for their brother and sister-in-law.   Miriam and Aaron are true to their characters; they are attempting to keep Moses' marriage intact.   The rules of behavior that apply to them, they reason, should likewise apply to Moses.   Being a prophet of God, they imply, is an *in*sufficient reason to separate from one's spouse.   Little do they know that God Himself will be championing his servant Moses in the upcoming verses, and that their well-intentioned reproof of their brother will end in punishment for them both.

In fact, the final words of Numbers 12:2 are *And God heard.* Yalkut Shimoni,[33] mindful that the *p'shat* or simple reading of the verse is that Miriam and Aaron were speaking only between themselves when discussing prophecy and celibacy, suggests a subtler reading of the verse. The commentary proposes that *Moses was present* at this portion of the conversation because of the next words, appearing at the beginning of verse 3: *And the man Moses . . . .* Read together, then, the phrase would be *And God heard, and the man Moses [also heard] . . . .*   Therefore, reasons the commentary, assuming that Moses was indeed present *and silent* in the face of their rebuke, verse 3's characterization of Moses as *more humble than any man on the face of the earth* would make sense.

Alschich focuses on the Bible's phrase at the end of verse 2, *And God heard.*   The text indicates that there are two reasons to infer that it was *only God*—and not Moses—who heard Miriam and Aaron's conversation.   First, because the text does not mention that

Moses was present during Miriam and Aaron's rebuke, notwithstanding Yalkut Shimoni and Ohr HaChayim. And second, Alschich suggests that even if Moses *were* present, he could not possibly have responded effectively to his siblings' argument about prophecy and celibacy without aggrandizing himself above them in an unseemly manner. That is the reason, says the commentator, that upon hearing their rebuke God stepped in to respond to them in Moses' stead.[34]

According to the Netziv, the text's statements that *God heard; and the man Moses was very humble* are a signpost for the Torah reader in our quest to understand the man Moses and his relationship with the women and men who surrounded him.[35] The commentator says that Moses paid absolutely no heed to his sister and brother's criticism in verse 1, but not because of any anger or resentment. To the contrary; Moses' character was so "humble," so disassociated from the affairs of the everyday, so preoccupied with realizing God's mission, that his siblings' comments—if he even heard them—did not ruffle him. It is therefore on account of Moses' humility and quiescence in the face of their criticism that the text explains that God heard their words. Thus, verse 3's explanation of Moses' humble character reflects the biblical defense of God's chosen messenger. The Netziv points out that in order to understand the essense of Moses the redeemer, Moses the lawgiver, and Moses the prophet, the Torah here gives us the distilled essence of Moses the man: his humility, or his nullification of self, even in the face of potentially hurtful criticism by two of his closest confidants. His silence in the face of their words invites the Torah text to explain and defend him. The reader is expected to appreciate the height of Moses' strength of character by the paradoxical illustration of his restraint here. Says the commentator, Moses was at the pinnacle of prophetic ability and closeness to God, a level never before—and never since—reached by any other.

We will see that in upcoming verses (4 through 14) God explicitly comes to Moses' defense in a fierce response to Miriam and Aaron's criticism of Moses in verses 1 and 2. Ramban includes verse 3 (*And the man Moses was very humble . . .*) as an implicit part of God's defense.[36] The commentator explains that specifically because of Moses' humility, knowing that Moses would never respond to any verbal provocation, God responds on Moses' behalf.

The reader might well ask why the text injects the issue of Moses' "humility"at this juncture. Is Moses' exceedingly humble nature emphasized here because it precipitated the necessity for God to rise to Moses' defense? Or was the fact of Moses' humble nature an enabling cause of Miriam and Aaron's criticism of him? Until now, the commentaries have all based their explanations on the supposition that because Moses was too humble to defend himself, God came to his defense. In contrast, Sha'arei Aharon seizes upon the alternative explanation.[37] Miriam and Aaron's criticism of their brother was undertaken because they viewed him as an ordinary humble man, on a par with themselves. Had Miriam and Aaron appreciated that their brother was no ordinary humble man—that he had evolved from the son of a Hebrew slave, to a prince of Egypt, to a fugitive, to a nomadic shepherd, into an exalted man of God—they would never have presumed to chastise him. It is because they viewed Moses in his humble, unheroic presona that Miriam and Aaron were emboldened to speak thus to him. And that, in turn, is the reason God defends him so eloquently in the coming verses.

Sifrei adds an overarching caution. The commentary warns the Torah reader not to bend too far in the opposite direction from Miriam and Aaron. They viewed Moses as their brother and felt on a par with him. The Torah text might even seem to support this, saying that Moses is more humble than any human on the face of the earth.[38] Paradoxically, however, Moses also occupies a higher spiritual plane than they do, and is to be revered as a prophet and teacher without peer. In upcoming verses we will read that God states unequivocally that none can compare with Moses, as only Moses speaks to God in an intimate manner, as if mouth-to-mouth. But while he certainly surpasses his sister and brother in his level of prophecy and influence with God, even so, cautions Sifre, Moses is never to be personally exalted to the angelic or God-like. He remains at all times a mortal man.

The issue of Moses' "humility" has preoccupied the commentaries for centuries. The obvious query is why—of all the heroic and obvious qualities exhibited by Moses—the only one ever highlighted by the Bible is his humility. Yeshayahu Leibowitz, a modern Israeli Torah scholar, addresses this precise question in an essay on the weekly Torah readings as he considers Numbers 12 (the portion of Beha'alotcha).[39] Leibowitz explains that while Moses' humility is his only characteristic to be explicitly described in the Torah text, other qualities are present, but are left for the Torah reader to infer from Moses' behavior. Moses' life fairly begs exegesis and analysis, then, if one follows Leibowitz's thesis.

Focusing on the singular quality of humility, Leibowitz explains that it is—perhaps mirroring Moses himself—deceptively simple and at the same time fathomless in its philosophical complexity. Looked at objectively, it is *un*natural for a great man to be humble; his deeds and status would fly in the face of humility. Still, because true humility can nevertheless exist, there are perhaps three reasons for its existence in the character of a great man: First, if upon self-reflection the person actually sees and appreciates his defects. Second, if the great person can, with much effort, overcome his haughtiness or pride and can legitimately present himself as humble. And third, as Leibowitz applies this notion of humility uniquely to Moses, is the category of one who is *more humble than any human.*

Moses' interaction with God was on a unique level that is recognized both philosophically and religiously. Surely Moses himself appreciated this, so that he was able to uniquely and personally behold God's greatness. We note (in verses to come) that while all other prophets view the presence of God as "through a glass darkly," Moses sees God's presence through a clear glass. How extraordinary! We are told that God spoke to Moses face-to-face. At that level, Moses was distinguished from all past, present and future prophets, says the commentary, because with his clarity of vision he was in a unique position to *know that he did not know.* Moses was aware—more than any other human on the face of the earth—that despite his proximity to God, still *he did not know God.* This quality of *knowing that he truly did not know God* is what the Torah is referring to in Numbers 12:3 when it injects the comment *and the man Moses was very humble, more than any human on the face of the earth.*

It would be a natural reaction for a prophet of Moses' greatness to be the antithesis of "humble." Thus the Torah takes pains to stress Moses' greatness in shorthand by pointing out his self-awareness, his humility, his *in*ablility to know God. It is we, the students of the text, who are humbled in turn. If Moses *knew that he did not know God*, what chance do we have to know the divine? This is a lifelong quest.

If humility is the only express quality in the Torah text describing Moses, a serious reader could well ask if the biblical portrait of Moses is perhaps lacking in depth and perspective? After all, it takes more than humility to guide a people, receive and disseminate a system of laws, and converse with God. The rabbis of the Talmud[40] (in Nedarim 38a) discuss the qualities of character that a person must possess in order for God to entrust him with the gift of prophecy, the *shechina*. Rabbi Yochanan teaches that God will only entrust the divine spirit to a person who possesses the qualities of heroism, wealth, wisdom *and* humility, "all qualities possessed by Moses." From where does the Talmud infer that Moses possessed these essential characteristics? We know that Moses was of a heroic height and build, says the Talmud, because it is written in the Torah that Moses single-handedly spread the tent over the entire Tabernacle, which was 10 cubits high and of great depth. Such an act required a man of great height and strength. It also required heroic strength to lift up the solid blocks of the stone tablets of the ten commandments above his head, and to smash them down with momentum, which Moses did. We learn that he was rich because the Torah states that God granted him the shavings of precious stone which were not used to form the tablets of the law; and we learn that he was humble from our verse in Numbers 12:3. As to Moses' wisdom, the Talmud teaches that God created fifty gates of wisdom in the world, and that Moses attained forty-nine of them, a level never reached by any other prophet. Yeshayahu Leibowitz agrees with the Ra"N, the 14th-century Talmudist, who said that the one level of knowledge that Moses lacked was knowledge of the absolute essence of God.[41]

The Rambam in his Mishneh Torah (Hilchot Ysodei HaTorah 7:1)[42] elevates the Talmud's Mosaic qualities from the purely physical plane to the spiritual. "Heroism and strength," says the Rambam, indicate Moses' strength of character to resist wrong-doing. "Riches" refers to Moses' ability to embrace his destiny. The reason for the Talmud's and the commentaries' dwelling upon all of Moses' actual and implied character traits is to emphasize that the people's liberator, leader and teacher was a man who commanded and merited their respect and awe. No one short of Moses' heroic stature—literally and figuratively—could have guided the Hebrews from slavery to nationhood.

THIRTY-NINE

৪৩৬৪৩৬৪৩

Miriam and Aaron are Chastised

NUMBERS 12:4-5

Suddenly, God spoke to Moses and to Aaron and to Miriam [saying], "Come out, the three of you, [into] the Tent of Meeting ;" and the three of them went out. And God came down in a pillar of cloud to stand at the tent door; and He called out, "Aaron and Miriam!" and the two of them emerged.[1]

In a surprising turn of phrase the Bible states that "suddenly" God interrupted the siblings' conversation. Why did God intercede at this juncture? After Miriam and Aaron's rebuke to their brother regarding his wife, and their comment about their level of prophecy being equal to his, God stepped in. Da'at Zekeinim says that God had overheard their words, and sought immediately to defend Moses on both counts.[2] But importantly, according to the commentary, God steps in almost before the siblings have ceased speaking, so that they will know that God was listening in—and not that Moses in any way complained to God about them.

Interestingly, because Moses was *always* prepared to receive God's prophecy, God's interruption would not have seemed "sudden" to Moses himself. Says Ramban, God routinely appeared "suddenly" to Moses; the text's use of the word "suddenly" here is an indication to the reader that God's voice had never before been heard suddenly by Miriam and Aaron; they were at a lesser level of prophetic preparedness than was Moses.[3] For this reason the

219

Torah says God "suddenly" spoke *to the three of them*. According to the Netziv, the only reason Aaron and Miriam were privileged to hear God's sudden voice in this verse—an occurrence they had never before experienced and, according to Ohr HaChayim,[4] they would never experience again—is due solely to the fact that they were in Moses' proximity.[5]

Miriam and Aaron, accustomed to God appearing to them "as through a glass darkly," were unprepared for God to address them directly. According to Rashi, their unpreparedness stemmed from their having had intimate relations with their respective spouses just hours before their conversation. They were thus ritually "unclean" when they heard God's voice, and, says the commentator, were in a state of shock, fear and confusion, shouting for "water, water!"[6] Rashi is revealing to the reader that Miriam and Aaron were desperate to avail themselves immediately of the purifying waters of a *mikveh*, or ritual bath. They knew that they could not receive God's word in an unclean state, for that would mean courting death. Never before had they heard God's ineffable word in a sudden or surprise manner; they learn in this frenzied moment that Moses is much closer to God than they are. They may all be termed "prophets," but Moses is in a category by himself.

At this time God has summoned Moses, Aaron and Miriam to the Tent of Meeting. Some amount of time has passed, sufficient so that Miriam and Aaron can become ritually pure so that they can receive God's word along with Moses. God proceeds now to address only Aaron and Miriam from the midst of the pillar of cloud, as they stand at the opening of the Tent. According to the Netziv,[7] while God had summoned the three siblings to the exclusive Tent of Meeting, He is presently addressing *only* Aaron and Miriam, and only from the midst of the pillar of cloud, and not face-to-face. The commentator stresses that Aaron and Miriam are to be addressed by God in the manner that befits them as lower prophets than their brother Moses. Alschich explains[8] that God has separated Aaron and Miriam from Moses at this point and addresses them as they stand *outside* the hallowed Tent of Meeting because—as the text will bear out—God is preparing a stern rebuke of them prefatory to meting out punishment.

The rebuke is intended by the Almighty to be for their ears only. God's intent is not to humiliate Miriam and Aaron before their brother, Moses. Yalkut Shimoni[9] explains that Moses is not asked to leave the Tent because God does not wish the people of Israel to suspect even for an instant that Moses has done anything to warrant being ejected from God's presence. God does have a stern agenda for Miriam and Aaron, however, and that is the reason *they* are summoned out of the Tent. Additionally, the *midrash* stresses that Moses, in his humility, is concerned lest God agree with the criticisms leveled against him by his siblings. Allowing Moses to remain within the Tent while they are commanded to exit its holy proximity serves to assure Moses that God has sanctioned his actions. It also solidifies Moses' position in the eyes of the entire nation. The commentator continues[10] that Moses' presence in the Tent of Meeting has the advantage of putting him out of earshot of God's words to his brother and sister. God does not wish Moses to hear His laudatory praise of him and to suffer embarrassment.

FORTY

ಬಂಙಬಂಙ

GOD IDENTIFIES MOSES
AS *HIS* PROPHET

NUMBERS 12:6-9

*And [God] said, Heed my words; if [among you] is a prophet
of the Lord, I would make myself known to him in a vision; I
would speak to him in a dream. This is not so with my
servant Moses; in all my house he is [most] faithful. Mouth-
to-mouth do I speak with him so I am manifest, and not
through enigmatic speeches; he beholds the semblance of
God; How could you not fear to speak against my servant,
against Moses?! And God was wroth with anger at them,
and He departed.*[1]

We can imagine the scene. God is addressing Miriam and Aaron
from the midst of the cloud as they stand outside the Tent of
Meeting. The speech—in point of fact the dressing down—that
God is about to impart will be the divine response to Aaron and
Miriam's rebuke of Moses in verses 1 and 2. Biblical readers hold
their breath as God launches into the famed explanation of the stark
differences between Moses' prophetic abilities and those of all other
prophets. This book will not embark on a lengthy philosophical
explanation of "prophecy." We will, however, bring to bear the

explanations of the Talmud, Rambam and several select commentaries who address these verses and help illustrate Moses' greatness as the prototypical man of God.

The Talmud[2] (Yevamot 49b), in discussing when a prophet can be said to "behold God," makes its notable statement that all prophets experience or "see" the divine "as through an unilluminated glass." This is to be contrasted with Moses, who views God clearly, as through an illuminated glass. The talmudic term for "glass" is of Greek derivation: *aspakloriya*. Any discussion, then, of divinely-inspired prophecy, will at the very least touch upon the meaning of the word *aspakloriya*.

A fascinating *midrashic* discussion ensues throughout the generations as the commentaries vie to define and differentiate *aspakloriya she-lo me'ira*—the unilluminated glass through which ordinary prophets experience God—and *aspakloriya me'ira*—the illuminated glass—through which only Moses beholds God. For our purposes, an important difference between them is that the *aspakloriya* of all other prophets in some way distorts the divine image or presents a barrier between the prophet and the divine. In contrast, Moses' *aspakloriya* is unique, presenting Moses with a clear, undistorted vision of the divine.

Vayikra Rabba (1:14)[3] presents examples of these rabbinic attempts to illustrate the differences between the two types of *aspakloriya*. One such example describes that the *aspakloriya* experience of all other prophets is akin to looking at an object through a lineup of nine lenses; the image that one can see in this manner is quite distorted. In contrast, Moses' *aspakloriya* allows him to see the divine through one clear lens. The *midrash* also suggests that other prophets' *aspakloriya* is a dusty or soiled glass, while Moses' *aspakloriya* is crystal-clear.

Sha'arei Aharon[4] suggests that the prophets' *aspakloriya* is a mirror rather than a pane of glass, so that it reflects back to the prophet some likeness of himself rather than of the divine. This mirror experience allows the other prophets to view only a limited, mirror-image reflection rather than reality, and of course they are prevented from beholding that which is behind the mirror. The *aspakloriya* examples presented by the commentaries emphasize that the prophecies of all the prophets with the exception of Moses are, to some degree, defined by the distortions and limitations of their visions. Other prophets' expressions of God's word are by definition limited, as the prophets never beheld God's word directly. Their prophecies are dilutions or interpretations, sometimes even distortions of the divine message, since their *aspakloriya* was the barrier to their appreciation of God. Moses' *aspakloriya*, on the other hand, was clear, and his path to prophecy unhindered by mirrors or lenses. Moses spoke to God face-to-face.

It is in this fascinating context that the Rambam[5] (Sefer HaMada, Hilchot Yesodei HaTorah ch. 7), in explaining prophecy, begins with the precept that it is of course the Almighty who invests mankind with the gift of prophecy. He then continues by discussing the nature of the prophet himself rather than by dissecting the term *aspakloriya*. Rambam explains that while all prophets possess certain common personality characteristics including wisdom, breadth of understanding and physical and moral strength, Moses is in a prophetic category all his own. Moses, the master of all prophets past, present and future, is set apart from other prophets because his thoughts must be open to God's word *at all times*. Also, he is permitted to open a dialogue with the Almighty at whatever moment he so desires. And it is for this latter reason that Moses continued to refrain from all marital intimacy at the time of the Revelation at Sinai even *after* the rest of Israel—including the other prophets such as Miriam and Aaron—were permitted to resume marital relations. Says Rambam, Moses understood that he needed to keep himself at attention, so-to-speak, standing before God like no other mortal man past, present or future, as if he were a ministering angel.

Rambam continues that while all other prophets may experience God in a dream, or through indistinct images during a "vision," Moses is awake and standing upright, conversing with God mouth-to-mouth, as directly as one speaks to a friend. This radical differentiation between Moses and all other prophets—dramatized by Moses' refraining from marital intimacy while his siblings do not—allows God's glory to reside within him and emanate from him at all times, for all the days of his life. According to Alschich,[6] this uniqueness illucidates Moses' greatness.

> This is not so with my servant Moses; in all my house he is
> [most] faithful. (Numbers 12:7)

The S'fat Emet[7] strives to explain that in this verse God is stressing for Miriam and Aaron that, in effect, Moses dwells within His house, while Miriam and Aaron, however valued, are forever at the threshold. The commentary teaches us a stark lesson: Miriam and Aaron are ordinary people elevated to prophecy from time to time as God sees fit. Contrast this with Moses, who at his intrinsic essence is *at all times* God's prophet, and who can *initiate* dialogue with the Almighty as well as *receive* His word. This is the reason, says the commentary, that Miriam and Aaron are at ease with their Israelite brethren, and are able to communicate with them harmoniously. In contrast, Moses is at all times a man of God, and in order to communicate with the people he assumes a different persona. All ordinary prophets must elevate themselves spiritually— even physically purify themselves—in order to prepare themselves to accept God's prophecy. Moses stands out in perfect contrast, as he is always God's vehicle, and in order to interact with the *non-*divine he must withdraw from God's presence; even, according to the *midrash,* to don a veil to speak with the people. For this reason God here refers to Moses as "my most faithful servant;" of all the prophets, only Moses is always in readiness to do God's bidding.

> **Mouth-to-mouth** *do I speak with him so I am manifest, and not through enigmatic speeches; he beholds the semblance of God . . .* (Numbers 12:8)

God continues to exalt Moses as He addresses Aaron and Miriam, uttering the immortal statement that He speaks with Moses "mouth-to-mouth." Alschich asks, Should not the text rather have said *mouth-to-**ear** do I speak with him*? How could God's words be transmitted mouth-to-**mouth**?[8] His response is that God's words exited the divine mouth, so-to-speak, and entered directly into Moses' mouth. God so trusted his servant Moses not to alter His law in any way that in speaking with Moses God's "mouth" and Moses' "mouth" were one. God's law thereby came down to the people intact. Adds Ibn Ezra, *mouth-to-mouth* means that God spoke directly to Moses, without an intermediary medium.[9] God's words, no sooner spoken, became clear images in Moses' mind, and thereby could be communicated to the people directly from

Moses' own mouth. Sforno[10] offers his explanation of the meaning of the "mouth-to-mouth" communication between God and Moses, saying that unique among the prophets, Moses' senses remained sharp as he heard God's words. Moses did not fall into a deep sleep or slip into a trance before God transmitted His words to his mind and mouth; Moses was awake and alert. God spoke with Moses one-on-one.

> . . . How could you not fear to speak against my servant, against Moses?! And God was wroth with anger at them, and He departed. (Numbers 12:8-9)

The first half of verse 8, as we discussed above, contains God's unparalleled description of Moses as his most trusted servant, distinguishing Moses from all other prophets, including his own brother and sister. The second half of verse 8 and verse 9 as well, translated here, jump to God's chastisement of Miriam and Aaron for speaking ill of Moses. God has just explained to them that of all the prophets in the world, past and future, *only* Moses is so trusted that God speaks to him mouth-to-mouth, or in God's words, *peh-el-peh*. He is angry that they would implicitly challenge His judgement by rebuking Moses.

The question that arises for Rashi is, what, specifically, angered God about what Miriam and Aaron had said? Rashi's answer harks back to the troublesome topic of Moses' separation from his wife, Zipporah, and Miriam and Aaron's *midrashic* discussion of Moses' unnecessary marital austerity. Their complaint was that Moses should *not* have held himself above them; that *they* returned to their familial obligations and intimacies after the revelation at Sinai, and so should Moses have done.[†] Here, Rashi explains, at the very phrase that distinguishes Moses forever from all ordinary prophets—*peh-el-peh*—God turns Miriam and Aaron's words back at them, and rebukes them, saying, "*I* told him to separate from his wife!"[11] The implication is, "Would you also challenge *me*?"

[†]Readers are invited to refer back to chapter 37, where we discuss at length Moses' unique relationship with God and the lifelong austerity that it engendered.

Sforno adds to our understanding of the scene.[12]   He relates an elaborate *midrash* where God in His anger takes Miriam and Aaron to task. "How could you both not have trusted my knowledge and understanding of Moses' heart and mind?   Were you both so mean-spirited that you presumed to know that Moses overstepped his bounds while I remained unaware of this?   Did you imagine that I would have chosen as my most trusted prophet a man who was arrogant and held himself above you?   My knowledge is perfect! And you have no true understanding of Moses.   You should have been fearful of speaking so against him!"

God's anger at Miriam and Aaron derives from their criticism of Moses' having assumed marital celibacy beyond the general three-day prohibition at Mount Sinai.   They are personally insulted that Moses—in their eyes—held himself to a higher prophetic standard than they did.   Faced now with God's rebuke, Miriam and Aaron are stunned into silence.   God chastised them from the midst of the cloud, confronting them with their offence, according to Rashi.[13]   Bechor Schor explains that it was actually their silence that kindled God's anger,[14] leading to their punishment.   Sforno suggests[15] that if they had offered some credible justification for judging Moses harshly, or demonstrated some contrition, perhaps God might not have departed from their midst and meted out punishment.

The Talmud (Shabbat 97a)[16] presents a fascinating debate between Rabbi Akiva and Rabbi Yehuda on the nature of the punishment.   Rabbi Akiva, picking up on the plural wording of verse 9—*And God was wroth with anger **at them***[17]—teaches that the indisputable inference from the text is that Aaron *and* Miriam *both* suffer a similar physical punishment; that they are *both* stricken with *tzora'at*, or leprosy.   On the other hand, Rabbi Yehuda's opinion is that Aaron *escaped* physical punishment, but still suffered God's rebuke.

The Sifrei Zutra, in its commentary on the verse, sides unequivocally with Rabbi Akiva, saying that the reason the verse specifies that God's anger was directed at *them* is that *both* Aaron and Miriam are culpable in God's eyes.[18]   The commentary does ask, however, if both are culpable, why, then, does the upcoming verse specify explicitly that Miriam was punished, while it only hints at Aaron's punishment?   Its response is that Numbers 12:1 opens with Miriam initiating the conversation, and for that reason her punishment is explicit. Still, says the Sifrei, it stands to reason that because both Aaron and Miriam spoke, both were stricken. The commentary offers an additional insight into Miriam and Aaron's offense. Their primary sin was not that they spoke against their brother Moses; their sin was their failure to comprehend that Moses was a prophet without peer. Their complaint in 12:2 that they are on the same prophetic plane as Moses sealed their punishment in God's eyes.

After God's anger has been vented upon Miriam and Aaron, the text tells us at the end of verse 9 *and He departed.* Sa'adia Gaon explains the *p'shat,* or simple meaning of the Torah's words, to mean precisely what the reader would think: When He ceased to chastise them his *shechina*—or holy presence—departed.[19]

Torah Temima goes so far as to explain that the Bible text states that *God was wroth with anger* **at them** as a hint to us that both Miriam and Aaron will feel God's anger as well as His punishment.[20] The anger is described here in verse 12:9; the upcoming text will describe the swiftness of God's punishment. With the aid of the Talmud and the commentaries the reader is now poised to witness both an explicit as well as a more subtle expression of God's wrath, and the heartbreaking human drama surrounding Miriam, Aaron and Moses.

PART VII

MIRIAM'S CODA: TRIAL AND REDEMPTION

ഌൠഌൠ

FORTY-ONE

৪০৫৪৩৪০৫৪৩

The Punishment of Leprosy

NUMBERS 12:10

And the cloud lifted from atop the tent, and behold! Miriam is leprous, as white as the snow; and Aaron turned toward Miriam, and behold, she was leprous.[1]

T his verse describes the sudden and devastating punishment that God inflicted upon Moses' siblings. According to the *p'shat* or simple reading of the text, after God's chastisement of Miriam and Aaron, His presence—clad in the pillar of cloud—departs from the Tent of Meeting. It was a fact of life for the wandering Israelites that the pillar of cloud signaled to them when to cease wandering and encamp, and also when to break camp and resume their march. According to the Malbim,[2] when this verse tells us that *the cloud lifted from atop the tent*, we must appreciate that this was the signal to the Israelites that it was time to move on from Hatzerot where they had encamped. The tribal buglers had already sounded the call to the people—some 600,000 in number—to pack up their gear, their tents and their cattle, and to prepare to break camp. It is in the midst of this tumult of motion and determined activity that Miriam is stricken with *tzora'at*, with leprosy. According to the Netziv,[3] at the moment she is aware of her punishment Miriam is struck speechless and motionless with terror,

231

watching her skin as it is transformed from healthy to corroded in an instant.

From the *p'shat* it appears that only Miriam—and not Aaron—was stricken with leprosy. But the Talmud as well as numerous commentaries do not allow the *p'shat* to rest. As we discussed in the prior chapter, the text is clear that God was angered at *both* Miriam and Aaron (the Bible uses the plural pronoun: *God was wroth with anger at them*[4]) for their disturbing conversation about Moses, and that *both* suffered punishment.

According to the Talmud's Rabbi Akiva (Shabbat 97a),[5] this plural pronoun indicates that Aaron *also* became leprous! Rabbi Yehuda is aghast at Rabbi Akiva's interpretation. He cautions Akiva, "If you are correct, you have disclosed something that the Torah has deliberately concealed: that Aaron, the high priest of Israel, suffered the arch-punishment of *tzora'at*. How could you dare disclose it in the Talmud? And further, if you are wrong, then your statement that Aaron, too, became leprous, is slanderous."

Rabbi Yehuda's concern is legitimate, because according to Sifrei Zuta a priest of Israel with such a leprous blemish would be barred from performing the holy sacrifices.[6] Thus, if Aaron had suffered the punishment of leprosy the consequences would have been severe, indeed: not only to suffer the agony of leprosy, but also the prohibition from performing his priestly rites. Can we believe, then, with Rabbi Akiva, Rashi and others, that Aaron was leprous, too? Perhaps the better question is, can we believe that he was *not*?

Torah Temima is certain that Aaron was punished with leprosy along with Miriam.[7] The commentary derives this from the phrase in this verse *and Aaron turned toward Miriam*. Says the commentary, the Hebrew word for "turned *toward*"—PaNaH—implies that he turned *away* from something. In this context Aaron "turned away" from his own leprous affliction, and beheld that Miriam was in a leprous state. Sha'arei Aharon steers a middle course.[8] The commentary stresses that while Aaron was also deserving of the severe punishment of *tzora'at*, given his exalted position as high priest of the Israelites, he was spared in order that he be able to function as priest and healer.

Rashi in this portion of Talmud agrees implicitly with Rabbi Akiva, saying that the verse has Aaron turning *toward Miriam* for the simple reason that his *tzora'at* was cured before hers![9] And Ohr HaChayim adds that no one in all of Israel knew that Aaron was stricken, as his *tzora'at* was short-lived in the extreme. He was leprous and healed almost instantaneously, while Miriam remained leprous for all to see.[10]

Alschich remains rooted in the *p'shat*, however, stating that Miriam alone was stricken with *tzora'at*.[11] According to the commentary the prime reason that she—and not Aaron—bore this physical punishment, is that the Torah text states that she spoke first; true, her intention was honorable, as she was troubled by her sister-in-law's predicament, but in God's eyes her speech doomed her.

FORTY-TWO

Aaron Pleads for Miriam

NUMBERS 12:11-12

And Aaron said to Moses, "Pray, sir, do not hold us culpable for a sin which we have foolishly committed, and which we have transgressed. Do not commit her to a [living] death, so that she should be like a stillborn whose skin is half wasted!"[1]

The affliction of *tzora'at* is loosely interpreted as leprosy, but in biblical terms is so much more. It is not the "leprosy" known to modern physicians, but in the case of Miriam, was a spontaneous "living death," recognized by all as divine punishment for having transgressed the divine will. We derive from the *p'shat* that Aaron almost instantly realized her plight and its cause, and immediately appealed to Moses to pray to God on her behalf.

The reader is extremely troubled by the events presented thus far in Number 12:1-12. Miriam and Aaron have had a conversation concerning their brother Moses that, from the standpoint of the *p'shat*, and regardless of their benign or justified motivation, belittled the level of Moses' prophetic ability while aggrandizing their own. God has taken offence on behalf of His servant Moses, has chastized both Miriam and Aaron, and has stricken Miriam with leprosy. In these present verses Aaron is begging intercession from Moses.

234

Aaron's plea to his brother Moses is telling. A first question that arises is why Aaron bids Moses to pray on Miriam's behalf; why does *Aaron* not appeal to God directly?

Alschich asks the reader to focus on the *p'shat* of Aaron's plea.[2] Aaron begins with the words *Bi, Adoni.* The commentator explains that the words do not only mean "Please, sir;" they also mean "it is **within me**, my master." The *p'shat* reading, then, according to Alschich, could be that Aaron is eloquently, albeit laconically, confessing *and* pleading to Moses. Read in this light, Aaron's plea to Moses can be interpreted as, "The transgression is *my* fault as well as hers, my master." Aaron keenly feels as responsible as Miriam for the sin for which God is meting out the punishment of *tzora'at.* Thus, he does not feel worthy to plead directly to God on her behalf. This makes sense in light of the rest of his words, where he uses the *plural* pronoun *we.* Aaron includes himself in Miriam's blameworthiness. And it would be unseemly for Aaron to act as the primary advocate for his sister when he himself is likewise implicated in the identical sin.[3]

Perhaps Aaron approaches Moses in a servile fashion here for the reason that he also has just endured God's chastisement, and he assumes that Moses, as well as God, was offended by his conversation with Miriam. The fact of the matter, according to Ohr HaChayim,[4] is that Moses was *not* personally offended by his siblings' words. We must recall that only several verses ago (Numbers 12:3) the Bible referred to Moses as the most humble man on the face of the earth. His humility is proven in his failure to take offence here. Still, says the commentary, regardless of his personal humility, Moses, as the leader of the Israelites, is akin to a king, and a king's honor must be upheld. The conversation that Miriam initiated with Aaron dishonored Moses; that is the reason God punishes her. This is why Aaron is here appealing to Moses, presuming that only Moses' words of forgiveness could cure Miriam's *tzora'at.*

Torat HaChidah[5] explains that Aaron's plea to Moses on behalf of his stricken sister goes beyond his feelings of guilt. In fact, Aaron is also ashamed. God's admonishment impressed upon him that his and Miriam's sin slandered Moses when they compared their level of prophetic ability to his. Therefore, Aaron reasons that his appeal must be *to Moses*—to him who was sinned *against*—

thinking that Moses alone can sway the Almighty to reverse His punishment. For this reason Aaron does not approach his younger brother in a fraternal manner, as perhaps was his wont. Rather, as Aaron perceives that he has slandered a man whose prophetic greatness is unsurpassed, he must now approach a Moses who is his superior or master. Hence the introduction *Bi Adoni*, or *Please, my lord.*

The Netziv explains[6] that Aaron is appealing to Moses because he, Aaron, is powerless to help dispel Miriam's leprosy. In order to appreciate Aaron's helplessness, notwithstanding his role as high priest, the commentator explains the types of biblical leprosy, and the practical and communal consequences for Aaron, Miriam, and all of the Israelites.

There are two overarching categories of *tzora'at*, or biblical leprosy. The first category is a spontaneous appearance of a type of affliction that arises instantaneously on a person's skin as a punishment for having spoken *lashon ha-ra* about another. *Lashon ha-ra* is defined as tale-bearing (its literal translation is "the evil tongue"). A person is guilty of speaking *lashon ha-ra* when the tale he has borne is *true.* This form of *tzora'at* is evanescent and disappears as instantaneously as it appears. It might even be considered a brief but dire warning to the tale-bearer.

The second type of *tzora'at* is also an instantaneous appearance of a corrosive skin affliction, but it is distinguished from the first type described here by its duration—it can last a very long time, even forever; it requires a priest, or *kohen*, to diagnose it, pronounce it and absolve the victim; and it is visited upon a person as a punishment for having spoken *falsely* about another. This more serious type of tale-bearing is known as *motzi-shem-ra* (literally, "one who exposes another to a bad name").

The signal and devastating difference between the punishment of *tzora'at* for the sin of *motzi-shem-ra* over that of *lashon ha-ra* is that in the case of *motzi-shem-ra* the leprous person remains so in a visible and public fashion, suffering the double humiliation of having his or her skin stricken and visibly decaying, *as well as* the stigma of public banishment. The Torah's rubric governing *tzora'at* is strict: when a person has told a falsehood about another—that is, has spoken *motzi-shem-ra*—and as a consequence is stricken with *tzora'at*, the leprous one is required to remain alone and estranged from the community until the leprosy is pronounced cured. The leprous tale-bearer, who has spoken slanderously about another, must now suffer, paradoxically, both a public *and* a solitary punishment. Further, there is no interpersonal absolution possible in the case of *motzi-shem-ra*; the slandered person cannot effect a cure by forgiving the tale-bearer. This harsher level of punishment is divinely visited. The reader can therefore appreciate that a close examination of the words **tzora'at** and **motzi**-*shem-ra* will reveal the commonality of the terms. *Motzi-shem-***ra** contains *within it* the term *tzora'at!* The sin virtually dictates the consequence.

Within the Netziv's instructive framework, then, we can now view Miriam's punishment and Aaron's plea to Moses. The slanderous statement that has caused this instantaneous, cascading tragedy was uttered by both Aaron and Miriam in Numbers 12:2: *And they said, 'Is it only through Moses that God speaks? For He also speaks through us!'* According to the commentator, Aaron is appealing to Moses here, nine verses later, in the hope that the offending statement can be construed as the less-serious *lashon ha-ra.*[†]

In approaching Moses in a respectful, supplicating manner (*Bi, adoni*), the Netziv believes that Aaron is making his case that his

---

[†]The Netziv and Rashi point out that earlier in the Bible the text describes an incident where Moses, too, experienced *tzora'at* or leprosy. At Exodus 4:2, a reluctant Moses is in conversation with the Almighty at the burning bush. Moses bemoans aloud to God that the Hebrew slaves in Egypt will not believe him, nor will they heed his voice speaking to them of impending redemption; that they will surely doubt that God had shown Himself to him. God demonstrates His greatness as well as His displeasure to Moses when He tells Moses to place his hand within his tunic. When Moses withdraws his erstwhile healthy hand, behold! it is leprous, as white as snow (Ex. 4:6). The commentators explain that Moses suffered the punishment for *lashon ha-ra* for slandering the Children of Israel before God. The Netziv even relates that Moses' leprous hand was extremely painful. Therefore, in our chapter, not only is Miriam stricken head-to-toe with leprosy, but we have also seen that the Talmud and midrash have proposed that Aaron, too, suffered an instantaneous form of the disease. The lesson to be drawn is that no one is immune from the prohibition against tale-bearing and its dreaded punishment. To be sure, Aaron understands this, and is begging for intercession for Miriam from Moses, who himself had a fleeting taste of the pain and fear she must be experiencing.

and his sister's offending statement, while false, was merely thoughtless and foolish rather than malicious and deliberate. Aaron and Miriam, in all good faith, thought that what they said was the truth. Aaron is thus desperate on his sister's behalf to stave off the harsher, humiliating and terrifying punishment that accompanies *motzi-shem-ra*. In effect, he is attempting—unsuccessfully, as it happens—to fashion a third category of *tzora'at*: a middle-level of punishment for a slanderous falsehood mitigated by the fact that it is spoken out of thoughtlessness.

But Miriam is in a more serious predicament even than being guilty of *motzi-shem-ra* would ordinarily dictate. The one person who could pronounce her stricken and ultimately free of *tzora'at* is Aaron, the high priest. But because of his close filial relationship to her, he is legally barred from ruling on the state of Miriam's contamination. According to the commentator, this could condemn Miriam to a miserable life of limbo: existing forever under the pall of the dreaded *tzora'at* outside the Israelite encampment even after her affliction has disappeared.

In verse 12 Aaron appeals blatantly to the filial imperative of keeping their beloved sister from the fate of a stillborn which emerges from its mother's womb with withered and corroded flesh. This visceral image is certainly not lost on Moses, who owes his very life to his sister Miriam, the woman who is also credited with serving as midwife to many thousands of Hebrew newborns during the darkest days of slavery under Pharaoh. For all these reasons Aaron is desperate to heal her.

Is there no one who can relieve Miriam of her *tzora'at* and pronounce her fit to rejoin the Israelite camp? The Talmud[7] (Zevachim 101b) discusses Miriam's impossible predicament. While God has stricken her skin with leprosy, Miriam cannot begin to be healed until, as we have learned, the rubric of biblical *tzora'at* is called into play. Step one is a formal pronouncement by a priest of the stricken person's leprous state; the second stage is banishment of the leprous person from the camp; and the third and final stage is the eventual declaration by the priest that the leprous person is free of all disease, and thereby entitled to rejoin the community.

Miriam's predicament is exacerbated because there is no priest among the Israelites to begin the three-stage process. Moses is a Levite but is not a priest, and Aaron is ineligible to issue the ritual pronouncements because he is her brother. Truly, explains the Talmud, Miriam could have been trapped in this living purgatory for the rest of her days! Amazingly, it is God Himself who resolves Miriam's terrible stalemate and accords the prophetess Miriam a great honor by coming to her aid. According to the Talmud, the Almighty intervened at the moment of her great despair and pronounced, "I am like a priest, so *I* hereby pronounce Miriam leprous; *I* hereby banish her; and *I also* will declare her free of the *tzora'at* and thus fit to re-enter the Israelite community."

So traumatic both to Miriam and to the Israelite psyche is the divine visitation of leprosy upon Miriam in this verse, that later on in the last book of the Bible, Moses cautions the Israelites in notably stern language to hew carefully and precisely to the rules governing *tzora'at*:

> Take special heed in the plague of tzora'at, to diligently observe and perform all that the priests and Levites will teach you; just as I commanded them, so shall you observe and do. Remember what the Lord your God did to Miriam, along the way following the exodus from Egypt! (Deuteronomy 24:8-9)[8]

The commentaries interpret these two verses in Deuteronomy both as a warning to the Israelites against tale-bearing as well as a tribute to Miriam (their *midrashic* elaboration on the *p'shat*). According to Sha'arei Aharon,[9] the verses imply that even Miriam—prophetess and sister of Moses, likened to the "king" of the Israelites, and Aaron, their high priest—is not exempt from the strict prohibition against tale-bearing and its draconian punishment of utter isolation and banishment. Ramban[10] explains that we must bear in mind that Miriam's ill-fated words were not spoken to Moses' face in anger; nor were they spoken about him in public so as to cause him embarrassment. Rather, she spoke in a whisper and for Aaron's ears only, out of love for her brother Moses coupled with sincere sisterly concern that Moses should reunite with Zipporah, alleviating his wife's loneliness and averting future barrenness. Miriam's words even elevated the status of God's prophets, pointing out that they are permitted—even encouraged—not only to receive God's word, but also to live full family lives.

Even so, notwithstanding the righteous life she led, or a lineage as exalted as Miriam's, or her words privately spoken, or her nearly pure motivation; even though Moses took no offense at her words, spoken as they were by the sister who raised him and saved him from death on the Nile river (Rambam's Mishneh Torah, Taharah: Laws of Impurity and *Tzora'at*, ch. 17, para. 10),[11] the commentators emphasize that *still*, Miriam must suffer the extreme punishment and follow the humiliating biblical rubric of *tzora'at*. The lesson Moses is teaching the Israelites is that they must take serious heed from what the Lord God did to Miriam, and must refrain from tale-bearing. For there is no exit from the inexorable punishment that the people will suffer otherwise. They can expect no leniency for their behavior if even Miriam was accorded none.

Ramban[12] considers the command in Deuteronomy 24:9 (*Remember what the Lord your God did to Miriam . . .*) to be one of the positive commandments, for the dual purpose of exhortation to proper behavior, and, adds Rashbam,[13] in order to accord Miriam the importance she deserves. The commentator reminds us that the Israelite encampment tarried at its stopping place for a period of seven days—the period of time that a leprous Miriam was in an enforced cloister outside the camp—until she was cured of her *tzora'at* and re-admitted into the fold. This was not a trivial honor that the Israelites paid their beloved leader. According to Sifrei,[14] this voluntary waiting period actually delayed the Israelites' redemption for a full week! The tribal standards were at-the-ready, flying at the heads of the twelve stationary encampments. Nevertheless, the people put off their march until the full complement of *three* leaders—Moses, Aaron *and Miriam*—took their rightful places at the front of the column.

We can liken this waiting period to a collective holding of the Israelites' breath, as they watched anxiously and from a distance for Miriam's affliction to pass. She was exalted, yet always remained one of them. As such, the people never forgot the brave duality that Miriam embodied: she birthed their babies yet prophesied from God. She stood her ground in the face of the Pharaoh yet danced among the people communing in their ecstasy at the miracle of the Red Sea. And of course, while it was God who daily fed the Israelites *mannah* from heaven, the people credited Miriam with the life-sustaining water that they found in the wilderness. The *midrash* and commentaries (Sha'arei Aharon)[15] point out that during Miriam's seven days of banishment the people recalled that it was Miriam's Well that magically traveled with them from one desert encampment to the other. The people adored Miriam, and it was a strong object lesson for them to witness her suffering with *tzora'at* for her whispered confidences with her brother Aaron. And as a visible measure of her greatness the Cloud of Glory continued to hover over the camp (Sha'arei Aharon),[16] a signal that even God sanctioned awaiting Miriam's return. Moses' lesson to the Children of Israel was thus crystal clear: no one—neither Miriam, nor, as the commentaries point out, even Moses and Aaron—is above the law.

The Netziv[17] explains that Aaron's attempt to lessen his sister's punishment for the reason that their words were uttered foolishly and in error *but without malice*, was doomed to failure. God rejected Aaron's plea to Moses and sentenced Miriam to the strictest consequence for speaking falsely about Moses' level of prophecy. According to the commentary, God refused to accept any extenuating circumstances attendant to speaking falsely about His servant Moses. Miriam's sin was between her and her fellow man, and as such was beyond even God's ability to forgive. She was required to bear the harsher punishment of *tzora'at* and banishment.

Do not commit her to a [living] death, so that she should be like a stillborn whose skin is half wasted!" (Numbers 12:12)

Aaron's second salvo in appealing to Moses for relief for Miriam is to appeal to Moses' emotional attachment to the sister who saved and raised him. Aaron, in his fear for his sister, exclaims to Moses, "Please do not condemn our sister to a twilight life with decayed and rotting skin! This would be like a living death for her!" Rashbam[18] explains that Aaron is appealing to Moses *sub silencio* to imagine himself in Miriam's place. This is not so far off the mark, as Moses, who owes his very life to Miriam, can well imagine that a part of himself will die off with her as she wastes away.

Pirkei d'Rabi Eliezer[19] envisions the scene graphically. Aaron has drawn near to Moses, who is, at his core, a brother to him and to Miriam. Once within Moses' personal space Aaron appeals to his brother saying, "My Lord, certainly you agree that siblings must remain close to one another while there is still breath in our bodies. As long as our sister still breathes, how can we allow her to be banished from among us as if she were already among the dead?" The commentary continues that Moses was moved by Aaron's words, and, won over, he uttered his immortal prayer to God on Miriam's behalf.

In addition to asking Moses to imagine himself suffering the leprosy along with his sister, Abarbanel[20] adds that Aaron appealed to Moses to pray for Miriam. "We need your prayers!" says Aaron. Following Aaron's two-pronged appeal we are told that Moses, hearing Aaron's words *and witnessing Miriam's leprosy consume her flesh*, quickly interceded with God and uttered his famed prayer on her behalf.

The next verse presents Moses' eloquent response to Aaron's heartfelt plea for Miriam.

FORTY-THREE

ഇഃരൃഃരൃ

Moses Prays for Miriam

NUMBERS 12:13

And Moses cried out to God saying, 'Lord, I beseech you! Please heal her!'[1]

Moses' prayer to God on behalf of his stricken sister is a scant five words long. It is uttered as the three siblings stand outside of the Tent of Meeting, set apart from the encamped Israelites. The three are enacting a private, tragic tableau of words misspoken, divine anger and punishment, and agonized regret. Moses' prayer is uttered spontanously, as Moses watches his sister's skin begin to turn white and leprous, and as their brother Aaron, in anguished terror, begs Moses' intercession.

The first word of the verse indicates Moses' state of mind at that instant: the word is *VaYiTZ'aK*, meaning *He [Moses] cried out*, and according to Ibn Ezra[2] signifies Moses' torment on his sister's behalf. Moses is desperate to help her, to arrest the progression of the wasting skin disease. Ohr HaChayim[3] focuses on the first word of Moses' prayer, the word *EL*, one of the innumerable names of God. This particular name incorporates the quality of mercy, and is Moses' intuitive entree to his appeal. Rabbeinu Bachya[4] adds that the name *EL* embodies the qualities of justice *and* lenient compassion. Moses, accustomed to entreating

God, has begun his prayer with the name of God that hints at Moses' ultimate request: mercy for Miriam.

The commentator points out that this verse, in introducing Moses' prayer, narrates that Moses cried out to God *saying* . . . . This last word seems redundant. In a powerful interpretation the commentator explains that the text's use of the word "saying" indicates that Moses' prayer was an articulated one, not a silent plea.[5] By giving sound to his words Moses could infuse his prayer with strong emotion that perhaps would have been absent or softened had he only *thought* his prayer. This verbalization of his plea literally breathed life into his words, in effect increasing their power. Each letter of each word of Moses' prayer held sway with God, more so for having been uttered into reality, literally trembling in the air, given force by the breath of Moses' anguished soul. It is these articulated words of prayer that will rise of their own volition to God's ear.

Abarbanel[6] deconstructs Moses' prayer to its essential components and emphasizes that it is a mere *eleven letters* long! The commentator states that it is difficult to conceive of a briefer prayer. Its almost cryptic format is a strong indication that Moses was on such intimate terms with the Almighty that his most fervent prayer need only have consisted of the barest elements of entreaty; God would intuit the rest. Their relationship allowed Moses to pray to God almost in abbreviated code, confident that God would appreciate his request without extra verbiage.

In this vein, it is interesting to note that nowhere in his prayer does Moses state Miriam's name. It is a mark of the intimacy and immediacy of the action that Moses needed only to refer to "her" in order to enlist God's attention. Moses was confident that God would know to whom he was referring. The Talmud[7] (Brachot 34a) points specifically to this prayer for the proposition that it is *not required*, when praying for compassion for another, to speak that person's name aloud. After all, Moses did not speak Miriam's name.

The second word of Moses' prayer, *Na*, or *please*, is also repeated as the fourth word of his five-word petition. Chizkuni[8] explains that the first time he speaks the word *Na* Moses uses it as a word of supplication; the second time he uses it he is pleading for immediacy. Sforno[9] agrees that the essence of Moses' plea was that God heal her speedily. He did not want his sister to suffer either the physical pain of leprosy or the humiliation of banishment for any longer than the time it took for his words to reach God's ears.

In fact, according to Sha'arei Aharon[10] the sooner Moses completed his prayer, the faster God could grant his plea and heal her. In this situation, implies the commentator, the brevity of Moses' prayer was essential to its effectiveness, for with every moment of delay Miriam suffered as her skin decayed. Rashi[11] also touches on the brevity of Moses' prayer saying that had Moses gone on at length in a prayer to the Almighty on behalf of Miriam perhaps the Israelites—who loved and revered her—might have complained, "Your sister is in dire pain! Why, then, do you go on in a protracted manner?" Alternatively, a brief prayer on her behalf might have prompted the people to say, as is suggested in the Talmud[12] (Brachot 34a), "Yet you prayed on *our* behalf for forty days and forty nights after the sin of the Golden Calf!"

Alschich[13] acknowledges that Moses is poised on the horns of a dilemma. The commentator explains that Moses solved it by keeping his prayer brief in the extreme, as befitted the dire circumstances, yet praying aloud and in anguish within the hearing of all the Israelites, so that they could witness that the prayer's brevity in no way relegated the subject of the prayer to secondary status. On the contrary; Moses' unusual agonized outcry to God was a proxy for a lengthy prayer, which would have been inappropriate with his sister standing by in pain.

Moses' prayer was granted by God at the moment his words were uttered. Pirkei d'Rabi Eliezer[14] states that God allowed Himself to be entreated by Moses' prayer, granting him the urgent relief he sought for his sister.

According to the Malbim[15] (Deut. 24:9), Miriam's public humiliation and banishment for seven days formed the crux of her punishment. Her exile was an object lesson that taught her as well as the Israelites to take special care when speaking about another. The commentator states plainly that Miriam did not go into exile as a leper. Rather, once Moses witnessed the sickening speed with which his sister's leprosy progressed and spread, he prayed to God to heal her instantly, to prevent her decaying and dying in front of his eyes. God granted Moses' plea and Miriam's leprosy was immediately healed. (This meshes with earlier *midrashim* that have explained that Moses' and Aaron's brief bouts with leprosy had also been healed virtually instantaneously.)

Ohr HaChayim[16] concurs, stating that Miriam had been cured of her leprosy at the moment of Moses' prayer, and that *thereafter* she was isolated for seven days. Those seven days were a period of shock, consideration, and reflection for both Miriam and the people-at-large. The days spent waiting for Miriam's re-entry into the camp constituted a time of hushed worry, and caused the kind of introspection that was perhaps intended by God's punishment of Miriam in the first place.

FORTY-FOUR

ಶಿ൧ೞಶಿ൧ೞ

God Sentences Miriam
to a Brief Exile

NUMBERS 12:14

And God said to Moses: Had her father but spit into her face, she certainly would have been in disgrace for seven days; therefore shall she be isolated for a period of seven days outside the camp, and thereafter shall she be gathered back in.[1]

Following Moses' brief but impassioned plea to God to heal Miriam, the Bible presents us with the Almighty's one-verse response to His servant Moses. God does not state outright that Miriam's punishment must stand; rather, in an unusual explanation of His punishment of Miriam, God takes pains to explain His will to Moses in a brief parable. God says, *If the situation had been different, and Miriam had caused her father to become angry with her and reprimand her, showing her his displeasure* (Onkelos),[2] *surely it is only natural that she would be embarrassed to face her father afterwards* (Ibn Ezra)[3] *for an appropriate week-long period* (Sforno)[4]. God desires Moses to understand that even in prosaic circumstances a seven-day respite would both allow Miriam to reflect on her behavior and would also afford her father a necessary cooling-off period (Abarbanel).[5] How much more so, then, explains Rashi,[6] when Miriam has spoken in such a way that angered *God*; out of embarrassment before the Almighty we would expect that she would logically remain out of His sight for even *longer* than seven days!

Fortunately for Miriam, according to Sha'arei Aharon,[7] God nevertheless graciously acceded somewhat to Moses' prayer on her behalf, and she was cured of the leprosy *before* she began her period of exile outside the Israelite camp. Also, her isolation was kept to only a seven-day period. The commentator explains[8] that God told Moses: "Out of honor to Miriam, I will not remove the cloud of glory—and the Israelites will not march—until Miriam has completed her seven days of exile. In this way, since the people of Israel were standing at a distance and did not witness Miriam's leprosy, at least the people will be able to draw a lesson from Miriam's period of banishment. They will know that *this* is how the Lord God visits punishment upon one who carries tales, even if that person acted with all good intentions as did Miriam the prophetess!"

FORTY-FIVE

ಬಂಗಬಂಗ

The Israelites Wait for Miriam

NUMBERS 12:15-16

So Miriam was confined outside the camp for seven days, and the people did not travel until Miriam rejoined the camp. And then the people journeyed from Hatzerot, and they encamped in the Wilderness of Paran.[1]

T he *midrash* and commentaries embellish on the Torah's brief but richly eloquent statement of the people's devotion to Miriam. We read that *Miriam was confined outside the camp for seven days, and the people did not travel until Miriam rejoined the camp.* Torah Shlema[2] relates that in order to mark the fact that Miriam had been *left outside the camp* for seven days, she acquired the additional Hebrew name of "Azuva" (I Chronicles 2:19), meaning "the one who was left out." Because that name is not commonly known or used with respect to Miriam, it is possible that the people referred to her as Azuva only during her week-long period of exile.[†]

Ohr HaChayim[3] points out that the Torah places the word *Ha'aM*, meaning "the people," at the fulcrum of the second half of

---

[†]The reader will recall that in chapter 35 above we mentioned the other names attributed to Miriam.

verse 15, denoting that *they* affirmatively refused to march until Miriam returned to the camp. The Bible does not state this fact in the passive, narrative voice. It does not even mention in this verse what the reader knows to be true: that the people's leave-taking was dependent upon the presence or absence of the divine cloud hovering over their encampment. According to the commentary, the essence of the verse is that *the people's will* was that they not break camp and continue their march to the chosen land until Miriam rejoined them. Sha'arei Aharon[4] states that the fact that God's cloud also waited for her is the Bible's unambiguous statement that Miriam is accorded honor by the Almighty as well as devotion by the people.

It must be emphasized that the prime purpose of the Israelites' wanderings is to reach the Promised Land. They have pined for it and dreamed of it for over two centuries. They have suffered the torments of slavery and all but lost hope of ever reaching it. Every march they make takes them closer to their real and long-imagined goal: a land they can call their own that is also the designated place to worship the One God. They yearn to end their desert encampments and pitch their tents on chosen soil at last. It is therefore revealing and breathtaking that the people are willing, even insistent, that they delay breaking camp until Miriam has served out her period of exile and rejoined them. Even more telling is the fact that God, who possessed overarching control over the Israelites' wanderings, also delayed their march.

According to Sifrei[5] and the Talmud (Sotah 11a) so great was the honor shown to Miriam and so pervasive the people's love for her that in actuality the exodus actually came to a standstill for the seven days of her exile from the camp! The *midrash* and the Talmud reason that Miriam was reaping what she had sown, and that she was justly measured by the yardstick against which she measured herself. Says the Talmud, Miriam waited in the bullrushes and watched over her baby brother Moses so many years ago; it is only just that she be repaid in kind now, as *all* await *her* return. The holy ark, the priests, the Levites, all of Israel, as well as the seven clouds of God's glory all remain suspended, as it were, in a state of concern and expectation.

FORTY-SIX

༄ ༀ ༄ ༀ

The Death of Miriam

NUMBERS 20:1-2

And the children of Israel, the entire congregation, reached the Wilderness of Zin in the first month, and the people settled in Kadesh; and Miriam died there, and she was buried there. And there was no [longer] water for the congregation; and they gathered before Moses and before Aaron.[1]

Nearly forty years have passed since the exodus from Egypt (Ibn Ezra).[2] Miriam's episode with leprosy and her banishment from the camp have long ago passed into communal memory. The Israelites have continued their dogged march through the wilderness, and we are told here in briefest outline that Miriam died in the place called Kadesh, and that she was buried there. On the heels of that statement we learn that the people's source of water dried up and that they rounded on Moses and Aaron to complain and bemoan their state. The Bible does not elaborate, but the Talmud and the commentaries fill in some exquisite details.

Rashbam[3] pinpoints Miriam's death to the first month of *the fortieth year* of the Israelites' desert wanderings. This becomes significant in upcoming verses, because as Ibn Ezra[4] explains, the narration of Miriam's death in verse 1 is the harbinger of further tragedy. The first misfortune that follows is narrated in verse 2, where we learn that virtually coincident with Miriam's death the life-sustaining waters disappeared from the midst of the Israelite camp. While we will discuss the water's disappearance in some detail, for present purposes the people's vociferous preoccupation with their need for water foretells the undoing and subsequent demise of the remaining leadership of the exodus. For, as Rashbam[5] indicates, here we learn that Miriam's death occurred in the first month of the fortieth year after the exodus; soon we will learn of Aaron's death, which occurred four months later, on the first day of the fifth month of that year; and lastly, the Talmud[6] (Kiddushin 38a) tells us that Moses' death occurred in the seventh day of the twelfth month of that same year.

The three deaths are linked by the Talmud and commentaries for reasons other than their temporal proximity. Focusing on the few words in verse 1 that starkly recount Miriam's death, Rashi[7] states that Miriam died via the rarified divine kiss. We are surprised at this embellishment, because, as the commentary himself notes, nowhere in the text is God's kiss mentioned; we are expected to infer it. Rashi posits that perhaps it would have been a touch unseemly for the Torah text to state that Miriam died by God's kiss. Rashi's opinion might reflect the mores of the commentaries in the absence of any explanation in the Torah itself. We deduce Miriam's death "by divine kiss" by examining the textual references to the deaths of all three leaders and noting the verbal similarities.

The Bible narrates Aaron's death (Numbers 33:38) stating, *And Aaron the priest went up to Mount Hor **by the word [mouth] of God and he died there**; in the fortieth year after the exodus of the Children of Israel from the land of Egypt, in the fifth month, on the first day of that month.*[8] And we are told of Moses' death (Deuteronomy 34:5) as follows: *And Moses, the servant of the Lord, **died there**, in the land of Moab, **by the word [mouth] of God**.*[9] Both textual statements contain two common elements: First, that Aaron and Moses *died there*; and second, that each died *by the word[mouth] of God.*

Returning now to the declaration of Miriam's death, the text includes only *one* of the two common elements. Numbers 20:1 states that *Miriam **died there**, and she was buried there.* Conspicuously absent is a reference to "the word [mouth] of God."

Rashi, the Maharal[10] and the Talmud (Moed Katan 28a[11] and Bava Batra 17a) insert the missing phrase and credit Miriam with the death worthy of a righteous heroine, called to heaven by the word or mouth of God, as were her brothers. The commentaries reason that since the Torah texts narrating the deaths of all three heroes of the exodus specifiy precisely *where* they died (in Hebrew, the word *SHaM*, meaning "there,"appears in all three verses), it surely also meant us to infer that Miriam died *there* in the same manner as her brothers, that is, by a divine kiss. The phrase was implied rather than expressed as regards Miriam only for the sake of propriety. In fact, we learn from the Talmud that the exceptional honor accorded to her brothers was accorded to her as well.

In explaining the significance of dying by a divine kiss, the Talmud[12] (Bava Batra 17a) tells of the six biblical figures who were rewarded by God for their years of steadfast service, so that their deaths were gentle slidings from this world to the next rather than wrenching struggles with the angel of death. The six who died without experiencing the slicing of that angel's scythe were the patriarchs Abraham, Isaac and Jacob, and Moses, Aaron *and Miriam*, the leaders of the exodus. Torah Temima[13] explains that God spared these chosen few the agony of death; that Miriam's righteous soul passed from life to life everlasting cushioned by a sense of peace, carried from this world by God Himself. It is this singular quality of dying that the commentators term "death by the divine kiss." Ohr HaChayim's commentary on Miriam's death[14] compares the righteous ones to the choicest of pearls, stored by the Almighty in a treasure chest that He keeps at His side. Whenever God has need of one of the pearls he removes it from the chest and places it as an adornment to a prized piece of jewelry. So it is here; Miriam's glory will continue to shine even as she is removed from God's treasure chest in this world.

Miriam's death as recorded in this verse signals the beginning of the end for the venerable leaders of the exodus. We have seen that the commentaries group Miriam with her brothers even this one last time, and hint to us that her death portends more adversity for the desert-weary Israelites. As we have described, her two brothers—two other gems in the Almighty's treasure chest—will also die before this fortieth year is out. So we learn that here, in the desert settlement of Kadesh, the Torah is sounding a death knell not only for Miriam, but for Aaron, Moses and the entire generation that was slaves to Pharaoh in Egypt. The commentaries urge us to hear it.

There is no narrative transition from the textual farewell to Miriam in verse 1 to the statement that the people's source of water disappeared with her death. In fact, there is no textual mention whatever of the people's mourning Miriam's death![†] Kli Yakar[15] intuits that Miriam's death in verse 1 and its proximity to verse 2's pronouncement that their water disappeared, actually teaches us that their failure to mourn her *brought about* the disappearance of their water source. Their ungrateful failure to mourn Miriam—as was her due after serving the people for more than forty years in the desert as well as in Egypt—angered the Almighty. God was saddened that Miriam's righteous memory seemed erased from their hearts. So He caused their source of water to run dry so as to invite the people to infer that they only enjoyed the plentiful water on Miriam's merit, and that she was deserving of their weeping over and eulogizing her. Moreover, says Sha'arei Aharon,[16] had the people understood and mourned her even belatedly, the magical well would have returned to them full-force. Unfortunately, this did not occur.

Alternatively, we must bear in mind that since the moment of Miriam's death the Israelites are literally dying of thirst. We can therefore appreciate that the people were still reeling from Miriam's death and that the coincident disappearance of her magical well of water was a one-two blow that brought them to their knees before Moses and Aaron. The swiftness of the text's movement from Miriam's death to the absence of the source of water in the wilderness is not lost on the commentaries, the Talmud and the *midrash*.

Rashi[17] makes the connection, saying that we learn from these contiguous verses—the first narrates Miriam's death and the second the absence of water—that it was because of Miriam's presence in their midst that the Israelites had water for the forty years of their desert wanderings. Her death harbingers a tremendous change in

---

[†]Whereas the text clearly states that the congregation mourned the deaths of Aaron and Moses for thirty days apiece (see Numbers 20:21and Deuteronomy 34:8, respectively).

the Israelites' fate. The first portend of this is their *en masse* convergence on Moses and Aaron to complain of their thirst.

Torah Shlema[18] explains that when the Israelites congregated before their two remaining leaders to complain about the lack of water, they interrupted the brothers as they sat in mourning for their sister. The commentary juxtaposes the brothers' weeping for their sister as they sit inside their tent, with the cries of the people as they stand just outside, calling for Moses and Aaron to hear their plea. A grieving Moses does not at first appreciate the exigency, so bereaved is he. The *midrash* elaborates: "Why are the people calling for me? Don't they know that I mourn for my sister who died?" And the people cry out, "Would you sit and mourn for just *one* soul while *all* of us perish?!" God thus allowed the brothers to interrupt their grieving period to tend to the people's needs. Moses immediately arises and follows the people to the site of Miriam's well; he sees that indeed, it is dry as dust. In this instant, the commentary tells us, mere hours after his beloved sister's burial, with the people's cries clamoring in his ears, a weary Moses foresees that his days as their leader are numbered.

And so whatever became of the Well of Miriam? As we have already described in a prior chapter explaining its advent, the miraculous well that followed the Israelites as they wandered the wilderness from Egypt to Canaan is attributed by the *midrash* to Miriam the prophetess.[†] The Talmud[19] (Taanit 9a) explains that Miriam's Well is one of the three supernatural phenomena that accompanied the Israelites after their exodus from Egypt and that are ascribed to one of the three leaders. It is on Miriam's merit that the well of water followed and sustained the people; it is on Aaron's merit that the divine cloud hovered over the Israelites' encampments and guided their march; and it is credited to Moses that daily, for the forty years of their wandering, the *mannah* appeared and fed the hungry multitude. Therefore, says the Talmud, by rights, with Miriam's death the people should have been forced to rely on their own devices to find water in the wilderness. That they were not; that Miriam's Well—while it ceased to provide water at her death but eventually resumed a moderate flow of water

---

[†]Please refer to Chapter 33 above, where we describe in detail the story of Miriam's Well and its miraculous occurrence.

until the Israelites entered Canaan—is said to have miraculously reappeared to sustain them, is attributed specifically to the combined merit of Miriam's two brothers.

The *midrash* is reluctant to relegate Miriam's Well to post-Egypt myth. The Talmud[20] (Shabbat 35a) ignites in the reader's imagination the exciting possibility that Miriam's Well survived the wilderness and became a natural wonder that is visible to this day. If you desire to behold Miriam's Well, says the Talmud, one need only climb Mount Carmel. From its pinnacle and looking seaward, a fountainhead would be visible; *this* is Miriam's Well.

> *And from there to Be'er; this is the well about which God spoke to Moses saying, 'Gather the congregation and I will give them water.' Then Israel sang this song: Spring up, O well, [let us] sing to it . . . .*[21] (Numbers 21:16-17)

Interestingly, in the wake of the disappearance of Miriam's Well after her death in chapter 20, the Bible's next chapter (Numbers 21:16-20) records a song of praise for a *Be'eR*—Hebrew for "well." Is this Miriam's Well, returned to life? Some Torah commentators answer this question in the affirmative, saying that it *is* Miriam's Well, albeit in a diminished state (Hirsch[22]). Or, that this reference to a well indicates that it is Miriam's Well's last stand, (Netziv[23]); that the well in the form of the magical, rolling rock[†] materialized here and then was no more. It appeared here only because the people needed it desperately, and so they sang it into existence (Targum Yonatan[24]). Hereinafter, the land provided its water naturally. Others (Malbim,[25] Ibn Ezra[26]) disagree, reiterating that Miriam's magical well disappeared utterly at her death, and that this reference to a well in Numbers 21 is to a new well of water created for the thirsty people by God's hand, *not* attributable to either Miriam, Aaron or Moses. Regardless, *this* song is the ecstatic Israelites' song of thanks after their victory over the Canaanites and a short paean to the Almighty for the life-giving waters (Sha'arei Aharon[27]).

Modern Israeli Bible scholar Binyamin Lau[28] wrote that Miriam and Moses differed in an important aspect in their styles of

---

[†]Please refer to Chapter 33 above, where we describe the honeycomb-shaped rock that miraculously spouted water for the Israelites.

leadership, and that these leadership methodologies were best exemplified by their versions of "The Song of the Sea" in Exodus Chapter 15. Moses' Song begins with the words, *So sang Moses and the Children of Israel (aZ YaSHiR MoSHe . . .).* In contrast, Miriam's Song begins, first, with her leading the women in music and dance, followed by the Torah's words, *And Miriam answered them, 'Sing unto the Lord . . .'* Says Lau, Moses is accustomed to leading the people as in a catechism. First he teaches them, and then the people *repeat* his teaching. His Song of the Sea reflected that successful and tautological manner of leading a nation of slaves.

But Miriam is ahead of her time! Her method of leadership is to attempt to awaken within the people the desire to break out in song. She prompts them not with words but in an outpouring of exuberance. Only then, after they dance and sing *of their own accord* does she "answer" them with her Song of the Sea to echo Moses'.

The people responded to *both* Moses and Miriam. However, says Lau, as the slave generation dies out over the course of their forty years of wandering, Moses' method of leading them has not changed with them. Moses still *strikes the rock* in order to bring forth water for the people, because that is the methodology he has used in the past and which has always worked. The difference now, however, is that the people have matured. God tells Moses to *speak to the rock*, but Moses, set in his ways, perhaps, strikes the rock instead. Following this episode, Moses is forbidden to enter the promised land.

It is therefore instructive and emotionally satisfying that even after Miriam has died, the third "Song" that is sung by the Children of Israel as a free people, in Numbers 21:17—entitled the "Song of the Well"—while it begins in the same way that Moses' Song of the Sea began forty years ago (*So sang . . .* or *aZ YaSHiR . . .*), continues in Miriam's fashion: *So sang **Israel** this Song . . . .* It is the people—all Israel—who sing out, of their own volition, without Moses leading them and obviously without Miriam either. The people have been taught well: they know that the proper manner of expressing their ecstatic gratitude to God is to break out in a song of thanksgiving. According to Lau, the people, on the brink of entering the promised land, are a generation born in freedom, and sing jubilantly without need of a teacher or conductor. They no longer need Moses' manner of leadership, they are bereft of Miriam's and Aaron's, and they will begin this new chapter in their destiny in a new land and under the banner of a new leader.

Perhaps it is the inexplicable, somewhat magical quality of the appearance of this new well, and the short biblical poem praising its origin (Numbers 21:18-20) that leads some *midrashists* to suggest that these verses supply a precious textual hint to the existence of the oral Torah. Alschich and S'fat Emet[29] pick up on the poem's references to the labor of *digging* the well, and that it is a divine *gift* to the people in the desert.[30] They derives from these allusions that the Well of Miriam *is* the wellspring of the oral Torah. Alschich says that the written Torah which the Israelites received at Sinai actually contains within it the oral tradition; it is necessary to dig deeply into the Torah text in order to reach these hidden well-springs of insight. S'fat Emet concurs, stating that the Torah's reference here to *this* well—forty years after Miriam's Well's first appearance—is a metaphorical hint to the existence of the gift of the oral Torah. The reader should appreciate this interpretation, recalling that nowhere in the Torah text do we find a reference to Miriam's Well. How fitting it is that the Well of Miriam is itself a product of the Oral Torah, which the commentaries attribute to these verses in the text describing the well's reappearance. Miriam's death and the well's disappearance have given rise to a body of commentary on the origin of *midrash!*

FORTY-SEVEN

ನ೦ಲ೩ನ೦ಲ೩

The Survival of the Women of the Exodus

NUMBERS 20:1

And the children of Israel, the entire congregation, reached the Wilderness of Zin in the first month . . . .

The death of Miriam pinpoints the beginning of the end of the lives of the leaders of the generation of the exodus. Miriam's death occurred at the beginning of the Israelites' fortieth year of wandering in the wilderness, and the deaths of Aaron and Moses follow soon thereafter, in the fifth and eleventh months of that same year. The Torah text (in Numbers 20:12[1]) relates the enigmatic reason for Aaron and Moses' deaths, the reason that God prevents them from entering the promised land: They disobeyed God's express command about providing water to the complaining congregation, and thereby forfeited the opportunity to sanctify God's name after Miriam's death in the wilderness of Zin.

Likewise, earlier, the Torah text (in Numbers chapters 13 and 14) explains in detail and in dialogue that *the adult male Israelites who were over the age of twenty at time of the second year after the exodus from Egypt* would suffer the same fate as Aaron and

Moses. They, too, will die in the desert without setting foot in the promised land.

The reason for such a dire punishment having been visited upon the male Israelites is less complex than the reason that their male leaders perish in the wilderness. The males' pessimistic and rebellious response to the report of the spies that had been sent to explore the new land was an unforgivable betrayal after having been delivered from Egyptian bondage by the hand of God, having witnessed His miracles, and received His commandments. Their faithlessness presages forty years of complaints and defamations against God. In response to the spies' account the men raised their voices and cried, complaining as one to Moses and Aaron, "If only we had died in Egypt or perished in this wilderness! Our deaths would have been preferable to coming into the land where God has led us; falling to the swords of the Canaanites, and our wives and children taken captive as spoils of war." The men turned to each other crying, "Let us instead return to Egypt rather than enter this new land!"

Standing alone, Joshua and Caleb rent their garments in abject misery upon hearing their brethren's blasphemous cries. And they spoke up in defense of God's plan, saying: "On the contrary—the land we passed through was extremely good! If God saw fit to bring us here and give us this land flowing with milk and honey, would you still rebel and shake with fear? God will turn the Canaanites into fodder for us. He will remove their protection and will stand with us so we will have no need to fear!"

In response, the angry men turned on Joshua and Caleb, resolved to pelt them to death with stones. It was at that instant that God's cloud of honor appeared over the Tent of Meeting and was visible to all the men of Israel. God's store of patience with the rebellious men of Israel had finally been been depleted when He heard their defamatory and abusive speech and witnessed their attempted lynching of Joshua and Caleb. God's wrenching words to Moses depict a deity bereft of faith in the people He has saved time and time again. "Until when will these men continue to spurn me?! Will they never believe in me, even after all the signs and wonders that I have brought into their midst?" God even thought to destroy them all at once with a sudden plague, leaving the new land to Moses' seed, allowing for the growth of a new nation in their stead. It was Moses at his eloquent and valiant best who prevailed on the Almighty not to act precipitously. "If you were to wipe out this people as one man, all the other nations of the world would hear of it and would say that the God of the Israelites stopped short of taking His people into the promised land because He was unable to do so, and therefore He destroyed them in the wilderness. For this reason, O Lord, allow your great power to be manifest. Let the Lord be slow to anger, filled with lovingkindness, forgiving of sin. After all, you took them out of Egypt and brought them to this place, forgiving them at every turn."

God heeded Moses' impassioned plea and said, "I will forgive them, as you say. But still, as I live, God's glory will fill the land. And the men who have spurned me and my miracles that they have witnessed both in Egypt and in the wilderness, and who have not heeded my voice, **and who have blasphemed against me** and mutinied, *they will not live to see the land that I promised to their forefathers!* Tell them that their carcasses will rot in the desert; all Israelite men twenty years and over, with the exception of Caleb and Joshua. But your children—the ones you feared would be spoils for the triumphant Canaanites—*they* are the ones I will bring into the new land. Only your children will know the land that you have spurned!"[2]

Because of their blaspheming and unrelenting faithless complaints (Numbers 14:29), God condemned all the adult Israelite males to death in the wilderness. According to a plain reading of the Torah text, only Israelite males who were less than twenty years old *at the time of the spies' account* during the second year of their desert wanderings would survive to enter the promised land at the end of forty years. Ohr HaChayim's[3] reading adds two years' worth of young men to those who are spared. He bases his interpretation on the fact that if God is visiting punishment because of the men's bitter complaints, a better reading would include their bitter complaints immediately after the exodus from Egypt two years earlier (Exodus 15:24[4]). The commentary's reading interprets the text to mean that God will therefore *also* spare the lives of those Israelite males who were under twenty *at the time of the redemption from Egypt.*

There is *midrashic* discussion (Torah Shlema,[5] the Netziv[6]) that some men of the tribe of Levi were spared God's wrath, as they were not among the blasphemers. The commentaries base this on the verse in the book of Joshua (19:41[7]) that states that Elazar the Priest allocates portions of territory to the various Israelite tribes after they have crossed into the promised land. This Elazar, quite possibly the son of Aaron, may have been only one of a number of Levites who was spared God's death sentence and allowed to cross over into the new land.

The Israelite *women* of the Egyptian slave generation, on the other hand, were spared. Rashi's commentary (to Numbers 26:64, which narrates God's punishment of the Israelite *males*) states that God's punishment of death in the wilderness did not extend to the *women* of the generation that left Egypt.[8] He reasons that the women were conspicuously absent from the angry, blaspheming mob that descended on Moses and Aaron in the wake of the spies' report that the new land was unconquerable. The women had had no hand in the spies' report, nor did they dishonor God and clamour to return to Egypt after hearing it, as did the men. In fact, according to the Maharaz,[9] it was known among the desert generation that *none* of the Israelite women believed any of the spies' deeply nihilistic reports about the promised land. To emphasize this the commentary goes on to say that so stout-of-heart were the women that even the wives of the ten spies disbelieved their own husbands' defamatory reports!

Also to their enduring credit, according to Bamidbar Rabbah (21:10),[10] the women of Israel had refused point-blank to cede their jewelry to their husbands when the men were in a frenzy to melt down all the gold booty taken from Egypt in order to fashion the Golden Calf. The commentary elaborates that the desert generation was comprised of polar opposites, divided by gender: The men were intent upon destruction of their own nascent morality and of God's redemptive ideal, while the women steadfastly guarded themselves and their children against slipping back into the depraved Egyptian mode. It was this overriding moral restraint, according to Kli Yakar,[11] more than any single behavior, that marked the Israelite women. For this reason they were exempt from the divine death sentence pronounced upon the Israelite men. In the words of Sifrei, "the women's strength of character eclipsed that of the men."[12] Is it any wonder, then, says Kli Yakar, that it was on the merit of that generation's righteous *women* that the Israelites were redeemed from Egypt?

And finally, according to Rashi, the women possessed a love for the land they were promised but had never seen; the land of their ancestors. It was this powerful yearning to return there that impelled them throughout the forty years of wandering through the wilderness. The men cried out to return to Egypt (Numbers 14:4); the women, on the other hand (Numbers 27:4), represented here by the daughters of Zelophchad, beseeched Moses for a portion of the new land.[†]

Torah Shlema[13] boldly states that not only were the women who survived the forty-year desert trek permitted to enter the land; in actuality, with the exception of Miriam, *no Israelite women* died in the wilderness! The commentary cites the Torah text that Serach, the daughter of Asher and granddaughter of Jacob,[‡] was among those who came into Egypt generations before, and who is followed through the *midrash* until, as one of the Israelite women, she enters the promised land. She is notably the oldest living Israelite to re-enter the land of Canaan.

The reader will be expecting to learn the fate of the one other ancient and seminal female figure who was unveiled in this book's first chapter, and who went on to become a heroine to her people during the darkest days of Pharaoh's holocaust. It is, of course, Yocheved, first-cousin to Serach, daughter of Asher, midwife to the enslaved and persecuted Hebrews, and mother of Miriam, Aaron and Moses.

––––––––––

[†]In point of fact, in Numbers 27:1 the five grown daughters of Zelophchad approach Moses and Aaron in the desert and petition for a ruling allowing them them their rightful portion of land when the nation conquers it and takes possession. The women reason that their father had already died in the wilderness, and that he had no male heir. They sought to retain their father's portion so that it would not be subsumed within the portions of the other tribes. Moses seeks the counsel of the Almighty, who replies that the daughters of Zelophchad are correct, and instructs Moses to give them their father's portion among the holdings of their tribe. God also instructs Moses to generalize a law for future generations so that daughters can inherit the land in the absence of a male heir.

[‡]We discuss the magical story surrounding Serach the daughter Asher in chapters 1 and 25 above.

Torah Shlema[14] highlights her, and reminds us that the midrash names Yocheved as the seventieth soul who arrived in Egypt along with Jacob and his family so many years ago. She is named here in the Bible (in Numbers 26:59, as she was in Exodus 6:20), at the close of the exodus story, unambiguously as wife of Amram, daughter of Jacob's son, Levi, and mother of the three leaders of the Israelites. The midrash wants us to appreciate the fitting closure: This story opened at Exodus 1 with the naming of the family of Jacob who first arrived in Egypt, and the midrash identifies her as Levi's daughter, born as her mother's wagon crossed over into Egypt.

The story effectively winds to a close here in Numbers 20 with the death of Miriam and her brothers in future verses. The dramatic, sweeping story of the brave women of the exodus began by highlighting Yocheved, and now the midrash reminds us that she, along with Serach, personally experienced the gamut of the collective Israelite experience: the rigors of enslavement, the jubilant exodus from slavery, the receiving of the ten commandments, the wandering in the wilderness, and now the immense privilege of entering the promised land. These two women of Israel embody the Israelite history and memory, and are privileged to enter the new land.

According to the commentary, the death and burial of Miriam, chronicled in Numbers 20:1-2 simply and without panoply, records the single death of a female Israelite from the post-Egypt generation.

One might wonder, Why, then—if all the women of the post-Egypt generation survived to enter the promised land—did Miriam die in the wilderness of Kadesh? The Netziv[15] echoes this rhetorical question when he reiterates that even though she was exempt from God's death sentence—and so by rights her bones should have been buried in the promised land—still Miriam died in the wilderness and was buried there. Torah Shlema posits an astonishing notion, responding that Miriam's death was, ironically, on account of the magical well of water that was gifted to the Israelites in her merit. The commentary asks, How could the well disappear at the end of the forty years of wandering, and Miriam survive its demise? The commentary reasons that she could not survive if the well disappeared; the two are inextricably linked. This is the reason verse 1 relates Miriam's death and burial, and immediately on its heels we learn of the disappearance of the water in verse 2.

Reading these two verses prompts the Netziv to pronounce that we are in essence reading the Bible's introduction to its conclusion of the exodus story. Numbers 20:1 states with particularity that the children of Israel all arrived in the Wilderness of Zin in the first month (of the fortieth year), and that they settled in Kadesh. The commentator views this first part of the verse as a formalized beginning of the end of the tale of the Israelites' forty years of wandering in the wilderness. Even though Miriam should rightfully have been included in the miracle of female survival along with all her Israelite "sisters," the Bible is winding down its narration and, as we have seen, will next narrate Aaron's death and then finally Moses'. Neither of her brothers survives to enter the promised land. Torah Shlema suggests that Miriam, an equal partner with Aaron and Moses and an essential component of the ruling triumverate, could not survive the desert experience while her brothers perished.

Miriam's earthly mission was complete. Her burial here is symbolic of the sea-change that she helped bring about. The reader will recall that as a girl Miriam assisted her mother Yocheved at the births of a generation of Hebrews under the nose of the murdering Pharaoh. She also was charged by her mother with the task of watching over her baby brother as he floated in his basket on the Nile; she facilitated Moses' rescue when Pharaoh's daughter drew him from the water and sought to raise him as a prince. Miriam's astonishing depths of courage and optimism were forged during her youth as a Hebrew slave and tested as the last of the slave generation wandered in the wilderness. Her valiant essence, coupled with her prophetic persona, graphically depicted by the well of water that flowed for her people during her lifetime, endeared her to the entire generation of Israelites that wandered in the wilderness for forty years. They did not but know it, but Miriam was at their side only and until the children of her midwifed generation had grown to maturity and were ready to carry their parents' standard into the promised land.

Miriam's life symbolized the female imperative of faith in the face of unrelenting repression, and her legacy was a generation of Israelite women who mirrored her deeply-rooted spiritual constancy and ingenuity born of the drive to endure despite their lifelong burdens. Sha'arei Aharon[16] explains that it is this abiding faith that contrasted with the spiritual desertion of the males of the post-exodus generation. The women of Miriam's generation were *not* partners with the men in their betrayal of God born of bone-deep despair. Quite simply, because of their strength of character, the women were able to retain their optimism, their life-force, their desire to bear children and their will to survive.

It is for this reason, according to the *midrash*, that the death sentence proclaimed by God upon the generation of the exodus did not extend to the women. And the consequence of this reprieve is that the multitude that was poised to enter the promised land, while it consisted of no males over the age of sixty (except for Joshua, Caleb and perhaps some Levite priests), was populated by mothers, grandmothers *and great-grandmothers.* These ancient women were privileged to carry in their hearts and collective memories the weight of God's gifts to the Israelites: the gift of a life of freedom bound by God's Torah, and the additional immeasurable gift of leading their children and children's children into the promised land. The privilege of linking hands with their grandchildren and great-grandchildren as they crossed over into the new land was a gift born of Miriam's legacy to them.

The commentary stresses that while both the Israelite women and men drank from the sustaining waters of Miriam's well, only the women *additionally* imbibed Miriam's lesson of drawing nourishment from the well of God's spiritual sustenance. Against tremendous odds Miriam enabled a multi-generational matriarchy of Israelites worthy to be called her "children." In a real sense, the *midrash* teaches us, the greatness of Miriam's prophecy was that she modeled ecstatic and enduring belief for the Israelite women.

Miriam's death and burial in Numbers 20:1-2 narrates more than just the death of this beloved and extraordinary woman. It presages the end of the leadership of the generation of the exodus. The next generation of Israelites, poised to enter the promised land, would do so under the guidance of a new leader, who would also write the next chapter of the story of their nationhood.

NOTES

ONE: Yocheved, the Seventieth Soul

1 ויאמר ישראל, רב עוד יוסף בני חי; אלכה ואראנו בטרם אמות.

2 כל הנפש הבאה ליעקב מצרימה, יוצאי ירכו...כל הנפש ששים ושש. ובני יוסף אשר ילד לו במצרים, נפש שנים; כל הנפש לבית יעקב הבאה מצרים שבעים.

3 ויסע ישראל וכל אשר לו, ויבא בארה שבע; ויזבח זבחים לאלקי אביו יצחק. ויאמר אלקים לישראל במראת הלילה ויאמר יעקב, יעקב! ויאמר הנני. ויאמר אנכי אלקי אביך, אל תירא מרדת מצרימה כי לגוי גדול אשימך שם.

4 ששים ושש שבאו עם יעקב, וג' של יוסף.

5 שיעקב ובניו היו שבעים.

6 כי יעקב נכנס בחשבון, כי נפש יש לו והוא העיקר.

7 אסנת היתה בת דינה שנתעברה משכם ונשאת ליוסף. אפשר לומר אסנת השלימה החשבון [של מספר שבעים נפש].

8 היתה בתו של יעקב יושבת אהלים, ולא היתה יוצאת החוצה. מה עשה שכם בן חמור? הביא משחקות נערות חוצה לה, מתופפות בתפים. יצאה דינה לראות בבנות המשחקות, ושללה ושכב אותה, והרתה וילדה את אסנת. ואמרו בני ישראל להרגה, שעכשו יאמרו כל הארץ שיש בית-זנות באהלי יעקב. מה עשה יעקב? הביא צי"ץ וכתב עליו שם הקדש, ותלה על צוארה, ושלחה והלכה לה . . . וירד מיכאל המלאך והורידה למצרים לביתו של פוטיפרא, שהיתה אסנת ראויה ליוסף לאשה. והיתה אשתו של פוטיפרא עקרה, וגדלה אותה כבת.

9 מה עשה יעקב לה? כתב בצוארה וכתוב בו כל המדבק בך מדבק בזרעו של יעקב.

10 וכשירד יוסף למצרים לקחה לו, שנאמר, 'ויתן לו את אסנת בת פרע כהן אן לאשה.'

11 נסתכל בו יוסף שהיתה בת בתו של יעקב, ונשאה לו לאשה.

12 רבי לוי בשם רבי שמואל בר נחמן: ראית מימיך אדם נותן לחבירו ששים וששה כוסות וחוזר ונותן לו אף שלשה, והוא מונה אותם שבעים?! **אלא זו יוכבד**, שהשלימה מנין של ישראל במצרים.

13 בכללן אתה מוצא שבעים, בפרטן אתה מוצא שבעים חסר אחד!...**זו יוכבד**, שהורתה בדרך, ולידתה בין החומות, שנאמר: "אשר ילדה אותה ללוי במצרים."

THREE: Seductions by Righteous Women

1 ובכל עבודה בשדה. וכי **בשדה** היו עובדין ולא **בעיר!** אלא שגזרו עליהן: אנשים ילינו בשדה, והנשים בעיר, כדי למעטן בפריה ורביה.

2 חריש וקציר.

3 כגון החפירות והוצאת הזבלים; הכל נתנו עליהם...שלא ינוחו. ומכים ומקללים אותם.

4 ונשיהם היו מחממין להם חמין, ומביאות לבעליהן כל מאכל ומשתה, ומנחמות אותם ואומרות: לעולם לא משתעבדין בנו.

267

5 בשכר נשים צדקניות שהיו באותו הדור נגאלו ישראל ממצרים. בשעה שהולכות לשאוב מים
הקב"ה מזמן להם דגים קטנים בכדיהן, ושואבות מחצה מים ומחצה דגים, ובאות ושופתות
שתי קדירות, אחת של חמין ואחת של דגים, ומוליכות אצל בעליהן לשדה. ומרחיצות אותן,
וסכות אותן, ומאכילות אותן, ונזקקות להן בין שפתים...וכן שמתעברות, באות לבתיהם.
וכיון שמגיע זמן מולדיהן, הולכות ויולדות בשדה.

6 במראות צבאות. בנות ישראל היו בידן מראות שרואות בהן כשהן מתקשטות, ואף אותן לא
עכבו מלהביא לנדבת המשכן. והיה מואס משה בהן מפני שעשויים ליצר הרע. אמר לו
הקב"ה: קבל! כי אלו חביבין עלי מן הכל, שעל ידיהם העמידו הנשים צבאות רבות במצרים.
כשהיו בעליהן יגעים בעבודת פרך, היו הולכות ומוליכות להם מאכל ומשתה, ומאכילות
אותם, ונוטלות המראות, וכל אחת רואה עצמה עם בעלה במראה, ומשדלתו בדברים לאמר:
אני נאה ממך. ומתוך כך מביאות בעליהן לידי תאוה ונזקקות להם, ומתעברות, ויולדות שם
7 בפרך...וכשראו שאין זה מועיל להם שלא יפרו, ולקחו להם צד אחר: להמית הבנים.

FOUR: The Midwives Foil the Pharaoh's Schemes

1 ויאמר מלך מצרים למילדת העברית אשר שם האחת שפרה ושם השנית פועה. ויאמר:
בילדכם את העבריות וראיתן על האבנים, אם בן הוא והמתן אותו; ואם בת היא וחיה.
ותיראן המילדת את האלקים ולא עשו כאשר דבר אליהן מלך מצרים; ותחיין את הילדים.

2 ויאמר מלך מצרים...שכל המעשה האומר בענין, אמר לשון רבים. דכתיב, וישימו...ויעבידו,
וימררו. כי לא המלך לבדו עושה, אלא הוא ועמו. **דבר זה עשאו המלך לבדו** כדי שיהיה
הדבר בסוד, שלא ירגישו העבריות להסתיר הריונם, שלא ירחיקו המילדות מילד אותם.

3 שרות היו על כל המילדות, כי אין ספק כי יותר מחמש מאות מילדות היו, אלא אילו שתיהן
שרות היו עליהן...לתת מס למלך מהשכר.

4 ויאמר מלך מצרים למילדת העברית וגו'. יש אומרים שהמילדות היו **מצריות** וכאלו אמר
למילדות **את** העבריות. דאם לא כן מאי רבותיה דקאמר: "ותיראן המילדות את האלקים."

5 הנה אמר 'ויאמר' בפסוק שאחר זה הוא מיותר. כי הלא בפסוק זה לא הוזכר שאמר להן דבר
לבד בו מזכיר שמותן. והנה אפשר כי זה כוונו רז"ל, באומרם שתבען למשכב. וכבוד עלהים
הסתר דבר כזה.

6 ולא עשו כאשר **דבר** אליהן... כאשר **אמר** להן מבעי ליה. מהו כאשר **דבר** אליהן...כתיב
הכא "כאשר דבר," וכתיב התם (בר' לט:י) "**כדברה** אל יוסף יום יום." מה להלן לדבר
עבירה? אף כאן דבר עבירה.

7 כל עבירות שבתורה אם אומרים לאדם עבור ואל תהרג, יעבור ואל יהרג, חוץ מעבודה זרה,
וגלוי עריות, ושפיכת דמים.

8 שהמצוה למסור נפשו ולא לעבור בעריות היא **רק בגבר**.

9 ותיראן המילדות את האלקים. ולא למאמר המלך. **וזאת** היראה היה בלב.

10 ולא עשו כאשר דבר **אליהן.** **להן** מיבעי ליה! אמר רבי יוסי ברבי חנינא: מלמד שתבען
לדבר עבירה, ולא נתבעו.

11 ובריב"א כתב שהדרשה כאן דורשת "**אליהן**" כאילו היה כתוב "**עליהן**," שהוא ודאי ענין של
ביאה...ועניינו שבקש לשלוט בהן שליטה גמורה.

12 אליהן משמע על עסקי ביאה. לשון "ויבא אליה " (בר' כט).

13 יותר היה לו להרוג הנקבות מהזכרים, שהרי במיעוט הנקבות יתמעט פריה ורביה. ואלו
במיעוט הזכרים לא יתמעט פריה ורביה. כי זכר אחד יכול לעבר אלף נשים ויותר בשנה . . .
14 כל אחת ואחת ילדה ששה בכרס אחד.

15 ואם בת היא...לא ירגישו בדבר הנשים היולדות כשיראו שלפעמים ולדותיהן מתקיימין, לא יחשדו במילדות והם לא יבחינו כי הורגו הזכרים ולא הנקבות.

16 אם בן הוא והמת אתו. אמר רבי חנינא, סימן גדול מסר להן. בן, פניו למטה, בת, פניה למעלה.

17 אם בן הוא . . . האם היה פרעה צריך להורות סימני לדה?! והלא מילדות ובקיאות היו! ובספר רביד הזהב כתב דכונת הגמרא בזה שחשש פרעה שלא תשמענה לו המילדות לאבד נפשות. ולכן הסביר להן שיכולות הן להרגן קודם שיצא לאויר העולם . . . ולא תעבורנה על אבידת נפש.

18 אפילו היא משימה אצבעה על חוטמו, הוא מת.

19 העלו חז"ל שלא צוה אותן שישתדלו להחיותן. אלא איך שהיה עם הולד כן יהיה...ולא שיראו להבריא את הולד.

20 אם בן הוא והמית אותו. ותאמרו "הפילה," כי לא רצה עדיין לעשות רציחה בפרהסיא.

21 אם בן הוא וגו'. לא היה מקפיד אלא על הזכרים, שאמרו לו אצטגניניו שעתיד להולד בן המושיע אותם.

22 בן זכרים, בן נקבות. וכן פרשו כל המפרשים.

23 לא דיין שלא המיתו אותן, אלא שהיו מספיקות להם מים ומזון.

24 ותחיין. בכל כוחן.

25 יש קילוס בתוך קילוס. לא דיין שלא קיימו את דבריו, אלא הוסיפו לעשות עמהם טובות. יש מהם שהיו עניות, והולכות המילדות ומגבות מים ומזון מבתיהם של עשירות ובאות ונותנות לעניות.

26 מקודם לא נתנו דעתם על מצוה זו לספק מים ומזון. ואחר שצוה להם פרעה חששו שהיו נחשדים אם ימות אחד מהנולדים שהם הרגוהו. לזה, להוציא עצמן מהחשד השתדלו להחיות החיות אפילו מי שימות מיתת עצמן, מהחסרון הספוק.

27 ד"א ותחיין את הילדים. יש מהם שראואים לצאת חגרים או סומים או בעלי מומין או לחתוך בו אבר שיצא יפה. ומה היו עושות? עומדות בתפלה ואומרות לפני הקב"ה: אתה יודע שלא קיימנו דברי פרעה של פרעה; דבריך אנו מבקשות לקיים. רבון העולם, יצא הולד לשלום . . . מיד היה הקב"ה שומע קולן ויוצאין שלמים.

FIVE: The Midwives are Called to Task

1 ויקרא מלך מצרים למילדות ויאמר להן מדוע עשיתן הדבר הזה; ותחיין את הילדים. ותאמרן המילדות אל פרעה כי לא כנשים המצריות העבריות; כי חיות הנה בטרם תבוא אלהן המילדת וילדו.

2 מה הוא המעשה שעשו, שעליו הוא אומר "מדוע עשיתן?" ואם שלא המיתו את הילדים, זה יקרא שלילת המעשה, והיה צריך לומר מדוע **לא** עשיתם.

3 מדוע עשיתן. שבגדתן בי.

4 אם שאל מדוע לא עשו כדברי להמית בידים. שעל זה היה התשובה פשוטה בדין ישראל דעל שפיכת דמים יהרג ולא יעבור. ואין להם רשות בשום אופן לעשות כן. אבל מדוע הם מסכנות א"ע להחיות את אחרים.

5 הרי הן משולות לחיות השדה שאינן צריכות מילדות.

6 יודעות כל אחת לילד את עצמה.

7 ומילדות זו לזו.

8 ארי חכימן אנין.

9 בקיאות במלאכת המילדת, ואם נחפוץ לעשות דבר או לדבר שלא כהוגן, תהיינה מרגישות
בדבר ולא תקראנה עוד אותנו ליילד.

10 שאמרו שהמה אינן מולידין העבריות כי חיות הנה. אך עיקר מלאכתן לשפר הולד ולצעוק לו
אחר שנולד כבר.

11 שקודם שתבא אליהן המילדת תלדנה להן. ואחרי זה שולחות בעדנו לתקן עצמן, לא לחתול
הילדים כלל, כי חשודות אנו בעיניהן.

12 היו מתחכמות להרחיק להם זמן לידתם, כי הרגישו בדבר, וכל זה נכלל בתיבת חיות.

13 כי חיות הנה. יש להם כח חיים בלב.

SIX: The Midwives are Favored by God

1 וייטב אלקים למילדת. וירב העם ויעמצו מאד.

2 ומה היא הטובה? וירב העם. שבזה יגדל זכותם כי כולם יחשבו להם כשלא הרגום.

3 וייטב אלקים למילדות . . . ולא נחשדו על שפיכת דמים. שאם **לא** היו פרים ורבים בתחילה
היו סבורים שהם היו עושים , אע"פ שכל אחת יודעת שלא עשו **לה** רק טוב.

4 מה היה הטובה הזאת? שקבל דבריהם מלך מצרים ולא הזיק להן.

5 שנתקבל דבריהן ושוב לא השגיח המלך עליהן כלל.

SEVEN: Shifra and Puah Defy the King

1 אשר שם האחת שפרה ושם השנית פועה.

2 לפי הפשט, שהן שמותיהן.

3 הזכיר הקב"ה שמם לכבודן, שתזכרן לטוב, כי שמו נפשם בכפם על ישראל לעבור מצוות
המלך.

4 ולא סתם שתי נשים.

5 רב ושמואל: חד אמר אשה ובתה, והד אמר כלה וחמותה. מאן דאמר אשה ובתה? יוכבד
ומרים. ומאן דאמר כלה וחמותה? יוכבד ואלישבע.

6 ואם תאמר למה לא הזכיר את שם יוכבד ושם מרים בפירוש, ויראה שאין הכתוב מזכיר שם
יוכבד ומרים ואהרן עד אחר לידת משה.

7 ואז מזכירים את שמות עמרם, יוכבד, ואהרן [להלן ו, כ], ומרים [להלן טו, כ].

8 שפרה, שהיתה משפרת את התינוק כשהוא יוצא מלא דם . . . ד"א שפרה, שפרו ורבו
ישראל עליה . . . ד"א שפרה, ששפרה מעשיה לפני האלקים.

9 כי דרך המילדות שלפעמים שהולד נוצר מת. לוקחת המילדת שפופרת של קנה ומשימה תוך
. . . היילד ומנפחת בו ומשיבה רוח ליילד. וזהו שפרה, לשון שפופרת.

10 . . . שפועה ומדברת והוגה לולד כדרך הנשים המפייסות תינוק הבוכה.

11 שהיתה פועה לולד . . . לוחשת לחישה ויוצא הולד, כמו שעושים אלו עכשיו באזני האשה.

12 ד"א פועה שהופיעה פנים כנגד פרעה. וזקפה חוטמה בו ואמרה לו: אוי לו לאותו האיש
כשיבא האלקים ליפרע ממנו. נתמלא עליה חמה להרגה. שפרה, שהיתה משפרת על דברי
בתה ומפייסת עליה, אמרה לו: אתה משגיח עליה תינוקת היא, ואינה יודעת כלום.

13 פועה. שהיתה פועה ברוח הקודש, ואומרת: עתידה אמי שתלד בן שמושיע את ישראל.

14 ורז"ל אמרו **שפרה זו יוכבד ופועה זו מרים** . . . שפועה לשון דבור, וזה מורה ממש על
מרים שהיתה נביאה . . . וייוכבד היינו שפרה, על שם שחזרה לשופרה ונערותה . . . כמו
שקרה לשרה. וגם נס זה היה מופת שיולד ממנה בן מושיעה בן מושיעה לישראל, כי לא בחנם נעשה לה
נס זה . . . ושמות אלו מורים על לידת הגואל.

EIGHT: The Midwives' Reward

1 ויהי כי יראו המילדת את האלקים, ויעש להם בתים.

2 כשיראה פרעה שלא היו מקיימין מצותיו וישם להם בתים אצל עבדיו כדי שיראו אם הולכות אצל העבריות.

3 לא יכלו ללכת מן הבתים בלא רשות ובלא הודעה.

4 ויעש להם בתים. לא פירש הכתוב מי עשה, ללמד ששני משמעות יש בזה. אם האלקים, והוא בתורת שכר . . . אם המלך, והוא הכנה לגזרה הבאה אחריה.

5 ולכן התיאש מהפיק זממו עוד על ידי המילדות. שידע שלא ימלאו פקודתו, עמד ותקן בתים.

6 יראת בשר ודם כשאדם מתירא מפני אדם, אין בו ישוב הדעת, כי יראה הוא היפך מזה: אך יראת השי"י יש בה נייחא. ועל זה מורה "ויעש להם בתים" כי בית מורה על ישוב הדעת, וממילא כאשר היה ישוב הדעת מחמת יראת אלקים לא היה להם שום פחד מגזירת פרעה.

7 בתי כהנה, ולויה, ומלכות שקרויין בתים.

8 זהו הכלל, דכל משפחה שהראש שלה הוא חשוב, כל המשפחה מתיחסת אליו . . . ולכן הם נקראים בית אהרן, בית הלוי, בית המלך.

9 ויעש להם בתים. רב ושמואל. חד אמר: בתי כהונה ולויה. וחד אמר: בתי מלכות. מאן דאמר בתי כהונה ולויה. אהרן ומשה. ומאן דאמר בתי מלכות. דוד נמי ממרים קאתי.

10 חור. בנה של מרים היה, וכלב בעלה.

NINE: "Death by Drowning to All Newborn Sons!"

1 ויצו פרעה לכל עמו לאמר: כל הבן הילוד היארה תשליכהו וכל הבת תחיון.

2 יום שנולד משה אמרו לו אצטגניניו, היום נולד מושיען, ואין אנו יודעים אם ממצרים אם מישראל. ורואין אנו שסופו ללקות במים. לפיכך גזר אותו היום אף על המצרים, שלא נאמר: הילוד לעברים.

3 לא היו האיצטגנינים רואים על תולדות אם מישראל; שהרי נקרא בן לבת פרעה, וגם לא אם ממצריים הוא. מפני שילדה אותו יוכבד, ולא היה מורה האצטגנינות לא שהוא מישראל, ולא שהוא ממצרים.

4 עשה הדבר בפרהסיה . . . כי חשב כי אין נמלט מהם לצד היותם רבים.

5 באותה שעה כנס פרעה כל המצרים ואמר להם: השאילו לי את בניכם ט' חדשים, שאשליכם ליאור . . . ולא רצו לקבל ממנו שאמרו "בן מצרי לא יגאל אותן לעולם, אלא מן העבריות."

6 ומה נכבד טעם כל הבן הילוד, בלי פירוש? והנה ראה לגלות דעתו אל בני עמו לעשותו כן מרוב חפצו שימעטו וישוחו.

7 ויש לאמר שלא העביר הגזירה אלא מעל עמו אבל הגזירה שגזר קודם לכן על בני ישראל במקומה, היתה עד יום שהושלך משה ליאור.

TEN: A Wedding, A Divorce and A Remarriage

1 וילך איש מבית לוי, ויקח את בת לוי.

2 וילך איש מבית לוי. הוא עמרם. ויקח את יוכבד בת לוי.

3 ולפי הפשט מעשה זה לפני גזרת פרעה היה. שהרי נולדו להם אהרן ומרים קודם לכן. אלא משבא לספר מה שאירע להן בשעת גזירה מבניהם, התחיל לספר גם מתחילת נשואיהם.

4 וילך איש מבית לוי. להיכן הלך? . . . שהלך בעצת בתו. תנא: עמרם גדול הדור היה, כיון

שראה שאמר פרעה הרשע "כל הבן הילוד היארה תשליכהו" אמר: לשוא אנו עמלין, עמד
וגירש את אשתו. עמדו כולן וגרשו את נשותיהן. אמרה לו בתו: אבא, קשה גזירתך יותר
משל פרעה. שפרעה לא גזר אלא על הזכרים, ואתה גזרת על הזכרים ועל הנקיבות. פרעה
לא גזר אלא בעולם הזה, ואתה בעולם הזה ולעולם הבא. פרעה הרשע, ספק מתקיימת
גזירתו, ספק אינה מתקיימת. אתה צדיק; בודאי שגזירתך מתקיימת . . . עמד והחזיר את
אשתו, עמדו כולן והחזירו את נשותיהן. וילד? ויחזור מיבעי ליה! . . . שעשה לו מעשה
ליקוחין, הושיבה באפריון, ואהרן ומרים מרקדין לפניה, ומלאכי השרת אמרו, אם הבנים
שמחה.

את בת לוי. אפשר בת מאה ושלשים שנה הויא וקרא לה בת? דאמר רבי חמא ברבי חנינא:
זו יוכבד שהורתה בדרך, ולידתה בין החומות, שנאמר, "אשר ילדה אתה ללוי במצרים"
. . . אמר רב יהודה, שנולדו בה סימני נערות.

5 אלא לפי שמעינו, לשון שליחה בגירושין.

6 לפי שלא באה למצרים אלא בבטן אמה.

7 ואמאי קרו לה בת? . . . מלמד שנולדו בה סימני נערות, חתעדן הבשר, נתפשטו הקמטין,
וחזר היופי למקומו. ויקח. ויחזור מיבעי ליה! . . . מלמד שעשה לה מעשה ליקוחין.

ELEVEN: Yocheved Gives Birth to a Son

1 ותהר האשה ותלד בן; ותרא אתו כי טוב הוא ותצפנהו שלשה ירחים.

2 להלן בפרשת וארא מספרת התורה ביתר אריכות על יחוסו, אך כאן היא מדגישה רק פרט
אחד בלבד, שהוא היה ילוד אשה, להבדיל מכל אותם הגבורים במיתולוגיה, המיוחסים ל"בן
אלים" . . . התורה מבליטה שרשה ומהותה של יהדות בכך, שהאדם הולך וגדל מלמטה
למעלה, ולא להיפך.

3 נסתכל והביט כל מעשיו וכל פעולותיו.

4 כי טוב הוא. שהיה יפה מראה.

5 ראתהו יפה יותר ממה שהיה מורגל.

6 לא כדרך הולדת הזקנות שהולד חלש מאד.

7 כי טוב פירושו, שלא היה בוכה, ולכן היה עליה נקל להצפינו.

8 אחרים אומרים נולד כשהוא מהול, וחכמים אומרים בשעה שנולד משה נתמלא הבית כולו
אור כתיב הכא "ותרא אתו כי טוב הוא," וכתיב התם "וירא אלקים את האור כי טוב."

9 אי נמי הברית נקרא אות, ודריש "ותרא אותו" פירוש "אות שלו" שהוא הברית כי טוב,
ומוכרח שהיה מהול.

10 וכוונת רז"ל שדרשו "טוב הוא" מהול.

11 ותצפנהו שלשה ירחים. דלא מנו מצרים אלא משעה דאהדרה, והיא הות מיעברא ביה תלתא
ירחי מעיקרא.

12 לא הלכו לחפש בבתיהם אם יולד זכר כי ידעו שקודם ט' חדשים אי אפשר שיולד למו, כי
הנשים היו גלמודות מבעליהם.

13 שמנו לה המצריים מיום שהחזירה, והיא ילדתו לששה חדשים ויום אחד . . . והם בדקו
אחריה לסוף תשעה.

14 שראתה המשגיחים דופקים על דלתי ביתה.

15 בדקו אחריו לסוף ו' חדשים משהחזירה, שהם ט' חדשים משנתעברה ממנו. שיודעים היו
יולדת לשבעה יולדת למקוטעים, **והוא נולד לסוף ג' חדשים מן החזרה.**

16 אמרה להם: נפל היה והשלכתיו היאורה.

17 ותחביאהו בבית תחת הארץ שלשה חדשים.

TWELVE: Yocheved Builds an Ark

1 ולא יכלה עוד הצפינו ותקח לו תבת גמא ותחמרה בחמר ובזפת; ותשם בה את הילד ותשם בסוף על שפת היאור.

2 כששלמו תשעה מליל חלומו של פרעה יצאו לחפש בכל המקומות. מיד "ותקח לו תבת גמא . . .".

3 ולא יכלה עוד להצפינו. למה? לפי שהמצרים היו הולכין בכל בית ובית שהיו חושבין בו שנולד שם תינוק, ומוליכין לשם תינוק מצרי קטן, והיו מבכין אותו כדי שישמע תינוק ישראל קולו, ויבכה עמו.

4 אולי השכנות המצריות שמעו קולו, כי לא היו לבדם דרים בארץ רעמסס.

5 ויוכבד עשתה כן כי אמרה אל אראה במות הילד.

6 ועומד בפני רך ובפני קשה.

7 והטעם שלקחה גומא . . . דבר קל הוא הגומא . . . שאם יבואו גלי היאור וישליכו התיבה על הסלעים לא תשבר, אלא היא תקפוץ לאחוריה.

8 לו לתועלתו והצלתו. ודבר חכמה עשתה יוכבד אמו, ותחבולה גדולה שהניחתו על שפת היאור כדי שיראו אצטגניני פרעה ויאמרו, "כבר השלך המושיע ביאור." כי ידעו זה מכח אצטגנינותם, ויגידו הדבר לפרעה, ואז תבטל הגזרה, כי לא יחקרו אם ימות אחר השלחתו ליאור אם לא, ולא יחפשו אחריו.

9 ודעתה לגנוב משם.

10 שלא נעשה דבר על ידי בעל; רק היא **לבדה**. כאומרו, ותקח לו תבת גומא ותחמרה **בעצמה**, ותשם בסוף **בעצמה**, כי לא דבר ריק הוא. כי הלא יותר הם אלו מלאכות אנשים ממלאכות נשים. אך עשתה בחכמה כי בידים אשר בהן היתה משפרת את ילדי העברים . . . ותחיה את הילדים בהן, תטפל בהצלת בנה.

11 בסוף . . . והוא צמח מן היאור.

12 ותקח לו תבת גומא . . . ותשם בסוף. סוף וגומא אחד הוא, [והתיבה] אין נראית וניכרת שם. משום שהסוף והגומא דמו להדדי.

13 ותשם בסוף אשר סמוך לשפת היאור והטמינתהו יפה, שהולכים על שפת היאר לא יכלו לראות התיבה. אבל הרוחצים בתוך הנהר יכלו לראותה כי יוכבד לא נכנסה בנהר להצפינו מכל צדדיו היטב.

14 רבי אליעזר אומר ים סוף.

15 היאור: נילוס.

16 שים סוף מגיע עד הנהר נילוס שבמצרים.

17 להפוך גזרת השלכתו ביאור.

18 כדי להטעות לאיצטגניני פרעה, כדי שיתיאשו ממנו ולא יבקשו אחריו, שהרי הושלך במים.

THIRTEEN: Miriam Guards Her Brother

1 ותתצב אחותו מרחק, לדעה מה יעשה לו.

2 דאמה העמידתה שם וציותה לה לראות מה יעלה בנער . . . אם יטריפו היאור או לא.

3 ותתצב אחותו מרחוק: **אמה** העמדתה שם, וצותה לה לראות מה יעלה בנער.

4 ותתצב . . . אכן משמעות הלשון שהיה גם זה השגחה פרטית מן השמים שתהיה האחות

ניצבת מרחוק.

5 שחשבה שיקחהו איזה מצרי, כשאר אסופי.

6 עמדה אמה וטפחה לה על ראשה. אמרה לה, בתי, והיכן נבואתיך?

7 וכיון שנולד משה . . . עמד אביה ונשקה על ראשה. אמר לה, בתי, נתקיימה נבואתיך. כיון שהטילוהו ליאור עמד אביה וטפחה על ראשה. אמר לה, בתי, היכן נבואתיך?!

8 על דרך הפשט זו מרים, שהרי מרים נתנבאה, "עתידה אמי שתלד בן שמושיע את ישראל." וזהו שאמר "לדעת מה יעשה לו," לדעת מה יהא בסוף נבואתה.

9 מה יעשה לו. איזה אופן יעשה לו להיות ניצל.

10 אמר רבי יצחק, פסוק זה כולו על שם שכינה.

11 ותתצב אחותו. זו שכינה, ולמדך הכתיב כשהצדיק מצטער, שכינה מזדמנת לו להצילו.

12 כי אלו היה גדל בין אחיו ויכירוהו מנעוריו, לא היו יראים ממנו.

13 [שמות ד', י'] וזה היה מהשגחת ד' שיגדל בבית מלך **ושם** למד כל חכמת מצרים והיה לו לב אמיץ בגבורים, **כי היה מבני פלטין.**

14 [שמות ד', יא'] שמינהו פרעה על ביתו.

FOURTEEN: Pharaoh's Daughter Discovers the Floating Basket

1 ותרד בת־פרעה לרחץ על היאר ונערותיה הלכת על־יד היאר ותרא את התבה בתוך הסוף ותשלח את אמתה ותקחה. ותפתח ותראהו את הילד והנה נער בכה; ותחמל עליו ותאמר מילדי העברים זה.

2 להקר מפני החום.

3 בזמן שהיתה רוחצת שהוצרכו נערותיה ממוסר המלכות שלא לעמוד לפניה, ולא נשארה עמה אלא אחת המיוחדת.

4 בת פרעה מצורעת היתה, לפיכך ירדה לרחוץ.

5 והיתה בתיה בת פרעה מנגעת בנגעים קשים ולא היתה יכולה לרחץ בחמין, וירדה לרחץ ביאור.

6 א) הזמין ד' שבת פרעה , אשר כל כבודה בת מלך פנימה, תרד ממעלתה לרחוץ על היאר במקום גלוי ומעבר לרבים. שלולא זה לא היתה אחותו מגיע אליה! ב) שנערותיה לא היו אתה, רק היו הולכות על יד היאר. שאם היו אתה היתה יראה מפנייהם לעבור על מצות אביה . . . ג) . . . הגם ש[התבה] היתה בתוך הסוף, טמון ומכוסה . . . ד) שלקחה אותו על ידי אמתה הפחותה, שלא בושה מלפניה לעשות כל חפצה. ויש הבדל בין נערות ובין אמהות, שהנערות הם הנתונות לה . . . והם נכבדות ובנות שרים, והאמהות הם . . . עומדים לשרתה.

7 ונערתיה הולכות על יד היאר לבקש ילדי העברים להשליכם ליאר לקיים גזרת אביה.

8 וידוע דפרעה היה עובד לנהר . . . ועל כן לא היה משמש באותו הנהר לרחיצת תענוג. ואם היתה בתו כרוכה אחרי דעותיו לא היתה רוחצת גם היא בו, ומדהלכה לרחוץ שמע מינא שבטלה עבודה זרה שלו.

9 ותרד בת פרעה לרחוץ על היאר. שכשנשפטר יעקב מאת פני פרעה, ברכו שנתעלה נילוס לרגלו. ומאז פסק הרעב ונתברך מצרים. . . . אך **פרעה זה** מלך חדש, שנתחדשו גזירותיו ועשה עצמו עבודה זרה ואמר "לי יאור ואני עשיתיני". . . . בת פרעה . . . רחצה . . . מגילולי בית אביה, שלא האמינה שאביה אלוה היאור . . . והיא האמינה שמברכת יעקב נתברך היאור. ואם כן הצילה ילד העברים מן היאור כי נראה לה עול לדון בני יעקב במי היאור.

10 אמר רבי יוחנן משום רבי שמעון בן יוחי: מלמד שירדה לרחוץ מגלולי אביה.

11 לרחוץ. לטבול שם לשם גירות.

12 ממש **פנימה.**

13 היה שהיתה צדקת ותחמול עליו.

14 וראתה נער בוכה, ושלחה ידה והחזיקה בו ונתרפאה, ואמרה, הנער הזה מישראל, וקימתו
לחיים.

15 וכל המקים נפש אחת מישראל, כאלו קיים עולם מלא. וכל המאבד נפש אחת מישראל, כאלו
מאבד עולם מלא. ולפיכך זכתה בת פרעה לדבק תחת כנפי השכינה ונקראה "בתו של
מקום."

16 ואשתו היהודיה . . . בתיה בת פרעה.

17 ואשתו היהודיה ילדה את ירד . . . אמאי קרי לה יהודיה? על שום שכפרה בעבודה זרה
. . . ילדה? והא רבויי רביתיה לומר לך שכל המגדל יתום ויתומה בתוך ביתו מעלה עליו
הכתוב כאלו ילדו. ירד זה משה.

18 יוכבד ילדה ובתיה גידלה, לפיכך נקרא על שמה.

19 הנה בתיה בהוצאת הילד מן היאור הוה ליה כמו שילדתו, כי הצילתו לשטף מים רבים אליו
לא יגיעו, ואם לא היה נטבע ואבד, וזה חשוב כאשר ילדתו בעצם . . . וכך כתיב "ויהי לה
לבן" ממש, דהרי איכא גידול ולידה.

20 התורה אינה מזכירה את שמה של בת פרעה, ואילו בדברי-הימים א' (ד:יח) מוזכר שמה:
"בתיה." חכמינו אמרו, כי השם "בתיה" ניתן לה רק לאחר-מכן, כאות תודה על אשר
הצילה את משה, וכך אמר לה הקב"ה את קראת לבני משה, הריני קורא לך בתי -- בתיה.
. . . כי על-ידי מעשיה הטובים נעשתה לבת קל חי.

21 מדותיה נבדלות ממדות אביה . . . הוא בתכלית הרשע, והיא בתכלית היושר.

22 בתיה . . . אשר לקח מרד. וכי מרד שמו? והלא כלב שמו! אמר הקב"ה: יבא כלב
שמרד בעצת המרגלים, וישא את בת פרעה שמרדה בגלולי בית אביה.

FIFTEEN: Princess Batya Rescues the Baby

1 ותרד בת-פרעה לרחץ על היאר ונערותיה הלכת על-יד היאר ותרא את התבה בתוך הסוף
ותשלח את אמתה ותקחה. ותפתח ותראהו את הילד והנה נער בכה; ותחמל עליו ותאמר
מילדי העברים זה.

2 היה השגחה פרטית שלא יהיה נודע לפרעה ולשריו כל הנעשה שהצילה בת פרעה ילד מן
היאור. והיה ההשגחה שבאותה שעה היו נערותיה הולכות ומיללות סמוך ליאור בגובה
החוף, ולא ראו מה שעשתה אדונית שלהן במורד.

3 ונערתיה. שלשים נערות היו עמה, ושום אחת לא ראתה, אלא היא, שנאמר "ותרא את
התבה."

4 ותרא את התבה . . . כיון דחזו דקא באו לאצולי למשה אמרו לה: גבירתנו, מנהגו של עולם
מלך בשר ודם גוזר גזרה, אם כל העולם כולו אין מקיימין אותה, בניו ובני ביתו מקיימין
אותה. ואת עוברת על גזירת אביך? בא גבריאל וחבטן בקרקע.

5 את שפחתה.

6 "ותשלח את אמתה ותקחה." רבי יהודה ורבי נחמיה; חד אמר ידה, וחד אמר שפחתה.

7 שני המשמעות נכללל בפשט המלה. היינו ששלחה את שפחתה שנשתיירה אצלה לאיזה דבר,
והיא בעצמה שלחה ידה ותקחה. ומשום זה לא נודע דבר.

8 מאן דאמר ידה, ששים אמה נשתרבבה אמתה של בת פרעה.

9   והנה אף על פי שידעה בת פרעה מדת ידה . . . ושבשום אופן לא תשיג בידה את התבה
ששטה בתוך האגם, מ"מ לא נמנעה משלוח את ידה להצילו . . . ומשם ואילך תעשה מלאכת
ההצלה מאליו בדרך נס, **או היד תשתרבב, או התבה תתקרב ביותר אל החוף**, וכן הוא
טבע הנס.

10   וכי מי אינו יודע שאם פתחה את התיבה שתראה את הילד. אלא כך פרושו: פתחה את
התיבה והביטה

11   "ותרא" מיבעי ליה! אמר רבי יוסי ברבי חנינא: שראתה שכינה עמו.

12   שזכתה לראות פני שכינה אחר שנתגיירה.

13   לשון הגמרא שמא לא אזכה לחופתו. עם כן עשתה לו חופה בתיבה לקינה ואבל.

14   כסבורה שמצאה ילד שנולד באותו יום או יומים. והנה הוא נער כבן ג' חדשים. מקרי נער
לגבי בן יומו. ומזה הבינה כי מילדי העברים זה. ודרך העברים להשתדל ולחפש עצות
להציל כפי האפשרי. ע"כ עלה ביד אמו להצפינו איזה משך עד שהוכרחה באחרונה להניחהו
כאן.

15   ואיך רחם ארחמנו ושמע אבי והרגני? כי לא יחפוץ בחיים של ילדי העברים. ומה גם
לגדלו בביתו ובחומותיו! אז עודנה במבוכה זו מבקשת להטיב, וחוששת על היותו מילדי
העבריים, שנואי נפש אביה.

16   כי לא היה בהצלתו של משה משום עבירה על חוקת אביה, שהרי השליכוהו ליאור.

SIXTEEN: Miriam Confronts the Princess

1   ותאמר אחתו אל בת־פרעה האלך וקראתי לך אשה מינקת מן העבריות ותינק לך את הילד.
ותאמר לה בת־פרעה לכי; ותלך העלמה ותקרא את אם הילד.

2   שנאמר על מרים ושהיא היתה אז כמו בת ט"ו שנים.

3   היה מהשגחת ה' שאחותו תערב לבה לדבר כזאת אל בת מלך בלא פחד שתענש.

4   ואחותו מרים כשראתה לקיחת התיבה, נתקרבה שמה לבת פרעה לראות מה תעשה בנער.
וכששמעה ממנה דברי חמלה . . . לפי כוונתה ואמרה "האלך . . .".

5   רצה לאמר שאם תתניהו לאשה מצרית תשלח פן תשלח בו יד להמיתו בסתר משנאתם ילדי
העברים, וצריך מינקת **עברית**, ובזה יש חשש שיקחוהו המצריים מידה וישליכוהו ליאור.

6   ומאי שנא מעבריות? מלמד שהחזירוהו למשה על כל המצריות כולן, ולא ינק.

7   שבקשה להניקו

8   אם היה מכירה. . . . עד כמה? . . . אמר רב: שלשה חדשים. . . כל זמן שמכירה.

9   דייקת שתי פעמים תיבת "לך." דבל"ז היה סכנה לה ולהמינקת להציל ולד מן היאור. אבל
כאשר היא קוראה להמינקת בשם בת פרעה, והיא תינק בשבילה, אשיג מינקת לזה.

10   בענין שיקרא ההנקה על שמך, ואך לא יערב איש לפגוע בו.

11   "העלמה:" שהעלימה את דבריה.

12   שלא אמרה שהיא אחותו, ושהיא מביאה את אמו.

13   **שנתעלמה** מן האדונית ולא שבה בחזרה עם אם הילד . . . שלא לבקש ולא לקבל שכר על
מלוי רצון.

14   ובזה היה ההשגחה שימצא משה בבית אביו ויכיר עמו ומולדתו.

SEVENTEEN: Princess Batya Commissions Yocheved
to Nurse the Baby

1 ותאמר לה בת־פרעה היליכי את הילד הזה והינקיהו לי ואני אתן את שכרך; ותקח האשה
הילד ותניקהו.

2 הוליכי.

3 והיה ראוי שיאמר **קחי**. וחז"ל תרצו זה על דרך שדרשו שהוא כמו **הי ליכי**; הוא שלך.

4 אמר רבי חמא ברבי חנינא: מתנבאה ואינה יודעת מה מתנבאה, "היליכי -- הא שליכי (זה
שלך)."

5 לבדו ולא אחר עמו.

6 והניקהו **לי** כאלו את מינקת בן המלך **לי**, דייקא בכל כבוד וזריזות וחמלה, ושאת תאכלי
מאכלים טובים ומעדנים לזכך החלב, כי את מנקת בן בת המלך. ואל תחושי לצרכי הוצאה
במאכלים היקרים והסגולים והפסדת מלאכתך בשומך כל חריצותך וזריזותך עליו, כי אני
מלכה אתן את שכרך.

7 אמרה לה "יראה אני מגזרה שגזר אביך." אמרה לה, "**לי** את מיניקתו."

8 ותקח האשה את הילד ותניקהו. באותה שעה נתן לה הקב"ה מקצת שכרה. שהיא היתה
מחיה את הילדים וכן הקב"ה החזיר לה את בנה ונתן לה שכרה.

EIGHTEEN: Yocheved Brings Her Son to Princess Batya
and He is Named Moses

1 ויגדל הילד ותבאהו לבת־פרעה ויהי לה לבן; ותקרא שמו משה ותאמר כי מן המים משיתהו.

2 כ"ד חדש הניקתהו.

3 והיה מהשגחתא ד' שגם אחר שגדל, שכבר עברה החמלה שעורר לבה עליו בעת שמצאה אותו
עזוב ומושלך, בכל זאת לקחה אותו לבן.

4 שם משה. מתורגם מלשון מצרים בלשון הקדש. ושמו בלשון מצרים היה מוניוס.

5 ולכן קראתו משה על שם שהוציאתו מהנהר, להורות דכלו **שלה**, ויהי **לה** לבן ממש . . . כי
בתיה הצילתו מהמות **במקום לידה**, ועל כן קראה שמו משה, לזכר עולם.

6 אולי למדה בת פרעה את לשוננו או שאלה.

7 שנתגיירה והיתה לומדת לשון הקדש על שם הנס שננמשה מן המים, להזכיר כי מן העברים
הוא.

8 הנקבה הנזכר בזה הפסוק היא כנוי לצדקת אם משה, לא לבת פרעה. כמו שאמר **ותקח**
האשה את הילד, **ותניקהו, ותביאהו** לבת פרעה . . . גם כן **ותקרא** שמו משה . . .
וכשהביאתהו לפניו קראה שמו משה . . . אמו של משה אמרה לבת פרעה . . . "גברתי, הלא
קראתי אותו משה על שם המאורע שהיה לך עמו כי מן המים משית אותו." ותדע ותשכיל
מזה . . . משיתהו שפירושו משית אותו . . . שהיא אמרה לבת פרעה "הנה אנכי קראתי שמו
משה בלשוננו העברית לפי שאת משית אותו מן המים."

9 ולא קראו הקדוש ברוך הוא בשם אחר אלא בו.

10 כי הנה אדון הנביאים נקרא משה מתחלה עד יום מותו, ולא הועתק שמו, ולא נשתנה.

11 שמזכיר שמשתה אותו מן המים.

12 כי לא היה בהצלתו של משה משום עבירה על חוקת אביה, שהרי השליחוהו ליאור, ומן המים
משיתהו. ונמצא הוא ניצל מבלי שתופר פקודתו של פרעה. ולפיכך יכולה היתה להכניסו
לבית אביה ולגדלו כבן.

¹³ שהיה גדל שלא כדרך כל הארץ . . . היתה בת פרעה מנשקת ומחבקת ומחבבת אותו כאלו
הוא בנה, ולא היתה מוציאתו מפלטרין של מלך. ולפי שהיה יפה, הכל מתאוים לראותו. מי
שהיה רואהו לא היה מעביר עצמו מעליו. והיה פרעה מנשקו ומחבקו. והוא נוטל כתרו של
פרעה ומשימו על ראשו כמו שעתיד לעשות לו כשהיה גדול . . . והיו שם יושבין חרטומי
מצרים ואמרו מתייראין אנו מזה שנוטל כתרך ונותנו על ראשו . . . שאנו אומרים שעתיד
ליטול מלכות ממך. מהם אומרים להורגו, מהם אומרים לשורפו. והיה יתרו יושב ביניהן
ואומר להם הנער הזה אין בו דעת . . . בחנו אותו. והביאו לפניו קערה זהב וגחלת. אם
יושיט ידו לזהב . . . יהרגו אותו, ואם יושיט ידו לגחלת . . . ואין עליו משפט מות. מיד
הביאו לפניו ושלח ידו ליקח הזהב, ובא גבריאל ודחה את ידו ותפס את הגחלת, והכניס ידו
עם הגחלת לתוך פיו, ונכוה לשונו. וממנו נעשה כבד פה וכבד לשון.

¹⁴ וישלך אלקים מלאך מ ממלאכים קדושים ושמו גבריאל.

¹⁵ ממלט ומושה את אחרים מצרה.

¹⁶ אולי סבב השם זה שיגדל משה בבית המלכות להיות נפשו על מדרגה העליונה בדרך הלימוד
וההרגלות . . . ועוד דבר אחר, כי אלו היה גדל בין אחיו ויכירוהו מנעוריו, לא היו יראים
ממנו, כי יחשבוהו כאחד מהם.

TWENTY: Moses and the Kushite Woman

¹ וישמע פרעה את הדבר הזה ויבקש להרג את משה ויברח משה מפני פרעה . . .

² ויברח משה מפני פרעה . . . וישמע פרעה את הדבר ויבקש להרוג את משה. ומסרו
לקוסטינר להרגו ולא שלטה בו החרב. ועשה הקב"ה נס עמו . . . ומה עשה האלקים?
וישלח את מיכאל, שר צבא מרום, ודמותו דמות שר הטבחים. ויקח חרבו והמית שר
הטבחים, כי נהפך דמותו לדמות משה. ויחזיק המלאך ביד משה ויוציאהו ממצרים ויניחהו
מחוץ לגבול מצרים רחוק מהלך ג' ימים . . .

וכשראה בלעם שלא נעשתה עצתו ולא יצא הדבר לפועל לכלות את בני ישראל כפי מחשבתו
הרעה אשר חשב יצא ממצרים וילך לו למלך ניקנוס. . . . ומלך ניקנוס הוא מלך אדום.
בימים ההם היתה מלחמה בין כוש ובין בני קדם . . . ויהי בצאת ניקנוס להלחם בבני קדם
ויעזוב בלעם הקוסם ושני בניו . . . לשמור את העיר. וישבו שם . . ויועץ בלעם את עם
הארץ למרוד במלך ניקנוס לבלתי תת בוא העירה. וישמעו אליו עם הארץ וישבעו לו,
וימליכו אותו עליהם למלך. ואת בניו הפקיד עליהם שרי צבאות בראש העם. ויגבהו
החומות משני צדי העיר ומן העבר השלישי חפרו בארות רבים לאין מספר, וישימו שם מי
הנהר הסובב את כל ארץ כוש. ומן העבר הב' קצבו נחשים ועקרבים רבים בלהטיהם, ואין
יוצא ואין בא אל העיר. ויהי בשוב ניקנוס וכל שרי החילים מהמלחמה, וישאו עיניהם ויראו
חומות העיר גבוהה מאד. ויתמהו איש אל רעהו ויאמרו ביניהם, ראו בני העיר כי נתאחרנו
במלחמה ויגבהו חומות העיר ויחזקוה לבלתי בא אליהם מלכי כנען. ויהי כאשר קרב אל
העיר ויראו שערי העיר סגורות. ויקראו לשוערים לפתוח אליהם לבוא העיר, וימאנו
השוערים לפתוח להם במצות בלעם הקוסם, ולא נתנום לבוא העירה. ויערכו מלחמה בפתח
השער, ויפלו מחיל ניקנוס . . . ולא יכלו ליכנס אל העיר . . . ויחדלו מלהלחם על כוש,
ויצורו עליה ט' שנים, אין יוצא ואין בא.ויהי בהיות המצור על כוש ברח משה ממצרים,
ויבוא אל מחנה ניקנוס מלך כוש.

ומשה בן שלשים שנה בבואו אל מחנה ניקנוס הצרים על כוש . . . ויהי משה הולך ובא
עמהם, וימצא חן בעיניהם, ויאהבוהו המלך, וכל השרים וכל חיל המלחמה,כי הוא הולך וגדל
. . . ויאהבהו המלך מאד, וישימהו שר צבא. וישבו שם ימים רבים עד שחלה המלך ניקנוס

וימת. ויאמרו עבדיו, מה נעשה?‏ . . . וייעצו יחדו להמליך עליהם את משה למלך, כי אין
כמוהו בעם. ויעשו כן, **ויתנו לו למשה הגבירה אשת ניקנוס.** ויזכור משה את ברית ד'
אלקיו, ולא קרב אליה. וישם חרבו בינו לבינה, ולא חטא עמה.

ויהי ביום הג' למלכו ויאמרו לו עבדיו , תן לנו עצה ודבר מה נעשה, כי ט' שנים זה לא ראינו
נשינו וטפינו, ואנו מתאים לראותם. ויאמר להם משה, אם תשמעו בקולי תצליחו ותשובו
אל בתיכם לשלום. ויאמרו לו, כל אשר תצוונו נעשה. ויאמר להם, הרה לכו וקחו לכם
מאפרוחי החסידה . . . וילכו מהרה ויעשו כן . . . ויאמר להם, רכבו איש על סוסו ולבשוה
שריונות, וקחו לכם איש כלי מלחמתו, ובואו אחרי מן הצד אשר הנחשים שם. ובעת אשר
יצאו הנחשים השליכו עליהם אפרוחי החסידה, ויאכלום, ונקה העיר. ויעשו כן ויקרבו אל
העיר, ויכהו לפני חרב. וכראות בלעם בן פעור כי נלכדה העיר, עונן ונחש ופרח באויר הוא
ובניו, וינוסו אל מצרים אל פרעה, וישבו עמו. וישובו איש לביתו. וכראות העם כי המלך
הושיעם . . . ויאהבוהו מאד. ויירא משה את ד' אלקיו, ולא סר מחוקות אבותיו . . . והימים
אשר מלך משה על כוש מ' שנה.

ויהי היום והוא יושב על כסאו **והגבירה יושבת אצלו.** ותאמר הגבירה לשרים, ראו המלך
אשר המלכתם עליכם. זה מ' שנה לא קרב אלי. ועתה שימו עליכם מלך בן אדוניכם ניקנוס,
כי לו משפט המלוכה. ולא תמליכו עליכם איש נכרי. ויאמרו כל שרי החיילים למשה, טוב
אתה בעינינו מאד, אך כל עם המדינות יועצים להמליך עליהם בן אדוניהם. ועתה קח לך
עושר ונכסים, ולך מעמנו, ושוב אל מקומך בשלום. וילך משה לארץ מדין וישב על הבאר.

	ידמה שהיה משה כבן כ' שנה כשנהרג את המצרי וברח מלפני פרעה. וכל מה שכתוב בדברי
הימים של משה אפשר שיהיה אמת. ושקודם שהגיע לארץ מדין מלך בארץ כוש ארבעים
שנה ולקח שם אשה כושית. ואחר כך ירד למדין . . . האמנם קצרה התורה בספור מה
שקרה לו בארץ כוש לפי שכל מה שעשה משה בזה היה אבוד זמן.

TWENTY-ONE: Moses and the Seven Shepherdesses

	ויברח משה מפני פרעה וישב בארץ מדין וישב על הבאר. ולכהן מדין שבע בנות; ותבאנה
ותדלנה ותמלאנה את הרהטים להשקות צאן אביהן. ויבאו הרעים ויגרשום; ויקם משה
ויושען וישק את צאנם. ותבאנה אל רעואל אביהן; ויאמר מדוע מהרתן בא היום. ותאמרן
איש מצרי הצילנו מיד הרעים; וגם דלה דלה לנו וישק את הצאן. ויאמר אל בנותיו ואיו;
למה זה עזבתן את האיש; קראן לו ויאכל לחם.

	ב' פעמים וישב, להגיד שלא קרה הספור הזה מבנות מדין מיד כשברח מארץ המצרים ונכנס
בארץ מדין . . . ואולי אחרי שבא מארץ כוש כמו שכתוב בדברי הימים [של משה] . . .
ואחר כך קרה שיום אחד נזדמן לו שישב על הבאר.

	ארץ מדין סרים היו אל משמעת פרעה. על כן הוצרך להיות רועה צאן, שלא יעמוד בישוב,
אולי יכירוהו.

	למד מיעקב שנזדווג לו זווגו מן הבאר.

	מיעקב למד שנזדווג לו זוגתו מן הבאר . . . כי יעקב ידע זה מאליעזר שנזדמנה לו רבקה על
הבאר לזווג ליצחק . . . ואז ישב לו על הבאר והתפלל שתזדמן לו אחת על ידי יציאת
השקאת הצאן.

	והנה אמר שהיו לכהן מדין . . . שבע בנות בתולות, והגדולה והנכבדת שבהן היתה צפורה.

	הוא יתרו.

	יתרו ראש כומרים של מדין היה.

	אמרו רבותינו יתרו כומר לעבודת כוכבים היה, וראה שאין בה ממש, וביסר עליה והרהר

לעשות תשובה עד שלא בא משה. וקרא לבני עירו ואמר להם, עד עכשיו הייתי משמש
אתכם; מעתה זקן אני. בחרו לכם כומר אחר. עמד והוציא כלי תשמישי עבודת כוכבים,
ונתן להם הכל. עמדו ונדוהו, שלא יזדקק לו אדם, ולא יעשו לו מלאכה, ולא ירעה את צאנו
. . . לפיכך הוציא בנותיו . . . מלמד שהיו מקדימות לבא מפני פחד הרועים.

10 בשביל שהיה עסק ההשקאה מרובה לדלות ולמלאות, והיו הרועים מתאחרים בגללם.

11 כי הכיר בהן צניעות. כי דרך נשים בבואן בארה לדבר עם האיש אשר ימצא שם ומה גם
בהיותו איש זר אשר לא מארצן הוא, כי שאול ישאלו מה ארצך . . . או לפחות לדבר אלו
עם אלו. אך לא כאלה חלק נשים אלו, כי אם ותבאנה ומיד ותדלנה, ותמלאנה וכו'. ולא
הוטפלו בדבור אפילו אלו עם אלו, כי בשו ממנו.

12 לא היה להן קירוב דעת עם הרועים, כי הלא אדרבה, ויבאו הרועים ויגרשום.

13 מלמד שהרועים נטלום ושפכום למים.

14 שרצו הרועים לאנסם.

15 על כן שם את נפשו מנגד, לקום לבדו על רועים רבים, ולא חש פן ירוצו את גולגלתו . . .
חרה אפו ויקם ויושיען.

16 ראה בנות יתרו מצטערות. ולא נתגאה מלעמוד ולדלות להן, והוא היה בנפשו כבן בתו של
מלך . . . שהיה לו לב אמיץ, להציל . . . אע"פ שהוא גר בורח.

17 אז השיב רעואל . . . כי אשר לו כח גדול כזה לא איש הוא, ומן הסתם נתעלם ופרח.

18 שהיה מדבר בלשון מצרים.

19 מאחר שהוא אורח ואיש חסד, היה לכן לגמול עמו חסד הכנסת אורחים.

20 שמא ישא אחת מכם. ואין אכילת לחם האמור כאן אלא אשה.

21 מיד רצתה צפורה אחריו כצפור והביאה אותו.

TWENTY-TWO: Zipporah Marries Moses

1 ויואל משה לשבת את האיש, ויתן את צפורה בתו למשה.

2 אם נפרש אכילת לחם כפשוטה, מדוע נכתב אח"כ 'ויואל משה לשבת את האיש?' היכן
מוזכר בתורה שביקש ממנו יתרו לשבת עמו? הרי ביקש ממנו רק שיאכל לחם. אלא ע"כ
שביקש ממנו גם זאת שישב אצלו, [וגם] וישא את בתו.

3 כתרגומו.

4 לרעות את צאנו.

5 "ויואל משה," אין אלה אלא שבועה.

6 לשון אלה. נשבע לו שלא יזוז ממדין כי אם ברשותו.

7 ולמה השביעו? אמר לו, יודע אני שיעקב אביכם כשנתן לו לבן בנותיו נטלן והלך לו חוץ
מדעתו. שמא אם אתן לך את בתי אתה עושה לי כך. מיד נשבע לו ונתן לו את צפורה.

8 אמר לו, הבן שיהיה לך תחלה יהיה לע"ז.

9 היתכן האיש משה יעשה כדבר הרע הזה לתת מזרעו . . . אמנם . . . שהוליד אברהם את
ישמעאל . . . כיון יתרו, כי חש פן יקרא למשה כהם . . . נושא אשה שלא מאומתך, אולי
תכוין לעשות כאברהם שלקח הגר . . . בהולדה אם בו בחינת זוהמא יטיל אותה בראשון,
והשאר יהיו טהורים.

10 הלא נמס כל לב איש שומע דבר כזה.

11 דידע משה שיחזיר את חמיו למוטב כמו שעשה, שהרי נתגייר.

12 ויואל משה. . . . היה משה בורח מפני פרעה, ומתירא ממנו שמא . . . יהרגוהו . . . מפני
שהיו כל נכסיהם בני חורין, אין למלך [פרעה] עליהם שום נגישה . . . רק אדמת הכהנים

לבדם לא היתה לפרעה . . . ועל כן רצה להתחתן עם אחד מהם, ושישא בתו אחר שנתגיר.

13 אמר לו רעואל, מאין תבוא, מה ארצך . . . ויאמר לו, אני משה. ויספר לו כל המוצאות אותו במצרים. אז אמר בלבו יתרו, זה האיש אשר שלח ידו בכתר המלך. ועתה אקחנו ואמסרנו ביד פרעה. ויצו לכלכלו בלחם צר ומים לחץ. וימצא חן בעיני צפורה בתו, ותחמול עליו. ובכל יום ויום מעת לעת היתה מספקת לו לחם ומזון, וישב שם שבע שנים. ויהי מקץ שבע שנים אמרה צפורה לאביה, השבוי והאסור אשר השלכת לבור זה כמה ימים ושנים, הלוא תדרשנו, כי בכל יום צועק עליו לאלקיו והיה בך חטא. ויאמר לה יתרו, מי שמע כזאת אדם שלא אכל ושתה כמה שנים ועודנו חי! הלכו לבית האסורים ומצאוהו עומד על רגליו ומתפלל לאלקיו, ויוציאוהו משם.

14 מאמרו במדרש שמטה האלקים היה נטוע בפרדס של יתרו, ולא היה שום אדם לזוזו ממקומו, רק משה. ועל זה נתן לו את צפורה בתו לאשה.

15 רבי לוי אומר, המטה שנברא בין השמשות נמסר לאדם הראשון מגן עדן . . . מסרו לנח . . . מסרו לאברהם, ואברהם מסרו ליצחק, ויצחק מסרו ליעקב, ויעקב הורידו למצרים ומסרו ליוסף בנו. וכשמת יוסף נשלל כל ביתו ונתן בפלטרין של פרעה. והיה יתרו אחד מחרטמי מצרים וראה את המטה . . . וחמד [אותו] בלבו ולקחו והביאו ונטעו בתוך גן ביתו . . . ולא היה אדם יכול לקרב אליו עוד. וכשבא משה לביתו לכנס לגן ביתו של יתרו ראה את המטה, וקרא את האותות אשר עליו, ושלח ידו ולקחו. וראה יתרו את משה ואמר, זה עתיד לגאל את ישראל ממצרים. לפיכך נתן לו את צפורה בתו לאשה.

16 כי כל חפצו לא היה רק **לשבת את האיש בלבד**, ולא לחיבת חיתון.

17 לא **"ויקח** משה את צפורה בתו," אלא **"ויתן** את צפורה בתו." לא משה חיזר אחרי צפורה, אלא יתרו חיזר אחרי משה.

18 משה שהיה מובדל מאנשים, ולא היתה לו לעזר.

19 מצאתי צפורה וראיתי אותה צנועה ביותר. אמרתי לה שאשאנה.

20 צפורה היתה היפה ביותר בין שבע הבנות . . . צפורה היתה יפה ומאירה כבקר דמתרגמין "צפרא."

21 נקראת צפורה מלשון צפור, שהוא עוף טהור, על שם שעתידה להתגיר ולהטהר מטמאת עבודת גלולים ולהזדווג למשה.

22 טעם שכפל הזכרת שמו ולא הספיק לומר ויתן **לו** את [צפורה בתו] כיון הכתוב להודיע כי היא בת זוגו.

23 צפורה הלכה בדרך הצדקניות שרה ורבקה רחל ולאה, ותלך בדרך ה' כאשר צוה עליה משה בעלה.

TWENTY-THREE: Zipporah Bears a Son for Moses

1 ותלד בן יקרא את שמו גרשם, כי אמר גר הייתי בארץ נכריה.

2 ותהר לא נאמר. ללמד שהיתה בחורה והריון אין ניכר בה.

3 משה קראו.

4 **צפורה** קראה שם בנה גרשום . . . דסמך משה . . . על צדקת צפורה . . . כלומר שאין לבעלה רשות, ומה שנתרצה היה בעל כרחו. וזהו כי אמר גר הייתי בארץ נכריה ואני איני מתרצה.

5 שכך משמע גרשם: גר **שם**, בארץ רחוקה.

6 יש לדקדק **הייתי** לשון עבר הוא, והלא עתה היה גר בארץ נכריה, כי מצרים עיר מולדתו היה, יאמר כי גר אנכי בארץ נכריה . . . אבל אם עתה טוב לו מאז, ובעיניו נדמה כי היה כי היה אז

בארץ מולדתו כגר . . . וזה היה אצל משה שהיה נרדף מפרעה ומעבדיו עד שברח. ושם
היה לו עונג ושלוה ושלום שקט ושאנן ואין מחריד, הודה להקב"ה על זה ויקרא שמו שם בנו
"גרשם" כי אמר גר הייתי בארץ נכריה. פירושו שהיה גר בארץ נכריה **לו עתה,** דהיינו
ארץ מצרים.

⁷ ואולי שרמז אל ארץ כוש, אשר גר שם בראשונה, באמרו גר **הייתי** בארץ נכריה ולא גר
אנכי.

⁸ ד"א כשנולד גרשום עדיין היה משה חדש במקומו ונחשב כגר.

⁹ לא שכח אהבת עמו, והיה עינו ולבו שם כל הימים, לשוב אליהם ולהושיעם, ומדין היתה
ארץ נכריה בעיניו, וישיבתו שם כגרות וטלטול.

TWENTY-FOUR: Moses Encounters God

¹ שמ' ג, טז: פקד פקדתי אתכם

² שמ' ג, כב: ושאלה אשה משכנתה . . . כלי כסף וכלי זהב

TWENTY-FIVE: Serach, Asher's Daughter,
Heralds the Redemption

¹ לך ואספת את זקני ישראל ואמרת אלהם ד' אלקי אבתיכם נראה אלי אלקי אברהם יצחק
ויעקב לאמר; **פקד פקדתי אתכם** ואת העשוי לכם במצרים.

² ושאלה אשה משכנתה ומגרת ביתה כלי כסף וכלי זהב ושמלות; ושמתם על בניכם ועל
בנתיכם ונצלתם את מצרים.

³ ויאמן העם, וישמעו כי **פקד ד'** את בני ישראל . . .

⁴ פ' מח: ולא נמסרו האותיות אלא לאברהם אבינו, ואברהם מסרן ליצחק, ויצחק מסרן
ליעקב, ויעקב מסרן ליוסף, ויוסף מסרן לאחיו, ואשר בן יעקב מסר סוד הגאולה לסרח בת
אשר. וכשבאו משה ואהרן אצל זקני ישראל ועשו האותות לעיניהם, הלכו זקני ישראל אצל
זקנתם סרח בת אשר ואמרו לה, בא איש ועשה אותות לעינינו כך וכך. אמרה להם, אין
באותות האלו ממש. אמרו לה, והלא אמר לנו, **פקד פקדתי** אתכם. אמרה להם, הוא האיש
שעתיד לגאל את ישראל ממצרים.

⁵ סרח בת אשר נשתיירה מאותו הדור.

⁶ אחר ששמעו כי **פקד ה'** עמו, כי הגיע הקץ האמור לאברהם.

⁷ תשעה נכנסו בחייהם לגן עדן ואלו הן . . . סרח בת אשר.

⁸ למה מצוה זו נאמרה לנשים? . . . שכיון שגזר פרעה כל הבן הילוד היארה תשליכוהו היו
בנות ישראל משחדות מתשכיטיהן לעבדי פרעה, ומשחידות למצרים שלא יגלו, ומשליכין
מבניהם מקצת, ומניחין מקצת.

TWENTY-SIX: Moses, Zipporah and their Sons
Take Leave of Yitro

¹ וילך משה וישב אל יתר חתנו ויאמר לו אלכה נא ואשובה אל אחי אשר במצרים ואראה
העודם חיים; ויאמר יתרו למשה לך לשלום. ויאמר ד' אל משה במדין לך שב מצרים; כי
מתו כל האנשים המבקשים את נפשך. ויקח משה את אשתו ואת בניו וירכבם על החמר וישב
ארצה מצרים; ויקח משה את מטה האלקים בידו.

² מן המדבר להביא לו צאנו, שלא יודע מתי ישוב.

3   ליטול רשות, שהרי נשבע לו.

4   אמר לו: במדין נדרת—לך והתר נדרך במדין.

5   ויתכן כי קודם הדבור הנדבר לו בהר האלקים, לא נולד לו רק גרשום. אבל היתה צפורה
הרה, וכאשר שב אל יתר חותנו ילדה. ובעבור כי היה דבר המלך נחוץ . . .

6   אשתו ובניו היו אתו בהר חורב אצל הצאן, כי שם אהלו, וכיון שרצה ללכת למצרים, חזר
למקום המרעה ויקח את אשתו ובניו . . . להשיבה אל בית אביה.

7   אמר לו יתרו: להיכן אתה מוליכן? למצרים. אמר לו: משהם מבקשים לצאת, את מוליכן
למצרים! אמר לו: למחר עתידין לצאת לעמוד על הר סיני ולשמוע מפי הגבורה 'אנכי ד'
אלקיך אשר הוצאתיך מארץ מצרים.'

8   הוא חשש פן לא יאמינו לו. לכן הכניס בניו ואשתו, כי הוא בטוח בדבר ד' להוציאן
ממצרים. כי אם לא, מי יכנס את בניו ואשתו אל מקום עבדות ומסוכן כזה?!

9   שמות כג (קכג) אימתי עשה הקב"ה בקולו נפלאות, בשעה שביקש הקב"ה לשלח משה
בשליחותו לגאול את ישראל, והיה במדין מתירא שברח מפני פרעה שמא יהרגנו . . . כיון
שנגלה עליו הדיבר במדין ואמר לו שיחזור למצרים, שנאמר ויאמר ד' אל משה במדין 'לך
שוב מצרימה.' נחלק הדיבור לשני קולות, ונעשה דיו פרצופין, ושמע משה במדין 'לך שוב
מצרים,' ואהרן שמע במצרים 'לך לקראת משה המדברה.' ומה שבאמצע לא היו שומעים
כלום, הוי ירעם קל בקולו נפלאות.

TWENTY-SEVEN: The Incident at the Inn

1   ויהי בדרך במלון ויפגשהו ד' ויבקש המיתו." ותקח צפרה צר ותכרת את ערלת בנה ותגע
לרגליו ותאמר כי חתן־דמים אתה לי. וירף ממנו אז אמרה חתן דמים למולות.

2   פרשת ד' בספר שמות, מפסוק כ"ד עד פסוק כ"ו, היא הפרשה הסתומה ביותר בין הפרשיות.
השם שולח את משה לגאול את ישראל, ופתאום הוא מפתיע אותו בדרך, ובקש המיתו, למה
זה ומדוע? . . . דברי חז"ל כי משה נתחייב מיתה על שלא מל את אליעזר בנו, אבל אם כן
למה פגשו גזר־הדין, דווקא "בדרך במלון?" ואם כבר באו משה ואשתו לידי מסקנה כי יש
למולו, למה מלה אותו צפורה ולא משה? . . . צפורה גם אומרת קודם: "חתן דמים אתה
לי," וכאשר המלאך הרפה מהם היא אומרת: "חתן דמים למולות." לא מבואר במקרא את
מי ביקש המלאך להמית, את משה או את הילד? המעיין בפסוקים יראה כי ללא הסברה של
חז"ל ומפרשים אין למצוא ידים ורגלים בהם.

3   לפי שלא מל את אליעזר בנו, ועל שנתרשל נענש מיתה.

4   "ויפגשהו ד' ויבקש המיתו." אמר רבי: חס ושלום שמשה רבינו נתרשל מן המילה; אלא כך
אמר: אמול ואצא־־סכנה היא . . . אמול ואשהא שלשה ימים־־הקדוש ברוך הוא אמר לי
'לך שב מצרים." אלא מפני מה נענש משה? מפני שנתעסק במלון תחלה, שנאמר "ויהי
בדרך במלון."

5   כי באמת היה לו למול את בנו בזמנו ולהניח אשתו ובניו אצל חתנו. כי מה חפצו בביתו
אחריו ושתצא אשתו עמו? הנה נראה שהיתה חביבה עליו בראשיתו יותר מבאחריתו . . .
על שנתעסק במלון תחלה שהלשון הזה הוא כנוי לעסק אהבת הבית הכוללת חברת האשה
. . . והצד היותר נאות הינו נסתר מעיניו והוא למולו ולהניחו שם עם אמו.

6   שנתעסק במלון, וסר ממעלתו כרגע שנתחייב לשול נעלו מעל רגליו . . . כשהגיע בין אנשים
זרים ממנו שלא יהא נראה בפניהם שהוא מורם מכל אדם . . . שהיה המראה בדרך פגישה
שלא במקומו, משום דמשה רבינו כבר נתקדש להיות מרכבה לשכינה. הגיע אליו מראה ד'
. . . גם בהיותו מתעסק בהליכות עולם.

7 ויש שכתב שנענש על שום שדאג קודם לצרכיו הגשמיים ולא עסק ראשונה בצרכים רוחניים.

8 מה היה החיוב של משה לקיים מצות מילה? הא עוסק במצוה פטור מן המצוה, דמשה היה עסוק במצות הקב"ה שילך ויחזור מצרימה . . . העוסק במצוה פטור מן המצוה הוא דוקא כשא"א לקיים שניהם, אבל ביכול לקיים שניהם אין פטור.

9 ויפגשהו ד': המלאך.

10 מלאך הברית, המקדש את הנימול . . . ביקש להרוג את משה בשביל שנתרשל.

11 לפי שלא מל את אליעזר בנו.

12 רבן שמעון בן גמליאל אומר: לא למשה רבינו בקש שטן להרוג אלא לאותו תינוק.

13 ויש אומרים שהבן הזה היה גרשום ולא אליעזר, כי הוא היה הבן הראשון של משה . . . ויתרו חותנו התנה עמו בשעה שנשא את צפורה, שאת הבן הראשון לא ימול . . . אמנם עכשיו בהיות במלון, שלא פחד מיתרו, היה יכול למולו. אבל משה אמר, "מכיון שעד עכשיו לא מלתי אותו, אמול אותו כשאבוא למצרים, ועל כן נענש.

14 וכתבו במדרש, מדכתיב מלאך **ד'**, ולא כתיב מלאך **אלקים**, מוכח שהיה מלאך של רחמים . . . לכן המתין לו עד המלון, ולא פגע בו בדרך, דאם היה פוגעו בדרך, היה מסתכן מאד.

15 בא מצד הרחמים כדי לזרזו במצוות, ולא שחפץ להורגו ממש.

16 לא היתה זו פגישה לרעה, אלא הופעת השכינה על שהגיעה זמן המילה . . . מכיון שכבוד השם הופיע והמילה לא נתקיימה, ביקש המלאך הממונה להמית את משה.

17 שפגש אותו השפע העליון בהיותו בלתי מוכן, ולכן נסתכן והגיע לשערי מות. וזהו . . . על שנתעסק במלון תחלה, רצה לאמר שהיה לו להתבודד ראשונה בנבואתו. שיום ליום יביע אומר ולילה לילה יחוה דעת באמצעותם.

18 ותפעם רוחו.

19 חלה עד מות.

20 היה כבוד ד' שפגשו . . . כמו אם היא באה על מי שאינו ראוי לישא מרכבת הקדושה. ורובץ תחת משאו עד שמת.

21 שנתפלצו מוסדי גויתו משכינת ד' שפגש אותו פתאום בשלא היה מוכן לזה.

22 והנה צפורה בצדקתה ובחכמתה חשבה . . .

23 היתה מפשפשת במעשיו, על איזה עון חלה.

24 מנין ידעה צפורה שעל עסקי מילה נסתכן משה? אלא בא המלאך ובלע למשה מראשו עד המילה. כיון שראתה צפורה שלא בלע אותו אלא עד המילה, הכירה שעל עסקי המילה הוא ניזוק.

25 דרש רבי יהודה בר ביזנא: בשעה שנתרשל משה רבינו מן המילה באו אף וחמה ובלעוהו ולא שיירו ממנו אלא רגליו.

26 אז ראתה צפורה ותבהל, ותהי לבה בקרבה אם על מילת בנה היה הדבר, או על מילת בעלה שלא היה רצונו יתברך יטמאו במדינת עתה שנתחייד לו הדבור . . . אמרה . . . שעל ידי מילה יתוקן. ראתה לעשות מצות מילה על ידי עצמה לשתי הכוונות. אם על בנה, הרי כורתת ערלתו; אם על עצמה, הרי על ידי עשתה בעצמה תיקון זה יהיה לה התיקון.

27 על ידי החלשות שנפלה על משה לא יכול למולו עד שנגלה הדבר לאשתו **והיא** מלתהו.

28 ומי איכא למאן דאמר אשה לא? והכתיב: "ותקח צפרה צר!" . . . אתיא איהי ואתחלה, ואתא משה ואגמרה.

29 ספר אהבה הלכות מילה, פ"ב ה"א. הכל כשרין למול ואפילו . . . אשה . . . מלין במקים שאין שם איש . . . ובכל מלין ואפילו בצור.

30 השליכתו לפני רגליו של משה.

31 לרגלי משה. ולא יתן המשחית.

³² בדם המצוה יסתלק לו הנגף.

³³ ותקח צפורה צר ותגע הצר לרגליו **של ילד** ותכרות את ערלת בנה.

³⁴ לרגלוי דמלאך.

³⁵ ר' יודה, ור' נחמיה, ורבנין, חד אמר לרגליו של משה, וחרנא אמר לרגליו של מלאך, וחרנה אמר לרגליו של תינוק. מן דמר לרגליו של משה הילך גזי חובך. מן דמר לרגליו של מלאך הילך עבד שליחתך. מן דמר לרגליו של תינוק נגעה בגוף התינוק.

³⁶ אתה היית גורם להיות החתן שלי נרצח עליך.

³⁷ אמרה חתני תהיה אתה נתון לי בזכות דמים הללו של מילה, שהרי קיימתי המצוה.

³⁸ והנשים קוראות לנער כאשר יכנס לברית "חתן."

³⁹ כי עיקר מלת "חתן" פירושו התחדשות השמחה . . . ביום המילה.

⁴⁰ ותאמר **אל משה** כי חתן דמים אתה **לי**. בשבילי. מה שבקש המלאך להרגך הוא בשביל שנתחתנת **בי**, שאנכי מדינית ואתה עברי, ואין אני ראויה לך.

⁴¹ בדמים הללו ישאר לי חתני. חתני, בעלי.

⁴² וירף ממנו ר"ל המות.

⁴³ סר כח הפגישה הנוראה ממשה.

⁴⁴ ולולי היא, לא ניצל.

⁴⁵ שנוציא דמים בשתי מילות, שהן כריתת המילה והפריעה.

⁴⁶ ואמרה "למולות" בלשון רבים לפי שלא ידעה האם נתחייב מיתה בעבור שלא מל את הילד במדין קודם או מפני שלא מל אותו שם במלון.

⁴⁷ אז ידעה דבשביל חשיבות המילה היה . . . לא בא לענוש את החטא.

⁴⁸ היית חתן דמים מסתכן ומת **מפני מילת הנער** שמנעת מעשותה עד כה. **לא בעבורי** כמו שאמרתי בראשונה.

⁴⁹ **אז אמרה. אז** ישיר משה. למה התחיל משה רבינו ע"ה את השירה ב**אז** וכו'? אמר משה, ב**אז** ניתנה המילה, וניתנה לי נפשי שנאמר **אז** אמרה חתן דמים למולות.

TWENTY-EIGHT: Zipporah is Sent Away

¹ ויאמר ד' אל אהרן לך לקראת משה המדברה וילך ויפגשהו בהר האלקים וישק לו. ויגד משה לאהרן את כל דברי ד' אשר שלחו ואת כל האתת אשר צוהו. **וילך** משה ואהרן . . .

² יצא [אהרן] לקראתו והיה מגפפו ומחבקו ומנשקו. אמר ליה, משה אחי, היכן היית כל השנים הללו? אמר ליה, במדין.

³ ויצא אהרן לקראתו ויפגשהו בהר האלקים. אמר לו, מי הם הללו? אמר לו, זו היא אשתי שנשאתי במדין ואלו בני. אמר לו, להיכן אתה מוליכן? אמר לו, למצרים. אמר לו, על הראשונים אנו מצטערים ואתה בא להוסיף עליהם! אמר לה, לכי אל בית אביך. נטלה שני בניה והלכה לה.

⁴ משום דמשה . . . הקפיד . . . על אשתו שלא ישתעבדו בה מצרים.

⁵ לא היה אדם עמו רק אהרן.

THIRTY: Moses' Provenance

¹ אלה ראשי בית אבתם: בני ראובן בכר ישראל . . . ובני שמעון . . . ואלה שמות בני לוי לתלדתם; גרשון וקהת ומררי . . . ובני קהת עמרם . . . ויקח עמרם את יוכבד דדתו לו לאשה ותלד לו את אהרן ואת משה . . . הוא אהרן ומשה אשר אמר ד' להם הוציאו את בני

ישראל מארץ מצרים על צבאתם.

2 הזכיר כי הקב"ה בחר בשני האחים האלה לענין הגדול הזה, שהם יהיו שלוחים בין קל
ישראל, בין אל פרעה. ראה הכתוב להזכיר יחוסם וקדושת אבותיהם לתולדותיהם לבית
אבותם, לברר כי הם היו רואים למעלה זאת מכל ישראל . . . והוא [עמרם] לקח את יוכבד
דודתו מן האב, ומבין שניהם . . . יצאו שני בנים שנבחרו לשליחות הגדול הזה.

3 ושם אשת עמרם יוכבד בת לוי אשר ילדה אתה ללוי במצרים; ותלד לעמרם את אהרן ואת
משה ואת מרים אחתם.

4 משה ואהרן נולדו ככל בשר ודם להורים רגילים, ובכל זאת נעשו לגדולי הנביאים והמנהיגים
של עמנו. הודות לפעולותיהם ומעשיהם הם אשר בחרו לעצמם, ולא שירדו לעולם כמלאכי
מרום. מכאן עלינו ללמוד . . . כי כל אדם ואדם מסוגל על ידי עבודתו ובחירתו להגיע למדרגות
העליוניות ביותר, ואפילו להיות בבחינת משה ואהרן.

THIRTY-TWO: Miriam the Prophetess Leads the Women
in Dance and Song

1 ותקח מרים הנביאה אחות אהרן את התף בידה; ותצאן כל הנשים אחריה בתפים ובמחלת.
ותען להם מרים: שירו לד' כי גאה גאה סוס ורכבו רמה בים.

2 ומכאן שמרים נביאה היתה.

3 אחות אהרן ולא אחות משה? . . . מלמד שהיתה מתנבאה כשהיא אחות אהרן, ואומרת:
עתידה אמי שתלד בן שמושיע את ישראל.

4 נתנבא כשהיתה אחות אהרן קודם שנולד משה.

5 אחות אהרן. לפי שהיתה דומה לו בנבואה, אבל לא למשה.

6 מובטחות היו הצדקניות שבדור שהקב"ה עושה להם נסים והוציאו תפים ממצרים.

7 וכתב בספר מעם לועז, הטעם שלקחה התף בידה לומר שירה, ולא עשו כן האנשים, מפני
שקול באשה ערוה, ואסור לאשה לזמר בפני אנשים. ולכן לקחו הכלים האלו, כדי שלא
ישמעו קולם.

8 דקול באשה ערוה, שלא שייך הכא דאיכא אימתא דשכינתא.

9 קול באשה ערוה, שנאמר 'קולך ערב ומראך נאוה.'

10 משה אמר שירה לאנשים. הוא אמר והם עונין אחריו. ומרים אמרה שירה לנשים.

11 מגיד הכתוב כשם שאמר משה שירה לאנשים, כך אמרה מרים שירה לנשים, שנאמר שירה
לד' וגו'.

12 מרים הנביאה עוררה התלהבות כה גדולה להודות ולהלל להשם יתברך.

13 ואמרו **כל השירה** , אלא על ידי שכתב כבר כל השירה לא הזכיר כאן אלא אלא תחלתה.

14 הנשים עשו להם שיר ארוך . . . אבל הסוגר מכל בית היה על פי מרים ברוח הקודש.

15 שהנשים צדקניות האמינו בתשועת ד' . . . נהפכו מנשים לגבורת אנשים להיותם אמיצי לב.

16 הם אמרו שכל זה נעשה בזכותן, ועל כן שרו ביחוד, כי היה להם חלק בנסים אלה.

17 נשים חייבות במקרא מגילה, שאף הן היו באותו הנס.

18 רש"י . . . והרשב"ם סוברים כי הכוונה היא ש**בנס זה היו הנשים עיקר.** שהרי עיקר הנס
נעשה על ידי אסתר.

19 שעיקר הנס היה על ידן; בפורים, על ידי אסתר; בחנוכה, על ידי יהודית; בפסח, שבזכות
צדקניות שבאותו הדור נגאלו.

20 נשים חייבות במגילה . . . גם בארבע כוסות, וכן בנר חנוכה.

THIRTY-THREE: The Well of Miriam

1 ותען להם מרים. והבאר בזכות מרים שאמרה שירה על המים.

2 מרים הנביאה

3 כי העלתיך מארץ מצרים ומבית עבדים פדיתיך ואשלח לפניך את משה אהרן ומרים.

4 לפני צאתך שלחתי לך בעבודתך **מבשרים** שבשרו לך בא הגאולה . . . והמבשרים היו
שלשה נביאים, משה ואהרן ומרים.

5 שלחתי לפניך **מנהיגים**, והם משה אהרן ומרים.

6 ושלחית קדמך תלתא נביין. משה לאלפא מסירת דינין; אהרן לכפרא על עמא; ומרים
לאוראה לנשיא.

7 אמר הקב״ה: בוא וראה מה ביני לבין בשר ודם. מלך בשר ודם משלח שלוחים למדינה, בני
המדינה מספיקין להם מזון. אבל אני לא עשיתי כן, אלא שלחתי לפניך גואלים שלשה, ולא
הייתם זקוקים לזון אותם. אלא הם היו זנים אתכם! המן בזכות משה, ענני כבוד בזכות
אהרן, הבאר בזכות מרים.

8 . . . ותמת שם מרים ותקבר שם. ולא היה מים לעדה; ויקהלו על משה ועל אהרן. וירב
העם עם משה . . .

9 באר בזכות מרים . . . מתה מרים, נסתלק הבאר . . . וחזרה בזכות שניהן.

10 אם הבאר יכלה לחזור בזכות משה ואהרן, משום מה נסתלקה אחרי מות מרים? ויש אומרים
שלא חזרה כפי שהיתה. ואחרים פרשו שנסתלקה כדי להראות לישראל **שעיקרה בזכות**
מרים היתה.

11 ותמת שם מרים ותקבר שם. ומה כתיב אחר כך? ולא היה מים לעדה. והיאך היתה הבאר
עשויה? סלע כמין כוורת היתה, ומתגלגלת, ובאת עמהם במסעות. וכיון שהיו הדגלים חונים
והמשכן עומד היה אותו הסלע בא ויושב לו בחצר אהל מועד, והנשיאים באים ועומדים על
גביו ואומרים, 'עלי, באר!' והיתה עולה.

12 והוא הסלע שבו הכה משה, שלא היה רוצה להציל מימיו בשבילו, לפי שמתה מרים.

13 . . . יען לא האמנתם בי להקדישני לעיני בני ישראל, לכן לא תביאו את הקהל הזה אל הארץ
אשר נתתי להם.

THIRTY-FOUR: Batya, the Egyptian Princess, is Also Saved

1 בתיה בת פרעה בכורה היתה.

2 מהו כל בכור? בכור לאיש, בכור לאשה, ואפילו **נקבות הבכורות מתו באותו הלילה**; לכך
נאמר '**כל** בכור.'

3 הנקבות הבכורות אף הן מתות חוץ מבתיה בת פרעה.

4 סמכו דרש זה שבת פרעה ניצולה, על הפסוק 'ותקם בעוד לילה.' באיזה לילה? 'ויהי בחצי
הלילה.' וזהו הפירוש במדרש משלי, 'ותקם בעוד לילה.' זו בתיה בת פרעה.

5 יש נשים חסידות, גמורות, כשרות מן הגוים, ואלו הן: אסנת, צפורה, שפרה, פועה, בת
פרעה.

6 בתיה בת פרעה . . . בתפלתו של משה נצולה.

7 תשעה נכנסו בחייהם בגן עדן, ומונה גם בתיה בת פרעה.

THIRTY-FIVE: Hur, Miriam's Son

1 ויבא עמלק וילחם עם ישראל ברפידם. ויאמר משה אל יהושע בחר לנו אנשים וצא הלחם

בעמלק; מחר אנכי נצב על ראש הגבעה ומטה האלקים בידי. ויעש יהושע כאשר אמר לו
משה. . . . ומשה אהרן וחור עלו ראש הגבעה. והיה כאשר ירים משה ידו וגבר ישראל;
וכאשר יניח ידו וגבר עמלק. וידי משה כבדים ויקחו אבן וישימו תחתיו וישב עליה; ואהרן
וחור תמכו בידיו מזה אחד ומה אחד ויהי ידיו אמונה עד בא השמש.

2 ומשה אהרן **וחור**. פירש״י חור בנה של מרים היה . . . ואביו כלב, שנאמר 'ויקח לו כלב
את אפרת ותלד לו את חור.' **אפרת זו מרים** . . . ולפיכך אני אומר ששם מפרש כל שמות
כלב וכל שמות מרים ועזובה ויריעות ואפרת, ונקראת אפרת . . . ויקח לו כלב את אפרת
דהיינו נמי מרים.

3 חור, בנה של מרים היה, וכלב בעלה.

4 חור בנה של מרים היה. הוצרך להודיע זה מפני שחור לא נזכר בשום מקום קודם זה. ואיך
יכתבנו כמו ידוע באמרו 'ומשה ואהרן והור.' לפיכך הוצרך לומר בנה של מרים היה, שהיה
מפורסם בימים ההם.

5 חור בנה של מרים היה. דאם לא כן, למה חור ולא נדב ואביהו? אלא מפני שהוא בנה של
מרים, ובזכות משה ואהרן **ומרים** ינצח האויב, כי הם שלשה רועי ישראל. ולפיכך **היה חור
שיש לו זכות מרים**.

6 וחלק זה של מרים **הוצרך** בכדי להתגבר על עמלק.

7 ואל הזקנים אמר שבו לנו בזה עד אשר נשוב אליכם; והנה אהרן **וחור** עמכם מי בעל דברים
יגש אלהם.

8 וכשקבלו ישראל את הדברות, לאחר ארבעים יום שכחו את אלקים, ואמרו לאהרן, המצרים
היו נושאין את אלהיהם והיו משוררים ומזמרים לפניו ורואים אותו לפניהם. עשה לנו אלהים
כאלהי מצרים, ונראה אותו לפנינו! . . . הלכו להם אצל חבריו של משה, אהרן וחור בן
אחותו . . . מגדולי הדור היה . . . התחיל מוכיח לישראל דברים קשים. והבזויים
שבישראל עמדו עליו והרגוהו. וראה אהרן לחור שנהרג, ובנה מזבח.

9 חור. בנה של מרים היה ואביו כלב בן יפנה (ד״ה א) ויקח לו את אפרת ותלד לו את חור.
אפרת זו מרים כדאיתא בסוטה.

10 ותקח מרים הנביאה אחות אהרן את התף בידה ותצאנה כל הנשים אחריה. הנה **בהאנשים**
כתיב 'ויאמינו בד' ובמשה עבדו.' האמינו כי אם אין משה העושה נפלאות, אין ד' עושה על
ידי אחר. על כן אמרו כי זה משה האיש, לא ידענו מה היה לו . . . אך **הנשים** האמינו גם
במרים הנביאה אף על פי שלא עשתה נפלאות . . . על כן בעגל לא נתרצו הנשים, כי אמרו
אם אין משה יש נביאים אחרים. ועל כן התאספו אל **חור, בנה של מרים**, כי חשבו אם חור
יעשה להם אלהים, שהוא בנה של מרים, על ידי זה יתרצו גם הנשים. אבל **חור מסר נפשו**
וזכה לבצלאל בן בנו שעשה המשכן.

11 ויאמר ד' אל משה לאמר: ראה קראתי בשם **בצלאל בן אורי בן חור** למטה יהודה: ואמלא
אתו רוח אלקים בחכמה ובתבונה ובדעת ובכל מלאכה.

THIRTY-SIX: Zipporah Returns to Moses
with Their Two Sons

1 וישמע יתרו כהן מדין חתן משה את כל אשר עשה אלהים למשה ולישראל עמו כי הוציא ד'
את ישראל ממצרים. ויקח יתרו חתן משה את צפרה אשת משה אחר שלוחיה. ואת שני
בניה אשר שם האחד גרשם כי אמר גר הייתי בארץ נכריה. ושם האחד אליעזר כי אלהי אבי
בעזרי ויצלני מחרב פרעה. ויבא יתרו חתן משה ובניו ואשתו אל משה אל המדבר אשר הוא
חנה שם הר האלקים. ויאמר אל משה אני חתנך יתרו בא אליך ואשתך ושני בניה עמה.

ויצא משה לקראת חתנו וישתחו וישק לו וישאלו איש לרעהו לשלום ויבאו האהלה. ויספר משה לחתנו את כל אשר עשה ד' לפרעה ולמצרים על אודת ישראל את כל התלאה אשר מצאתם בדרך ויצלם ד'.

2 אחר שלוחיה. נטלה שני בניה והלכה לה.

3 אלמלא מקרה זה לא היינו יודעים ששלחה משה. אך היינו סבורים שהיתה עמו! דכתיב: וירכיבם על החמור. עכשו בא ולמדך כאן כשנפגשו אהרן ומשה, וישראל היו שרויין בצער, ויתרו ברוח, שלחה.

4 שהיא היתה אשת משה אחר שלוחיה. שלא הסיחה דעתה ממנו אף על גב ששלחה.

5 הגם ששלח אותה ונפרד ממנה לא חש לזה. כי לא עשה זה בעבור שמאס בה, כי היא עדיין אשת משה גם אחר שלוחיה. כי לא נפרד ממנה רק עד שעה לפי יפקוד ד' עמו.

6 אחר שלוחיה. ר' יהושע אומר מאחר שפטרה בגט. נאמר כאן שילוח, ונאמר להלן שילוח, וכתב לה ספר כריתות ונתן בידה ושלחה מביתה . . . ר' אליעזר המודעי אומר פטרה במאמר . . . באותו שעה אמר לה 'לכי לבית אביך,' ונטלה שני בניה והלכה לה. לכך נאמר 'אחר שלוחיה.'

7 כי יקח איש אשה ובעלה והיה אם לא תמצא חן בעיניו כי מצא בה ערות דבר וכתב לה ספר כריתת ונתן בידה **ושלחה** מביתו.

8 נראה לומר כי משה גרשה כשראה שהיה עוסק במצות שליחות ית', לא ידע שיעור הזמן, ושלחה מביתו, והבנים אליעזר קטן היה וצריך לאמו, שנולד בדרך במלון. וגרשם מן הסתם קטן היה.

9 ומכח זה שהוציא את ישראל ממצרים לקח את בתו ודן שהיא אשת משה שהוא אף שהוא אחר שלוחיה שפטרה בגט . . . ואז פטר אשתו בגט כמו שאמרו ז"ל, **והוי כגט על תנאי** שלא גרשה, אלא מפני שהיו ישראל בגלות מצרים, ועתה שיצאו, הגט בטל! . . . ועל ידי זה 'ויקח אשת משה,' נקראת 'אשת משה' אחר שלוחיה בגט, דהגט בטל, והיא אשתו.

10 ותימא היאך החזירה? והלא כהן היה, והגט פוסל בכהונה. ויש לומר ש**על תנאי גרשה**.

11 דאף שנשתלחה ממנו, עדיין החזיקה את עצמה כ"אשת משה" בכשרות ובצניעות, כך שלא נתעורר בה שום חשש זנות. ולפיכך שב ונשאה.

12 צפרה אשת משה. ראויה היתה לו.

13 להיות עקר מסדור הנהגת הבית להשגיח במה שיאות לאשה לפי כבודה לשבת בית בדרך מוסר וצניעות בהכנת כל צרכי השארה כסותה ועונתה . . . וכבר נפל משה בזה החטא במה ששלח אם על בנים ועזבם זה ימים. וגם עתה, אחר כל הכבוד ההוא, לא שם לבו עליהם אשר כל זה יגדיל עוד התלונה . . . לפי הסדר הביתיי צריך לנהוג בה יקר יותר וחשיבות, ותכבד לשבת בביתה. ואף אם תתעורר לשוב אליו כי תמשוך בחבלי אדם ובעבותות אהבה אין לבוא אביה החשוב עמה . . . נתעוררו מתחלה לחסות תחת כנפיו ראו למחול על כבודם . . . ולבוא אליו שם כלם כאחד.

14 התעורר יתרו מפי השמועה ההיא ששמע , לקחת את צפורה אשת משה . . . אבל משה כדי שלא להפסיק בדבקות האלקי והנהגתו לעם, ובהכנסו לקבל התורה לא הלך **למדין הקרוב אליו** לכבד חותנו, ולפיס אשתו, ולראות את בניו. והוצרך יתרו לבא לראותו . . . עם כל זקנתו . . . אל המקום שהיה משה תמיד חונה שם מתחלה כשהיה רועה את צאן יתרו. כי תמיד בהר ההוא היתה ישיבתו ודבקותו.

15 אחר שמשה לא חש לכבוד בתו [של יתרו] ולכבוד אביה להחזירה בעצמו למדין.

16 איך הוא יסביר את העובדה התמוהה שמשה לא עשה כל מעשה כדי להביא את אשתו ובניו אל מתן תורה . . . לעיני כל ישראל?

17 אשתו שהיתה כצפור נודדת מקנה, ובעבור צער זה שסבלה ראוי לכבדה.

¹⁸ יש לומר שמשה לא הביא את אשתו ובניו הקטנים אליו . . . כדי שידעו כל העולם שגירותם היא גירות אמת . . . רק עתה כשהיא באה אליו בלי שהוא שלח לקחת אותה, סימן שהיא באה להתגייר.

¹⁹ ואם גירותיה של צפורה גירות אמת היא, גם גירותם של בניה גירות אמת היא.

²⁰ פרש המקרא **בניה**, ולא כתיב **בניו**. ללמד שבניה המה המקשרים אותה למשה גם אחר שלוחיה. באשר היא גידלה אותם.

²¹ אמר לו יתרו, 'צא בגין אשתך צפורה, כי כצפור נודד מקנו כן איש נודד ממקומו, ובא להזכירו צער אשתו כל זמן היותה נודדת מביתה. ואם לא בגינה, כי אולי אין האדם מרגיש כל כך בצער אשתו, צא בגין בנך גרשום, על שם כי גר הייתי בארץ נכריה, ובא להזכיר צער בנים שאינם מסובים על שלחן אביהם, כי גרים המה.' ואמר לו, 'אתה ידעת את נפש הגר, כי גר היית גם אתה. ואם לא בגינו, צא בגין בנך אליעזר, שנקרא על שם כי אלקי אבי בעזרי. ושמו . . . דומה כאילו אתה מקבל פני השכינה.'

²² כלומר שיער בנפשו כי עוד היא אשת משה . . . ואם כן יקרים הם אצלו להיות הם זכרונים האלה רשומים בשמותם, ובאין ספק עוד ישוב ויפרוש כנפיו על אם הבנים.

²³ איך יאמר 'ויצלני מחרב פרעה,' וזה הטעם היה ראוי לבן הראשון. דע כי משה אף על פי שברח אל ארץ מדין היה לו פחד מפרעה. כי שלום היה בין מצרים ובין מדין. וכאשר אמר לו השם 'לך שוב מצרימה כי מתו כל האנשים,' וזה 'וימת מלך מצרים,' **אז** בטח לב משה.

²⁴ כי בלידת אליעזר כבר מת אותו מלך מצרים שהיה רודף את משה . . . עד מותו לא היה משה בטוח מחרבו.

²⁵ וזה האות שאהב את בניו כי הם ציינו את שמותם את כל קורותיו. ששם גרשום קרא מפני 'כי אמר גר הייתי,' כי בלידתו היה מתחבא מפני פרעה, והגם שגם בארץ מצרים היה גר ככל אחיו.

²⁶ בפרוש 'גר הייתי' שיכוין על גרותו בעולם הזה.

²⁷ ושם האחד אליעזר. **השני** מיבעי. ללמדנו שהוא המיוחד בבני משה, וממנו נשתלשל זרעו.

²⁸ אמר לו יתרו: קבל עליך דבר זה שאומר לך, ואני נותנו לך לאשה. אמר לו: מהו? אמר לו: בן שיהיה תחלה יהיה לעבודה זרה. מכאן ואילך לשם שמים. וקבל עליו. אמר לו: השבע! וישבע לו. שנאמר, "ויואל משה . . ."

²⁹ דרש זה המכילתא, ובאמת **אף על גב שאין משיבין על הדרש**, מכל מקום הוא כמו זר נחשב שמשה רבינו יתרצה שיהיה בנו הראשון לעבודה זרה, לא תהא כזאת בישראל.

³⁰ כי ידע שיחזיר את חמיו למוטב כמו שעשה שהרי נתגייר.

³¹ שאמרו ז"ל שהתנה עם יתרו שהבן הראשון יהיה לעבודה זרה . . . וכתב בפירוש המכילתא זה ניחמנו שמשה רבינו סמך על צדקת צפורה שיכולה לעכב וכו'. כי בלדת הילד הזה הראשון, יתרו אמר שיקוים תנאו. וצפורה השיבה שהיא המושלת בילד. ומשה אמר, מה בידי לעשותו? גר הייתי בארץ נכריה, ולא ידעתי הנימוס שלכם שהאשה מושלת . . . וצפורה הצדקת עשתה רצון ד' ורצון בעלה.

³² וכי לוי שמו? והלא יהונתן שמו. שנאמר: 'ויהונתן בן גרשם בן מנשה הוא ובניו היו כהנים לשבט הדני!' . . . וכי בן מנשה הוא? והלא **בן משה הוא**, דכתיב: 'בני משה גרשם ואליעזר.'

³³ בימים ההם אין מלך בישראל; איש הישר בעיניו יעשה.

³⁴ והוא לוי מן האם, ורבותינו אמרו . . . **והוא לוי בן גרשון, בן משה רבינו היה.**

³⁵ ויואל הלוי לשבת את האיש.

³⁶ ויואל משה לשבת את האיש.

³⁷ ויהי הנער לו אחד מבניו.

38 ויקימו להם בני דן את הפסל; **ויהונתן בן גרשם בן מֹנַשֶׁה** הוא ובניו היו כהנים לשבט הדני עד יום גלות הארץ.

39 יש כאן תמיהות הרבה! לא מזרעו של משה רבינו אתה?!

40 המה עם בית מיכה והמה הכירו את קול הנער הלוי; ויסורו שם ויאמרו לו מי הביאך הלם ומה אתה עושה בזה ומה לך פה?!

41 מפני כבודו של משה כתוב כאן נון, לשנות את השם; ונכתב תלויה לומר שלא היה מנשה אלא משה.

42 הנון תלויה, לפי שהיא יתרה, דבן **משה** הוא. ויהונתן בן גרשם . . . שגזלו שבט הדני פסלו של מיכה, והלוי הלך עמהם להיות להם לכהן . . . והלא בן משה הוא; דלכך הנון תלויה. וגם מדקרי ליה לוי, שהיה משבט לוי.

43 יש מסורת שהנון של מנשה תלויה, לרמז שאינה שייכת למלה, ויש לקרוא את המלה בלא נ': משה.

44 ושם האחד אליעזר. *השני* מיבעי. ללמדנו שהוא **המיוחד** בבני משה.

45 מה שלא קרא להראשון אליעזר כי לא רצה שיהיה בשמו שם 'קל', כי מאתו יצא יהונתן.

46 בשעה שעלה משה למרום שמע קולו של הקב"ה שיושב ועוסק בפרשת פרה, ואומר 'אליעזר בני אומר פרה בת שתים ועגלה בת שנתה.' אמר משה לפני הקב"ה, 'רבונו של עולם, העליונים והתחתונים ברשותך, ואתה יושב ואומר הלכה משמו של בשר ודם!' א"ל הקב"ה, 'משה, עתיד צדיק אחד לעמוד בעולמי, ועתיד לפתוח בפרשת פרה תחלה רבי אליעזר אומר . . .' אמר [משה] לפניו, 'רבש"ע, יהי רצון שיצא מחלצי!' א"ל הקב"ה, "חייך שיצא מחלציך"!

47 משה היה במדרגת מלך.

48 עשה בשביל בניה. היינו בניך, אלא אתה עוסק ללמד תורה ומצות לישראל, ואת בניך הנחת עמה והרחקתם מעליך.

49 לא מחמת אשתו ובניו, אלא מחמת חותנו.

50 והודיע והראה לכל שאינו פונה אלא לחותנו ולא לאשתו ובניו.

51 בעבור כבוד יתרו וחכמתו ולא לאשתו ובניו.

52 וישמע יתרו כהן מדין. מה שמועה שמע ובא ונתגייר? רבי יהושע אומר: מלחמת עמלק שמע . . . רבי אלעזר המודעי אומר: מתן תורה שמע [ובא] . . . רבי אליעזר אומר: ים סוף שמע ובא.

53 ונחלקו בענין זה חכמי ישראל לדורותיהם, תנאים ואמוראים, ראשונים ואחרונים.

54 מתן תורה שמע ובא. שנאמר שם 'אל תגשו אל אשה.' וחשב יתרו לדרוש אותו קל וחומר אשר דרש משה . . . על כן בא יתרו והביא למשה את אשתו כדי שתדור אצלו. כי תפארת אדם לשבת בית כדת משה וישראל.

THIRTY-SEVEN: Marital Abstinence in Preparation for Receiving God's Law

1 היו נכנים.

2 מבדלים מאשה.

3 כתיב הכא והיו נכנים וכתיב להלן היו נכנים אל תגשו אל אשה.

4 אלא היו נכנים והיו נכונים לגזרה שוה. מה היו נכונים כאן לפרוש מן האשה אף והיו נכונים האמור להלן לפרוש מן האשה.

5 שיהיה גם הגוף טהור ומוכן לנבואה. לא הנפש בלבד.

6 ופירש מן האשה. מאי דריש? נשא קל וחומר בעצמו. אמר: ומה ישראל שלא דברה
שכינה עמהן אלא שעה אחת, וקבע להן זמן, אמרה תורה 'והיו נכנים וגו' אל תגשו;' אני,
שכל שעה ושעה שכינה מדברת עמי, ואינו קובע לי זמן -- על אחת כמה וכמה!

7 ורשי פירש שרק משום שהשכינה היתה שורה על משה בכל עת היה לו לעשות מדעתו.
אבל שאר בני אדם אסור היה להם לעשות כן.

8 שלשה דברים עשה משה מדעתו, והסכימה דעתו לדעת המקום: פירש מן האשה . . .
והסכימה דעתו לדעת המקום, שנאמר 'לך אמר להם שובו לכם לאהליכם ואתה פה עמד
עמדי.'

9 מכיון שמשה מעצמו קיבל עליו פרישה כזו, הסכים לו גם הקב"ה.

10 ודילמא על פי צווי מהקב"ה, וצריך לומר דאם מהקב"ה היה צווי זה, לא היה מצוה אותו על
פרישה מוחלטת ונצחית, שאין דרכי הקב"ה על שנויי גבולי הטבע.

11 לך אמר להם שובו לכם לאהליכם. ואתה פה עמד עמדי.

12 להתיר נשותיכם לתשמיש, שאסרתי לכם.

13 הדרשה אין אהלו אלא אשתו.

14 ומדאמר לו אחר כך 'ואתה פה עמד עמדי' ש"מ שהסכים לו הקב"ה שפירש

15 **לגמרי**, לאחר מתן תורה, מיד משפירש עם חביריו, **שוב לא חזר לתשמיש**.

16 שתהיה כל נבואתו מעת מתן תורה והלאה 'פנים אל פנים.'

17 פה אל פה. **אמרתי לו לפריש מן האשה.** והיכן אמרתי לו, בסיני: לך אמור להם שובו
לכם לאהליכם, **ואתה פה עמוד עמדי**.

18 והודיע והראה לכל שאינו פונה אלא לחותנו, ולא לאשתו ובניו.

19 ויאמר יתרו ברוך ד' אשר הציל אתכם מיד מצרים ומיד פרעה; אשר הציל את העם מתחת יד
מצרים.   עתה ידעתי כי גדול ד' מכל האלהים . . .

THIRTY-EIGHT: Miriam and Aaron Speak about Moses' Kushite Woman

1 ותדבר מרים ואהרן במשה על אדות האשה הכשית אשר לקח כי אשה כשית לקח.

2 היא פתחה בדבור תחילה, לפיכך הקדימה הכתוב.

3 היא דברה, גם אהרן הסכים או החריש; על כן נענשו.

4 כדכתיב בדברי הימים דמשה רבינו, מלך היה בארץ כוש ארבעים שנה, ולקח מלכה אחת.

5 'על אדות האשה הכשית אשר לקח.' וכי **כושית** שמה? והלא **ציפורה** שמה! אלא, מה
כושית משונה בעורה, אף ציפורה משונה במעשיה.

6 נראה הכונה שהיתה משונה בצדקה ומעשים טובים מיתר הנשים בערך שנויי עור הכושי
מעור שאר בני אדם, ור"ל שהיתה צדקת מופלאה.

7 מגיד שהכל מודים ביפיה כשם שהכל מודים בשחרורתו של כושי.

8 שאמרו עליה 'ותלך צפורה בדרכי בית ישראל. לא חסרה דבר מהצדקות שרה, רבקה, רחל
ולאה.'

9 הכושית היא צפורה כי היא מדינית, ומדינים הם ישמעאלים, והם דרים באהלים . . . ובעבור
חום השמש אין להם לבן כלל.   **וצפורה היתה שחורה, ודומה לכושית.**

10 הנה אמרו הכושית לזר יחשב יקראנה כושית והיא מדינית! ומה גם אחר התגיירה כי
ליהודית תחשב אף היא.

11 כי אשה כושית לקח. אלא נתגיירה. וכסבורים אהרן ומרים הכי פירש משה ממנה,
משום שאינה לפי כבודו של משה. שתהיה אשתו מיחוסי ישראל. ודברו בזה שמכל

מקום אינו נכון . . . ואחר כך אינו ראוי לצערה ולפרוש ממנה.

12 שהיו אומרים, 'וכי לא מצא משה מבנות ישראל שיקח לו אשה, שהלך לקחת לו מבנות
הכושים . . . אשר במרחק.'

13 כי מצפורה בורח היה מפני פרעה ואנוס היה . . . מגיד לך הכתוב שלא מחמת גאוה לקחה,
אלא היתה סיבה ומזל.

14 קשים גרים לישראל היינו משום שמדקדקין במצות יותר מישראל . . . ונתגיירה וצדקת
מאד במעשים טובים.

15 ומנין היתה יודעת מרים שפרש משה מן האשה? . . . מרים היתה בצד צפורה בשעה שנאמר
למשה: אלדד ומידד מתנבאים במחנה. כיון ששמעה צפורה אמרה: אוי לנשותיהן של אלו.
אם הם נזקקים לנבואה שיהיו פורשין מנשותיהן כדרך שפרש בעלי ממני. ומשם ידעה מרים
והגידה לאהרן.

16 מרים היתה עיקר, כדרך נשים, לקנא על כבוד אשה כמה יותר מאיש, ואהרן נטפל אליה
ונגררה אחריה.

17 דאם לא כן, וכי דרך הנשים הצנועות, כמו צפורה, לפרסם הדבר איך בעליהן נוהגים עמהם
בתשמיש!

18 אספה לי שבעים איש כיון שנתמנו זקנים, הדליקו להן כל ישראל נרות ושמחו להם. מרים
רואה את הנרות דולקות אמרה לצפורה מה עסק של נרות הללו דולקין אמרה הענין. אמרה
מרים 'אשריהן נשים של אלו. מה הן רואות היאך עלו על בעליהן לשררה.' אמרה לה צפורה,
'אוי להן שמעכשיו אינם נזקקים להן לתשמיש; אלא הן לעקרות מעכשיו.' אמרה להם 'מנין
את יודעת?' אמרה לה, 'מאחיך, שממשעה שנתקדש לדבור אינו מכיר למטתו.'

19 מנין היתה מרים יודעת שפירש משה מפריה ורביה? אלא שראת צפורה שאינה מתקשטת
בתכשיטי נשים. אמרה לה, 'מה לך שאין את מתקשטת בתכשיטי נשים?' אמרה לה, 'אין
אחיך מקפיד בדבר.' לכן ידעה מרים ואמרה לאחיה, ושניהם דברו בו.

20 ותדבר מרים ואהרן ב**משה** . . .

21 עמו לבדו.

22 אינו כונת הפסוק שהקב"ה דיבר אודות משה, אלא **עם** משה. 'במשה' הוא במקום 'עם משה.'

23 ב**משה**

24 ב**נו**

25 ב**משה.** אולי שדברו בפניו של משה . . . אמרו דבריהם דרך תוכחה, והוא שומע מלתם.

26 והאיש משה ענו מאד מכל האדם אשר על פני האדמה.

27 ויאמרו הרק אך ב**משה** דבר ד' הלא גם בנו דבר; וישמע ד'. והאיש משה ענו מאד מכל האדם
אשר על פני האדמה.

28 הרק אך. עמו לבדו דבר ד'. הלא גם בנו. ולא פירשנו מדרך ארץ.

29 הלא גם בנו דבר. ולא פירשנו מפריה ורביה.

30 כי לא עשה זה לקדושת ד', כי הם היו נביאים, ואין המשכב אסור להם.

31 היינו דתניא בספרי והלא עם אברהם, יצחק ויעקב דבר ד', ולא פרשו מן האשה.

32 לזה אמרו דרך חבה, שאין זה טעם מספיק.

33 מלמד שלא היה שם בריה, אלא בינם לבין עצמן דברו בו. שנאמר 'וישמע ד'.' רבי נתן אומר
בפניו של משה דברו בו, שנאמר 'וישמע ד', והאיש משה.' אלא שכבש משה על הדבר.

34 לומר תדע למה שתק עד בא דבר ד'. הלא הוא למה, הלא האיש משה ענו מאד מכל האדם
אשר על פני האדמה. ואם כן איפה היה בלתי אפשר לו להסביר דבר. כי הלא התשובה היא
לומר שהוא גדול מכל האדם, שנבואתו עולה מעלה מעלה מכל הנביאים. ואיככה יכול לומר
דרך התנצלות שהוא גדול מכל אדם, והוא ענו מכל אדם! . . . ואיך יענה התנצלותו האמתי,

שהוא נאמן ביתו יתברך העליון, ולא ידמה לשכוני ארץ. **אם כן הוכרח שהאלקים יענה במקומו.**

35 **והאיש משה ענו וגו'.** ביאר הכתוב דלא משום משה וצערו ענה ד' . . . אבל באמת משה לא חשש כלל לזה דהאיש משה ענו וגו'. אלא משום שנוגע לעיקר התורה לדעת כח מעלתו של משה שהוא למעלה מכל נביא שבעולם . . . הוא היה כאדם שאינו עוד על פני האדמה . . . ישפיל שלא ירגיש בצער ובהעדר הרצון והכבוד. וזה היה מדתו של משה רבינו.

36 וטעם והאיש משה ענו מאד, להגיד כי ד' קנא לו בעבור ענותנותו, כי הוא לא יענה על ריב לעולם, אף אם ידע.

37 ויש מפרשים דיתכן לומר שהמאמר הזה רומז לסיבה שהביאה אותם לדון את משה כך. כלומר ענוונותו היתרה של משה גרמה, שלא ידעו דבר על דרגתו המיוחדת בנבואה, כי הוא הראה את עצמו תמיד אחד מהם.

38 מכל אדם. ולא ממלאכי השרת.

39 הפרשה המפורסמת (שאין אנו מבינים אותה על-בוריה) של מה שאירע בין מרים ואהרן לבין אחיהם משה. ובמסגרת סיפור המעשה הזה נמצאת הערה המתייחסת למשה: . . . 'והאיש משה ענו מאד מכל האדם אשר על פני האדמה.' אנו מכירים את משה רבנו ממפעלו: הגואל הראשון שעמד לישראל, ומחוקקם של ישראל, אשר על-ידו ניתנה תורה לישראל, ואשר עשה את האותות והמופתים . . . אבל התורה איננה מתארת את אישיותו במפורש, פרט למקרה הזה, שבו היא מציינת בפירוש אחת מתכונותיו. בשום מקום אין התורה אומרת בפירוש שהאיש משה היה חכם מכל אדם, ואיננו אומרת שהיה צדיק מכל אדם, ואיננו אומרת שהיה גיבור מכל אדם, אף-על-פי שאנחנו **למדים מן הדברים** שהיה . . . אבל התורה מוצאת לנכון . . . להטעים דבר אחד בלבד: שהאיש משה היה **ענו** מכל האדם. ובזה יש להרהר הרבה. **ענווה**, ללא כל ספק, היא דרגה גבוהה בשלמות האנושית. בדרך-כלל הטבע האנושי הוא שהאדם גדול וחשוב בעיני עצמו -- אם לא במודע, על-כל-פנים בבלתי-מודע. לשון אחר: אין זה טבעו של אדם להיות ענו. אבל יש ענווים. והענווה המצויה בקרב בני-אדם בעלי רמה אנושית, מוסרית והכרתית גבוהה יכולה להיות תוצאה של אחת משתי סיבות: או שהם, בביקורת עצמית, מכירים פגמים וחולשות בעצמם, או שהם מתגברים על יצר האדם להחשיב את עצמו . . . ומופיעים כענווים . . . **והם ענווים**. אבל על משה נאמר: 'והאיש משה ענו מכל האדם . . .' **במה היה ענו?** משה רבנו הוא האדם אשר הגיע להכרת אלקים במידה העילאית שאדם מסוגל להגיע אליה; דבר זה מוסכם ומקובל על ההוגים באמונה ובעולמה של היהדות . . . אפשר לחשוב שאם האדם מגיע לדרגה גבוהה זאת לא ייתכן שלא יכיר ברמה שהגיע אליה . . . ועל כך נאמר בגמרא: 'כל הנביאים נסתכלו באספקלריא שאינה מאירה, ומשה רבנו נסתכל באספקלריא המאירה.' מי שהגיע לדרגת משה רבנו, והוא באמת 'משכיל ויודע את ד',', דווקא **הוא מכיר שהאדם איננו מכיר ויודע את ד'**. **הוא** מגיע לענווה האמיתית והגבוהה ביותר. הנביא -- הכרתו אומרת לו שהוא הכיר את אלקים, ולכן יש לו במה להתהלל. אבל אם האדם מגיע לרמתו של משה רבנו -- אשר עליו נאמר שד' דיבר עמו 'פנים אל פנים' . . . -- מי שהגיע לדרגה הזאת, **הוא המסוגל להכיר ולהבין** . . . שהאדם **איננו** מכיר את האלקים . . . **וזאת היה הענווה העמוקה ביותר, אשר רק משה רבנו היה מסוגל להגיע אליה.** על אותו מאמר חז"ל אומר רש"י מלים אחדות נוקבות: 'כל הנביאים נסתכלו באספקלריא שאינה מאירה, וחשבו שראו אותו. ומשה רבנו נסתכל באספקלריא המאירה [זאת אומרת, הוא, לכאורה, זכה לראות את אלקים], **וידע שלא ראהו בפניו**.'

40 אמר רבי יוחנן: אין הקדוש ברוך הוא משרה שכינתו אלא על **גבור ועשיר וחכם ועניו,**

וכולן ממשה. גבור, דכתיב 'ויפרש את האהל על המשכן' . . . 'ואתפש בשני הלחות ואשלכם מעל שתי ידיו ואשברם' . . . עשיר, 'פסל לכ' . . . חכם, . . . חמשים שערי בינה נבראו בעולם, וכולם נתנו למשה חסר אחת, שנאמר 'ותחסרהו מעט מאלקים.' עניו, דכתיב 'והאיש משה ענו מאד.'

41   **חוץ מאחת.** ידיעת השם יתברך על אמיתתו.

42   מיסודי הדת לדעת שהקל מנבא את בני האדם. ואין הנבואה חלה אלא על חכם גדול בחכמה, גבור במדותיו . . . דעתו תמיד פנויה למעלה.

THIRTY-NINE: Miriam and Aaron are Chastised

1   ויאמר ד' פתאם אל משה ואל אהרן ואל מרים צאו שלשתכם אל אהל מועד ויצאו שלשתם. וירד ד' בעמוד ענן ויעמד פתח האהל ויקרא אהרן ומרים ויצאו שניהם.

2   **פתאום.** שלא יוכלו לומר משה צעק עלינו והתפלל לפני הקב"ה.

3   **וטעם פתאום.** שלא היו בעת ההיא נותנים לבם ומתכנים לנבואה . . . כי משה רבינו ראוי לנבואה בכל עת . . . קרא להם פתאום בעודם אינם מוכנים לנבואה, נמצא שלא היה להם פנאי להתיישב כראוי לעמוד לפני מלך מלכי המלכים, הקב"ה.

4   שרמז להם שלא ידבר עמהם עוד אלא עתה לבל יחשדו בדעתם כי הוכשרו לנבואה עליונה כזאת.

5   ואמר בלשון **שלשתכם** ללמד לאהרן ומרים שאינם ראוים לדבור לולי **שגם משה עומד עמהם** בפתח אהל מועד.

6   **פתאם.** נגלה עליהם פתאום והם טמאין בדרך ארץ, והיו צועקים: 'מים, מים!' להודיעם שיפה עשה משה שפירש מן האשה.

7   **ויצאו שניהם.** יצאו מאוהל מועד. דמתחלה נכנסו שלשתם לאהל מועד כמו שהיה רגיל משה להיות לדבר עמו באוהל מועד. אבל הם לא זכו לכך באותה שעה. אבל הענן עמד פתח האהל והמה נצטוו לצאת לחוץ.

8   היה דעתו יתברך להוכיח את שניהם על דבר משה. אך לא רצה לביישם שתהיה התוכחה בפני משה עצמו. רק ממנו יתברך אליהם . . . אם כך מה עשה? צוה יבאו אל אהל מועד וישאר משה בפנים, ושניהם יצאו אל הפתח למען תקן את הכל.

9   ולמה יצאו חוץ לאהל מועד? שלא יהא משה אומר, דומה שנמצא בי פגם, שכן נדחתי מן האהל, ושלא יהיו ישראל אומרים דומה שנמצא במשה פגם, שכן נדחתי מן האהל.

10   מקצת שבחו של אדם בפניו וכולו שלא בפניו.

FORTY: God Identifies Moses as *His* Prophet

1   ויאמר שמעו־נא דברי אם יהיה נביאכם ד' במראה אליו אתודע בחלום אדבר בו. לא כן עבדי משה בכל ביתי נאמן הוא. פה אל פה אדבר בו ומראה ולא בחידת ותמנת ד' יביט; ומדוע לא יראתם לדבר בעבדי במשה.

2   כל הנביאים נסתכלו באספקלריא שאינה מאירה; משה רבינו נסתכל באספקלריא המאירה.

3   מה בין משה לכל הנביאים? . . . אומר מתוך תשע איספקלריות היו הנביאים רואים . . . ומשה ראה מתוך איספקלריא אחת . . . רבנן אמרין כל הנביאים ראו מתוך איספקלריא מלוכלכת . . . ומשה ראה מתוך איספקלריא מצוחצחת.

4   והנה הרואה בשפיגל לא יוכל לראות הצורה העומדת מצד האחר אחורי המראה, רק הצורה העומדת בצד שהוא עומד בה לפני המראה . . . שהצורה הנראית במראה אינה הצורה עצמה

העומדת נוכח המראה; רק תמונה של הצורה . . . כן לא ישיגו את האלקות כמו שהיא
בעצמה . . . משה רבינו ע"ה ראה באספקלריא המאירה, שהוא הזכוכית שכח הראיה עובר
בו אל העבר השני.

5   מיסודי הדת לידע שהקל מנבא את בני האדם.   ואין הנבואה חלה אלא על חכם גדול בחכמה,
גבור במדותיו . . . דעתו תמיד פנויה למעלה . . . חוץ ממשה רבינו ורבן של כל הנביאים.
ומה הפרש יש בין נבואת משה לשאר כל הנביאים?   שכל הנביאים בחלום או במראה, ומשה
רבינו והוא ער ועומד . . . כל הנביאים על ידי מלאך . . . משה רבינו לא על ידי מלאך.
שנאמר פה אל פה אדבר בו . . . הוא שהכתוב אומר כאשר ידבר איש אל רעהו . . . כל
הנביאים אין מתנבאים בכל עת שירצו.   משה רבינו אינו כן, אלא כל זמן שיחפוץ רוח הקדש
לבשתו, ונבואה שורה עליו, ואינו צריך לכוין דעתו . . . שהרי הוא מכוון ומזומן ועומד
כמלאכי השרת . . . ובזה הבטיחו הקל שנאמר לך אמר להם שובו לכם לאהליכם, ואתה פה
עמוד עמדי.   הא למדת שכל הנביאים כשהנבואה מסתלקת חוזרין לאהלם, שהוא צרכי הגוף
כולן כאשר העם, לפיכך אינן פורשין מנשותיהן.   ומשה רבינו לא חזר לאהלו הראשון,
לפיכך פרש מן האשה לעולם . . . ונתקשרה דעתו בצור העולמים ולא נסתלק ההוד מעליו
לעולם, וקרן אור פניו ונתקדש כמלאכים.

6   נכלל גודל השגת רוממות נבואתו, והן זאת אשר עשה הוא יתברך עיקר בשבחו אותו.

7   דכל הנביאים היו צריכין להשתנות בעת הנבואה על ידי התפשטות הגשמיות . . . אבל במשה
רבינו ע"ה אדרבא כשהוצרך לדבר עמהם הושם לפניו מסוה . . . וכשהנבואה דיברה בו, היה
בעצם תבניתו פה אל פה אדבר.   וזה נקרא נאמן.   ולכן הם לא הוצרכו לפרוש
מנשותיהם . . . שמשה שלמטה הוא משה שלמעלה: איש אלקים.   אבל שאר נביאים רק
בשעת הנבואה היה להם דביקות בשורש שלמעלה.

8   בשום לב אל אומרו פה אל **פה** כי אלא פה אל **אזן** הוא . . . כי היה הדבור יצא מפיו יתברך
ובא לפיו של משה.

9   פה אל פה.   הטעם בלא אמצאי.

10 בלי תרדמת חושיו.

11 פה אל פה.   אמרתי לו לפרוש מן האשה.

12 ומדוע לא יראתם.   לא ימלט שאין זה כי אם רוע לב.   שאם חשבתם שאני מכיר במעשיו, אם
כן חשבתם עלי תועה שאני חפץ ברשעים, היפך מה שהיה לכם לחשוב, שלא הייתי מזכה
אותו לזאת המעלה אלא מפני שהוא ראוי לכך.   ובכן היה לכם לירא מלדבר באיש כזה.   ואם
אולי חשבתם שאיני מכיר במעשיו ושאתם מכירים בו יותר ממני.

13 ויחר אף ד' בם.   מאחר שהודיעם סרחונם, גזר עליהם נדוי.

14 וכשלא מצאו תשובה, ויחר אף ד' בם.

15 ויחר אף ד' בם.   שלא נכנעו תיכף.

16 ויחר אף ד' בם וילך.   מלמד שאף אהרן נצטרע.   דברי רבי עקיבא.   אמר לו רבי יהודה בן
בתירא . . . ואלא הכתיב **בם**?   ההוא בנזיפה בעלמא.

17 ויחר אף ד' **בם**.

18 ויחר אף ד' בם.   ולמה פרסם הכתוב במרים, ורמז באהרן?   לפי שהיא התחילה בדבר . . .
שניהם דברו, ושניהם לקו . . . ואף אהרן היה ראוי לכך.   לכך נאמר **בם** . . . אלו שדברו
באחיהם הקטן מהן, ולא דברו בגנותו, אלא שהשוו אותו לשאר נביאים.

19 וילך.   ויסתלק שכינתו.

20 דמשמע **שבשניהם** היה שוה החרון והעונש.

FORTY-ONE: The Punishment of Leprosy

1. והענן סר מעל האהל והנה מרים מצרעת כשלג ויפן אהרן אל מרים והנה מצרעת.

2. יש לאמר שלכן סר הענן. שזה היה סימן למסע העם, כמו שלאמר 'ובהעלותו יסעו.' וכיון שסר הענן תקעו בחצוצרות והתחילו לנסוע. ובתוך כך נצטערה מרים.

3. והנה מצרעת. היא מובהלת ונאלמת דומיה מרוב צער.

4. ויחר אף ד' **בם.**

5. מלמד שאף אהרן נצטרע, דברי רבי עקיבא. אמר לו רבי יהודה בן בתירא: עקיבא, בין כך ובין כך אתה עתיד ליתן את הדין. אם כדבריך -- התורה כסתו ואתה מגלה אותו! ואם לאו -- אתה מוציא לעז על אותו צדיק . . . תניא כמאן דאמר אף אהרן נצטרע, דכתיב 'ויפן אהרן אל מרים והנה מצרעת.' תנא: שפנה מצרעתו.

6. אמר הקב"ה, אם יצטרע אהרן אין כהן בעל מום יכול להקריב על גבי המזבח.

7. ויפן אהרן. מהו 'ויפן?' שפנה מצרעתו.

8. ויפן אהרן. שגנה מצרעתו . . . **שהוא היה ראוי לצרעת** . . . אלא שמפני כבוד כהונתו חיסך הקב"ה עליו.

9. שפנה מצרעתו קדם ונתרפא.

10. ויפן. פנה מצרעתו, אלא שמרים לא נתרפאה כאהרן תכף ומיד, ולא ידע אדם מצרעתו . . . שגם אהרן נצטרע. ירצה לומר הנה **היא עדיין מצורעת** ולא פרחה ממנה כאהרן.

11. אך הצרעת היה בלבד במרים . . . שאהרן לא היה אשם כמרים.

FORTY-TWO: Aaron Pleads for Miriam

1. ויאמר אהרן אל משה, **בי אדני** אל־נא תשת עלינו חטאת אשר נואלנו ואשר הטאנו. אל־נא תהי כמת; אשר בצאתו מרחם אמו ויאכל חצי בשרו.

2. זה יאמר פה אהרן: 'בי אדני,' כלומר **'בי הוא העון** בעצם.'

3. בי אדני לומר שבי עצמי גם הוא חטא, וזה כמדובר. או יאמר הנה הנה לבבוא על אחותי, **ואני גם כן חטאתי.** ואיך אבקש על חבוש להתירו טרם אתיר עצמי תחלה.

4. כי משה לא הקפיד על הדבר ולזה נתחכם הכתוב וסמך לדברם בו אמר 'והאיש משה עניו מאד.'. . . וטעם העונש . . . שיש לנו לדון משה משפט מלך, שכן כתיב . . . 'ומלך שמחל על כבודו אין כבודו מחול.'

5. ויאמר אהרן אל משה, בי אדני . . . והלא אחיו הקטן ממנו היה, אלא עשאו רבו . . . דאהרן ומרים סברו דנבואת משה היא שוה כנבואתם . . . וד' הוכיחם דנבואת משה גדולה מהן, ואין יחס ביניהם לבינו. ובו בפרק נתבייש אהרן על שהשוה עצמו לו. לכך אמר 'בי אדני.'

6. כונת בקשה זו . . . אמר אהרן, נמצאת מפסיד לאחותנו שאיני יכול להסגירה ולא לטומאה ולא לטהרה . . . במה היה מפסידה? הא כיון שאין אדם רואה את הנגעים, הרי היא טהורה. אבל מתחלה יש להבין מוצא זה הדרש שאמר כן אהרן . . . דעיקר כפרה שבצרעת הוא מנהג דיני מצורע שמלמד יסורין של צרעת עוד הוא בזיון לפרסם עצמו ולשבת בדד מחוץ למחנה ועוד . . . מצורע זאת תהיה תורת המצורע **המוציא שם רע.** למדנו דאע"ג דצרעת בא על **לשון הרע אפילו באמת,** כמו שנענש משה בצרעת על שדבר על ישראל. מ"מ די להתכפר ביסורין כרגע לחוד. **משא"כ מוציא שם רע היינו לשון הרע בשקר,** אינו מתכפר עד שיהיה נוהג תורת המצורע. מעתה עם היה אהרן ומרים מדברים על משה דבר **אמת,** היה כפרה שלהם בצרעת לחוד. אבל כשדברו **בלא אמת** וה"ז בכלל הוצאת שם רע, עונשם בדיני צרעת. **ובלי זה, אין לה כפרה. וביקש אהרן ממשה שלא יהא חושב חטאם בכלל**

מוציא שם רע, אלא בכלל לשון הרע. והסביר טעם שהרי מוציא שם רע הוא בזדון, שיודע שאינו כן והוא מדבר. משא"כ המה אך נואלנו ולסבורים שכן הוא. ואם כן אינו אלא חטא לשון הרע של אמת ולא של מוציא שם רע . . . והיינו דבר אהרן.

7 מרים מי הסגירה? אם תאמר **משה** הסגירה, משה זר הוא, ואין זר רואה את הנגעים. ואם תאמר **אהרן** הסגירה, אהרן קרוב הוא, ואין קרוב רואה את הנגעים! אלא, כבוד גדול חלק לה הקדוש ברוך הוא למרים אותה שעה: "**אני** כהן, ו**אני** מסגירה, **אני** חולטה, ו**אני** פוטרה."

8 השמר בנגע הצרעת לשמר מאד ולעשות ככל אשר יורו אתכם הכהנים הלוים כאשר צויתם תשמרו לעשות. **זכור את אשר עשה ד' אלקיך למרים** בדרך בצאתכם ממצרים.

9 ואפילו הוא מלך . . . לא יכבדוהו, אלא יסגירוהו וישלחוהו ובדד ישב. שהרי זכור את אשר עשה ד' אלקיך למרים, שהיתה אחות למלך וכהן גדול, ואף על פי כן נסגרה מחוץ למחנה שבעת ימים.

10 העונש הגדול שעשה ד' לצדקת הנביאה שלא דברה אלא באחיה . . . אשר אהבתו כנפשה, ולא דברה בפניו שיבוש, ולא בפני רבים. רק בינה לבין אחיה . . . וכל מעשיה הטובים לא הועילוה, גם אתה, אם תשב באחיך תדבר . . . לא תנצל.

11 התבוננו מה אירע למרים הנביאה, שדברה באחיה שהיתה גדולה ממנו בשנים וגידלתו על ברכה, וסיכנה בעצמה להצילו מן הים. והיא לא דברה בגנותו, אלא טעתה שהשותה לשאר נביאים. והוא לא הקפיד על כל הדברים האלו. ואע"פ כן מיד נענשה בצרעת.

12 לפי דעתי היא מצות עשה ממש, כמו 'זכור אן יום השבת לקדשו.'

13 המאמר זה בא להגדיל חשיבתה של מרים . . . אע"פ שהיו טרודים בדרך, מכל מקום לא נסע העם עד האסף מרים. ואף על פי כן לא חלקו לה כבוד, אלא תסגר שבעת ימים [כמו] שאר בן אדם.

14 ועכבו הכל בשבילה . . . להגדיל את העונש, כלומר לא רק ענש פרטי היה לה, אלא נתעכב הגאולה לכל העם! . . . כל זמן שהיו הדגלים נוסעים, לא היו הולכים עד שמרים מקדמת לפניהם. 'ואשלח לפניך את משה, אהרן ומרים.'

15 מרים היתה חשובה, אחת בכל העולם שהיה הבאר לכל ישראל בזכותה.

16 הכוונה שהענן נתעכב לה.

17 אהרן בקש ממשה שלא יחשוב לעון מה שנואלנו והוציאו שם רע. וזה העון חמור מלשון הרע לחוד. ואינו מתכפר אלא בתורת המצורע ולא בצרעת לחוד. **והנה הקב"ה לא קיבל בקשת אהרן** ואמר תסגר מרים, ודן אותה בעונש מוציא שם רע, **אף על גב שבשוגג וטעות דברה על משה בשקר.** דבחטאים שבין אדם לחבירו אדם מועד לעולם, בין שוגג בין מזיד. וזהו דבר הכתוב כאן, שלא יקל בעצמו ויחשוב דכבר יש לו כפרה בצער צרעת לחוד.

18 הרי נאכל חצי בשרו של משה . . . אל תהיה **אתה** כמת.

19 הלך אהרן אצל משה. אמר לו, אדוני משה, אין האחים מתפרשים אלא מתוך המות . . . אחותנו עד שהיא בחיים, נתפרשה ממנו כמות. ונתרצה משה בדברים, והתפלל עליה.

20 בשעה הזאת התפלל בעדה כי צריכים אנחנו את תפלתך . . . וכאשר שמע משה דברי אהרן וראה צרתה של מרים, התפלל אל השם.

FORTY-THREE: Moses Prays for Miriam

1 ויצעק משה אל ד' לאמר; קל נא רפא נא לה.

2 זה יורה שהיה בצער על אחותו.

3   קל נא לשון בקשה ופיוס לעורר הרחמים.

4   השם הזה דין כלול ברחמים.

5   וטעם 'לאמר' כי התפלה היתה באמירה מחלטת, לא במחשבה . . . וטעם החתוך כדי שיצטירו האותיות ברוח פיו של אדם בקול, ורוח, ודבור, ותעלה התפלה מצירת ברוח לפניו יתעלה.

6   אי אפשר תפלה יותר קצרה מזו **שהם אחת עשרה אותיות!** וגם זה להורות להם שהיה משה בן בית ועבד נאמן לפני אדוניו שבראשי דברים היה שואל ממנו שאלה כזאת. והשם השיבו: שמעתי תפלתך ואני ארפא אותה.

7   כל המבקש רחמים על חבירו אין צריך להזכיר שמו.

8   הראשון לשון בקשה, והשני לשון עכשיו. ולכך, השיבו הקב"ה אם היא תרפא מיד, לא תהא נזופה אפילו יום אחד.

9   בבקשה אני שואל שתרפא **עתה** לה, ולא נצטרך לביישה להוציאה חוץ למחנה.

10   הלא בודאי לא יעננו הקב"ה עד שיגמור תפלתו, ובתוך כך תצטער אחותו.

11   מה לא האריך משה בתפלה, שלא יהיו ישראל אומרים, אחותו נתונה בצרה והוא עומד ומרבה בתפלה.

12   'את ארבעים היום ואת ארבעים הלילה.'

13   שהיתה בצער, **והצעקה במקום אריכות**, להורות כי צר לו עליה . . . צעקו יורה כי מר לו מאד.

14   והתפלל עליה ונעתר לו.

15   הסגר מרים לא בשביל הצרעת היתה, כי צרעתה היה גדול כל כך עד שאלו לא נרפאת **מיד**, היתה מתה. . . . וכאשר משה התפלל עליה, תיכף נתרפאה, וההסגר היה מטעם הנאמר שם.

16   אלא ודאי שכבר נתרפאה.

FORTY-FOUR: God Sentences Miriam to a Brief Exile

1   ויאמר ד' אל משה ואביה ירק ירק בפניה הלא תכלם שבעת ימים; תסגר שבעת ימים מחוץ למחנה ואחר תאסף.

2   ואלו אבוהא מזף, נזף בה.

3   הלא תכלם לראות פניו שבעת ימים.

4   ראויה היא לזאת הבושה.

5   תכלם שבעת ימים עד שוב אף אביה ממנה.

6   ואם אביה הראה לה פנים זועפות, הלא תכלם שבעת ימים. **קל וחומר** לשכינה . . . אלא דיו לבא מן הדין להיות כנדון. לפיכך אף בנזיפתי תסגר שבעת ימים. אלא שתפלתו עשתה זאת.

7

8   גם כאן אמר הקב"ה, אני לא אסיר עמוד הענן עד האסף מרים. ובזה אראה שבחה לכל, אבל עתה תסגר מחוץ למחנה . . . וישראל רחוקים ממנה ולא ידעו בצרעתה. עתה תצא מחוץ למחנה, כדין המצורע . . . כדי שידעו כל ישראל כמה הוא עונש לשון הרע.

FORTY-FIVE: The Israelites Wait for Miriam

1   ותסגר מרים מחוץ למחנה שבעת ימים; והעם לא נסע עד האסף מרים. ואחר נסעו העם מחצרות; ויחנו במדבר פארן.

2   **עזובה היא מרים.** ולמה נקרא שמה עזובה? שהכל עזובה במדבר. וכתיב 'ותסגר מרים.'

3   והעם לא נסע. תלה הדבר בעם, ולא אמר ולא נסע העם להודיע כי העם הסכימו לבל יסעו

עד האסף מרים. והגם שהדבר היה תלוי בנסיעת הענן! התורה מעידה כי גם הם היו חפצים בעכבה לכבודה.

4 אמר הקב"ה, אני לא אסיר עמוד הענן עד האסף מרים . . . זה הכבוד חלק לה המקום, כוונתו שהענן נתעכב לה.

5 שבעת ימים. ללמדך שבמידה שאדם מודד בה מודדים לו. מרים המתינה למשה שעה אחת, שנאמר ותתצב אחותו מרחוק. לפיכך עיכב לה שכינה, וארון, כהנים, ולוים, וישראל, ושבעה ענני כבוד.

FORTY-SIX: The Death of Miriam

1 ויבאו בני ישראל כל העדה מדבר־צן בחדש הראשון וישב העם בקדש; ותמת שם מרים ותקבר שם. ולא היה מים לעדה; ויקהלו על משה ועל אהרן.

2 בחדש הראשון. **בשנת הארבעים.**

3 ותמת שם מרים. בחדש הראשון שלסוף ארבעים שנה.

4 ספר הכתוב שנים מאורעים. האחד מות מרים, והשני מות אהרן ומשה, ולא יכנסו לארץ.

5 שהרי מת אהרן אחריה בחדש החמישי בשנת ארבעים לצאת בני ישראל.

6 ובני ישראל אכלו את המן **ארבעים שנה** . . . בשבעה באדר מת משה, ופסח מן מלירד . . . מנין שבשבעה באדר מת?. . . וכתיב, ויבכו בני ישראל את משה בערבת מואב שלשים יום; . . . [וכתיב] הכינו לכם צדה כי בעוד שלשת ימים תעברו את הירדן; . . . וכתיב, והעם עלו מן הירדן בעשור לחדש הראשון. צא מהן שלשים ושלשה ימים למפרע, **הא למדת שבשבעה באדר מת משה.**

7 ותמת שם מרים. אף היא בנשיקה מתה. ומפני מה לא נאמר בה 'על פי ד'? שאינו דרך כבוד של מעלה.

8 ויעל אהרן הכהן אל הר ההר **על פי ד' וימת שם** בשנת הארבעים לצאת בני ישראל מארץ מצרים בחדש החמישי באחד לחדש.

9 **וימת שם** משה עבד ד' בארץ מואב **על פי ד'.**

10 אף היא בנשיקה מתה . . . דלא הוי צריך למכתב **שם** ,רק 'ותמת מרים.' אלא לכך כתב **שם**, למילף בגזרה שוה מאהרן, דכתיב אצלו גם כן **שם**, ואהרן מת בנשיקה, דכתיב אצלו 'על פי ד'.

11 אף מרים בנשיקה מתה. **אתיא שם, שם ממשה.** ומפני מה לא נאמר בה 'על פי ד'? מפני שגנאי הדבר לאומרו.

12 תנו רבנן: ששה לא שלט בהן מלאך המות, ואלו הן: אברהם, יצחק ויעקב, משה, אהרן ומרים. אברהם, יצחק ויעקב, דכתיב בהו: בכל, מכל, כל. משה, אהרן ומרים, דכתיב בהו: על פי ד'. והא מרים לא כתיב בה על פי ד'! אמר רבי אלעזר: מרים נמי בנשיקה מתה, דאתיא שם, שם ממשה. ומפני מה לא נאמר בה על פי ד'? שגנאי הדבר לומר.

13 לא על ידי מלאך המות כדמפרש, וגם לא ביסורים . . . כשהמקום נוטל נשמתן של צדיקים נוטלה מהם בנחת רוח; וכינו חז"ל מיתה כזו בשם מיתת נשיקה.

14 כי הצדיקים דומים לפני הקב"ה למרגליות המונחים בארגז. כשהוא חפץ באחת מהם הוא מוציאה מהארגז וקובעה בתכשיט אחד מתכשיטיו.

15 על צד העונש חסרו המים לפי שלא הספידוה כראוי, כי במשה ואהרן נאמר 'ויבכו אותם בני ישראל,' וכאן לא נאמר ויבכו אותה.' ונאמר 'ותמת שם, ותקבר שם.' . . . ונשכחה כמת מלב ולא הרגישו בהעדרה כלל. על כן נחסרו להם המים. כדי שידעו למפרע שהבאר היה בזכות מרים.

16 ובאמת אם היו עושים כן, מסתבר שהיו המים חוזרים.

17 מכאן שכל ארבעים שנה היה להם הבאר בזכות מרים.

18 וכיון שנסתלק הבאר התחילו מתכנסין על משה ועל אהרן שנאמר 'ויקהלו על משה ועל
אהרן.' והיו משה ואהרן יושבין ומתאבלין על מרים.   אמר הקב"ה, 'בשביל שאתם אבלים
ימותו בצמא!   עמוד וקח מטך והשקית את העדה . . . .'   היו יושבין ובוכין בפנים, וישראל
בוכין בחוץ . . .   נכנסו אצלו ואמרו לו, 'עד מתי אתה בוכה?'   אמר להן, 'ולא אבכה על
אחותי שמתה?!'   אמרו לו, 'עד שאתה בוכה על **נפש אחת**, בכה **עלינו** שאין לנו מים
לשתות!'   מיד עמד ויצא עמהן וראה הבאר יבישה והם מריבין עמו.   אמר להן . . 'לא אוכל
לבדי שאת אתכם.'

19 שלשה פרנסים טובים עמדו לישראל; אלו הן: משה, ואהרן, ומרים.   ושלש מתנות טובות
ניתנו על ידם; ואלו הן: באר, וענן, ומן.   באר בזכות מרים, עמוד ענן בזכות אהרן, מן
בזכות משה.   מתה מרים, נסתלק הבאר, שנאמר, 'ותמת שם מרים.'   וכתיב בתריה, 'ולא היה
מים לעדה.'   וחזרה בזכות שניהן.

20 אמר רבי חייא: הרוצה לראות בארה של מרים יעלה לראש הכרמל ויצפה ויראה כמין כברה
בים.   **וזו היא בארה של מרים.**

21 ומשם בארה; הוא הבאר אשר אמר ד' למשה אסף את העם ואתנה להם מים.   אז ישיר
ישראל את השירה הזאת; עלי באר ענו לה.

22 שם הוחזרה להם הבאר שקבלו אותה מחורב לפני ארבעים שנה, ומימיה פסקו אחרי מות
מרים.

23 מקום שעמד הבאר מללכת עוד משום שלא היו נצרכים עוד לה . . . ושם אמרו שירה על
הבאר.

24 הא בכן שבח ישראל ית שבח שירתא הדא בזמן דאתכסיית והדרת בירא דאתיהיבת להון
בזכותא דמרים.

25 ושם נעלם הבאר ולא היה להם מים ולא רצה ד' לתת להם מים על ידי משה . . . .   ובכל זאת
השיגו באר מים.

26 ואיננה הבאר הנקרא באר מרים.

27 כשראו הנס שהבאר שהיתה נעלמת מהם, חזרה ונתנה מים.   נתמלא לבם שמחה ואמרו
שירה.

28 השירה [הבאר] מזכירה מאוד את שירת הים ששרו בזמן יציאת מצרים: "אז ישיר **משה ובני
ישראל**," אך בהבדל אחד משמעותי מאוד: במקום "אז ישיר משה ובני ישראל" נאמר כאן
"אז ישיר **ישראל**." . . . .   בסופה של שירת הים מובא
פסוק המתאר את שירת הנשים המובלות על ידי מרים אחות משה: "**ותען להן מרים** שירו
לד' כי גאה גאה." . . . .   בשירת משה **הוא** היוזם והמבצע, והעם עונה לו על כל דבר ודבר.
מרים אינה מוכנה לזה.   היא מבקשת מהעם לשיר . . .   מנהיגותה של מרים המנוסה לעורר
את העם לנבוע בשירה עצמית, **היתה מנהיגות טרם זמנה** . . . .   בשלב זה מבין העם שלא
משה יהיה ממשיך דרכה של מרים.   עכשיו, אחרי ארבעים שנה, מחלחלת לתודעה שלהם
הצוואה של מרים . . .   אז פורצת השירה **שלהם**.

29 אלשיך: רמזה תורה פה . . .   כי בארה של מרים היא מעין תורה של בעל פה . . .   אל יעלה
על רוחך חלילה שהתורה שהתורה שבעל פה הוא דבר חוץ מהתורה שבכתב; כי דע איפה כי בספר
הוא תורה שבכתב נמצא כל תורה שבעל פה.   שפת אמת: ענין שירה הזאת . . . .   הבאר
שהוא רמז לתורה שבעל פה.

30 באר **חפרוה** שרים . . .   וממדבר **מתנה**.

FORTY-SEVEN: The Survival of the Women of the Exodus

1   ויאמר ד' אל משה ואל אהרן: יען לא האמנתם בי להקדישני לעיני בני ישראל; לכן לא
תביאו את הקהל הזה אל הארץ אשר נתתי להם.

2   ואולם חי אני . . . אם יראו את הארץ אשר נשבעתי לאבתם; וכל מנאצי לא יראוה . . .
במדבר הזה יפלו פגריכם . . . **מבן עשרים שנה ומעלה אשר הלינתם עלי** . . . כי אם
כלב בן יפנה ויהושע בן נון.

3   מבן עשרים שנה . . . אין הכוונה כל מי **שהיום** בן עשרים. ולפי זה נמצא שבכלל הגזירה
נכללים גם מי שיצא ממצרים פחות מבן עשרים, כיון שבשנה השניה באו לכלל עשרים.
אלא הכוונה היא, מי שהיה בן עשרים בשעת יציאת מצרים . . . פירש מזמן **שהתחילו**
להלין.

4   **וילנו** העם אל משה
. . . .

5   בא אלעזר ללמד על שבטו, שכשם שנכנס הוא כן נכנסו הם.

6   ודאי **מן הלוים** הרבה נשתיירו.

7   אלא הנחלת אשר נחלו **אלעזר הכהן** ויהושע בן נון וראשי האבות למטות בני ישראל . . . .

8   אבל על הנשים לא נגזרה גזרת המרגלים, לפי שהן היו מחבבות את הארץ. האנשים אומרים
'נתנה ראש ונשובה מצרימה,' והנשים אומרות 'תנה לנו אחוזה.'

9   לא שמעו לדברי המרגלים . . . לא היו עמהם בעצה להאמין למרגלים . . . לא נותר איש
אבל נשים נותרו. ותקרבנה בנות צלפחד שהנשים בקשו הארץ ולא האמינו לעצת המרגלים.
ואם נשי המרגלים לא היו עם עצת המרגלים קל וחומר על שאר הנשים שלא שמעו.

10   הנשים גודרות מה שהאנשים פורצים . . . והנשים לא השתתפו עמהן במעשה העגל וכן
במרגלים . . . הנשים לא היו עמהם בעצה . . . ולא נותר מהם איש . . . איש ולא אשה על
מה שלא רצו ליכנס לארץ, אבל הנשים קרבו לבקש נחלה בארץ. לכך נכתבה פרשה זו
סמוך למיתת דור המדבר, שמשם פרצו האנשים וגדרו הנשים.

11   האנשים היו פרוצין בעריות . . . אבל הנשים היו כשרות וצנועות . . . הנשים של אותו דור
צדקניות היו . . . בזכות נשים צדקניות שהיו באותו דור נגאלו אבותינו ממצרים.

12   כאן יפה כח הנשים מכח האנשים.

13   זו מיתה בלבד מכל הנשים שיצאו ממצרים. **שלא מתה אשה במדבר**, שנאמר (יהושע ה:ד)
כל העם היוצא ממצרים הזכרים, כל אנשי המלחמה מתו, ולא הנקבות. וזו למה מתה [מרים]
מפני הבאר שנתנה בשבילה, שלא היה אפשר לה שתהא קיימת והבאר שנתנה בזכותה
מסתלקת. דבר אחר, מפני שהיא שוה למשה ולאהרן בגדולה, ששלשתם היו פרנסים טובים
לישראל, שאינו בדין שיסתלקו ומרים קיימת. לכך קדמה תחלה ומתה . . . ולא נותר מהם
איש. על האנשים היתה הגזירה ולא על הנשים, שהרי **שרח בת אשר היתה מבאי מצרים
ומבאי הארץ.**

14   יוכבד היתה מבאי מצרים ומיוצאיה . . . ומבאי הארץ, שנאמר, 'ושם אשת עמרם יוכבד בת
לוי אשר ילדה . . . .'

15   בחדש הראשון. של שנת הארבעים . . . ופירש הכתוב זמן ביאה זו ביחוד כדי שנדע יום
מתת מרים. ויותר מזה יבואר לפנינו דמאז התחילה הנהגה אחרת בישראל לא כמו שהיה עד
כה . . . שלא היתה הגזרה עליה שלא יבואו עצמותיה לארץ ישראל כמו שנגזר אחר כך על
משה ואהרן.

16   ותמת שם מרים ותקבר שם. היא סיימה את שליחותה עלי אדמות, קברה בקדש, יודיע לדור
אחרון, שלא הסתלקה מן העולם עד שלא היה זה הדור החדש מוכן לעתיד המובטח לו. במסע
הארוך והעשיר בנסיונות קשים, לא היו הנשים שותפות למעשה הבגידה בד' שבאו מתוך

יאוש. בשמחת לבב הן בטחו בד' ויחלו לו בהתמסרות. ולפיכך גזירת המיתה במדבר לא
נגזרה על הנשים. ועתה אמהות וסבתות עמדו לעלות עם הדור החדש אל הארץ המובטחת,
והן שמרו בלבן את הזכרון החי של העבר במצרים, ושל המסע במדבר על פי ד'. והן יכלו
לרוות את נפש הנכדים והנינים מן המעיין הרוחני של חוויותיהן עם ד'. ובאמת נשי ישראל
הקדימו להצטייד ברוח ישראל, והיו חדורות בה עד לעומק נפשן. ועבודה זו ראויה להיות
נזקפת לזכותה של מרים שהאירה לפניהן כנביאה.

GLOSSARY
OF TERMS AND SOURCES

෨෬ඐ෬ඐ

Abarbanel Rabbi (Don) Isaac Ben Yehuda (1437–1508) was a Spanish Bible commentator, philosopher and statesman. He suffered various misfortunes culminating in the expulsion of Spanish Jewry in 1492. Abarbanel's extensive commentaries to the Bible are arranged by chapters introduced by numerous questions that he then proceeds to resolve.

Aggadot Yam HaTalmud A multi-volume, modern compilation (by Rabbi Shimon Vanunu of Yeshiva Chayei Torah in Jerusalem) of "pearls" from the writings of several hundred Talmudic scholars. The volumes correspond to the books of the Babylonian Talmud.

Akeidat Yitzchak Isaac ben Moses Arama (1420–1494) was a Spanish rabbi, teacher, and philosopher. After the expulsion of the Jews from Spain in 1492 he settled in Naples, Italy. He delivered hundreds of sermons dealing with the weekly Torah readings, which were compiled under the title of "Akeidat Yitzchak," which was published in Salonika in 1522.

Alschich Rabbi Moshe Alschich (1508–c.1593) was a Torah scholar who spent most of his life in Safed, in Israel, and who was a disciple of Rabbi Yosef Karo, the author of the *Shulchan Aruch*, the Code of Jewish Law. His primary interest was *halacha*, Jewish law, but Alschich also studied Kabbalah, Jewish mysticism, and biblical exegesis. His Shabbat sermons formed the basis of his popular commentaries on most of the Bible.

Ba'al Haturim Rabbi Yaakov ben Asher (c.1270-1340), was born in Germany, but fled with his father to Spain, and there he served as the *dayan*, or Judge of Jewish law, in the City of Toledo. His father was "The Rosh," Reb Asher ben Yechiel, who wrote an authoritative commentary on the Mishna. He is called the Ba'al HaTurim because of his major work, entitled the *Arba'ah Turim*, which for 200 years, until the appearance of the *Shulchan Aruch*, was considered the standard code of Jewish law.

Bachya, Rabbeinu Rabbi (Rabbeinu) Bachya ben Asher (d. 1340) was a Spanish Bible commentator and kabbalist. He wrote his popular commentary on the Torah in 1291.

Bamidbar Rabbah A compilation (400 to 500 C.E.) of homilies and interpretive sources from *midrash* and the Babylonian and Jerusalem Talmud on the Book of Numbers, the fourth book of the Hebrew Bible. It is based on Palestinian sources dating from the time of the *Tanaim* (*mishnaic* teachers 20 to 200 C.E.) and *Amoraim* (sages of the Talmud 200 to 500 C.E.). The entire body of work encompasses the Five books of Moses, and also is referred to as **Midrash Rabbah.**

Bechor Schor Rabbi Joseph Bechor Schor, born in (c.) 1140 in Northern France, was a 12th-century Tosafist and renowned *p'shatist* who also wrote a commentary on the Five Books of Moses.

Bereishit Rabbah An early compilation of *midrash* and homilies for each verse of the Book of Genesis, the first book of the Hebrew Bible. It is based on Palestinian sources and is written for the most part in Aramaic. See entry for Bamidbar Rabbah above.

Berman, Saul Rabbi Saul J. Berman is a leading American Jewish activist, teacher, scholar and author specializing in the subject of women in Jewish law. He is an Associate Professor of Jewish Studies at Stern College for Women of Yeshiva University, as well as an adjunct Professor at Columbia University School of Law in New York City.

Chafetz Chayim Rabbi Israel Meir Ha-Kohen (1838-1933) was a widely influential rabbi, ethical writer and Talmudist who, teaching primarily in Vilna, wrote the well-known *Mishna Berura*, a six-volume commentary on the *Shulchan Aruch*. Among numerous other scholarly works, he also wrote a commentary on the Five Books of Moses.

Chatam Sofer Rabbi Moses Sofer (1762–1839), was born in Frankfurt, but moved to Hungary at a young age, where he remained until the end of his life. He served as rabbi of Pressburg, Hungary for 33 years, during which time he established the largest yeshiva, or house of Jewish study, since the Babylonian *yeshivot*. His many writings include commentaries on the Bible and Talmud, numerous responsa, sermons, letters, poems and a diary.

Chizkuni Hezekiah ben Manoah was a Bible scholar who lived in France in the mid-thirteenth century. He is known for his *midrashic* commentaries on the Torah and on Rashi's vast exegesis. His work was published in Venice in 1524.

Da'at Zekeinim Miba'alei Hatosfot Thirteenth-century compilation of commentaries on the Torah originating with the French Tosafists, the Talmudic commentators who were the disciples of Rashi.

Divrei HaYamim Shel Moshe A *midrashic* interpretation of the life of Moses written in the early Middle Ages. Authorship is unknown.

HaMa'or Shebatorah A modern (2005) collection of rabbinic interpretations on the Five Books of Moses edited by Israeli Rabbi Daniel Bitton.

Hartman, Yehoshua David A modern-day Israeli rabbi and commentator on the Bible and Talmud.

Hegyona Shel Torah A compilation of homiletic writings on the Five Books of Moses by Rabbi Bentzion Faher (Israel, 1967).

Hirsch, Rabbi Samson Raphael (1808–1888) The rabbi of Frankfurt-on-Main and the defender of Orthodox Judaism against the upsurge of the Reform movement. Among his many works is his monumental German translation of and commentary on the Torah.

Ibn Ezra (of Tudela), Rabbi Abraham (1089–1164) A Spanish poet, grammarian, philosopher, and physician whose commentary on the Bible dwells on the meaning, grammar and etymology of the words in their different contexts.

Kli Yakar A homiletic commentary on the Bible written by Rabbi Ephraim Solomon ben Haim of Luntshitz (1550–1619), the Rabbi of Prague and head of the yeshiva in Lemberg.

Lau, Binyamin Rabbi Dr. Binyamin Lau is a lecturer in Talmud at Bar-Ilan University, rabbi of the Rambam Synagogue in Jerusalem, and author of numerous articles on Torah and Jewish law.

Leibowitz, Nehama Born in Riga, Latvia, in 1905, "Nehama" was a twentieth-century Israeli teacher and Bible scholar. For a half-century her renowned "Pages" on the study of the weekly Torah portion reached Bible students the world over. She was a Professor of Bible at Tel Aviv University whose unique method of critical analysis of the Bible and its commentaries challenged generations of students to understand the nuances of meaning in the Torah text. She died in Israel in 1997.

Leibowitz, Yeshayahu (1903-1994) Born in Riga, Latvia, emigrated to Palestine in 1935 after having been awarded both PhD and MD degrees. He was professor of biochemistry and neurology at the Hebrew University as well as an outspoken thinker and prolific author on topics spanning politics, the State of Israel, Jewish culture, human values, and the teachings of Maimonides. He also authored essays on the weekly Torah portion. The noted Bible scholar, Nehama Leibowitz, was his younger sister.

Levush HaOrah A supercommentary to Rashi written by Rabbi Mordechai ben Avraham Jaffe (c.1535–1612), who succeeded the

Maharal as the *Av Beit Din*, head of the Jewish High Court, in Prague. He is known as the *Ba'al Halevushim* because he authored the "Ten Attires" (*Levushim*), commentaries on a range of Hebrew texts. It is the sixth *Levush* that is the supercommentary on Rashi.

Maharal Rabbi Judah Loew ben Bezalel (c.1525–1609), born to a noble Worms family, was a scholar of Bible, mathematics and astronomy, and served as Chief Rabbi of Moravia, Posen and Prague. His many writings on ethics, law, philosophy and homiletics had *kabbalistic* leanings. He is the author of the *Gur Aryeh*, a supercommentary on Rashi.

Maharaz Rabbi Ze'ev Wolf was a nineteenth-century Torah scholar writing in Vilna, Lithuania. He is noted for his commentary on the Midrash Rabbah.

Malbim The acronym of Rav Meir Leibush ben Yechiel Michel (1809–1879), known as the "illui [prodigy] of Volhynia" in the Ukraine. He was a staunch supporter of Orthodox exegesis, and wrote an esteemed commentary on the Torah.

Ma'ayna Shel Torah A twentieth-century anthology and commentary written by Rabbi Alexander Zushia Friedman. It combines ethical and moral teachings with the weekly biblical portions. Written originally in Yiddish in Warsaw, Poland, it was translated into Hebrew and published in Palestine in 1938.

Mechilta A *midrashic* compilation on the book of Exodus, written during the *mishnaic* period (c. 20-200 C.E.).

Mei HaShiluach Rabbi Mordechai Yosef Leiner (Poland, 1804-1854), known as the Ishbitzer, founded the Ishbitzer dynasty of Hassidic Judaism. He compiled his commentary on the weekly Torah portions in his book, *Mei HaShiluach*.

Mephorshim A generic term that refers to traditional Jewish biblical commentators whose words were recorded from the third century before the Common Era to the present day.

Meshech Chachma   A commentary on the Torah written by Rabbi Meir Simcha Hakohen of Dvinsk (1843–1926), where he served as rabbi for forty years. His commentary on the Torah combines Talmudic and *midrashic* material with philosophical insights. He also wrote commentaries on Maimonides' *Mishna Torah* and on the Talmud.

Metzudat David   Rabbi David Altschuler (Prague, seventeenth century) and his son, Rabbi Yechiel Altschuler, authored this popular commentary on the Prophets and Writings.

Midrash   From the Hebrew root-word *DaRoSH*, meaning to search, seek, examine or investigate. Commentaries that discuss the *legal* texts of the Torah comprise *midrash halacha*. *Midrash aggadah,* on the other hand, which is the essence of our book, is rabbinic interpretation whose focus is the biblical narrative combined with historical events, and ethical and philosophical matters. According to Daniel Boyarin in his book, *Intertextuality and the Reading of Midrash* (Indiana University Press, 1994), pages 10–20, *midrash* represents the "intertext" of the Bible, or the rabbis' attempts to fill in the gaps that may appear to exist in the Bible's spare narratives and dialogues. In Boyarin's words, the authors of the *midrash* are "lonely geniuses in communion with the biblical heroes," reproducing the "essences" of these biblical heroes. *Midrash* represents the timeless "double-voicedness" of the Torah, by setting up a dialectic between rabbinic interpretations. Certain biblical ambiguities naturally invite the *midrashic* intertexts, thereby generating more than one legitimate *midrashic* reading. Biblical *midrash* thus preserves intimate contact with and context for the Bible, and provides a rabbinic model of the relationship between the present and the past.

Midrash Lekach Tov A twelfth-century anthology of Torah commentaries ascribed to Rabbi Tuvia ben Reb Eliezer of Mainz (Mayence).

Midrash Tanchuma A collection of interpretations of the Torah originally written in Aramaic by the fourth-century Talmudic scholar Rabbi Tanchuma bar Abba. The work, first published in Venice in

1545, was comprised mainly of Tanchuma's sermons on the biblical text.

Mizrachi Rabbi Eliyahu Mizrachi (1450–1526) of Constantinople. Known as the Re'im, he is the premier supercommentary on Rashi. He served as the rabbinical authority throughout the Ottoman Empire, and was considered the greatest *posek*, or authority on Jewish law, of his time. Mizrachi's supercommentary itself became a subject for study of succeeding generations of rabbinic commentators.

Nachshoni, Yehuda Twentieth-century Israeli rabbi, scholar, and Torah commentator whose Hebrew-language work on the weekly Torah portions combines traditional commentaries with original exegesis.

Netziv The acronym of Rabbi Naphtali Zvi Yehuda Berlin (1817–1893), the prodigy Talmudist who served as the head of the Yeshiva of Volozhin for forty years, until the yeshiva was closed by the Russian authorities in 1892. Berlin's commentary, *Ha'amek Davar*, incorporated his daily lessons on the weekly Torah portion.

Ohr HaChayim Rabbi Chayim Ibn Attar (1696–1743), a Moroccan Torah scholar and kabbalist who encouraged resettlement of Palestine and established a yeshiva there. His commentaries on the Talmud, *halacha* and the Torah were widely circulated in Germany and Poland.

Onkelos The Torah commentary written *circa* first century c.e. by Onkelos the Proselyte, referred to in the Talmud (*Megilla* 3a) as a student of Rabbi Eliezer and Rabbi Yehoshua after the destruction of the Second Temple in Jerusalem in 70 c.e. Known as "the Targum," Onkelos' work aimed for literal translation of the Hebrew biblical text into Aramaic, but in fact it liberally employed paraphrase for clarity or in order to avoid anthropomorphism. It was highly valued by the Babylonian Talmudists, who referred to Onkelos as "our targum."

Otzar Ishei HaTanach   A one-volume encyclopedia of biblical personalities anthologized from the Talmud, *midrash*, and rabbinic writings. First published in Jerusalem in 1964 by Rabbi Yisrael Yitzchak (Yishai) Chasidah.

Perush Yonatan   An ancient biblical commentary on Targum Yonatan Ben Uziel/Yerushalmi, an Aramaic translation on the Torah of uncertain authorship.

Pirkei d'Rabi Eliezer   A commentary of *midrash aggadah* compiled in the eighth century, attributed to Rabbi Eliezer, son of Hyrkanos, who lived in the latter half of the first century c.e. He was renowned for his erudition, but was ultimately excommunicated for revealing kabbalistic mysteries in his commentary. He is cited in the Tosfot commentary to the Talmud (*Ketubot* 99a), as well as by Rashi and Maimonides, and it is believed that much of his commentary has been incorporated into the Zohar.

P'shat   The plain-sense meaning of the Bible text, or its strict textual reading.

Radak   Acronym of Rabbi David Kimchi (1160–1235), Bible commentator and grammarian of Provence, France. Known for his plain-sense commentary on the Bible, he was interested in science and philosophy, as well as the rationalism of Ibn Ezra and Maimonides.

Rambam   Acronym for Rabbi Moses ben Maimon [Maimonides] (1135–1204) of Fostat, the Old City of Cairo, Egypt. He was a brilliant Rabbinic authority, codifier, philosopher, and royal physician. Among his great works are his commentary to the Mishna, the *Mishna Torah,* and *Guide to the Perplexed.* Rambam is considered a towering figure of Judaism in the post-Talmudic era.

Ramban   Acronym for Rabbi Moshe ben Nachman [Nachmanides] (1194–1270) of Gerona, Spain. He was a physician as well as a Talmudic authority who authored biblical commentaries distinguished by an in-depth analysis of the larger significance of the Torah's stories and themes. His work on the Torah often quoted the writings of Rashi and Ibn Ezra as his point of departure, explaining or challenging their comments.

Ra"N Acronym of Rabbeinu Nissim ben Reuven Gerondi (c.1310-c.1375), a Spanish Talmud and Bible commentator, physician and philosopher. He is best known for his *halachic* works, notably his commentary on the Ri"f, Rabbi Isaac Alfasi. He authored responsa, a book of sermons and a commentary on the Torah.

Rashbam Acronym of Rabbi Shlomo ben Meir (1085–1174) of Troyes, France. The grandson of Rashi, Rashbam's Bible commentary favors the literal or plain-sense meaning of the Torah text. Rashbam was one of the earliest Tosafists.

Rashi The acronym of Rabbi Shlomo Yitzchaki (1040–1105) of Troyes, France. Rashi's exhaustive biblical exegesis, the first known Hebrew commentary to be printed in 1475, spawned more than 200 supercommentaries. He employed literal as well as *midrashic* interpretations, and said of his own commentaries (at Genesis 3:8): "As for me, I am only concerned with the literal meaning of the Scriptures and with such [*midrash*] *aggadot* as explain the biblical passages in a fitting manner." Rashi also wrote a commentary to virtually all of the Babylonian Talmud.

Ri"f Rabbi Isaac ben Jacob Alfasi (Fez, Morocco, 1013-1103) was a revered Talmudic scholar who authored an authoritative code, *Sefer Ha-Halakhot*, or *Talmud Katan*, encompassing the entire Babylonian Talmud. In his generation the Ri"f was regarded as the pre-eminent Talmudic authority in Spain and North Africa.

Sa'adia (ben Joseph) Gaon Born in Egypt (882–942), he translated the entire Torah into Arabic, incorporating into the translation his authoritative biblical commentary.

Samuels, Beth (1975-2007) A Drisha Scholar and Director of Drisha's High School Program, Beth Samuels received her PhD in Mathematics from Yale and was a Visiting Assistant Professor of Mathematics at UC Berkeley. Her Torah lectures were widely attended in Jewish communities across the U.S. until her untimely death.

S'fat Emet   The collected writings of Judah Aryeh Leib Alter (Poland, 1847-1905), the head of the Hassidim of Gur.

Sforno   Rabbi Ovadia ben Jacob Sforno (1475–1550) was an Italian Bible commentator and physician. In Bologna, Sforno established a *beit medrash*, or house of learning, over which he presided until his death. He is best known for his Bible commentary which often highlighted the medical and biological aspects of the text.

Sha'arei Aharon   The Torah commentary of Rabbi Aharon Yeshaya Rotter, a survivor of the holocaust of Eastern European Jewry. Rabbi Rotter fled the Nazis in Hungary and ultimately emigrated to Israel via the Ukraine, and a displaced persons camp in Cyprus. He is currently living in B'nei Brak, Israel. His encyclopedic work explains the Torah text, Rashi, Onkelos, and numerous other rabbinic sources. He also incorporates his original interpretations in a verse-by-verse explication of the Bible.

Sh'mot Rabbah   An early compilation of *midrash* and homilies for each verse of the Book of Exodus, the second book of the Hebrew Bible. It is based on Palestinian sources. See entry for Bamidbar Rabbah above.

Sifrei   *Tannaitic* (from the period of the mishna) *midrashim* on the books of Numbers and Deuteronomy.

Siftei Chachamim   The Torah commentary written by Rabbi Shabbetai Bass (1641–1718) is the most popular and widespread supercommentary on Rashi. Bass was born in Poland but was forced by a pogrom to flee to Prague in 1655, where he became a publisher and bibliographer. In 1680 he published this commentary as well as the first Jewish bibliography written in Hebrew.

Soloveitchik, Rabbi Joseph B.   (1903–1993) Known as "The Rav," Soloveitchik was born in Russia into a prominent rabbinic family. He earned a Doctorate of Philosophy from the University of Berlin in 1931, and emigrated to the United States the following year. From 1941 to 1985 the Rav served as *Rosh Yeshiva* at Yeshiva University. A talmudist and philosopher of vast erudition, he was one of the preeminent teachers and scholars of the twentieth-century.

Steinsaltz, Rabbi Adin   Born in Jerusalem in 1937, Rabbi Steinsaltz is a modern author and Torah scholar whose towering translation of the Babylonian Talmud into Hebrew includes his original commentary. Rabbi Steinsaltz also has written a commentary on the *Tanya*, the classic treatise of Lubavitch Chassidic thought, as well as numerous philosophical works. He lives and teaches in Jerusalem, and lectures worldwide.

Talmud, Babylonian and Jerusalem   Foundational multi-volume works consisting of discussion and commentary on the Mishna, or Oral Law, as expounded in the Jewish academies of study in Babylon and Palestine between the years 200 and 500 C.E. by the *amoraim*, the rabbinic scholars of that period. The Babylonian Talmud was completed in c.500 C.E., about a century later than the Jerusalem Talmud, and is considered more *halachically* authoritative.

Targum Yonatan ben Uziel   (first century B.C.E.-first century C.E.)   An outstanding pupil of Hillel the sage known for his *midrashic* translation of the Prophets into Aramaic (and to whom also is ascribed an Aramaic translation of the Torah, known as *Targum Yerushalmi*). Commentary to this translation is known as *Perush Yonatan*.

Torah Shlema A verse-by-verse, encyclopedic compilation of *midrashic* commentaries on the Torah, authored by Rabbi Menachem Mendel Kasher, and published in Jerusalem in 1992.

Torah Temima   The Bible commentary written by Rabbi Baruch Halevi Epstein (1860–1942), a Russian talmudic scholar whose father, Rabbi Yechiel Michel Epstein, authored the monumental work entitled the *Aruch Hashulchan,* and whose uncle was the

Netziv. In his introduction to his Torah commentary he explained that his aim was "to show that this Torah, the written law, is a twin sister . . . to the oral law. They are inseparable, as body and soul." Epstein perished at the hands of the Nazis in the Pinsk Ghetto.

Torat HaChidah   Rabbi Chayim Yosef David Azulai (1724–1806), author of *Torat HaChidah*, was a native of Jerusalem. Azulai, a leading scholar of his generation, traveled extensively in Europe as an emissary of the houses of Torah study in the Land of Israel, and was esteemed by the Jews of the Ottoman Empire, Italy and Germany. He authored literary diaries, *halachic* works, and mystical interpretations of the Bible.

Tosfot   Rabbinic commentary on the Babylonian Talmud which expanded upon Rashi's exhaustive Talmudic commentary.   Noted early Tosafists were Rabbi Meir, Rashi's son-in-law, the Rashbam, and Rabbeinu Tam.

Vayikra Rabbah   A collection of thirty-seven *midrashic* discourses pertaining to verses at the beginning of each Torah portion in Leviticus, the third book of the Hebrew Bible.   The *midrashim* in Vayikra Rabbah are of Palestinian origin and are written primarily in Aramaic.   See entry for Bamidbar Rabbah above.

Wiesel, Elie   Born in 1928 in Sighet, Transylvania, Elie Wiesel is professor of Humanities at Boston University; lecturer, thinker, and prolific author of thirty-six works dealing with Judaism, the Holocaust, and moral responsibility. He is the recipient of the 1986 Nobel Peace Prize.

Yalkut Shimoni   Considered the most extensive *midrashic* anthology, spanning the entire Torah, including the Prophets and the Writings. Its authorship is attributed to Rabbi Shimon Hadarshan of Frankfurt, in thirteenth-century Germany. The Yalkut collected more than 10,000 *halachic* and *aggadic* opinions.

Yefei To'ar   A commentary on *Midrash Rabbah* authored by Rabbi Shmuel Yafeh Ashkenazi (1525–1595) of Constantinople.

Zornberg, Dr. Avivah Gottlieb A modern-day Torah scholar and author of two books of biblical commentary on Genesis and Exodus. Born in England to a rabbinic family, she grew up in Glasgow, Scotland, where her father was head of the rabbinical court. She holds a Ph.D. from Cambridge University, and emigrated to Israel twenty-five years ago, where she lives with her husband, Eric, and their family. She now lectures widely in Israel, Europe and the United States.

INDEX OF SOURCES

ଈୠଔଐଈୠଔଐ

Abarbanel, 71–72, 77, 83–84,
94–95, 97, 100, 105, 111,
132–34, 138, 181, 242,
244, 247
Aggadot Yam HaTalmud, 69–70,
84
Akeidat Yitzchak, 40, 129, 180–
82
Alschich, 17, 53, 62–63, 69, 98–
100, 103, 106, 134, 137,
181, 207, 210, 214–15,
220, 224–25, 233, 235,
245, 258

Bechor Schor, 14, 22, 26, 28, 31,
54, 56, 133–34, 208–9, 227
Ba'al HaTurim, 32, 125
Babylonian Talmud
Avoda Zara, 135
Bava Batra, 8, 44, 189, 191,
253
Brachot, 159, 244–45
Kiddushin, 252
Megilla, 64, 157n, 161
Moed Katan, 206, 253
Nedarim, 102, 124, 129, 131,
134, 136, 218
Sanhedrin, 19, 64
Shabbat, 199, 227, 232, 256
Sotah, 12, 19, 22, 31, 33, 37,
43, 47–48, 54, 57, 62, 67–

68, 73–74, 77, 117, 119,
157, 171, 250
Yevamot, 200–201, 223
Zevachim, 195, 238
Bamidbar Rabbah, 163, 192, 262
Rabbi Saul Berman, 159n
Bereishit Rabbah, 7

Chafetz Chayim, 68
Chatam Sofer, 61, 111, 162, 174,
209
Chizkuni, 6, 42, 48–49, 53, 83,
97, 110–12, 123, 135–37,
151, 160, 177, 185, 206,
244

Da'at Zekeinim, 35, 99, 171, 208,
219
Divrei Hayamim Shel Moshe, 90,
104, 108, 206

HaMa'or Shebatorah, 102, 131–
32, 179n, 180
Hegyona Shel Torah, 106, 182–
83
Yehoshua David Hartman, 31
Samson Raphael Hirsch, 256

Ibn Ezra, 5, 16, 22, 27, 46, 52,
54, 57, 82–83, 86, 96–97,
110, 118, 135–37, 185,

195, 206–7, 213, 225, 243, 247, 251, 256

Ishbitzer, *see* Mei HaShiluach

Jerusalem Talmud
  Nedarim, 102, 124, 129, 131, 134, 136, 218

Kli Yakar, 16, 27, 34, 43, 151, 158, 182, 184, 195, 254, 262

Binyamin Lau, 256–57
Leibowitz, Nehama, 119–20
Leibowitz, Yeshayahu, 216–18
Levush HaOrah, 96

Ma'ayna Shel Torah, 64, 152, 160
Maharal, 32, 40, 139, 142, 172–73, 207, 210, 212, 253
Maharaz, 4, 69, 262
Malbim, 48, 58, 60, 71–72, 74, 81, 84, 112, 133, 151, 161, 177, 185, 231, 245, 256
Mechilta, 160, 178, 187, 199
Mei HaShiluach (the Ishbitzer), 36
Meshech Chachma, 125, 188–89, 192
Metzudat David, 164
Micah, 164, 189–91
Midrash Lekach Tov, 18
Midrash Tanchuma, 125–26
Mizrachi, 172

Yehuda Nachshoni, 46, 128–29, 132
Netziv, 21–22, 26, 29–30, 35–36, 46, 49, 51, 56–57, 66–69, 73–74, 98–99, 107, 130–31, 133, 138, 161, 177, 183, 186–87, 192, 194, 201, 208–9, 213, 215, 220, 231,

236–37n, 241, 256, 261, 264–65

Ohr HaChayim, 15, 21, 23, 25–28, 40, 47, 59, 73, 108, 178, 1–86, 212, 215, 220, 233, 235, 243, 246, 249, 253, 261
Onkelos, 27, 247
Otzar Ishei HaTanach, 119

Perush Yonatan, 136, 164, 256
Pirkei d'Rabi Eliezer, 5–6, 49, 60, 63, 105, 117, 173, 241, 245

Rabbeinu Bachya, 6, 53, 57, 68, 77, 83, 104, 108, 243
Radak, 164
Rambam (Maimonides), 135, 218, 223–24, 240
Ramban, 11, 124–25, 215, 219, 239–40
Ra"N, 218
Rashbam, 5, 11, 46, 54, 68, 111, 131, 137, 151, 206, 240–41, 251–52
Rashi, 13, 20, 22, 26, 32, 37–39, 44, 48, 52–53, 58, 62, 65, 67, 74, 96, 102–3, 123, 129, 131, 135–36, 141, 151, 157–58, 160, 166, 171–73, 177, 189, 191, 199–201, 206–7, 209–10, 212–13, 220, 226–27, 232, 237n, 245, 247, 252–54, 262–63

Sa'adia Gaon (RASA"G), 65, 228
Beth Samuels, 119
S'fat Emet, 225, 258
Sforno, 25, 27, 46, 56, 86, 100, 102, 131, 138, 185, 199, 201, 226–27, 244, 247

Sh'mot Rabbah, 21, 23–24, 29,
    32–33, 36n, 40, 52, 57, 60,
    79–80, , 97, 100, 103, 108,
    125, 134, 137–38, 166, 169
Sha'arei Aharon, 27, 36–37, 47,
    52, 55–56, 59, 77, 104,
    124, 131–32, 137, 159,
    161, 216, 223, 232, 239,
    241, 245, 248, 250, 254,
    256, 266
Siftei Chachamim, 20, 142, 199
Sifrei, 201, 211, 213, 216, 227–
    28, 232, 240, 250, 262
Rabbi Joseph B. Soloveitchik, 36,
    53, 62n, 81n
Song of Songs, 159
Rabbi Adin Steinsaltz, 19–20, 131,
    135, 161–62, 165–66, 191,
    195, 200

Targum Yonatan (ben Uziel), 136,
    164, 256
Torah Shlema, 60, 67, 78, 99,
    104, 107–8, 139, 164, 168–
    70, 180, 187, 193–94, 249,
    255, 261, 263–65
Torah Temima, 21, 54, 61, 157,
    200, 207, 228, 232, 253
Torat HaChidah, 5, 47, 64, 77,
    82, 110, 159, 179, 188, 235
Tosfot, 33, 162

Vayikra Rabbah, 223

Yalkut Shimoni, 11–12, , 103,
    141, 165, 168, 170, 192,
    210, 214–15, 221
Yefei To'ar, 41

Avivah Gottlieb Zornberg, 13–14,
    163

GENERAL INDEX

∂Ω∞∂Ω∞

Aaron
  advises Moses re Zipporah, 177
  and the daughters of
    Zelophchad, 263n
  and the death of Miriam, 251–
    56
  and the punishment of leprosy,
    231–33, 246
  and the spies' report, 262
  as leader, 164–65
  as prophet, 224–227
  at battle Amalek, 171–75
  brother of Miriam, 157–58
  brother of Moses, 32, 38n, 115,
    130, 193
  death of, 252, 258–60, 265
  is chastised by God, 219–22,
    228
  pleads for Miriam's recovery,
    234–243
  returns to Egypt, 118, 126,
    128, 140–142, 145–52
  son of Yocheved and Amram,
    37, 42, 44
  speaks about the Kushite
    Woman, 205–216
abandonment
  of God by Israelites, 205
  of Israelites by Moses, 173
  of Zipporah by Moses, 180–81,
    213

abduction of Dinah by Shechem, 5
ablutions of Pharaoh's daughter,
  59
Abraham
  and divine covenant, 113, 116–
    19
  and exile of Yishmael, 103
  and staff of wonders, 105
  as forefather, 6, 152n, 213
  change of name, 84
  death of, 253
  sons of, 187
abstinence from marital relations,
  198–200, 200n
Adam and staff of wonders, 105
admonishment
  of Miriam by Amram, 57
  of Aaron and Miriam, 235
adoption
  in the Talmud, 64
  of Asnat by Potiphar's wife, 6
  of Moses by Pharaoh, 90
  of Moses by Pharaoh's daughter,
    76, 81, 83, , 168, 170, 186,
affliction
  of Aaron and Miriam, 232, 234,
    236, 238, 240
  of Pharaoh's daughter with skin
    disease, 60
  alma, 74

323

Amalekites, 38n, 171–73, 177,
    193–195
Amram
    and loss of leadership, 54
    father of Miriam, 57
    father of Moses, 32 husband of
        Yocheved, 150–52, 264
    remarriage to Yocheved, 42–46,
        48–49
amulet of Asnat, 6
angel
    Gabriel, watches over Moses,
    Gabriel, watches over Pharaoh's
        daughter, 67
    Michael, watches over Asnat, 6
    Michael, watches over Moses, 91
    of death kills firstborns of Egypt,
        168
    of death threatens Moses, 129,
        131–32, 134, 136, 138–39,
        148
anger
    of God at Israelites, 254, 261–
        62
    of God at Miriam and Aaron,
        222, 226–28, 232, 243, 248
    of God at Moses, 131–138
    of Israelites at Hur, 173–74
    of Israelites at Joshua and Caleb,
        260
    of Israelites at Moses, 117
    of Moses at the Israelites, 166
    of Moses at the well in Midian,
        99
    of Pharaoh, 147
    of Puah, 33
ark
    built by Yocheved, 51–55
    holy ark waits for Miriam, 250
    rescued by princess, 59, 61, 66–
        68

watched over by Miriam, 72,
    250
arms
    of God, 149
    of Moses, held aloft by Aaron
        and Hur, 38n, 171–72
    of Princess, 62, 64, 67–68, 72
Asnat, 5–6, 170
aspakloriya, 223–24
astrologers, of the Pharaoh, 22,
        34, 39–41, 47, 51, 53, 55,
        91
attendants, of Pharaoh's daughter,
        60
Azuva, see Efrat, 172

baby
    of Dinah, 5–7
    of Pharaoh's daughter, 59–8,
        169
    of Yocheved and Amram, 45–
        49, 52–58
    of Zipporah and Moses, 130,
        135–37, 184, 189
babies
    Egyptian edict concerning, 14–
        15, 17, 20, 39–41, 43, 52,
        55
    and Israelite fecundity, 16
    of righteous women, 13
    saved by midwives, 19, 21–38
    saved by Miriam, 240
banishment
    as punishment for motzi–shem-
        ra (talebearing), 236, 238–39
    of Asnat, 6
    of Miriam, 241–42, 245, 248,
        251
barter
    by Hebrew mothers for babies'
        lives, 119–20

basins, of desert sanctuary 13
basket
    discovered by Pharaoh's
        daughter, 59–64, 67–69, 72,
        82, 84
    guarded by Miriam, 56, 58, 265
    of reeds woven by Yocheved, 49
bathing
    of husbands by righteous
        women, 12
    of Pharaoh's daughter in Nile,
        59–62, 66–67, 72
Batya
    is saved from plague of firstborn,
        168–70
    meets Yocheved, 76–82
    names Moses, 82–
    Pharaoh's daughter, receives
        Hebrew name, 64
    rescues Moses, 63–66, 163, 86
be'er (well of water), 256
betrayal
    of God by Israelite males, 205,
        260, 266
    of Moses by Israelites, 128
    of Pharaoh by midwives, 29
Bezalel, 13, 175
Bilaam, 91–93
blessing, of Yitro,103, 124–25,
        196, 202
blood
    bridegroom of, 127, 129, 136–
        39
    of afterbirth, 32
    of circumcision, 137–39
    prohibition against spilling, 26
    transformation of Nile waters
        into, 114, 118, 146
bricks
    and forced labor, 11, 146–47
bride
    Yocheved as, 44
    Zipporah as, 103, 105, 187

bridegroom of blood, 127, 129,
        136–39
brit
    angel of the (covenant), 131–32
    Zipporah performs
        (circumcision), 135–39
bullrushes
    ark of, 51–52, 54
    Miriam is concealed by, 72–73,
        250

Caleb, 38, 65, 171–73, 260–61,
        266
celibacy
    and Moses, 227
    and prophecy, 214–15
    of the Hebrew slaves, 48
Chanukah, women's role in, 162
chatan, and circumcision, 137
Chetzron, 38, 172
circumcision
    of Moses, 47, 68
    of Moses' and Zipporah's son,
        127–39
cloud
    of glory, 165, 241, 248, 250,
        255, 260
    pillar of, 219–20, 222, 227,
        231
convert
    Egyptian princess as, 64, 183
    Yitro as, 188
    Zipporah as, 108, 207–9
covenant
    angel of the, 131
    brit (circumcision) as sign of, 47,
        136
    divine, 113, 148–49, 152n,
        186–87

Dan, tribe of, 190–91
dance
    at Yocheved's remarriage, 44

of Miriam at Red Sea, 157–158, 160, 164, 170, 240, 257
decree
of divorcement for Zipporah, 178–79
Pharaoh's, against Moses, 91
Pharaoh's, against newborn males, 20, 55, 67, 70, 76, 78
Dinah, rape of, 5–7
divorce
conditional, 179n
of Amram and Yocheved, 43
of Zipporah, 178, 180
dream
and prophecy, 222, 224
of promised land, 250
Pharaoh's, of redeemer, 52
drowning
of Egyptians, 139, 158–59, 161, 163, 170, 174
of newborns, 39–40, 43, 47, 56, 63, 67, 81, 84, 117
drums of Miriam, 158–59, 174

Eden
Garden of (Serach bat Asher), 119
Garden of (staff of wonders), 105
Efrat, see Azuva, 171
Elazar, 262
Eldad, 210
Eliezer
Abraham's servant, 107
Moses' son, 127–29, 131, 136, 176, 183–87, 192,
Elisheva, wife of Aaron, 31–32
Eliyahu, 119
Ephraim, 170
Esav, 187
Esther, 157n
as heroine of Purim, 161–62

fertility, of Israelite women, 16, 29, 40
flint, of circumcision, 127, 134–35, 138

Gabriel, archangel, 67,
Gershom
father of Yehonatan, 189–92
son of Moses and Zipporah, 110–12, 124–25, 127, 131–32, 176, 178, 183–87
Gershon, son of Levi, 150
Goshen, Jewish settlement in Egypt, 9, 170, 211n

Haggadah, of Passover, 153n, 169
Haman, 162
handmaidens, 59, 66
Holofernes, 162
Horeb, God's Mountain at, 113, 124, 130, 132–33, 147–48, 166
Hur, 38, 171–75

immortality, of Serach, 119
Isaac, 44, 96, 105, 107, 113, 116–17, 152n, 187, 213, 253
Ishmaelites, 119

Jacob
and divine covenant, 113, 116–17, 198
and family in Egypt, 37, 61–63
and Rachel, 20, 20n, 106–7
and staff of wonders, 105
change of name, 84
children of, 150–52n, 213
death of, 253
descends into Egypt, 3–9, 264
grandfather of Serach, 118–19, 263

grandfather of Yocheved, 31, 44
great–grandfather of Moses, 96,
   103, 152n
son of Isaac, 18
Judah, tribe of, 38, 175
Judith, heroine of Chanukah, 162

Kehat, father of Amram, 150–51
kiss
   Aaron to Moses, 140–41
   divine, 252–53
   Moses to Yitro, 176, 193–94,
      201
   Pharaoh to Moses,
Kush, kingdom of, 90–94, 96,
   111, 206
Kushite
   king, see Nikonos, 92
   queen, 90, 92–94
   woman, 205–9, 212

lashon ha–ra, 236–37n
Lavan, 20, 103
Leah
   as matriarch, 109, 207
   grandmother of Yocheved, 7
   wife of Jacob, 20n, 106
leprosy
   of Aaron, 227, 232–33
   of Miriam, 227, 231–39, 242–
      48, 251
   of Moses, 114, 118, 146
   of Pharaoh's daughter, 60
Levi, father of Yocheved, 7, 31,
   38,
   grandfather of Amram, 42–45,
      150–52, 261, 264
   great–grandfather of Moses
      (through mother), 4
Levite
   Aaron the, 115
   as teachers, 239, 250
   dynasty, 37–38, 54, 266

Elazar the, 262
Moses, the, 238
son of Gershom the, 189–91
lynching
   of Hur, 174
   of Joshua and Caleb, 260

mannah, 165, 240, 255
Meidad, 210
Menashe
   son of Asnat 170
   the Danite priest, 190–91
Merari, brother of Amram, 150
meyaldot (see midwives), 37
Micah
   the prophet, 164
   the Danite, 189–91
Michael, archangel, 6, 91
Midian, 90–91, 94–98, 100, 102–
   113, 123–27, 129–31, 135–
   38, 141–42, 147, 176–82,
   184–87, 189–90, 193–95,
   202, 207, 209
midwives, 15, 25–28, 29, 31–32,
   35, 37, 38, 42, 238, 263,
   265
Miriam, 31–34, 37–39, 42–44,
   54–58, 61, 63, 65, 70–74,
   76, 151–52, 157–61, 163–
   67, 170–75, 205–16, 219–
   22, 224–28, 231–59, 263–
   66
mirrors
   of Israelite women, 13–14
   of prophecy (see aspakloriya),
      223–24
Moses, 3–4, 7, 13, 30–33, 37–42,
   44, 46, 49, 58, 64–65, 74–
   77, 80–86, 89–100, 102–20,
   123–42, 145–53, 157–61,
   163–202, 205–28, 231–32,
   234–48, 250–63n, 265
Munius, see Moses, 82

Nikonos, 91–93, 206
Nile
    and Miriam, 63, 240, 265
    and plague of blood, 114, 118,
        146
    and the Egyptian Princess, 62–
        67, 81, 169
    as a god, 61
    as instrument of death, 39, 41,
        43, 46–47
    receives Yocheved's reed basket,
        54, 163
nursemaid, Yocheved as, 71–79

Padan–Aram, 96, 107
PaKoD PaKaD'Ti, (code of the
    redemption), 114, 116–19,
    146
Passover, 153n, 169
    women's role in, 162
Potiphar, 6, 18
prayer
    of Moses for Batya, 170
    of Moses for Miriam, 235, 242–
        248
    of the midwives, 24
    of Yocheved, 69, 242
priest
    and leprosy, 236, 238–39
    Elazar, the, 262
    God as, 239
    high (Aaron), 232
    kingdom of, 198
    Levite, 266
    of Dan, 189–91
    of Midian (see Yitro), 91, 95,
        97–98, 100, 104, 107, 135,
        176, 180, 183, 188, 195, 202
priestly, dynasty, 37, 38
prince
    Moses as Egyptian, 4, 58, 79,
        81, 86, 91, 99, 170, 208–9,
        216, 265

princes, Israelite, 166, 170, 193
princess, Batya, Egyptian, 59–74,
        76–78, 81–86, 163, 168
prophet
    Aaron and Moses as, 164
prophetess
    Miriam the, 157–60, 174, 239,
        248, 255
prophetesses, seven biblical, 157
Puah, 15, 30–34, 170
Purim, women's role in, 162

queen of Kush, 90, 92–93, 206

Rachel
    as matriarch, 207
    at the well, 107
    wife of Jacob, 20, 96, 106–7,
        109, 207
rape
    of Dinah, 5
    shepherds' intention to, 99
Rebecca,
    as matriarch, 96, 109, 207
    at the well, 107
    wife of Isaac, 107
reeds, e
    as hiding place for ark, 51, 58–
        63, 66–68
    as hiding place for Miriam, 70–
        72, 163
    basket woven of, 52–53
Reeds, Sea of (Yam Suf), 54
Refidim, 171, 195
remarriage, of Yocheved and
        Amram, 42, 48–49
Reu'el (see Yitro), 95
Reuven, firstborn of Israel, 150,
        187
ritual bath (mikveh), 220

Sarah, 34, 44, 84, 108, 118n,
        157n, as matriarch, 207

Sarai, 84

seder, 153n, 162, 169

seductions, by righteous women, 11, 13, 18, 19

Serach, daughter of Asher, 6–7, 116–119, 119n, 263–64

Shechem, 5

shechina (divine presence), 57, 228
  and gift of prophecy, 218
  as seen by Batya, 69
  watched over floating baby, 57

Shifra, 15, 30–34, 170

Sinai, 124–25, 173, 182, 198, 200–202, 205, 207, 210–11, 213, 224, 226–27, 258

slander
  and the punishment of leprosy, 232, 237–38
  of Moses, 232, 235–38

tzora'at (see leprosy), 227, 231–41

wedding,
  of Amram and Yocheved, 42
  of Kushite queen, 92

well
  in Midian, 94–100, 104–8, 111–12, 207, 209
  Jacob at the, 96
  of Miriam, 163, 165–67, 254–58, 264–66
  of Miriam and Oral Torah, 258
  Rebecca at the, 96
  song of the, 257

Yehonatan, the Danite priest, 190–92

Yephuneh, father of Caleb, 38, 65, 172

Yeter (see Yitro), 123

Yishmael, son of Abraham, 103, 187

Yitro, , 91, 97, 100–108, 110–13, 123–25, 131–32, 176–77, 179–84, 187–91, 193–96, 201–2, 209

Yocheved, 3, 7–8, 31–34, 37–39, 41–49, 51–57, 60–61, 63–64, 66, 69–70, 73–84, 150–52, 163, 170, 186, 263–65

Zelophchad, daughters of , 263, 263n

Zin, Wilderness of 251, 259, 265

Zipporah
  abandoned by Moses, 199–201, 213–14, 226, 239
  as Kushite Woman, 206–214
  a righteous Gentile, 170
  at the Inn, 127–39
  bears a son for Moses (Gershom), 110–112
  daughter of Yitro, 97
  marries Moses, 100–108
  mother of Eliezer, 192
  returns to Midian, 140–42, 148
  returns to Moses, 176–90, 193–97
  takes leave of Yitro, 123–26

ABOUT THE AUTHORS

Shera Aranoff Tuchman has been teaching weekly classes in biblical commentary at Congregation Kehilath Jeshurun for the past fifteen years. She was recently interviewed on the CUNY television series "Jewish Women in America." Besides writing, studying and teaching Bible, which has been her passion, she is a dermatologist in private practice in Manhattan and at Lenox Hill Hospital. She and her husband Alan Tuchman live in Manhattan and enjoy their children and grandchildren.

Sandra E. Rapoport was a litigating attorney when she met her co-author in her women's Bible class fifteen years ago. Sandra, who has written for law reviews and *Commentary* magazine, once again combines her love for Bible study and her passion for writing as co-author in this, the authors' second book. She continues to consult to an auction house specializing in rare Hebrew books and manuscripts, and lives in Manhattan with her husband, Sam, where they raised their three children.